MY LAST MILLION READERS

MY
LAST MILLION
READERS

By

EMILE GAUVREAU

1941

E. P. DUTTON & CO., Inc.
NEW YORK

First Printing . . . August, 1941
Second Printing . . . August, 1941
Third Printing . . September, 1941
Fourth Printing . . September, 1941
Fifth Printing . . September, 1941

TO
WINIFRED

CONTENTS

BOOK I

THE MIRACLE

CHAPTER I

PROFESSOR BILLY HEGEL lowered the ebony flute from his lips, fingering the silver keys with the sensitive fondness of a musician who loves his instrument. For a few moments, conscious of his little nods of encouragement, I played alone, my head turned away from the music rack. I felt the absence of his full tones and I withdrew the flute from my lips and faced the Master. We were rehearsing *l'Après-midi d'un Faune* and I knew the flute part by heart. I loved its formlessness, its sense of release. I could hear it and see trees swaying in the wind, fluffy clouds, a purple mantle of grass. I was in my early 'teens and music came to me in light breezes and color. It disentangled my thoughts.

"You're playing by ear, you little devil! But you're getting better in the low octave. You need bigger lungs. Practicing will develop that little ridge on your lower lip. Later, little drinking and almost no kissing. Self-denial and hard work lead to the symphony. You've picked a tough instrument. You have to be a saint to get the most out of it."

When the Professor sermonized, the lesson was at an end. I replaced my second-hand Boehm flute in its black leather case, not bothering to swab it out, and clicked the lock.

"Do you want that thing to crack? Dry the inside of it when you put it away. Just because you like Debussy you don't have to become the absent-minded musical nihilist that he was. You can feel; that's good! But wake up when it's over."

Suddenly he twirled me around and gripped my arm.

"Something wrong today or just a little temperament?"

I liked his human, instinctive understanding. It was in 1909 when we had with us the pre-war type of kindly, musical German, long since gone. Professor Hegel lived in a warbling heaven and played in the New Haven Symphony with an indescribably ecstatic pleasure. A concert to him was a ritual. He taught me the reverence that has clung to me ever since for good music.

The teacher searched me with his brown gimlet eyes. He has been my tyrant for almost four years and had built in me hopes that, at times, made my heart beat faster. Once he had taken me to the Metropolitan Opera in New York where first I watched the flutes, the reedy oboe, the bows on precision, the swaying double bass, the glittering brasses and crashing percussions. I paid no attention to the bellowing commotion on the stage. What fascinated me was in the pit, this managing and combining of sounds under the rapier thrusts of a suave gentleman in evening dress who brought it all out. Now it was over, and I had to tell the Professor.

I faced him, taking in his little puckish figure, rounding stomach and almost ascetic face, at times a mask combining dissipation and remorse. He liked merry company, and tiny veins were coming out on his nose. He was a little musical snuffbox of a man.

"I'll have to give up the lessons, Professor," I said. "My father had to take a cut in salary at the gun factory and the music is over. It will take too long to make any money in concert work. I've got to get a job. You wouldn't want your pupil to play in dance halls, anyhow."

Hegel turned away and began to blow on his flute—little arpeggios, winged, slurred notes, rasping, double-tonguing repetitions in minor keys. This he would do, swaying between dismay and anger when things went wrong. He placed his flute down tenderly on a piano, pulled out a long handkerchief and wiped his eyes.

"Why does it always have to be like this?" His high pitched voice choked. "You have it in you. You love it. And our duet in the symphony—that will never happen! All this practicing—*Gott in Himmel*—and you have to earn a living already!"

He puffed about the room while I bit the little ridge on my under lip. He slumped into a corner exhaling a deep sigh.

"What are you going to do? You can't work at a machine. You'll never be much bigger than I am. You'll have to work with your mind." He dropped his billiard-ball head on his chest. "Maybe it's just as well. Playing in dance halls! Mutilating a beautiful instrument. But the flute is through in the dance halls. What do people care about the flute? Schoenberger across the street makes more money than I do, teaching the saxophone." He lowered his voice as if about to describe the theft of the eucharist from the altar. "He's even teaching saxophonists to play the flute as a side line if they need it to fill in! It's this damned ragtime noise, drums, jungle music. And it took Adolph Sax, a good German, to invent the saxophone. Maybe we'll be playing on ferry boats and windy street corners together. Wait and see what this ragtime comes to!"

He was speaking with true prophecy but he was to die before the madness had reached its height.

"Do you want to write? Maybe I can start you off on a newspaper. What a hell of a business after classical music! I know the boss of the *Journal-Courier*. I can have a drink with him anytime at the Aschenbrödel. I found a music critic for him. But the editor won't ask you to write anything about music. He wants young reporters. He'll show you how to ask the why and things of people, and when you no longer know how to mind your own business you'll have a steady job. Good-by to your only free delight, your time for music. Good-by to Debussy!"

CHAPTER II

OUR home had never been without music. When my sister Laura wasn't dragging out the threadbare melodies of *Poet and Peasant* on the piano like a reluctant penance, my younger sister, Jeannette, sawed *Hearts and Flowers* to its gizzards on a violin. My brother practiced the trap drummer's triple roll and its taradiddles on a cigar box back in the kitchen where my mother thought such music belonged. When the practicing was over, my mother sang at her work. With us, perhaps, music was the overflowing of a buoyant impulse; with her it was the language of a once cheerful heart.

There was another note, in a high, harsh key, that regulated our affairs. It was the whistle of the gun factory. It blew at six forty-five in the morning, a warning to the toilers who had to be at their machines at seven. At night it blew again at six, releasing them for another day. When there were no revolutions in South America, and people had enough guns to kill themselves with in various parts of the world, the whistle didn't blow at all. Then times were described as bad in our neighborhood.

My father was among the exhausted army that trudged home up the railroad tracks which skirted our backyard when the whistle blew at six. He had learned to scamper aside with the others to give the Northampton express the right of its roaring way. Once I remember, one worker had been too weary to scamper. There had been a little piece in the paper about it.

When my father got home, no matter how hard the day had been, he picked up his alto horn, pulled its glittering bell from its green flannel bag and blew a few reassuring roulades into its brass convolutions, unscrewing a piston or two, spitting on their scalloped valves, fingering them briskly and giving a final, defiant toot before he sat down to supper.

The percussion influence in our family came from a noisy gentleman who lived above us—my Uncle Napoleon. He was

14

the trap drummer at Poli's Vaudeville House in New Haven, and his instruments made up in force what they lacked in dignity. He made music pay. When I was a boy, his front room fascinated me. Sometimes I would go up there when my buxom Aunt Lena was downstairs practicing the tarantella, and lose myself in the most remarkable collection of sound producers ever invented to assault the ear's anatomy. There was the side drum, the bass drum and cymbals. In a corner stood a Hungarian cembalo which my uncle had won at a raffle. It was rather dusty and my father said my uncle didn't play it because its vibrations might have blown down the house. There were cow bells, sleigh bells, a steamboat whistle and a gadget which made noises like a skyrocket. I amused myself with the triangles, xylophone and a glockenspiel that imitated a carillon. In a case containing Chinese gongs and castanets there was a .32 calibre revolver and when I finally reached it in my explorations I was hustled out of the room.

On some occasions my uncle, a tall, thin, dark man with a haunted look, departed at night to play for the Yale dances. He went jingling down the street carrying his bass drum, snare drum and a bulging valise full of noise makers. I envied him and was always worried by the fear that he had forgotten something. He came home quite late because the musicians stopped at the Aschenbrödel for refreshments when they had played themselves out. One night, upon his return, heavily laden, he stumbled on the stoop, the valise flew open and his revolver went off. My Aunt Lena, planted solidly at the top of the stairs in a nightgown, held an oil lamp and swore in French. When the warning factory whistle blew that morning my father still roared with laughter.

There were nights when my father put his alto horn aside and described the sensation of the bullets that had whined by his ears in 1885 when, as a Canadian Volunteer, he helped to crush Louis Riel, the fanatical half-breed who flung Canada into the turmoil of the Northwest Rebellion. Winter evenings when neighbors, Canadian immigrants, gathered in the kitchen, my father fought the campaign of the hardy Canadians from their trek up to the head of frozen Lake Superior, through five hundred miles of wilderness. Riel had escaped them, then, but they had saved Fort Garry, which had become Winnipeg. The rebel came back and with him a dangerous Indian uprising inflaming the half-breeds.   There had been fierce battles before Riel was hanged.

We were on our chairs' edges when my father drew from the stove a poker, red hot almost up to his hand, and plunged it into a hissing can of beer as he led his men once more in the bayonet charge that obliterated the Indian rifle pits at Bloody Batoche.   With his left hand he throbbed the rhythmical war whoop over his military mustache.   While I drowned my terrors in the hot mug of shandygaff I was permitted to quaff on these occasions, my father in his excitement, the poker still in his hand, dashed into my mother's bedroom and emerged with his Queen Victoria medal, which had been pinned on him for valor at Saskatchewan.   A few more sips from my mug and I might have seen the Indians peering in, but for the frosty rime on the windows.   The story always had the same ending.

"Fort Garry was nothing but a prairie.   Now Winnipeg is a great city.   They gave us acres of it.   I sold my scrip for $2,500.   *Beaucoup d'argent* then.   Now, I would be a millionaire!"   The veteran lapsed excitedly into his Canadian accent.   "I was crazee!   *Nom d'un chien!*   But l'Angleterre find out that les Canayens fight the sam as bes' English man.   *Hein?*"

One final sputtering stab into the protesting beer, the philosophical puff, puff, from six or seven understanding pipes and the story was gone, like the last slide of our magic lantern. The dense smoke from "tabac Canayen" draped us into blue phantoms.   My father would pick me up and sigh.   "But you! You can never be a soldier."

I was taken to bed, but not to sleep, for the prelude made me the subject of a discussion lasting far into the night.   I heard it many times, from my bed off the kitchen, where I could see some of the smoky specters, silent and listening.   It was comfortable in the dark where I could not be turned into an exhibit.   My mind raced ahead of the story my father told, for I knew more about it than he did.   I was living it.

My first recollection of any beginning places me in a dining room in a frame dwelling on the fringes of New Haven, Connecticut.   It was in late June and my father, home from work in the gun factory, was rehearsing a little orchestra in the parlor.   The windows were open and people were gathered outside, along our picket fence.   My mother was teaching me the steps of the schottische in time with the music.   She was seventeen when I was born and this night was five years later. Even then she was just a girl. She was lithe of figure, wore a clinging dark dress with white ruffles at her neck and wrists and her black hair, parted in the middle, shone in the lamp light. Her eyes sparkled in her sweet face. She loved songs, books and painted flowers on silk.

My father passed through the room with a tray of glasses. "Dancing already, the little devil," he laughed. "Dancing leads the way to romance. He'll find that out as I did. But his drill lessons come first. Don't forget that, *mon petit diable!*"

I was well acquainted with the drill lessons. In the morning my father hustled me in my nightgown to the parlor before a life-size bust of Napoleon, placed a broomstick in my hand and snapped me through the infantry drill and the manual of the bayonet.

"Eyes FRONT!" His voice would jump to a querulous pitch on the last word, a command with a questioning ring. I stood up straight in the parlor, holding my broomstick between my thumb and fingers so that it touched my bare right foot.

"Present ARMS! Port ARMS! Order ARMS! Right shoulder, ARMS! Mark time!"

I swung into the cadence of the movement by alternately raising each foot and planting it in line with the other.

"Halt! Fix bayonet! CHARGE!" And he rushed me off to bed again at the double-quick, with a laugh. "At rest," he said as I dove into the pillows and he looked down at me, square shoulders, chest out, his strong chin under his bristling mustache.

"He'll be more than a captain—a colonel, maybe!" He was at the breakfast table gulping his coffee which my mother poured out for him.

The warning whistle blew at the factory and he was off, his firm military step resounding on the wooden sidewalk. Sometimes he sang something in French that had carried his men through the Saskatchewan:

> *"Brigadier! repondit Pandore,*
> *Brigadier! vous avez raison!"*

It was the time of clanking horse cars making way for the

trolley; the time of limber-legged gentlemen with handle-bar mustaches, "scorching" on bicycles and giggling ladies on tandems, webby veils holding down their sailor hats. Even my Aunt Lena perched her ample form over two uncertain wheels and pedaled herself about.

It was the time of the "Glorious Fourth" when people really celebrated and those who survived with four limbs had another year ahead to think of more hilarious methods of self-destruction. One Fourth of July we had driven away in a cabriolet from Jack McGrail's livery stable. A cannon cracker had thrown our horse to its haunches and we had gone rearing through the country side. My mother held me and screamed. I watched the jiggling black fringes on the calash top as my father lashed away, bracing his back, amid explosions. I wasn't frightened until we reached my father's abandoned farm in Centerville when the outhouse was blown up. Men were scurrying off laughing.

On the Fourth of July that I was to remember we did not go to the farm. My mother was nervous. Even days before the holiday people couldn't wait to shoot things off. Small bangs, then loud, near the house, made me jump. It was this way until the night before everything happened. My father made me say my prayers as he said them out loud himself at his own bed. I had to shout the words to be heard above the bombs.

Some of the neighbors did not like my father who had fought under the British colors. His military bearing irritated them. Early in the morning a drunken crowd of them had dragged a brass cannon on a wheeled platform to the side of our house and loaded it to the muzzle to give us a good taste of powder. All this was under my open bedroom window. I was sleeping when they touched off the fuse.

I remember being on the floor. Gray daylight came from a broken window through clouds of powder smoke. I had a burning, acrid taste. I can describe it better now. My mother was holding a shaking lamp. My father was trying to stand me up. He caught me as I crumbled like the inflated paper bags he used to blow up and smack between his hands and laugh when the noise startled me. A grave man with handle-bar mustache, Dr. Hotchkiss, whose name still remains in my mind because, for a long time, he saw me every day, was bend-ing over me. He had a black box that hummed and hissed and he was touching two silver handles over me. My father said it was electricity. The doctor swung a little knob clear over to the end of its arc and blue sparks snapped, but I couldn't feel anything where the handles touched me. I screamed when one of them fell on my left leg and sizzled.

CHAPTER III

I TURNED instinctively at first to the tender consideration of the household and the neighbors. Weeks stretched into months and finally I gave up thinking how long ago it was when I could run and play. The growing weariness of those about me developed into an attitude of toleration that turned my existence into a siege. When I was seven I could see the widening chasm that so quickly separates the halt from the quick. My weakness and pain were a fixed idea among all whom I knew. The affection with which I had been surrounded was hardening day by day. Absorption in the contemplation of my plight narrowed my world to a little circle of which my wheel chair was the center.

My father left the United States with his family and went to Canada and settled in Montreal. Connecticut, where I was born, was a state we no longer mentioned. My sister Laura had arrived and I wondered why she kept my mother in bed day after day. I lived in a big house with three flights of stairs, but I pushed myself about in the basement. I knew there were many rooms above me by the sound of feet ascending until they clumped dimly into silence mysteriously high up. Through an oblong aperture with bars, on a level with the sidewalk, I could see many feet, cut off at the ankles, passing left and right.

At night the house was full of people. They ate merrily and later the piano played. I could see it all when the shades of the French windows were up and their activities were reflected in the plate-glass windows of a department store across the street. A lady in black silk that frou-froued down the stairs came to see me every night. When I saw her the first time I thought she might have been the Queen on my father's medal. One time she hugged me and cried and ran away, her ruffled skirts to her knees, and I never saw her again. My father said she was an actress and kissed everybody. My Aunt Mary, my father's sister, red-headed and flaming, who wore black, dead silk that didn't rustle, and a little, heaving gold watch over her ample bosom, said: "Never mention that woman." My Uncle Ferdinand, who was present, plunged his brown Vandyke beard into a copy of *La Presse*.

A long time later when I was able to clank up to the street level in a brace and explore the big rooms where the music came from, I learned that the carefree ladies and whiskered gentlemen were boarders and the palace of the upper regions, with its red drapes, stuffed spiders, Union Jacks, sabres and maple-leaf banners were all a part of my Aunt Mary's boarding house.

Reading came to me as a prisoner might suddenly find a key in his cell to let himself out into daylight. By some magic the French alphabet formed quick words and books leaped at me. I couldn't get enough of them and I was at them upstairs before the household knew. I was learning French and English from a Jesuit tutor. Most of the books in the parlor were in French but there were two volumes of *John Halifax, Gentleman* and three of *Fire and Sword in the Sudan,* the story of some forgotten hero's years of captivity in the camp of the Mahdi. My Aunt Mary, blowing out the oil lamps would ignore mine as I read about the Battle of Om Waragat. She told me who Mr. Gladstone was and about other people that popped up as I turned the pages. My father tried to call a halt when he found me in the pillows with Zola's *Nana.* My Aunt told him it was the proper place in which to read it.

Before I was nine I had hurdled Hall Caine, Marie Corelli, Ouida and Mrs. Humphrey Ward, after a fashion. *Ishmael* by E. D. E. N. Southworth made me weep silently. The *Maxims of Napoleon* and *Plutarch's Lives* were devoured between gulps of *Voyages, Travels, Discoveries from the Time of Columbus.* There were seven volumes of this and I never finished them but they swept me far away from my basement bedroom. I read Poe's *Weird Tales* just late enough to escape convulsions. My questions were never too pointed for my Aunt Mary. I can remember her now, a stern sentinel in a family row over my reading, beating off the assaults while I decided from the diminishing book cupboard what my mental fare should be for the night.

In the room of the stuffed spiders, over the *fauteuil* and its blazing antimacassar which protected it from the oil in my

Uncle's hair was a painting of a saintly lady holding a violin. I became interested in her when I found the same picture in a huge tome, the last I was to read in my Aunt's library. The lady of the violin was the Virgin Martyr Saint Cecilia, patroness of music. In Irish homes I was to see her with a harp. Italians represented her with an organ. I was convinced that she could play anything. Her story was to have a strange effect on my life and the only book of my reading which seemed to have the unanimous approval of the household.

Those who surrounded me, except my Aunt Mary, believed that pain was the outcome of sin; that pain must follow pleasure as its shadow. To deny yourself of a pleasure was to please God who would keep pain away when you embraced holiness. Over again I read of Saint Cecilia:

"The Roman Almachius commands the maiden to be closely shut up in the bathroom in her house, and sevenfold quantities of wood are heaped on the furnaces beneath. But for a whole day and night she remains marvellously protected from on high, as in a cold place."

It was her faith, my father said. Didn't Almachius order a barbarian to cut off her head with an ax? "Whether overcome with fear to do so pitiful a deed or held back by an angel as Abraham of old, we do not know," the story said, "but thrice he smites her on the neck and she is not dead."

"Why didn't he hit her once more and end her suffering? She must have felt some of it?" I asked. "The law allowed no further stroke," my father said, "and she lived bathed in her own blood until her work was done and her house had been consecrated into a church."

I thought it all out at night as I put my iron brace silently on the floor. Did God insist on pain for those who could reach Him? I could not believe that it pleased Him that all the street should stare at me, that I should bring out all of the blind cruelties of the boys in the Jesuit academy I now attended.

I fell asleep with the story of Saint Cecilia in my bewildered head. "Richly clad, secretly she wore the hair shirt and fasted three days a week. Grown up to womanhood she was forced to marry Valerian, a pagan, noble of birth and character—this against her will, for secretly she was bound by the sacred ties of a vow of perpetual virginity.

"The day of her nuptials arrived and all the company rejoiced with *cantantibus organis*. But she sang to God: 'May my heart and body be undefiled, that I may not be confounded.' And her prayer was heard as she and her spouse entered the secrecy of their bedchamber. And she addressed him:

"'Oh sweet and loving youth, I wish thee to know that I have an angel of God for my lover, who guards me with exceeding zeal. If thou drawest nigh with an unholy love, his anger will be enkindled. But respect my firm purpose and he will love thee as he loves me.'

"And Valerian said: 'Show me this angel! If truly angel of God he be, I will do as you ask, but if you love another man, I will slay both you and him!'"

And Valerian had gone and confessed and been baptized and had come in a white robe to Cecilia and there in her bedchamber, "in glorious plumes and wings and shining as fire" was the angel, sure enough.

CHAPTER IV

We moved from my Aunt's boarding house to a French-Canadian canton where shabby little houses blinked sleepily and braced themselves against each other as though to summon some final effort to remain standing. We lived on a long street, at one end of which was a church with a sonorous bell, at the other, a parade ground. Stern priests in flowing black robes and wide hats knew everybody and marshaled us to mass as rigidly as the red-coated officers on the drill square gathered their platoons to the roll of drums. Recruiting sergeants passed up and down and all the talk was of the South African War. My mother silenced my father when he exploded about it at night. He supported the Boers and bought only French papers which gave prominence to their military skill. He was selling lightning rods and fell into spells of despondency because his manager had told him that fear of thunder and fiery bolts had to be implanted into the minds of prospective customers. My father felt there was something dishonest about this form of salesmanship and obtained employment as the driver of a jangling wagon from which he delivered tins of biscuits. When Saturday came he perched me high up with him on the driver's seat and we delivered the tins at a gallop and drove to Mile End, where the road was free in the fields and he sang the songs of the Rebellion. He gave me the reins and taught me how to handle horses. When we got back to the bakery in the dark he made me read articles from French and English newspapers to the night watchman who held a lantern and praised me for my accomplishments.

We lived near my school, a private academy under Jesuitical domination, whose discipline was law to the point of harshness. I knew my catechism by heart, so far ahead that I marked time while rulers cracked the knuckles of the tow heads, who gagged and retched, inarticulate under the questions bursting like grenades over them.

"What was mortal sin?" Whack! Crack! "What was

24

eternal damnation?" More cracks and howls. You had to know the meaning of eternal damnation until it seared your mind. If we were consigned to Hell, a place Father Chapdelaine, master of our form, indicated we were all headed for, although he never included himself in the terrifying journey, we would be there roasting forever. I couldn't shiver about it although some boys burst into tears. I went home with whole knuckles. I would have felt those cracks, too, if the teachers had known what I read at home.

I was able to get around by myself, glad to be rid, with a shudder, of the altar boys, appointed to escort me and who enjoyed a masochistic gratification in telling me of the activities I could never take part in.

The nest egg my father had acquired after selling his scrip on the thriving acres which were now Winnipeg had been swept away in a gale of doctors' bills. A new baby sister had made her appearance in a winter of bitter cold and mountainous snowdrifts. Almost immediately, it seemed, we had to set out with her, all bundled up, in an open sleigh to the Cathedral of Notre Dame to have her baptized. The wind lashed us with a merciless powder from the rim of the canyons which formed the streets.

The sleigh turned over on our way back. While my father got the groaning vehicle on its runners, my Aunt Mary, functioning as godmother, gave us a sip of Holland gin from a flask. My Uncle Ferdinand's Vandyke had been frozen into a spearhead. He denounced these expeditions which impelled the faithful to carry infants a few days old through wintry blasts and often to their little graves as a result.

In the house I was deposited behind a hot stove to thaw out and holding my sister Laura's wax doll which she childishly extended to me, I was dumfounded to see it cave in and melt into a sickening puddle before my eyes. Amid her lamentations I got my first whaling. But my new sister, Jeannette, had been saved from limbo and that was something I would no longer have to concern myself about.

Through gaps cut from the sidewalks into ravines of snow I saw, from my window, mournful sleighs. Riding in the rear were women in black. On the seat in front was the driver, and beside him a man, bent and muffled, his hat tangled in crepe and holding on his knees a little white casket.

I had acquired a close companion, a boy older than I, who loved books. He could run and jump and bat a ball but he had to do it defiantly by himself because he was a Jew. His name was Isaac Levy and his father, Moses, ran a grocery store across the street. I was known as the boy who played with the Jew.

One night at supper time there was an outcry of two words which had become familiar to me: "Christ killer! Christ killer!" It was taken up until the street rang with it. My father ran out and chased a taunting gang away from Isaac who stood in front of his store, his face white, his lips a scornful line.

We saw a parade together, Ike and I, on Sherbrook Street, gaudy with flags, waves of bayonets and stirring bands. Men were going to war. The Boers were losing but men still had to go. A brigade went by, swinging and jangling like the rest but in uniforms of sombre hue. From the crowds the cry went up, "The Jews! The Jews!" Apparently, they were going to war, too.

"They can fight as good as all of them," Ike said. "Maybe better, if they're given a chance!"

Ike told me Christ was a Jew. I told my Aunt Mary. "And not only that," she added, "but God chose a Jewess to be the Mother of His only Son." Ike said he knew it but his father told him to talk of anything but religion and avoid bloody noses. Ike could not fight more than three Gentiles at a time.

Books were Ike's passion and we had the same freedom in reading them. Sometimes he would rush across the street and shout: "Hey! Read this!" Over a paragraph I followed his trembling finger as though it were a guide holding a torch ahead in a tunnel which had an end into daylight. We made our own discoveries and when Ike found an unexpected door open to his mind, we pushed through together. His brown eyes, aflame with new light, made you forget his long, hooked nose and compressed lips. We compared notes in whispers like conspirators. He knew the daily taunts and jeers, but he had his side alleys, as I did, when we had to retreat. We sought the same objectives in life. We were looking for answers.

I could talk to Ike about anything, even the three hours at the Royal Victoria Hospital where I was stripped on a table in the bottom of a bowl lined with seats. Men in frock coats, in uniforms, some in white, sat leaning forward, every burning eye on me. One man with thick glasses and a bushy beard, in a white suit, lifted my ankle between his thumb and finger and talked and prodded me from the hip down. When they turned me over on my back I could see the clock. I thought somebody was holding back the hands.

Christmas came again and *la nuit de noël* enveloped us in a crisp, pure night of starry loveliness, of tenderness, so still that a low voice, scarcely audible outside at other times, could be heard through the soft rhythmic music of sleigh bells as we trudged to the church. The houses were lighted and hung with adornments and were no longer shabby. The great bell in the steeple boomed and clanged in divine satisfaction.

The church was a warm dazzlement of candle twinkle about the manger. The Christ Child held out little pink hands and the figures of Mary and Joseph bowed in adoration. They seemed to be coming to life and I should not have been surprised if they had spoken. They could not be of the family of plaster saints only a block away in a little shop where Mr. Bergeron painted red hearts on them dripping with drops of blood. Near the crèche you could light a candle if you put a coin in a box and my father helped me there and told me to pray. A poetry of notes came from the organ. Priests and altar boys moved in an exquisite glow. Here there was no dread of solitude. Thoughts seemed chastened when whispered on the lips and even the flaky darkness outside the stained glass windows was full of comfort. Nothing could be more beautiful than a midnight mass on Christmas Eve.

We did not get our presents on Christmas in the French-Canadian canton. We talked about the story of the Nativity, drank cool port and sherry and had a pungent dinner of roast pork, or duck. Candies and fancy wafers came from the bakery where my father worked. *Le Jour de l'An* was the big day for us. The neighbors celebrated by drinking together but the children were absorbed with their gifts and were oblivious of the harmless roistering.

My presents were books, largely. My father had thrown away the brigades of lead soldiers with their bent bayonets and shattered cannon wheels when I had been released from port arms and shoulder arms. I received a gift in wrapping paper which came from Moses Levy's store and tied with the same string he held in his teeth and twirled around his packages. I tore it open. A card said: *Compliment de bonne année—* Moses Levy and his son Isaac." It was an old book of green leather with fleur-de-lis in its corners. Crumbs of gold still remained on the edges of its leaves. It was well thumbed but of enduring beauty, mellowing like a fine old man, as good books do. I recognized it as one which had been frequently in the hands of Moses, lately, when he took off his glasses, adjusted his skull cap and blinked his mind back to my grocery order.

Inside the cover of this book, a strange cocked head peered out with a smile of tolerant skepticism. Yet it had an honesty and faith, a knowing, as if never blind to the snares laid for it. It had firmness, it was ageless and reminded you of someone trying to keep a straight face. The smile remained when my father closed the book and took it from me.

"Hm-m-m . . . Voltaire," he said and he put the book under his arm, stroking his mustache.

My Aunt Mary looked up from the business of opening packages and parcels with my mother. My Uncle Ferdinand, whose Vandyke never seemed to have recovered from the baptism, put down his glass so that it would not be spilled during the explosion which he knew was about to take place.

It was the last flare-up in our family about my reading. My Aunt let loose the temper under her red hair. One withering volley from her and it was over. My Uncle said he would not have agreed with her if Voltaire had come into my life before my first communion. My father gave me the book and I went back to the kitchen to read it slowly. Long after bedtime he put his hand tenderly on my shoulder and said: "Don't try to understand Voltaire all at once. He had to believe in God, too, finally, although he could never explain Him."

CHAPTER V

My father was a believer. The faith once delivered to the Saints was the root of his life. He believed with a staunchness and a sublime humility. This faith was not to be pried into by reason. It shone in his face at Mass. I sat beside him, looking at him, and saw it. To me this faith was like love, but somehow it couldn't be forced. It had been handed down to him. He was not made to question. If the world were harsh and life a terrific struggle, the only warmth and shelter lay in his faith. Stories of cruelty and deceit, he read without criticism. It was part of God's unfinished work. It would take time. To believe that was to keep a solemn promise, to stand to one's engagement.

I knew about my father's faith when I was very young and for years I heard him nightly beseeching heaven to guide his steps. I tried hard to feel this faith but having encountered troubles early in life and living in neighborhoods full of driven, hopeless toilers I couldn't believe there was hope for anyone if God, as I tried to picture him, was a benevolent old man with a white beard, sitting on a gold throne. I have always believed in God but even then I was developing a broader conception of Him as a force unseen but potent, motivating the universe.

As a boy I thanked God for saving my father's life from the Indians. My father believed that and I wanted it to be true. If it were true, I could ask God for the one favor I wanted. But supposing I asked for it and nothing came of it? I could never ask for it again. And yet, when I was brought to the churches to see clusters of crutches, braces, canes and wheel chairs I believed people had been cured by faith. It was not in me to believe that God, undoubtedly weary of troubles, some of which I saw with my own eyes, could take the time to single me out for a special dispensation.

While I read Voltaire at night I listened to the family plans in which I was involved. There was to be a novena at Sainte

Anne's Church in Montreal and there we were to ask for a
cure. Sainte Anne was the mother of the Virgin Mary and
had performed great miracles. I had seen her statue in the
basilica and at her feet all sorts of things people no longer had
to wear, because they were whole. Her great shrine was near
Quebec, where miracles were performed more frequently, my
father said. Sainte Anne could talk to the Blessed Virgin.
She was closer to Jesus than other saints. I was told to prepare my mind for the novena.

I put Voltaire and his smile aside. I read the New Testa-
ment, the ordeal of Sainte Cecilia over again, the lives of great
saints who obeyed divine visions and in the end died in flames
with the ecstasy of martyrdom. To them, Heaven was real.
Joan of Arc, at the head of her armies, led me up a different
road, as I dozed in bed, and almost immediately we were in a
hard press of men afoot and horseback, going from Chinon.
She was ahead in shining armor on a white horse and could
hear Voices which no one else could hear. Then she was kneel-
ing at an altar, just as it was shown in the steel engraving over
my bed. And in a flash we were in the thick of it at Orléans,
banners flying, the crash of battle axes on smashed helmets
blinding in the sun, and pikes driving back a whole cursing
horde and I was hacking at a vizor in front of me and split it
open, and behind it was Father Chapdelaine! He recognized
me and thundered: *"Ah! Mon petit polisson!"* And suddenly
I was badly frightened because I had struck a priest in the face!

My father was standing at my bed turning down the sputtering wick of my oil lamp, before blowing it out.

"You have been having a nightmare, *mon petit polisson!*
I have called you that twice, already." He adjusted the blankets and put my book on a table. "Joan of Arc was not a soft
saint. She had to be a hard saint. But see what she did when
she believed!"

Two events drove me in terror to my mother's knees that
week. Montreal was shaken by an earthquake that swayed the
buildings where we lived as though waves were under the
streets. My mother was lighting the lamp in the kitchen and
it crashed to the floor, before she could touch the match to
the wick. Pictures fell and chairs danced crazily and my
mother picked up the babies and I got out as fast as she did.
Outside, people were on their knees, praying in the street.

Chimneys were falling and bricks and mortar hit the roofs of
the porches. Women were crying: "Earthquake! Earthquake! Christ save us!" Before a full minute it was over,
but we did not go in until the big bell in the church at the end
of the street tolled reassuring strokes.

The next day I was to feel, for the first time, the stark terror that a newspaper headline can implant in a trusting soul.
A local prophet had been interviewed after the earthquake and
announced that the end of the world was coming that night. It
was smeared on the front page of *La Presse* and when I picked
the paper from the front steps and read it my heart almost
stopped. I hurried to my mother with it, speechless. She
read it and, curiously enough, I thought, continued her work.
If the world were coming to an end what was the use of doing
anything?

"If God saves those who suffer and try to be as uncomfort-
able as possible for Him, there is some hope for us," she said,
with something of bitterness, wiping her eyes on her apron.
These days, many times, I found her weeping. I was older
than my years. I had read much that people said I shouldn't.
Finally, my father had told me that the man plants the seed
of life into the woman and, instinctively, it came to me then
that my mother was with child again.

I went to the front stoop, carrying the paper and shook with
fear. The appalling realization of the headline was worse
than the night my flesh crept when, one Good Friday, in bed,
I heard neighbors in the kitchen over their mulled wine, tell of
the dreaded "Loup Garou" howling in the dark after he had
been changed from a human being for desecrating the church.
Hardy trappers had seen the animal in the woods near Three
Rivers. The headline in the paper was more horrible, even,
than the "revenant" they described, doomed to walk the earth
in chains as a ghost, begging for deliverance, because he had
given up confession and communion long before he died.

I dragged myself across the street to Moses Levy's, gave
him the paper and clung to the counter. He read French, and
he needed no glasses to see the headings. He came around the
counter and held me up.

"Son," he said, "how could a newspaper know? Think!
Think, as Voltaire can teach you. Read everything he wrote.
Millions of years this earth is old. Older than the Bible says.

Vy should it end now? Because a newspaper says so? Study nature. Man is unhappy because he is ignorant of our natural laws. He takes his ideas from others who themselves make mistakes or want to fool him."

And yet there it was in the paper, which I read always, industriously, and believed implicitly because it told you what happened. How could they print such a thing? How ashamed they would be the next day when they all had to go back to work as usual and the sun came out as it did the day before. How well I was to know later, how *that* felt!

The street was alive with papers. The newsboys had to go back for more. When my father came home he read the story through, flung the paper into the coal scuttle and snorted, *"Une blague!"* But trembling neighbors came in with it. I repeated what Moses Levy had said but one woman wailed, "What does he know? A Jew!" My father had a respect for the Jew and his reading and brought her up sharply.

That night people were on the roofs scanning the sky, the clearest in many weeks, dripping with stars. Many others went to church, its tolling bell calling the evening service. The sidewalks were crowded with them. "Those are the ones who missed Mass last Sunday," my father laughed. "That means hell fire for them if it comes tonight." He poured himself a snifter of port.

English Protestants who read the *Star* were trading in Levy's store as if nothing would happen and through the shop's smudgy window I could see the nodding skull cap, long hooked nose and quiet smile of the Jewish tradesman, making change, wrapping packages. There was an air of permanency about it. I crossed the street and pushed open the door which rang a bell behind the partition. Levy told me to sit down. Nobody talked about the end of anything. Ike stopped practicing on his violin in the rear and came out.

"It won't happen," he said.

When I came home my father was in the kitchen smoking a pipe and reading *La Patrie* with his feet in the oven. *La Presse* was still in the coal scuttle. "That's the last time that damned paper comes into this house," he said. The new paper looked thin and peaked but it had courageous headlines. The Boers were making a desperate stand and Sir Wilfred Laurier was trying to settle an argument with the United States about fishing. My father adored Laurier and could never read enough about him. He loved the Canadian statesman for his defense of Riel and the French half-breeds. The Rebellion was still fresh in the public mind and my father had taken part years ago in the fierce nationalist agitation which the rebel's execution had excited in Quebec. My father had helped to capture Riel but did not believe his life should have been taken from him.

For generations the Gauvreaus had been unable to forget the defeat of Montcalm. They had defended Quebec against General Wolfe and had bled on the Heights of Abraham and for a long time lived in a rebellious mood under the English. It was in the blood because Nicolas Gauvreau, the first of the family to come to Canada from France, had been a king's man under the fleur-de-lis. He had married in Quebec in 1668, a lady named Simone Bisson, daughter of Gervais Bisson and Marie Lebeau. It was a rugged and prolific union and their children, grand-children and great grand-children believed Canada belonged to the French. The men were soldiers and sea captains, rebels and hotheads.

Now that the Gauvreaus were loyal to Queen Victoria there were other parts of our family tree into which I was not permitted to climb. But one night in Montreal, my father had taken me to see a play called *The Death of Robert Emmet,* in which the poor man fell through a trap door with a rope around his neck, while a surly audience of Irish and Canadians drank from flasks and shouted "Let Erin remember!" I came home a mass of goose flesh and couldn't sleep. My Aunt Mary, who sat up with me, told me of one of my forebears who had bound himself with an oath of allegiance to the Irish Republic and had become a Fenian and had crossed the Niagara River with 800 men under John O'Neill and they had captured Fort Erie. At a place called Ridgeway they were beaten by Canadian volunteers. And my Aunt Mary had safely hidden the Gauvreau who had escaped.

Now my father wore his Queen Victoria medal on holidays and took me to Laurier political meetings. One of these rousing affairs I still remember. My father, wearing his medal, and accompanied by a number of veterans of the Rebellion, shook hands with the statesman and lifted me up so that Laurier could kiss me on the forehead. Amid the smoking torches

I was hit squarely in the face with a bad egg, which must have been aimed at somebody of more importance. I never forgot this episode, and after nearly four decades of time, when I read that Wendell Willkie had undergone the same experience, I put the paper down with a shudder.

The Gauvreaus of Canada were deeply religious, unquestioning in their faith. That my Aunt Mary was otherwise, some people said, was due to the fact that she had "read too much." She did not intrude herself in the plans of the novena but I remembered one day, when I had swallowed a large Canadian penny and somebody had given me a bottle of holy water to drink, she snatched it out of my hands and forced down my throat the most vicious dose of castor oil that ever passed my lips, and she kept at it until I had reported satisfactory results.

The excitement of the earthquake and the end of the world had disturbed my prayers, which I now repeated, at odd times of the day, perhaps to reach Sainte Anne unawares. At night I sat up in bed thinking about the cure, but I could not rationalize it. Would it happen right then and there in the church? What would become of my foot in the special shoe? Would it burst through it? Perhaps I should take my shoe off in front of everybody. But what difference would such humiliation make afterward? Then I would be permitted to have a gun and drill, and perhaps go to war.

The day of the novena came and we all went to the church and prayed for a long time. It was agreed, first, that we should pray for all those in trouble, and then ask for our special favor. When the time came my father took me from the pew to the basilica. We waited, but nothing happened, and I was the only one in the group who knew why I walked out of the church as I had come into it. A miracle had taken place but it had nothing to do with the brace I was wearing. A brace had been removed from my mind, and I thanked God for it. The brace of dogged fear that held in my consciousness the evil, grimacing goblins of inferiority had dropped off and lay at the foot of the statue with the other discarded props of human suffering which reposed there. It was what I really had wanted. And that night I asked God to try to understand my Aunt Mary.

BOOK II

THE LAND OF STEADY HABITS

CHAPTER I

PROFESSOR HEGEL knew much of my personal history when he helped me to become a reporter on the *Journal-Courier*. Due to my father's restlessness we had returned to New Haven where he resumed his work in the gun factory. He felt he should have gone to the Yukon where he believed the richest gravels had not been worked out, although the Klondike gold rush was almost forgotten.

He bought me a piccolo, the smallest instrument a musician may play in public and still maintain his self-respect. My Uncle Napoleon, a fellow member of the Second Regiment Band with Hegel, who was a noted piccoloist, was impressed with my improvisations and introduced me to the teacher who thought I had possibilities as a flutist virtuoso. My lessons had then begun.

I was sent to the Abraham Lincoln Grammar School in the neighborhood and translated my French education into English while I strove to subdue my Canadian accent which aroused guffaws of laughter in the classroom. The Jesuits had been thorough with me, however, and I skipped several grades. I developed a talent for drawing and sketched a railroad wreck in which the Northampton express had struck a trolley car, whose tracks crossed the New Haven Road line close to our home. Newspaper photographers were rare in those days and I hurried with my drawing to the office of the *New Haven Union* where a busy man under a green eyeshade looked at it and snatched it from me. He seemed to be working in a turmoil with a dozen men, most of whom were writing by hand around a large table. Three or four typewriters were being pecked at with hesitation.

I stood in the door, seeing for the first time a city room in action. No further attention was paid to me and I went home. To my astonishment, the paper, that evening, carried my drawing with my signature, on the front page. A line of type under the sketch said: "By a staff artist on the scene." I bought

37

six copies of the paper and was thrown into such a state of exaltation about my accomplishment that I forgot I had received no remuneration for it.

When my time was not taken up with practicing on the flute I found odd jobs to help pay for my keep. While these chapters inevitably fall into the tradition which seems to insist that childhood shall be a period of privation I was too busy to reflect upon the underprivileged. Boys in my social class were expected to be resourceful. If you didn't know what you were going to do by the time you were fifteen you were considered a failure. The matter of having a job, or not having a job was up to the individual. If he was any good he got a job. If he wasn't, he didn't. No one was pampered in this struggling school and later I interviewed successful men, high in life, who came from it. Many of them had sold newspapers. Times could never have been hard enough for such people to conceive the idea that the Government should support them.

The early struggles of men who have made their own way always have fascinated me, and I have little patience with those who look upon such accounts as concerned with frustration or futility or breast-beating awakenings. As a reporter I discovered that a number of men of importance, often inaccessible to the press, talked to me when I found they had read Horatio Alger. Memories of *The Erie Train Boy* frequently softened a railroad director to the point where he gave me the information I wanted.

During a period when I had abandoned Voltaire and Zola I went through the memorable "Dime Novel" experience, which was supposed to head a boy to perdition. I painted window signs for the owner of a stationery store who traded in newspapers and magazines and who paid me for my work with bundles of back copies of these lurid chronicles, which, incidentally, sold for five cents and not for a dime.

I must have read nearly all of *Frank Merriwell* and years later I met the author of this weekly classic who was looking for a job. Frank Reade's *Weekly* was one of my favorites. I remember *Six Weeks in the Clouds, Exploring a Submarine Mountain, or Lost in the Bottom of the Sea.* Another good story signed, "By an Old Scout," was *Custer's Last Shot, or the Boy Trailer of the Little Bighorn.* The *Pluck and Luck* series always outlasted the oil in my lamp. The best of them was *Harry Hook, the Boy Fireman of No. 1, or Always at His Post.* Here was a lesson in duty and fortitude. I still have a copy of *Young Wild West and the Arizona Boomers, or the Bad Men of Bullet Bar.* No patriotism ever excelled *The Liberty Boys of '76.* Through the years I saved one record of their fame: *The Liberty Boys' Bold Front, or Hot Times on Harlem Heights.* I became saturated with weird ideas of the American Revolution, but I learned about its battles even though the "Liberty Boys" won them all.

These pleasures came to an end one winter's night when my father found me reading *The Road to Ruin, or the Snares and Temptations of New York.* I was to discover that this account of life in the great city had not been exaggerated. My paper-covered periodicals were stacked so high under my bed that the mattress rested on them. My father dug out all that he could find and burned them in bundles in the cellar furnace. Collectors today would give hundreds of dollars for them as museum pieces. I don't believe a boy was ever injured by this rugged reading. There was a good American shout in it. When I was much older, as an editor in Hartford, I met the author of *Diamond Dick,* who found the going hard, and who told me that his hero had never shot a man without complete provocation, a fact which I had verified.

Newspaper reading had become a habit with me as a boy, and I found that in selling papers on competitive street corners New York extras with large headlines attracted more customers. One afternoon on my front porch, I was looking at a terrifying story in the *New York Journal* which gave a half-page display to the drawing of an insect, enlarged to immense proportions. The headline called it "The Kissing Bug," one sting from it on the lips bringing fatal results. I explained it all to my sister Laura who was looking at the picture over my shoulder. A fly settled upon her face and she ran screaming into the house. This was my introduction to the technique of Hearst journalism. Later I was to know more about its effect.

After school hours I dug wild horse-radish in the swamps of Beaver Hills near our home. I was often up to my knees in ooze which turned my brace into rust. I ground the radish, following a recipe passed along from one boy to another, and sold it in jars. My father liked it because its strength made his eyes stream. I am still a connoisseur of any dish which has to do with this powerful root. I obtained part-time work as a sign-painter's apprentice with a stern master of the lettering art named "Flash" Rawson who painted gigantic announcements of fire sales and bargain opportunities in a Church Street loft, a cold place which made me blow on my fingers to hold the brush. During Christmas vacation my salary was increased to $2 a week when I agreed to open the shop at six-thirty in the morning. I started a hellish fire in the stove with discarded creosote blocks piled high on the sidewalk during street repairs. I was fired by Rawson's assistant on Christmas Eve when I slipped on a ladder and fell through a plate-glass window of Childs' Restaurant, whose glittering facade I was adorning with goldleaf.

I was fired as part-time office boy in a spoon factory when I decided to clean a Hammond typewriter by taking it apart. Armed with a screw driver I released a number of screws from the machine, while the typist, a haughty brunette of the Gibson girl era, with tight waist, flaring skirt and pompadour hair, was stamping envelopes. To my horror the machine flattened out like a decimated spider, hundreds of its parts crawling off the table. The girl's screams attracted the office manager who stood white-faced in the door and finally recovered enough self-possession to order me out.

No story of this sort would be complete without an account of the fight with the bully in the schoolyard. My experience did not follow this tradition closely, however, but it had a surprising affect on my lameness.

In my classroom was a hunchback known to the cruel rabble of our house of learning as "Humpy" Gilbert. I avoided him because I thought that when we were together we drew conspicuous attention to each other. Some of the boys in our grade conceived the fiendish plan of forcing "Humpy" to fight it out with me. For days I knew this would happen and one afternoon, after the bell had let us out, I was aware the time had come for it. The taunting gang had closed the gate of the school-yard fence and the hunchback and I were hemmed in for combat. The insults seemed to be aimed mostly at "Humpy," who was mocked and called a coward who did not have the courage to knock me down. He was standing beside me, his face distorted with suffering. He dropped his school books and said:

"We've got to do it. Let's get it over with."

We grappled and struggled on our feet while the barbarians around us, hypnotized to silence, riveted their eyes on every movement of our tussle, slobbering at the mouth. I was stronger than Gilbert. I had learned to ride a bicycle and this exercise had developed my muscles. He crumbled under me and I fell on top of him trying to pin him on his back but he rolled on his hump in a horrible fashion and I couldn't make his shoulders touch the ground. My difficulty was perceived immediately by the brutish louts who had provoked the encounter and they burst into a savage jeering, a depraved howl of laughter, whose hardness of heart I couldn't believe was possible among human beings. Their outcries attracted the janitor who chased them away and "Humpy" and I got up.

My brace had been broken and the parts dragged as I walked and I ripped them off and threw them into the street. I never wore those steel ribs again.

CHAPTER II

Now I was a cub reporter on the *Journal-Courier* and under my coat lapel I wore a silver badge which permitted me to pass through police lines which held back less privileged people who gathered at scenes of fires, murders or suicides. My job was to cover the undertakers, obtain advance copies of Sunday sermons reflecting the views of the clashing denominations and lug from the post office sacks of newspapers which were called "exchanges." Our paper came out in the morning and we worked all night under gas lights in a large room separated by a partition from clattering machines. These activities took place on the second floor of a gloomy building on State Street, around the corner from Chapel Street, not far from the Yale Campus.

It was during the Christmas season of 1909 and New Haven was a happy town. Its inhabitants were singing *In My Merry Oldsmobile, Pony Boy* and *Has Anybody Here Seen Kelly?* Men of an amorous technique clung to *Love Me and the World Is Mine* and sang it in front parlors, accompanied on the piano by blushing young women. Even though the family purse was not so full as it might have been, people could afford a phonograph operated on cylinder records and *Cohen on the Telephone* was always good for a belly laugh. Song hits had a long life. For five years before the World War no banquet was complete without the roaring refrain of Bob Cole's inspiration, sung by carefree gentlemen, full of good food and liquor:

> *"Oh, didn't he ramble, r-a-m-b-l-e?*
> *He rambled all around,*
> *In and out of the town;*
> *Oh, didn't he ramble, r-a-m-b-l-e?*
> *He rambled 'till the butcher cut him down."* *

There seemed to be something serene and reassuring about

* Copyright by Edward B. Marks Music Corporation, and used in this book through its permission.

the future. The Connecticut Company had signed a ninety-nine year lease to protect its franchise to operate trolley cars until 2008 A.D. Maliciously skeptical persons driving buggies drew up their horses and watched optimistic pioneers struggling under stalled automobiles. I got my first automobile ride when the managing editor permitted me to hire one to hurry to some midnight blaze. He rode with me, at twenty miles an hour, but when we got there the fire was over. Editorial writers were still commenting about the journey Senator Chauncey M. Depew had taken from New York to Washington in his own horseless carriage. We refer pityingly to those days as "the horse and buggy age" but only a few families in a town could afford to own a horse and carriage. Now that 27,000,000 of us are driving automobiles we cannot understand how people got around in those good times.

I had left high school after two years of study; and Arthur J. Sloane, the managing editor who hired me, because of his friendship with Professor Hegel, opened a door through which I was to pass to see the best and the worst of what may be absorbed in a lifetime: from darkest Russia to the jungles of Nicaragua; from Presidents to paupers; from high idealism to the lowest depths into which humanity can crawl. Sloane hammered much nonsense out of me with the thoroughness of the Jesuits. He was a stocky man with a stern face which always seemed to be under the greenish pallor of an eyeshade he wore down to his nose. But his face shone from a living spark when he had a good story in his fist. Doing things in my own way is my chief peculiarity and we fought it out many times because of my stubbornness. But no man ever knew the value of news better than Arthur J. Sloane.

Our staff was made up largely of Yale men working their way through college and there was a general exodus of editorial brains when Commencement arrived. Sloane got a new staff together, year after year. Sinclair Lewis was one of Sloane's reporters and so was Waldo Frank, the brilliant liberal writer. There were others, now nationally recognized. Lewis dropped in to smell the ink when I was a cub. The intellectuals on the paper carried on great discussions. I sat back in my corner, when my obituaries were done, and listened to verbal explosions which were as illuminating as they were unprintable. I have heard Lewis tear the world to pieces, and as things turned out, his predictions were moderate. After he left the *Journal-Courier* he sent an autographed copy of his first novel, *Our Mr. Wrenn,* to Sloane who let everything slide and locked himself up in his cubby-hole to read a book written by one of his boys. Even then I understood the pride this unappreciated editor felt in his heart.

Norris G. Osborn, our editor in chief, was a tall dark gentleman of aristocratic features, who strolled out of his sanctum, occasionally, with his suspenders hanging down. He liked to watch the reporters working in the newsroom, which he called the "news rum," a description which was not always inappropriate. He believed the world revolved about Yale University and his editorials came out in floods. He had an assistant, a little old man who looked like Andrew Carnegie and whose name was, as I recall it, Epaphroditus Pratt, who many years before my time had written flaming fulminations against those who opposed the purchase of Alaska for $7,200,-000. He could show you reports to prove that the value of fur seals taken from the territory from 1868 to 1902 amounted to $35,000,000 alone. Sometimes he got going on the Klondike rush and I was the only one who listened to him, in my corner, with my list of the dead from the undertakers.

Editor Osborn discovered that I was more widely read than some of the other members of the staff. At times he called me in to read the "exchanges" while he went to lunch at the Graduates Club. He created the "Three Hours for Lunch Club" years before the idea came to the mind of Christopher Morley. I answered the telephone in the editor's office and one day I reported that a tradesman had called up and made some rather emphatic remarks about an unpaid bill. The editor kept his bills on a long spike and said he was working from the bottom of it. He explained to me, with a sardonic grin, that he was acting on the plan of Mirabeau, who never settled his baker's bill until it underwent a formidable transformation into a bill of exchange. The editor took his time at it but always paid his creditors.

One evening I was stunned by an episode which made me realize I was engaged in an unpredictable enterprise. The city editor, Paul Barnett, who later helped to turn the Yale football ticket office into big business, picked up his hat during a thunderous argument with Sloane about a story we had missed,

and quit his job. At that time a city editor impressed me with
the importance of some sort of minor god. A few weeks
before this excitement, on my way home, I had found a crowd
gathered about a dead man on the Yale Campus. I telephoned
frantically to the paper but our issue had gone to press. Returning to the scene I was shocked to discover that the victim
was "Pop" Haight, the city editor of the *New Haven Register*.
Those who identified him told me that he loved a girl on his
staff. She refused him and he had slashed his throat. I couldn't
understand how a man who had risen to the position of city
editor could be bothered by a woman's rebuffs. From a professional standpoint I regretted he had to kill himself at a time
which made it impossible for us to print the first story of his
self-destruction. Already, the fascination of recording sensational happenings in a newspaper had crept into my bone and
marrow.

Sloane told me to read the editorials of Arthur Brisbane
who, at that time, had begun to list the great books which have
opened the mind of mankind. The Hearst editor, whom I then
believed to be a great man, was performing an invaluable
service through his literary recommendations. His column
guided me to second-hand book shops where I picked up the
works of Samuel Johnson, Racine, Heine, Montaigne and
most of the immortals. It was through Brisbane that I read
enough to know why Homer, Dante, Goethe, Cervantes and
Shakespeare are the greatest writers that ever lived.

The Hearst papers were undergoing a heavy attack from
the conservative press and the church, and Brisbane traveled
about the country delivering talks in defense of sensational
journalism. He came to New Haven and I was permitted to
report his address for the reason that I was an unimportant
member of the staff and that nothing that I could write about
him would appear in print, unless he dropped dead on the platform. I was unacquainted with the humiliation of this assignment, and I wrote a long account of Brisbane's remarks. I
read our paper through the next day and I found a four-line
item on the last page, informing the public that the editor had
come and gone. Among other things in the defense of Hearst
journalism, Brisbane had said:

"The whole human race, according to the highest authority,
has been exterminated once already because it wasn't going

right and only the rainbow protects it from a repetition. They say that the Hearst papers are yellow. Remember that the sun is yellow and we need a little sunshine. Think of the colors of the rainbow!"

My duties increased and I had to cover meetings of The Sacred Stars of the Milky Way. While taking notes at one of these gatherings I sketched on my pad a vicious caricature of an ample, matronly lady who was entertaining the assemblage by singing a song of which I was weary. I had heard it poured out too many times by females of avoirdupois before women's clubs.

"Oh, the days of the Kerry dancing
"Oh, the ring of the piper's tune."

Some of the members peered over my shoulder, a common practice among the curious who want to see how a reporter functions. The soloist had reached the words: "Gone, alas, like our youth too soon." It made my drawing worthy of Daumier. There was a muffled scream of horror behind my back and a trembling Sacred Star asked:

"Is THAT going into the paper?"

The question pleased me as it seemed to brand my sketch as authentic. Although I did my best to explain that I merely was amusing myself there was considerable trouble over this episode. I never covered women's clubs again. Osborn who had received a complaint about me, asked me to produce the caricature. He roared with laughter, and I was then permitted to draw political cartoons which appeared on the front page. I studied the works of Thomas Nast and Homer Davenport and my mind was full of dreams of becoming a great cartoonist. But I had to watch my undertakers, lodge meetings and hotel arrivals.

I learned the first great lesson in journalism from my job as obituary editor. It is quite simple. Once a mistake has been made in print it should be honestly admitted, and immediately corrected. I absorbed this lesson through days of torture and when it was over I felt I was waking from a troubled dream.

I had many things to do, and through carelessness, or otherwise, I selected from the city directory the full name and address of a man who, I assumed, was the departed individual whose last name had been telephoned to me by an undertaker who was leaving immediately to embalm the corpse. The name was the only one of its kind in the directory and there was no telephone number listed for it. It was after midnight. Soon it would be too late to get anything into the paper. There was another important reason to consider. The obituary editor of the *Palladium,* our opposition, had been giving me some stiff competition. I wrote an item about the man, whose occupation was described in the directory as an inspector of gas meters, and drew over him the wings that bear the good to heaven.

When the next evening came and the man, one Francis Xavier McGoorty (whose name is seared into my brain), announced that he was still alive, I was so dumfounded as to ask him if he were sure of it. He said great damage had been done. Women fainted when he went into their homes to inspect the meters. I should have reported the facts to the managing editor, but for days Sloane had been in an ugly mood. There were threats of labor troubles in our plant and we had been late for press. The editor went about with eyes like glazed apple rings, having little time to sleep and I thought my mistake would be the last straw added to his burden and that I would lose my job. I gave the gas man fifty cents and told him to return in two days while I thought it over. The next time he came he wanted more and I gave him seventy-five cents. After a few days of these machinations I was broke.

I consulted Charles Kenney, our veteran proofreader, an ageless, Peter Pan sort of person, who had survived many crises. He was loaded down with toil but caught the drift of my story and said: "Tell him he's dead." It was too late to do this convincingly. I felt I was in human bondage for the rest of my life. But when Kenney heard that the gas man was collecting money from me he became sympathetic. When my oppressor came once more, the proofreader, who could put on an impressive and terrifying appearance, jumped up, faced him and roared:

"We're going to sue you for libel!"

The gas man ran for the door and we never saw him again.

Kenney became my guide and teacher while I remained on the paper. He performed an incredible amount of work every night, never too drunk to proofread the entire paper, including the advertisements, without any assistance. He claimed to be the last surviving member of a New York Suicide Club and after his last proof had been corrected he discussed the philosophic convenience of suicide until dawn came and milk wagons rattled in the street.

CHAPTER III

I was young in years, but, as Bacon puts it, old in hours. Half a decade on a newspaper had made me tougher than I appeared to be and I had no illusions left. Now I could understand the living conditions which disturbed me. The press was not responsible for them. But the press could speak out. Unfortunately, if the press crusaded, it was called sensational and cheap. Papers of old traditions had to maintain their self-respect.

As a police reporter I became interested in police raids which were made on a long row of houses on a notorious short-cut to nowhere called Prindle Alley, in the center of the city. The news of the raids was recorded placidly every month in the local press, names of girls given with the amount of their fines. The names changed occasionally as the months passed along.

Prindle Alley was the first place of note to be heard about as one of New Haven's attractions by visitors and particularly Yale freshmen looking for the usual temptations. I was not interested in improving the morals of the visitors. I was interested in the fact that girls in my neighborhood, risking their lives at starvation wages in the powder plant of the gun factory where my father worked, eventually went to Prindle Alley to make enough to live on. When some of them discovered that one day's work in Prindle Alley brought them more money than they could earn over the powder bins in a month, they gave up the art of powder mixing. Occasionally a girl lost an arm or a leg in the powder shop when things blew up. You could hear the noise of it and mothers rushed out of the little houses where we lived and appealed to Christ. I had heard the cry several times as a boy. "Oh, Christ, don't let it be Joan!" or "Oh, Christ, don't let it be Peggy!"

In Prindle Alley death did not come as quickly. There, at least, you could eat, have warm clothes in the winter and help your broken-down father who could no longer crawl along the

tracks to the factory. This thing was hitting close to home.
I had two beautiful sisters, as shapely and skylarking as the
French-Canadians know how to produce them. Their only
hope of existence was in the gun factory. Perhaps they might
marry some honest toilers in the neighborhood, have children
and watch pennies. My sister Laura soon tried this system of
living and died of tuberculosis. My father knew what our
neighborhood had to face. He sent us to confession and communion each month and every night he prayed at his bed. He
had developed a rheumatic heart, but he trudged to the factory
every day. Perhaps if I could have kicked the treadle of a
machine I would have earned less than my reporter's salary,
and I would have been stuck in the factory for life. I was
fortunate.

I attended a raid on Prindle Alley. The police dismounted
from a long line of hacks, knocked on the doors and the blue-
coated visitors were addressed by their first names by the
madames who were familiar with these social calls. The girls,
who were familiar with them also, were dressed and ready and
amid friendly bantering we proceeded to headquarters. The
men in the houses, students and such, were never bothered and
generally waited there until the legal formalities were over.

At the station house I recognized a number of the girls of
my neighborhood who looked at me pleadingly as I stood by the
police blotter with my pad and pencil. I changed my report to
such names as Penelope Devonshire, Doris Trowbridge or
Gladys Carrington-Peters. But I did something which was
more unorthodox. I began my story with the name of the
politician and deputy sheriff who accepted twenty-five dollars
as a bonus from each girl to arrange their bail. The scores
of girls going through these proceedings under the nose of the
desk sergeant were worth $1,500 each month to the political
panderer. The sum was lower when some of the girls were
ill. After the court had fined them, the next day, they returned to Prindle Alley to continue their traffic undisturbed
for another month. Out of respect for the surviving relatives
of the New Haven politician, who lived by these means and
left a good estate, I am omitting his name here, but it appeared plainly enough in the afternoon papers after my story
came out. He called the reporters together and gave them
an interview in which I was referred to by name as a "social-

istic trouble-making whipper-snapper, the kind of person that corrupted journalism and belonged with Emma Goldman."

I talked to the judge about these conditions. He was a tall, thin man, gray of hair, and a tired face lined with care. His name was John Tyner.

"If you think you can stop it, go ahead," he said. "I wish I could. How do you suppose I became a judge, for God's sake?"

Sloane printed my story as I wrote it, knowing full well the rumpus it would cause. When the strife became heavy and I was barred from headquarters, he launched me into a campaign to clean out the police department. At critical times, he backed me up as his reporter, which is the finest thing you can say about a managing editor. He came to headquarters to fight my battles with me. Captains and police sergeants were toppled from their nests of graft. I wrote the stories and found time to draw cartoons on the subject, copying Nast's style. Sloane printed them and had a difficult time with the directors of the paper, but we won our fight. A new chief of police was appointed named Philip Smith, who, I believe, is still at his post. I remember him as an honest, two-fisted cop. After he took up the reins, Prindle Alley no longer could exist by paying its money to political panderers at police headquarters. The system was broken.

I investigated the ownership of the Prindle Alley real estate which, I found, was owned by a church corporation whose agents collected the rent money from the houses each month. I knew then that I had gone as far as I could. A newspaper cannot attack a church. It was a house of worship, incidentally, which felt itself superior to the Catholic Church.

This experience changed the course of my newspaper life. I was no longer interested in printing surface facts, and my attitude, from then on, caused me to be whirled off into space from newspaper offices at regular intervals through the years. I was never turbulently cynical. I felt that the press had more to do than merely to print the accepted alibi. I knew that Sloane felt that way about it, but when my enthusiasm reached the point of embarrassment he saw to it that I had other things to occupy my mind. Why he made me a sporting editor, I never knew. I had no interest whatever in the contests I had to view, learning the rules of prowess, studying

handbooks to remember that Dodo Maher had knocked out
Spike Hickey in the third round of their last encounter; hob-
nobbing with prize fighters, taking fake wrestling matches
seriously, drinking with aristocratic football stars and watching swimming champions doing something I fairly ached to
duplicate. Old Sloane was a sardonic teacher.

One day I rebelled. My name on the masthead on the sporting pages suddenly stuck out as some ironic joke and I removed
it and turned my sporting department over to my assistant,
Bob Wilson, who was a better man at that sort of work than I
would ever be. I became an anonymous figure again and my
newly acquired friends who thought that a sporting editor was
a person who had reached the height of success, sought me
out to express their condolences. Even the telephone operators,
who represented my first feminine social contact, dropped me
from their list of possibilities.

But I had another plan in mind which was to result, only a
few years later, in my appointment as managing editor of the
most powerful Connecticut newspaper of the period and the
oldest journal of the nation. Of course, I didn't know about
that when I threw up my job as sporting editor. I have come
to believe that there is a purpose written on the forehead of
those who obey their honest inclinations and follow the in-
dwelling impulse. At such times opportunity tugs at the
elbow of the man engrossed in his little troubles, if he will but
feel.

Sloane was becoming irritated by a murder mystery which
had been dragging along in the newspapers for days and offered no prospects of solution. He believed, as I did, that the
machinery of the law could not always be depended upon to
fathom the suspicions of justice. He was convinced that a
reporter was the best detective in the world. The mystery that
bothered him bothered me as well, as it had come to light in
Beaver Hills, close to Hamden, where I used to dig my horse-
radish. I knew every inch of the neighborhood and everybody
in the district. I decided to solve the case for him.

I had identified a corpse in an undertaker's shop, back in
my obituary days, by the numerals on the dead man's watch.
He had a green cross tattooed on his arm and I had turned this
sad affair into a little mystery of my own called *The Man with
the Green Cross*. He was nothing but an itinerant workman

in shabby clothes but the *New York Journal* had picked up my story and described him as attired in a full dress suit with a top hat lying at his feet. This had been the only mystery to present itself to me for solution.

My reading had included the best detective stories written from the time of Edgar Allan Poe and Wilkie Collins. I still agree with Alexander Woollcott that *The Moonstone* is the best mystery story ever conceived. I adored Sergeant Cuff and followed the great thief-taker until he retired to cultivate his favorite roses in his hidden garden. But Monsieur Lecoq was no slouch and, at times, Sherlock Holmes was magnificent. Take the others from me, including Philo Vance, who is too damned supercilious. The modern crew stole everything from the grand old sleuths who plowed the field.

My solutions of crime in my newspaper work usually have been based on a simple method of putting two and two together with patient determination. I learned this as a police reporter. Intelligence is necessary, but a surpassing insight is all bosh. Outthinking the sick mind of a criminal can be done by any good police detective who sticks to his job.

Sloane's mystery, which was slowly disintegrating into half-columns on inside pages, had to do with a Jewish wholesaler who had been lured to Beaver Hills with $750 for which he was to receive a tremendous bargain in potatoes. He had been shot and the money taken from him. The Jew's family knew he had been enticed to the scene of the crime with the cash through the use, over the telephone, of the name of a rich farmer.

In my neighborhood lived one of my former schoolmates, George Redding, whose ambition was to be a playwright. He had brought his plays to me at the newspaper shop, with the hope that I would write a story about him and his efforts. He had left with me several of his photographs for which he had posed in dramatic attitudes. He had not been able to sell his wares and he was too obscure to be given attention.

Going over my district, where the crime had been committed, I discovered that Redding was spending money lavishly in taverns to entertain a comely woman who was a trained nurse. He had no means of support and I knew that literature could not so quickly have lined his bulging pockets. I was writing thousands of good, honest words for thirteen dollars a

week. I went to the house where the nurse lived and obtained
her photographs from a downstairs neighbor, and had the pictures re-photographed and returned the originals to their proper
place. I armed myself with the entire history of Redding and
his nursing companion. I remembered that, as my schoolmate,
he had been among those who had hooted and howled in their
depravity while I rolled in the dirt with poor "Humpy" Gilbert.

I went to Redding's closest male friend and when I mentioned the murder he was struck with terror. I obtained the
information that Redding had confessed everything to him in a
letter. I arranged to have the murderer arrested by the town
constable, Fred Sturtz, with the help of the New Haven Police
at a time to suit my own convenience. When the young playwright was locked up I was the only reporter in the city who
possessed the complete facts of the case, all of his photographs
and his forgotten plays which suddenly became news.

Sloane treated me with the consideration a director of our
company might have deserved. The editor played the story as
Paderewski might have played Beethoven's *Moonlight Sonata*
before a favorite audience. He bought me my first cocktail and
patted me on the back as I released, day by day, exclusively,
every phase of the case with new photographs. Joseph Connolly, then a smart reporter on the *New Haven Union* and
later to become general manager of the Hearst publications,
attempted to deny the authenticity of my reports by quoting
disgruntled police officials in his articles, but my competitors
were snowed under. I was merciless, as they would have been
with me, had circumstances been otherwise. When you are
fighting for a two-dollar increase in pay, war is war in newspaper work. Arnon Alling, the prosecuting attorney, came to
consult me about what I was to announce, to Sloane's unbounded amusement. Later, the editor had a fist fight with
Alling, and perhaps it was about this episode.

Redding confessed his crime to the police, leaving out a
number of important details which were in my possession and
which were vital to the prosecution of the case. He sat in court
as some figure in one of his melodramas while I covered his
trial. As a reward for my work, Sloane assigned me to report
the hanging of this poverty-stricken transgressor whose literary
frustrations in our drab neighborhood undoubtedly had unbalanced his mind. I stood a few feet away from him on the

night of his execution and he held me, fixed, with his burning brown eyes which seemed to grow larger and larger as we stared at each other until the black cap was finally pulled over his head and he was yanked up to the ceiling and his neck broken. On his way to the rope he had been required to walk by his own coffin, whose lid was held upright by an undertaker looking at his watch. When I left the prison to write my story I found out why newspaper men drank and I had my first half-tumbler of cognac.

I became a nine-day wonder as a reporter-detective, and fidgeted for another good murder mystery. One evening, a journalist of note, an apostle of Dana and a pupil of Boss Lord of the old *Sun* came to see me and introduced himself. He was Clifton L. Sherman, managing editor of the *Hartford Courant*, the state's greatest newspaper. He wanted to know how I had obtained my information about the Redding case, and I told him. He was a man of medium height, with a certain restless energy. He had piercing, bluish-gray eyes and a sharp nose in a keen, sensitive face, and he seemed to inhale as a perfume the details of my exploits. Before he left, he put his hand on my shoulder and said: "Boy, if you ever leave here, come up and see me. You can work for me anytime."

Sloane promoted me to the post of telegraph editor, giving me a title and more money. He was an expert in the handling of foreign news and I learned from him how to boil down 100,000 words a night from all parts of the world and give the reader a digest of all the things that happen in a day on this weary sphere. The work tied me to my post until the Associated Press wires closed at three A.M. "Flimsy" began to pour in on me at six o'clock in the evening. I had hardly become accustomed to the work when a Serbian student fired two shots at a royal couple in a place called Sarajevo. I gave the news the prominence I thought it deserved but I found in the morning that the *New York Times* had printed a headline larger than my own on the subject. My conservatism annoyed me. I bought myself some maps to study the territory in which the assassinations had taken place and I was in the middle of them, to familiarize myself with the geography of Europe, when the World War exploded on my desk.

The *Journal-Courier* was then the only morning paper in New Haven (the *Palladium* having expired) and I began to receive as visitors faculty members from Yale University who couldn't wait until the paper came out to absorb the news. A number of professors who introduced themselves to me, I soon perceived, were better acquainted than I was with the significance of the affairs I was attempting to interpret for the public. Professor Yandell Henderson, noted Yale physiologist, actually took me to task one night, absent-mindedly assuming that I was one of his students in class, when he looked over my shoulder at a headline I was writing about the Russian movements. The grave professors came in regularly, not only to find out what was happening, but, I believe, to see that I did not go entirely off the track on which world events were leading us. I abandoned my editorial dignity and listened, and I learned much from these scholarly men. I remember at least six of them who would have made first-class telegraph editors, but their work would have been worth more than fifteen dollars a week. At times I found myself wishing I were older. I thought that knowledge came with the years. I grew sideburns, which, I hoped would induce the professors to treat me with more respect.

One man who came to see me was more tolerant and sympathetic than my impatient professors of the night who were now appearing with less regularity. He was William Howard Taft, former President of the United States. He sat at my desk and read official statements from the powers at war. At first he seemed surprised that I was handling the avalanche of news by myself. "More and more," he said, "this is becoming a world of graver responsibilities for the young." His comments on the sweeping changes in Europe helped me and he often predicted turns in events which, when they happened, did not sweep me off my feet. I was becoming more pleased with myself when I compared my work with the treatment of the same news in the *New York Times*, whose telegraph editor did not have half of the Yale faculty and a former President of the United States to help him out.

Taft was at this time Kent professor of law at Yale but his mind still followed closely all events which affected our Government. We became friendly in our little chats. At times he was talkative, but his joviality, once characteristic of him, was gone. One evening while he was reading bulletins of appalling disasters to the Allies he said:

"As abhorrent as the German military system is, we will
have to adopt its method if civilization is to survive. The
Germans concentrate on such things while democracy leaves
defense to the last minute. If such a state of affairs continues,
some day, in your life time, because you are young, you may
see the end of democracy, such as we know it now. This
trouble will continue for half a century. Germany will always
have some kind of Bismarck. It would never be happy if it
conquered all Europe. We must safeguard our future. Nations do not quickly mend their ways, and human nature, like
one or two individuals I might mention, does not change over
night."

He laughed over his last remark and I made notes of his
comments after he left. He was not talking for publication
and felt free to chat with me. I fell into the habit of recording
the salient points of conversations I was privileged to have with
important people.

On the last occasion I saw the former President the dispatches emphasized critical reverses for the Allies on the Western Front. Taft read the official statements, interpreting the
communiqués from France and England as admissions of
grave retreats. "This will keep Mr. Wilson up tonight," he
said. "At least, I can sleep."

A boy brought in another handful of "flimsy" and Taft
waited for me to separate it. The news was on yellow tissue
and the carbon lettering was hard on the eyes. One story was
from New York and he read every word, holding the paper
close to his face. It was a statement by Theodore Roosevelt
who sounded grave warnings about the future state of the nation. While I read it, Taft said:

"If I were in your position I wouldn't give too much
prominence to that ass. Whatever he says from now on will
never carry any weight or significance. That's for your own
guidance."

I threw the news into the wastebasket, acting on what I
thought was fairly good authority.

Now when I came home in the morning at four o'clock I
found my father waiting for me in the kitchen where he read
my headlines and shook his head over the losses of the French.
He was working on war orders in the gun factory with an increased force of men. Long hours of overtime brought more

money to the neighborhood and, day and night, people were bobbing and jiggering madly at the machines in the gun plant. I saw them through the windows as I passed the factory which was ablaze with lights. The roar of activity rang in my ears until I reached my doorstep.

When the year of 1915 was well on its way the sound from the shop became an uproar and a clatter so powerful that voices had to be raised to be heard in the homes near by. My father, who still waited for me and my paper, had to sleep in a chair. His heart troubled him more when he lay on his back. The company physicians who examined him apparently saw no cause for alarm. He had new responsibilities which concerned the inspection of guns, and grew more haggard and worn. His military bearing was gone and he was beginning to stoop although he was barely approaching middle age. He talked of the rights of men to organize and said that if the people got together the Government would make unionism a law. Debs, he said, was an honest man and he would vote for him at the next election. There had been disturbances at the shop. Police guarding the plant had dispersed groups of toilers who were listening to a speaker who advocated collective bargaining. White-collar crowds from the offices had called the agitator an anarchist while he was hustled off in a patrol wagon. My father now read a paper called *The Appeal to Reason* which I found in his lap when he was asleep near the kitchen table, a bottle of "Father John's Medicine" at his elbow.

One morning he greeted me in trembling agitation. He had been comparing notes at the factory with a friend who was inspecting ammunition to be sent to Russia with a large order of rifles with which both men were familiar. The two, who had been soldiers together in the Northwest Rebellion, were alarmed by the discovery that some of the bullets would not fit the guns. My father believed that the pressure of the rushed order made minute inspection difficult and blamed officers of the Russian Army, two of whom he had seen in the factory under the influence of liquor during their tour of supervision. Perhaps, in his excitement, the affair had grown to exaggerated proportions in his mind, but he had been an infantryman, decorated for bravery, and he would have worried over a handful of soldiers of any race had he known that they were in the front line without the proper equipment with which to defend themselves. He was reassured when I told him I would seek out the Russians and deliver his message.

On the next evening, during the midnight hour which had become my dinner time, I visited Bishop's Hotel where a group of officers of the Czar's regime were quartered while they were ostensibly supervising the war orders for Russia. They were in uniforms, sitting at tables in a tap room roistering with actresses of a vaudeville troup, whose professional entertainments were over for the night. I proposed to impart my father's information to the officers but they had reached a stage of bewildered drunkenness, their heads rolling on the shoulders of their hysterical women companions. The men laughed as only Russians can laugh when they guzzle. They would not have understood a word I said. I prodded a good looking bearded man, with the rank of colonel, who was apparently the host. He pulled me down into his seat and broke into a maudlin song. I got away while he was pouring out a drink. My time was short and I had to get back to my war news.

I reported my experience to my father and he buried his face in his hands. Finally, he said:

"Maybe you can write a piece for the paper about it. You could put it on the telegraph and it would go all over the world. That would stop it."

During the previous year the news had fallen on my desk from the battlefield at Tannenberg, where the Russians clubbed their guns and their general committed suicide. The debauched officers of the Czar now supervising Russian war orders in American munitions plants were usually too drunk to discuss its significance.

One night, during the second year of the war, my father died in his chair on his day of rest. He had never feared death and as I looked into his face I saw in it the expression of a man who had left a darkroom to enter a large place full of light and divinely beautiful. I tried to open his right hand which gripped something tightly. His fingers clutched a rosary and I never removed it.

CHAPTER IV

SLOANE increased my pay after my father died. My two sisters became factory workers and a younger brother continued to go to school. My mother, with her usual bravery, restored the household to its family routine. I assumed additional duties which increased my salary to twenty-three dollars a week. Now I was telegraph editor, real-estate editor and automobile editor and I worked from one o'clock in the afternoon until three o'clock on the following morning. I was also financial editor, a duty which consisted of clipping columns of closing stock prices from final editions of New York evening papers and sending the quotations to the printers. By this method I supplied material for a page and a half of type in five minutes. I bought one share of New Haven Road stock to develop my interest in high finance.

While doing the breast stroke through waves of Associated Press "flimsy" which broke over my desk I thought editing was a deadly dull task. I could see no end to the war and I wrote my headings without emotion although dispatches describing the Kaiser as having bombed the statue of his own grandmother amused me. When memories of my father came to my mind I choked my grief by reflecting upon the fascinating hours I had spent with pad and pencil hunting news.

One night when I was a reporter, I had been sent to cover a meeting addressed by Emma Goldman in a crowded hall stirred into feverish agitation and surrounded by policemen. I fully expected a bomb to be thrown from the platform. I talked to the anarchist and she said: "Lad, when I read your piece in the paper in the morning I won't blame you for the names your editors will call me. Open your young mind and think of the workers."

I would not have believed then, that the fiery agitator, years later, would receive a kindly and understanding editorial in the *New York Times* when her struggle against the injustices of the world had come to an end.

Once Sloane had appointed me a "war correspondent" and I reported the military maneuvers at Niantic in Connecticut, where laughing men in khaki were put through strategical movements under the watchful eye of Colonel John Q. Tilson of the National Guard. I was with the "Blue Army," and we were planning to check an invasion by the "Red Army" coming at us from Rhode Island. It was furious fun. Later my army was to discover the ghastly realism behind this summer lark and send back the names of many of its soldiers to be inscribed on a roll of honor on the New Haven Green as heroes who died to save the world for Democracy.

On a grassy mound at Niantic, where I lay on my stomach observing with a pair of old-fashioned opera glasses an out-flanking movement by the Second Regiment, a wax bullet went through my hat, and I wore the headgear for months with a hole in it. Colonel Tilson admitted me into his tent where he perspired in his drab fighting togs and glued his eyes on large maps. At night I sent off my dispatches which always announced that he had saved Connecticut. One afternoon, my editor in chief, Norris G. Osborn, who was a colonel, too, left his desk to offer his cooperation and appeared at the headquarters tent in a brilliant uniform of blue with quivering epaulets, red stripes down his trousers and a polished sword on his hip. Tilson, bareheaded, sweating and dusty, looked up and said:

"My God, Norris, has war been declared?"

Richard Harding Davis arrived from New York to view the operations and sat in the Colonel's tent, asking significant questions. The famous correspondent paid no attention to me although I stared at him with such admiration that my eyes must have bulged. After I returned from the wars, Bessie McCoy came to New Haven as the "Yama Yama" girl in the musical comedy, *Three Twins*. She was supposed to have been injured when a curtain came down on her shoulder and I was sent to the Hotel Oneco to interview her and write a story that she would appear, regardless of the accident because "the show must go on." I was told to go right upstairs and I found the actress wrapped in a red lounging robe of silk and reclining in a Morris chair. Her injuries were not perceptible but I was struck with amazement to find Richard Harding Davis sitting by her side holding her hand. He did not recognize me as his fellow war correspondent. He sat back, poured out a Scotch highball and said:

"Sit down, Kid, and have a drink. What paper are you from? This is a front page story and I'll tell you how to write it."

I saw *Three Twins* on a press pass. I sat in the front row, close to the orchestra and I could have touched the musician who played the flute. He was superb but couldn't approach Billy Hegel. The house was darkened and the leader directed the music with a baton tipped with a little green light which swung about in rhythmic arcs. I thought the spectacle was as wonderful as the Metropolitan Opera. And Richard Harding Davis married Bessie McCoy because they were in love and all the papers carried stories of the romance I had seen with my own eyes. I pondered about how glorious the world could be for some people.

At times during my rounds, I dropped into a restaurant and cafe in the center of the city, around the corner from Church Street, to hear a girl sing. Professor Hegel had been struck by her voice and told me it had the most remarkable quality he had ever heard outside of the Metropolitan Opera. I wrote a little piece about her which was considered free advertising and thrown out of the paper. The singer was the daughter of an Italian coal dealer in Meriden, Connecticut and her name was Rosa Ponselle. Not many years later when she became the first American to make her debut with Caruso I managed to be in the gallery.

Sloane sent me to help report a railroad wreck in North Haven. More than twenty passengers had been killed and I stepped about the bodies in a melon patch while I chewed salted peanuts and made a bird's-eye-view sketch of the disaster. An old reporter from the *Register* told me the accident had been caused by "interlocking directorates" which had thrown the New Haven Railroad into chaos. That was beyond me and I waited until press time to see my drawing printed. When I became "financial editor," my one share of New Haven Road stock was to intrigue my interest in "interlocking directorates" by dropping fifty points almost in my face while I was clipping Wall Street closing prices for the printers.

I liked to think of the time I climbed to the second floor of the Hotel Oneco when flames were raging through the building. Firemen pulled me out while I clutched the hotel register. I was drenched but I had the list of the guests. I worked with an intensity born of desperation, a determination that I was not to be beaten on an assignment.

I had to be a reporter again. Occasionally, I tried to avoid these lingering looks behind, when I was free from my desk, by playing the flute with a dance orchestra from which I watched ecstatic crowds swing to the accelerated music of the period. I needed the money. I was engaged to play with Bob Eaton's minstrel show at the Town Hall in North Haven. Eaton paid me $10 for my work. He was an important Republican politician who had a daughter of almost ethereal beauty and I rehearsed a song with her called *Red Wing* in which I had to follow her sweet, poignant voice with a caressing obligato. On the gala night we repeated it to rocking applause. She stood above me on the stage, bright-eyed and flushed, wearing a white dress with red roses at her breast, her auburn hair caught in a circlet. From the pit I accompanied her with the modulated strains of other instruments. I watched the graceful girl, as I played my variations by heart, and I was swept by an irresistible emotion of love for her. It became something like a heart-pain when we went on to the celebrated numbers of Stephen Foster's music.

Eaton was well-to-do and I felt he would not have countenanced future visits to his daughter by an itinerant musician. As soon as the show was over she was surrounded by congratulatory admirers and I left the hall without saying good-by to her. I never saw her again.

Returning from a musical expedition early one Sunday morning I locked up my aged ebony flute in its case for the last time. I had been playing at the Second Regiment Armory for a dance whose music had reached the first stages of the hysteria to come. Victor Herbert's waltzes were flung aside for *Everybody's Doing It* and *When That Midnight Choo-choo Leaves for Alabam. Alexander's Ragtime Band* still reigned and the tempo whirled the breathless dancers about the floor. The *Midnight Choo-choo* was accompanied by blasts from a steamboat whistle blown by a percussionist whose foot meanwhile made the bass drum tremble. The melody was a blare of saxophones and shrieking clarinets. My contribution was lost in the din.   Dance music was on its way to the hey nonny-nonny and the hot-cha-cha, and the flute that was meant for Debussy had sobbed its last notes in this Devil's tattoo.

When I saw Professor Hegel once more I found him dejected to the point of despondency.   A good German-American, he was already feeling the sting of the war's lash.   Prejudice was rising against his race, whose simple character and good-natured sentiment was to become nothing but a memory.   The Germany of his musical and metaphysical abstractions was to be transformed into a force of hate, treachery and scientific murder.   He saw it all ahead and the spectre of its barbarism killed him.

One day I forgot my war desk and I went to see Managing Editor Sherman on the *Hartford Courant*.   He remembered me at once and hired me on the spot, giving me more money than I was receiving for my various editorships on the *Journal-Courier*.   I came back, told my mother I had found an opportunity for advancement and that as soon as I had established myself we would all move to Hartford.   Before I embarked on this enterprise I married Sarah Welles Joyner, society editor of the paper on which I had worked for seven years.   She had left Mount Holyoke College for journalism.   She was an active suffragette, tired of the humdrum of social affairs, and had influenced me in my decision to seek new pastures.

I would miss some interesting friends.   Among them was H. I. Phillips, then managing editor of the *Register*, who had talked to me about some way of getting out of New Haven. He was a cartoonist, also, and had a style which might have been described as "early James Thurber," whose bewildering drawings much later helped to make the *New Yorker* famous. All this was long before Phillips was to become the brilliant columnist of the *Sun* in the metropolis, but his drawings created such an impression on me that I have never forgotten them. With his unique pen, Phillips had a certain breath-taking daring.   One day he spread across the front page of the *Register* a cartoon strip he had drawn of a New Haven Chamber of Commerce banquet.   On the dais could be seen former President Taft, making a speech with one foot in a punch bowl.   Standing beside him was a local dignitary of power and prestige, Colonel Isaac M. Ullman, who was represented as juggling champagne bottles as Indian clubs.   Other notables were performing dumfounding acts of similar interest. When John Day Jackson, the publisher, recovered from the shock of this art after the paper appeared he ordered platoons of employees to rush about town to recall all the copies that had been distributed. I have always considered this episode a result of some frustration which finally made Phillips an outstanding humorist.

The closest friend whom I was to miss most of all was Clifford L. Weaver, who had contributed much to my mental relief during the months of grief which overcame me after my father died. Weaver developed into an amazing literary prophet and had made me acquainted with the books of Blasco Ibáñez, Arnold Bennett, H. G. Wells, D. H. Lawrence, Katherine Mansfield, Maurice Maeterlinck, Leonard Merrick and countless other noted moderns long before they finally became popular. He might have been one of the best literary critics of his time. Later, my exploits to capture millions of readers must have stunned him.

My experience on the *Courant* was to be more or less spectacular, due to Sherman who asked his tolerant city editor to permit me to hunt out my own news. I knew what he wanted and I had been on his staff but a short time when I uncovered in Connecticut an aged recluse whom I identified as Hermione Wallace, a woman of great wealth who had disappeared many years previously from Chicago where she was known as "The Diamond Queen." She had been a friend of Hetty Green, the fabulously rich eccentric, and had presented a jeweled altar to the Cathedral of St. John the Divine in New York. She had vanished and was said to be going about in tatters carrying precious unset jewels in a black bag. I had never heard of her but my attention was attracted to her as she passed me by, dressed in the shabbiest of clothes. At the throat of this apparently poor woman was a brooch of fiery diamonds which glittered in the sun. I could not reconcile this precious ornament with her attire, and I followed her. After two days of prowling around her shack I obtained from the hermit her photographs and life story. Sherman could hardly believe it until he telegraphed the *Chicago Tribune* which verified my facts and wired for all of the particulars. My new editor printed every word I wrote about it, pushing the war to a secondary position. His eyes twinkled with satisfaction and he asked me to remain in the office long after press time to chat about famous newspaper scoops when he was on the old *Sun.*

Droves of reporters and feature writers from all parts of New England and New York surrounded the hovel of the recluse, but by that time the story was over. "The Diamond Queen" had barred herself in. Among the visitors from the press was Nixola Greeley Smith, an important writer of the *Evening World* who offered to find a position for me on its staff. But Sherman would not let me go and increased my salary. I performed a number of similar feats, perhaps for the reason that all of my waking moments were devoted to the prospects of snatching the exclusive story ahead of the pack.

The managing editor taught me the routine of his office while scoops lay dormant and soon he had me sitting in for him on his night off, guiding me by telephone. On these occasions I found myself directing a large staff of men, most of whom were much older than I and some almost thrice as old. Perhaps they may have resented my authority for I drove them as hard as I drove myself. I was impatient with the unimaginative who were satisfied to accept the official hand-out and call it news.

Sherman, by this time, had run me through the mill of the paper from legislative reporter to Sunday editor and back again at his elbow. The *Courant* was his life, his meat and drink, and I sat at his table. I lived as he did. He walked home with me at night along Farmington Avenue and pointed out Mark Twain's former home along the way. He told me what a rebel the great writer had been. The author had shaken the dust of Hartford from his feet because of the old city's smug complacency. And always the editor talked of the stimulation of the story that infused life into type, the tingle, the quiver that came over a man who knew what news was when it broke. It was beyond science. It was a sixth sense. No woman could understand it, he said. And no woman could understand a man who could feel it. He had been divorced. His wife had not understood it.

Sherman went to Florida for a rest and I handled his desk. Late one evening a gang of bandits drove a truck to a silk mill in Manchester, an adjoining town, and murdered the watchman, loaded their vehicle with silk valued at thousands of dollars and got away. Some were in a car but were intercepted in their flight and had piled out of it and escaped on a corner of Farmington Avenue. It was a sensational story and I gave it the treatment it deserved. I sent the paper to press and drove to the spot where the thieves had scrambled for safety. I felt a clue might be found there, something that had been dropped in the excitement, a piece of wearing apparel, a ring, a watch, which might lead to the identification of the murderers. Under a street light, while patrolmen were placidly guarding the area, I picked up a brand new black cap, containing the fresh label of a Hoboken hat shop. I gave the cap to the State Police on a barter arrangement for exclusive rights to the news which I was sure would develop from my discovery. The gang was traced to New Jersey and rounded up and the *Courant* led the city with the story.

Sherman, who had been watching matters from Florida, returned with a beatific smile on his tanned face and promoted me to the post of assistant managing editor with more money in my pay envelope.

CHAPTER V

Now I lived in the first comfortable home I ever had, but I had little time for it. Sarah became reconciled to the routine which the wife of every newspaper man has to face when he works on a morning paper. A son had been born to us and I named him after my father, and the maiden name of my mother: Alphonse Perron Gauvreau. He was to grow into a tall, handsome, young man, a football player, swimmer, fine dancer, a mathematician and electrical expert. As I write this story he has left the Massachusetts Institute of Technology to become manager of a department in a widely known electrical testing laboratory. He could never see anything in the newspaper business.

I wanted security for my family and other relatives before I reached the age of thirty, and "30" is a number of peculiar significance to every man who has worked in a newspaper shop. It is an old code that closes a telegraphed story. It means the end of it.

Sherman taught me much. Such men pass on what they have acquired in knowledge and experience to others if they will listen, and my chief, at times impatient and fiery when I slipped, had much to hand down. It had come to him on the old *Sun* from Carr V. Van Anda and Chester S. Lord who, in turn had received it from Dana the Great. It was a competence of knowing, a proficiency, a craftsmanship that dealt with life itself. I was with a master who calmly handled news which shook the world: the United States at war, the casualty lists with their local implications, the false armistice, the victory. And through it all sat the cool editor, smoking his favorite "Milo" cigarette, his deliberate hand holding the stubby pencil which produced the sure words in the banner lines. I thought he ranked with Brisbane.

The last year of the war staggered by for us as though night had settled upon the world. It seemed that the billowing flags and bugles had hardly passed our doors when names came trickling over the wire in a crimson trail, of the youngsters who had swung down Main Street and waved from train windows amid cheers and tears. Theodore Roosevelt came to Hartford to address the Trinity College commencement exercises and I sat next to him as he spoke. He appeared to be looking forward to old age with dismay, a little, tired man, his eyes dim sparks in deep hollows, his brow loaded with forebodings. His voice cracked when he raised it in a speech full of bitterness and pessimism about the struggle he was forced to view from the sidelines.

"You can tell Mr. Clark," he said, "that he could perform no greater service than to hammer away at the prejudices of that mule-headed professor (Woodrow Wilson). That man has kept the best of us out of this war because he wants to run it himself. Too proud to fight; too obstinate to call for help. He shoved us into it stern foremost. Thank God, even under a Chinese Mandarin, we're unbeatable!"

Although men beyond the draft age predominated on our staff, several, much younger, soon found their little careers deflected, and shook hands, self-consciously, in their uniforms and packed off. I remember a bright reporter Wallace Brymner, frail but eager, constantly bothering me for a tough assignment. He found it in the Argonne Forest where he was blown to bits as a message carrier. It must have happened while we were reading one of his postal cards telling us of the fun he was having. I chafed helplessly, handling copy. Draft officials had rejected me and put in my lapel a bronze button labeled "exempt" which I threw into the street. Sherman, acquainted with my kindling misery, sent me off on spy hunts and one night beamed over one of my discoveries which exposed a group of pseudo-patriots and pro-German professors who were about to leave New York for Venezuela, ostensibly to obtain quinine for American troops but who were really seeking information for a German submarine base. The *New York Times* gave this story a front page display which pleased my chief to the point of adding a few more dollars to my salary, a gesture unusual enough to keep its memory green.

When there were no spies to be found I remained in the office thirteen hours a day, sending out for my food while I drew maps of the conflict, inking in a shaded line one inch steadily westward, a little space in France where thousands lay gasping of wounds, calling for water or dangling in a lifeless sprawl over barbed wire. Often Sherman permitted me to write the main headings, occasionally changing a word and smiling his satisfaction when he compared our results with the banner lines in the *Times*.

He went away one night, perhaps to put me through a test of fire, during the critical period between the false armistice and the real one. After press time in the early morning, the costs of holding open the Associated Press wires were high and there had been protests from the business department about expenses. Under such circumstances the entire plant had to be kept going. I was expected to save money. I had been criticized before for detaining an entire force for something which had not happened. The telegraph operator blinked when I told him to close the wire at three A.M. All the papers on the line were still on the job.

"Boy," he said, "if this war comes to an end this morning, you will have been scooped on the greatest story in history, and even a weekly wouldn't hire you!"

I went home and Sarah wondered why I couldn't sleep. At eight o'clock I hurried to the offices of the *Hartford Times*, our afternoon contemporary, and waited for the A. P. wire to open. The first bulletin to come through was that the Germans and the Allies had not yet made contact for a parley. The war was still on. I had saved several hundred dollars for the company. When I shaved that morning I noticed that my hair had touches of gray at the temples and my face had an old look.

Sherman was a man of sincere beliefs. He loathed the *Courant's* political policies, which were strongly influenced by J. Henry Roraback, Connecticut's Republican boss. The editor despised our continual attacks on Woodrow Wilson and our sneers at the League of Nations plan. We had called the President "the sick man of Europe" and our editorial attitude was to let the Europeans take in their own washing. Nothing that happened across the sea could ever affect us. We were among the earliest of the smug isolationists. Sherman believed that the *Courant*, the oldest paper in the nation, should see what was ahead and point out the pitfalls of the dreadful future which was to take so short a time to come upon us.

One night in September in 1919 my chief resigned, turned his roll-top desk over to me, picked up some trinkets and left

the paper he had toiled on for twenty-five years to make into
one of America's outstanding dailies. For twenty-two years
he had been its managing editor. I was shocked by his decision
and when we shook hands I couldn't see him because my eyes
were blind with the first tears since my father's death. I
slumped in Sherman's chair as he fumbled at the door.

"Keep it going, Boy," he said, "and don't let it break your
heart."

I was promoted to the position of managing editor with
the usual increase in pay which follows such ceremonies. I
hurried home to dinner with the story of what had happened.
I had become the youngest managing editor of an important
daily in the nation and I had been made a stockholder in the
company. I was well under thirty. My climb on the *Courant*
had been fast. It had taken three years.

I thought Sarah accepted the news of this event as though
I announced I had picked up a bargain in lamb chops on the
way from the office. She was serving portions of food on
little plates. Now we had two sons. Henry Welles Gauvreau
had arrived, and we were all sitting around the table.

"We will buy a house," Sarah said, "in West Hartford,
around the corner from Farmington Avenue. Now we can
afford to live in that neighborhood."

I became more occupied than I had been when I was helping Sherman. He had taken over the post of managing editor
of the *Hartford Times*, an excellent newspaper, whose liberal
policies of the period opened the eyes of New England journalism. He was familiar with every penny of my rather stinted
payroll and like a sharpshooter he picked off my best men who
left me, one by one, for more money. I snatched men from
other newspapers around the state to fill the gaps. Now, I had
no time to go out and scoop the town and Sherman knew it.
And he knew Hartford down to its last insurance dividend.
He must have been well beyond middle age then, but he began
to show me how it felt to be scooped off my feet. He had his
ear to the city's best news sources and raked me with exclusive
beats as though he might have been John Paul Jones firing
broadsides from the *Bonhomme Richard*. I gave up my days
off to hunt up front page local news, pulled my staff together,
and the battle became fairly even, but deadly. It was a good,

honest fight. Sherman respected sportsmanship but he had a jolting uppercut.

Charles Hopkins Clark, majority stockholder of the *Courant*, and its editor in chief, looked upon my battles with mild amusement. Struggles for circulation were incomprehensible to him. He had been with the paper since the night of the great Chicago fire in 1871, when fresh out of Yale University he applied for a job and was hired to help in handling the news of the conflagration. He wanted his paper to be read by the intelligent few. He followed the traditions of Charles Dudley Warner, one time editor of the *Courant*, gifted essayist, international figure in belles-lettres and a collaborator with Mark Twain. Clark believed the *Courant's* circulation had little influence on its advertising. Hartford was the insurance center of the nation and advertisements from this source helped the paper to be high in the field of newspaper financial advertising in the United States.

I respected Clark but I could never digest his policies. He was then close to seventy-two years of age, a large, impressive man, whose arborescent mustache and goatee sometimes shook with rage over President Wilson's pronouncements. The veteran editor, a figure of influence in National Republican politics, could not understand why God permitted Democrats to walk around on their hind legs like human beings. He was a close personal friend of Theodore Roosevelt, Taft and Coolidge, who was then Governor of Massachusetts. The editor actually hated Democratic victories. On the night when Wilson's first election had been confirmed and vast crowds were standing in front of the *Courant* building waiting for the returns before a huge screen, Clark ordered the street bulletin service choked off and the outside lights put out, leaving thousands in pitch darkness, and in complete ignorance of what had happened.

When the Democrats won, Clark's editorials ignored their victories. Under the masthead of his page, he printed a little line:

"We'll be happy yet, you bet!"

I have never seen anything to approach the venom that could be nourished from political animosities in Hartford. I recalled that Clark, calling me into his office when I was reporting affairs at the Capitol, had inquired about the condition of Governor Simeon Baldwin, an aged but two-fisted Democrat

who had slipped on the ice and had to go to bed. I informed
Clark that the Governor was improving. The editor looked up
despondently from his desk and said:

"That man will NEVER die!"

The editor was a Fellow of the Corporation of Yale University and a director in many rugged enterprises, including
fire insurance companies and the Associated Press. I remember his crushing disappointment when James Rowland Angell
was made President of Yale University.

"After Hadley," Clark said, "this is something to gulp
down!"

Music was an incomprehensible jumble of jarring sounds
to the old journalist, and a waste of time. Having been persuaded to attend a concert by Paderewski one night, when the
great artist was full of color and shook his heavy mane and
raised his hands high above the keys in a passion of eloquence,
the editor, in evening dress, sat at his desk when the performance was over and imitated the gestures of the master as
though he had been a clown in a circus. "We flock to see
these foreigners and pay ridiculous prices to watch their gym-
nastics because we think it's smart," he scoffed. "And they
go home loaded down with our money. They're smarter than
we are!"

The editor's financial interest in fire insurance companies
affected my work each year and resulted in the only newspaper
campaign he ever asked me to conduct. Annually I had to
wage a crusade against Christmas trees lighted with candles
which he believed were the cause of many fires. Clark had a
son, Horace, a kindly bachelor of middle age, and fires were
his chief interest in life. He lived with his father and mother
in a home of wealth and culture, and in his room, over his bed,
was a large brass bell, connected with the headquarters of the
fire department. Horace went to sleep with rubber boots and
fire helmet close to his side. When the bell clanged late at
night he telephoned me to climb to the roof of the *Courant*
building and scan the city's darkness while he held the wire.
When I saw a glare he was off. This became part of my
regular duties, even during blizzards. Horace and I covered
a destructive fire in the department store of G. Fox and Co., on
Main Street, one night, and how I managed to get back alive
is beyond me to describe.

I began to perceive some of the reasons which had finally impelled Sherman to resign his job. Our paper catered to the old-line aristocrats and an editor who could not conform with their dogmas might as well have packed off. There were in the city many older people of the ruling class whose parents had honored Charles Dickens at a great banquet in 1842 when he came to Hartford. Dickens had returned to England and had written his querulous *American Notes* and *Martin Chuzzlewit*, and in 1920 a number of the best people in town were still damning Dickens.

The Associated Press, about this time, prepared a system of advance obituaries of important persons. These stories were to be released only by the Grim Reaper himself. Clark, as a director of the A. P., was interested in this piece of enterprise and notified all people of consequence who were concerned in Hartford to call on me and read their own death notices. Not infrequently, a number of dignitaries sat in my office, putting the seal of approval upon their past activities after making favorable corrections.

Sinclair Lewis, who had become the literary sensation of the nation, moved to Hartford with his wife and young son. He appeared as a guest of honor at a banquet of the Hartford Press Club and following a number of speeches praising his genius, he got up and compared the people of Hartford with the Babbitts he had written about. He said it was regrettable that Hartford, in which he proposed to live, could be known only as the richest city of its size in the country, and for no other reason. I agreed with him and printed his speech under a two-column heading on the front page of the *Courant*. Lewis then was as completely ostracized as a man with the plague— and moved out.

During the election campaign of 1920 which had animated Editor Clark into a snorting war horse, I attended a political gathering on my day off in the southern part of the state and met Warren G. Harding, the Republican candidate. I was introduced to him by Benedict M. Holden, a prosperous lawyer active in Hartford affairs. The future President told me that no writer had ever equalled the efforts of Edgar Saltus, his favorite author. He quoted whole paragraphs from *The Imperial Orgy*, a new work, to illustrate his point. Later, upon reading the book, Harding's literary choice impressed me with a peculiar significance when I handled the news of the nation-rocking scandals of his administration.

"We've got to get back to the sanity of normalcy," Harding told me. "America must mind its own business. We are through with world meddling, and at election time we will awaken from it as if it had been a bad dream, and we'll all be prosperous."

Lawyer Holden, whom I knew intimately, and who handled some of my private business, visited Harding at the White House, soon after the Ohio Senator's election. "When it came time for me to go into his office," Holden informed me, "there sat Warren with a big smile. He put his feet on his desk, leaned back and said: 'Ben, now I can tell any son of a bitch in the United States to go to hell!' "

Boss Roraback, who played pinochle with Editor Clark at the Allyn House, had assured me that Harding would return the nation to Lincolnian principles and give it the greatest prosperity it ever had enjoyed. We were going back to normalcy. The *Courant* had come out for Harding, boots, breeches and saddle. But the *New York Times* in a front-page editorial had stunned Clark by calling Harding's nomination an act of cowardice and an appalling event. The editor who had attended the Republican convention as a delegate-at-large, told me that Nicholas Murray Butler and Will Hays were crushed almost to tearful disappointment when they were told they could not be nominated. Clark quoted Senator Frank Brandegee as having said: "The Republicans have no first-raters. We nominated the best of the second-raters. It doesn't matter, because any Republican can win."

But the editor was disturbed by the *Times* editorial. "Ochs has made a mistake," he said. "Any Republican is better than the greatest Democrat. That was an impulsive editorial. Jews are impulsive, but Ochs is a great Jew, even if he is a Democrat."

Our editorial campaign against James M. Cox and Franklin D. Roosevelt was conducted on vicious lines. Even in our news columns we referred to the Vice-Presidential candidate as the "maverick Roosevelt." On the eve of the election, Boss Roraback, whose voice trembled with excitement, telephoned me to spike a rumor, with a front-page headline, that Negro blood could be traced in Harding's veins.

I found myself in close contact with the business manager, Henry H. Conland, an ambitious Vermonter, who had climbed up the ladder from the counting room and who was eager for more circulation. With his approval I made a trip about the country, studying the circulation methods of such papers as the *Chicago Tribune* and the *Boston Post,* the latter then boasting 450,000 New England readers. Conland wanted to modernize the *Courant* and we injected into its aged columns the first comic strips it had ever carried. Editor Clark, meanwhile, could never reconcile himself to the chinless "Andy Gump" and similar characters whom he called monstrosities. When "Andy" was innocently slipped into the obituary page one morning I had to fight for his life.

One of our syndicated purchases created an unfortunate impression on the aged editor. I bought from Frank Markey, a popular salesman under whose hypnotic eye I seemed to be powerless, a continuous feature entitled, *The Funniest Story I Ever Heard.* Each day I inserted one of these anecdotes on the editorial page with the hope of spicing its dreary columns. One afternoon Clark called me into his office, holding the *Courant* in a trembling rage. Twenty old readers had canceled their subscriptions, and a number of others had been unable to eat breakfast as a result of the humor our page of opinion had presented to them that morning. A chill went up my back when I recalled that I had sent the latest batch of the "funniest stories" to the composing room without reading them. The offending tale, written by Irvin S. Cobb and which brought all humor on our editorial page to an end, needed no explanation as to its effect on our conservative followers. It went along somewhat as follows:

An inebriated "Butter and Egg Man," finding time on his hands before he could catch a train for his home in Glastonbury, Conn., after a night of celebration in New York, dropped into a Childs Restaurant and ordered a shredded vegetable salad smothered with Russian dressing and dabs of mayonnaise. While it was being prepared he fell asleep. Discovering the deposit in front of him when he was awakened by the waitress he turned to her wildly and cried: "Hey, Baby! Do I eat this or DID I?"

Following months of strategy we obtained Clark's permission to include colored comics into the Sunday *Courant.* He stipulated that he would not permit the paper to cross his door-step unless the comic section had been removed from it, an order which was rigidly observed. For years Clark had told syndicate salesmen that comics would never be sold to the *Courant* until his obituary had appeared in the *New York Times*. He advised them to read that exemplary journal and wait for the proper occasion.

Great changes came to pass in my time on the venerable newspaper which had printed the text of the *Declaration of Independence* as news, had numbered George Washington as a subscriber and had published the reports of General Israel Putnam, who was its war correspondent during the Revolution. The age of rugged, personal journalism was dying. The streamlined march of newspaper progress, as it was called, was merciless and we had to keep up with it, while Clark, who wanted to produce a paper for an influential and intellectual class of readers, shook his head resignedly

"Jazz it up!" Conland would say to me. "We've got to get 50,000 circulation for the Sunday *Courant*."

I got the 50,000 readers and brought up the daily circulation to 38,000, which was considered an impressive feat. I still addressed the business manager as "Mr. Conland." One day, after some exploit which attracted new readers, he clapped me on the back. "Call me Harry," he said. He had become a Rotarian.

Four years of my managing editorship flew by. I gave the paper every ounce of strength and energy I had. At times I found myself in hot arguments with old employees who could not understand my modern enterprises. I remember a vicious quarrel with an irate, white-haired gentleman, Dr. Edwin Pond Parker, our literary critic, whose grandson married Dorothy Rothschild, soon to be famous as Dorothy Parker. One tempestuous night when, among other matters, if my memory serves, the news of the Wall Street bomb explosion was pouring in, I threw Dr. Parker's literary criticisms into the "hell box" to make room for the growing columns describing the horror. He never forgave me for this imperious act.

In 1922 I established the first newspaper broadcasting station in New England in the *Courant* building. It was known as WDAK and its microphone was an upright telephone to which had been attached a megaphone of papier-mâché. Broad-

casting on WDAK required a speaker to insert his face into
this affair, as though preparing to inhale gas in the office of
an old-fashioned dentist. Weird sounds, occasionally intel-
ligible, were produced to which Editor Clark listened at home
in bewilderment with ear-pieces around his head. He staggered me one evening by bringing in Vice-President Calvin
Coolidge to broadcast a talk of more than twenty minutes from
our station, a cubby hole on a lower floor, on which rested two
unmuffled motors. I explained the tortuous operations to
Coolidge who listened, skeptically. It was to be his first radio
speech and he decided to risk it. I helped him to push his face
in the cone, into which he proceeded to talk Republicanism.
Shortly before his address came to an end our nervous photographer squeezed himself into the crowded cubicle and took
a blinding flash-light picture of the event, the powder fumes
choking us almost into insensibility. Coolidge staggered out,
his speech unfinished, and gasped:

"I hope they never put these damned things in the Senate!"

I had taken my first airplane flight, about this time, with a
circus aviator known as "Speed" Chadwick whose sky-climbing
was apparently less uncertain than his course on land. His
machine had the appearance of a repaired egg-crate. Later he
plunged into Hell Gate with it. I asked Coolidge what he
thought of the possibility of developing airplanes as powerful
engines of war.

"They are an interesting invention," he said, "and possibly
may be useful later for scouting purposes. They certainly
proved nothing in the World War."

On my trip about the country I had visited a number of
broadcasting stations. I was struck by the strides radio was
making, and on my return from the West I met at Schenectady,
the famous electrical wizard, Charles Proteus Steinmetz. I
rode with him on a train to Springfield. I burst into flights of
imagination about the possibilities of radio but in our conversation he went far beyond my speculations. He was an interesting man, cruelly incapacitated but, apparently, he gave his
handicap no thought.

"Radio," he said to me, "will some day turn your line of
business upside down. People will get up in the morning, press
a little button and not only hear what is happening but see it
taking place on a screen in their own houses. When that time

comes, my boy, people are not going to rush out to buy news-papers."

This prediction was too revolutionary for me to print in the *Hartford Courant*.

The electrical genius noticed my lameness and discussed it philosophically with me. "Such a thing," he commented, "I have found to be an asset in the struggles for accomplishment. It keeps your mind from frittering itself away on amusements in which you cannot indulge and which would waste most valuable time, if you could enjoy them. Time is everything." He died a year later.

A news episode in November of 1923 threw our editorial room into spasms of laughter. The telegraph editor had taken his weekly night off and the Associated Press news on his desk was being edited by a young man from Trinity College named John Bierck. During the evening he burst into cackles of merriment over a cabled dispatch and suggested a headline of buffoonery to be put over it as a piece of high humor. The story described a "putsch" which had been launched from a beer hall in Munich by an obscure creature named Hitler who had staggered into the street with General von Ludendorff to defy the German Government. They were taken to jail. The dispatch was passed around so that the whole staff might get a good laugh over it. I laughed as heartily as the others.

I made my first diplomatic blunder on the paper by start-ing a crusade to save Mark Twain's old Hartford home from destruction. The famous rambling house where the great hu-morist had written many of his well-known works, including *Huckleberry Finn, Tom Sawyer* and *A Connecticut Yankee at King Arthur's Court* was to be torn down to make way for a building to be known as "The Mark Twain Apartments." The property had been disposed of by an old Hartford family for a good price. The new owners tried to appease me with the assurance that Mark Twain's profile would appear in a plaster plaque over the new entrances. I believed Hartford would rise up in arms to prevent the outrage when I called for an appeal for help under large headlines. For days I found myself fight-ing the battle alone.

My campaign, however, attracted national attention. The outcries of the old *Life* magazine stirred New York papers to print the news of my commotion. The old *Herald,* among

other papers about the country, backed me up with big headings and the Federal Commissioner of Education in Washington offered his cooperation.   In the *Courant* office my activities
were accepted with glum resentment.   I couldn't understand
why the influential groups of the city remained aloof.   It was
finally explained to me by Harry Horton, our aged and doleful
city editor, a humorist himself, and the author of 25,000 jokes
which he had sold for years to such publications as *Life*, *Judge*,
Puck and London *Punch*.   He still lived in the humorous world
of Bill Nye, Eugene Field, Josh Billings and Artemus Ward.
    "Hartford never liked Mark Twain," Horton said sor-
rowfully.   "It is ashamed of him!"
    I was now in a serious predicament from which I could not
back out without losing face and I appealed to the school children of America to send in their pennies to save the home where
Huckleberry Finn had been cradled.   The pennies began to roll
in.   Those who came to my aid were struggling people of
meagre means who read Mark Twain's books.   I opened a campaign headquarters in the studio of an Italian artist, Nunzio
Vayana, who rushed into the battle like a matador in a bull
ring.   I appeared with my agitators before Marcus Holcomb,
the old War Governor of Connecticut, who assumed that the
uproar could not have been possible without the approval of
his friend, Charles Hopkins Clark.   Action was then forthcoming.   The Attorney General of the state issued an opinion
to the effect that the famous residence could be protected under
the laws of Connecticut by right of eminent domain as a place
of historical association.   The clamor of the outside press could
no longer be ignored and wealthy Hartford sheepishly took
hold of the project while the pennies were sent back to the
school children.   The home was saved and became a literary
shrine.   One evening I presented the silent motion picture of
Huckleberry Finn in the room where "Huck" was born, and
many eyes were moist, including my own.
    I created some influential enemies for myself in this battle
which perhaps helped to bring my Hartford experiences to an
untimely end.   The *Courant*, later, in its 175th anniversary
edition ignored the crusade completely, and my eight years on
the paper, five of them as managing editor, were treated as a
mysterious gap in the stretches of time.   I could find no reference whatever to Mark Twain in the huge number of com-

memoration, which was choked with advertising. The great
author was as dead to the *Courant* as the Charter Oak.

It reminded me of a bitter political feud which had thrived
for decades between Editor Clark and the noted Morgan G.
Bulkeley. During the election campaign of 1920, I innocently
attempted to patch it up on my own initiative while interview-
ing Bulkeley, from whom I sought an endorsement for Senator
Frank Brandegee, who had opposed woman suffrage and was
a somewhat nervous candidate. Bulkeley, who was a Republican to his toenails, gave me his approval to be published,
readily enough. He was then a grand old man of eighty-two,
one-time United States Senator, Governor, first President of
the National Baseball League and a power in the insurance
world, from which he had acquired vast wealth. When the
interview was over he said:

"How is Charlie Clark getting along?"

I told him my editor was as vigorous as ever and I expressed the hope that I might carry some message back to him
of a friendly nature from the insurance patriarch. At the risk
of being presumptuous, I said it was regrettable that the two
most illustrious living men in Connecticut had not spoken to
each other in years, after the warm friendship of their early
days. Bulkeley replied:

"Charlie must be over seventy-two now. Well, I'm eighty-
two and I want to tell you that the fine hate from that feud is
keeping us both alive!"

Clark expressed to me his displeasure over the Mark Twain
campaign in a manner which explained Hartford's animosity
toward the humorist:

"I knew Mark Twain," the editor said. "He used to come
to the *Courant* office and criticize the paper when Charles Dudley Warner was the editor. He was never satisfied with it.
Sam Clemens was a tramp printer who deserted the Con-
federate Army when the first shot was fired. He ran from
Missouri to Nevada, pellmell, like all Democrats under fire.
Everybody knows he ran away from the war. He told the
story himself, because he thought it was funny. What kind
of a sense of humor do you call that?

"When he came to Hartford he gave everybody the idea
that he was a Republican. I think he must have been a Democrat all the time. He and his crony, Holy Joe Twichell, voted

for Cleveland after we had come out for Blaine. I can prove Clemens voted for Cleveland. I know people who saw him do it! He was such a trouble-maker that he influenced Warner to keep his vote in his pocket and turned Warner's head so badly that he resigned his position when we endorsed Blaine. Mark Twain spent his time laughing at people and finally he had to move out of here. What in the world possessed you to stir up all this mess about his house? Do you think Hartford will ever forget that he voted for Cleveland?"

The old man grunted when I replied: "I did it for Huckleberry Finn."

CHAPTER VI

I REMEMBER the hedge which ran down the street where Sarah selected the house we bought and lived in. Behind this long belt of green stood homes, comforted by little blankets of lawn and sheltered by elms and maples. The hedge seemed to bristle over night and had to be clipped so that it would be even as it pursued its course to some mysterious perspective. On the corner where the hedge began its sweep, a property owner often stooped and cocked his eye down this natural paling and could tell at once where it stuck out like porcupine quills, revealing an inactive clipper. Hedge-husbands, good Rotarians and Kiwanians, clipped religiously before supper, squinting at each other between sliced openings. The hedge was even until it passed my house. In the neighborhood I was known as the man who was out all night and spoiled the contour of the street.

I had no time to enjoy my first fireplace in our ample living room from which an upper floor was reached by an attractive, open staircase. As soon as I got up after going to sleep at four A.M., I hurried to work. At six o'clock in the evening I had an hour and a half of time for supper at our family table. I was in the fifth year of my managing editorship, and Sarah believed our affairs had been settled for a lifetime. Her family, the Joyners, of old American stock, and thoroughly practical people who looked far ahead, had told me that when the time came we could all be buried happily together in the restricted plot of a historical cemetery, with Sarah's father, a soldier of the Civil War.

Another baby had come to us. He was a happy, smiling infant, whose tiny, pink fist clung to my finger when I had free moments to play with him. This boy we called Peter and I thought of his gurgling laughter at night while I sent off pages of type to make the presses roar.

Developments resulting from Conland's increasing authority at the office were making me unhappy. Editor Clark was seventy-six years old, coming in daily and writing mild editorials, now that his friend Coolidge was President. The old man showed his age and relied more and more on the business office for the paper's direction. Conland, in a sweeping move, had made an open shop of the *Courant's* entire mechanical departments. Old union printers, who had served the paper for years, were forced to uproot their families and leave town, to seek work elsewhere. A chain gang of typesetters, who went around the country to break strikes, moved into our plant and for a nerve-racking period we wallowed in a typographical mess. Clark penciled every error painfully in the *Courant's* columns and with trembling hand and increasing complaints deposited the paper each day on my desk. But Conland had won his fight. No organized group would tell him how to produce the *Courant*. He had cleaned unionism out of the shop. The Manufacturers Association of Connecticut supported his policy with a weekly page of advertisements of various enterprises operated on a policy of rugged individualism. Coolidge, the *Courant's* powerful friend, was President and he had shown the country how to handle matters during the Boston police strike. Regularly the *Courant* praised him as a great President.

I had launched the *Courant's* rotogravure section for the Sunday paper and I supervised the pictures edited by a well-meaning maiden lady of middle age named Mary Lally, a close friend of the Conland family. My conferences with her became matters that tried the soul. Meanwhile, Clark apparently did not dislike what seemed a spectacular way of handling news stories if the large headings reflected the sunshine that poured from the White House all over the land.

Old Horton, surprisingly enough, had become my silent partner in much of my pioneering and astonished me one day, in 1920, by assigning a writer to review a motion picture. He must have been one of the first editors in the country to see that such entertainment eventually would attract millions of people and deserved serious consideration. Horton's enterprise amazed Clark who said motion pictures would never be important enough to engage the attention of critics of any sort. He had not been pleased with the few films he had seen and referred to them as "pie-throwing contests" prepared for the great unwashed. The Roscoe ("Fatty") Arbuckle scandal convinced the editor that the "celluloid," as he called it, had reached a depth of iniquity in which it would remain.

In the summer of 1921 I involved the old paper in an adventure which Clark never forgot. I made preparations to print an extra on the result of the prize fight between Jack Dempsey and Georges Carpentier, who met at Boyle's Thirty Acres. The veteran editor was dubious about the project but let me go ahead with it. On the day of this revolutionary enterprise in Hartford, masses of people gathered in front of the *Courant* building to hear a description of the encounter from a megaphone while I rushed the round by round account to the typesetters. We took our time with the megaphone news to hold the crowds on the innocent theory that our extra could be flung to them for sale when the end of the combat had been reached.

Noble historians have recorded the unpleasant surprise Monsieur Carpentier experienced in the fourth round on that famous occasion. While I was watching a typesetter turn the account of the knockout into type I heard a disturbing roar from the street and hurried to the front windows. Excited customers were buying an extra of the *New York Journal* which announced the result in headlines a foot high. The pink papers were selling like hot cakes while we had not even reached the process of putting our type into the front page form. The *Journal* had printed two sets of fake extras and sent them to Hartford on the previous night. All that the newsdealers in charge had to do, after hearing the result of the fracas from an open telephone wire to New York, was to distribute the right extra which simply informed the public with staggering type that Dempsey had won. It satisfied the crowds, which had flown away like dried leaves in a gale, before the product of my useless toil reached the street.

Clark, who was watching this lamentable affair from his own window, and who perceived instantly what had happened, walked into my office to give me an emphatic lecture. I never needed consolation more in my life in a newspaper office.

"We don't have to compete with those tricks," the editor said. "In my opinion William Randolph Hearst is the most unscrupulous man in the newspaper business. As a director of the Associated Press I know what his organization has done. They will stoop to nearly anything for circulation. You have just seen a rather embarrassing example of it. We are buying too much of their syndicated material already. When they

have finally loaded us up with their Sunday comics they might
well snatch them away from us and start their own Sunday
paper in Hartford. Then, where would we be? I didn't make
my money by getting into newspaper brawls. We were much
happier when we had 18,000 intelligent readers. This paper is
institutional. It doesn't need more circulation.

"You're making a lot of trouble for yourself. The right
people in this town will not believe what happens until they
read it in the *Courant*. From Bunker Hill to the funeral of
George Washington we gave them the news and we took our
time doing it and we're still printing after nearly 160 years.
We were better off when we adhered to the idea that the future
is only a prolongation of the past. Connecticut is the land of
steady habits."

Until he died at the age of seventy-eight, the veteran
journalist was faithful to that dogma, and I admired him for
his loyalty but his era was done, as that of Dana was done,
and those of Greeley and Watterson. Looking back through
the years I wish I had been born with them.

I remember Clark's laughter when, over my shoulder, he
looked at one of the early copies of the New York tabloid,
Daily News. He considered it a curiosity. I was intensely
interested in the new paper.

"Some publishers," Clark said, "don't care what they do
with their money. That sheet is a hopeless venture. Readers
will never be satisfied with a paper that throws its news out to
print pictures."

He made one prediction, however, which was closer to
accuracy. He spoke to me of two young gentlemen of imagination and energy named Henry R. Luce and Britten Hadden,
who were planning an editorial review of the news once a
week to be called *Time*. He believed there was a field for such
a publication. "Two smart Yale boys with an idea," he said,
"often achieve surprising results."

The change coming over our old paper was happening all
over the land to publications trying to cling to the sober methods of the past. The World War had created a new people.
Women were growing up from "flappers." Young men were
restless and questioning. F. Scott Fitzgerald was trying to
describe the new yearning of the fresh generation in his best
book, *This Side of Paradise*. I was under thirty, then, editing

the oldest paper in the country and the invasion of new methods suggested thousands of reflections to me. I would go down
into the bowels of the building and read our accounts of the
great events in history from the time the nation was born.
The *Courant* was always skeptical of anything indicating progress. Before the gay nineties it was shouting that something
would have to be done to stop the reckless idiots who were rushing down Main Street on bicycles at ten miles an hour. I remember the fight Clark conducted against daylight-saving time.
He ordered us to keep our office clocks on standard time. "The
nation's oldest newspaper will not change God's time," the
editor said. But time was changing us.

I tried to understand Conland, who was as much of a slave
in the business end of the paper, as I was in the editorial rooms.
In this new day, if you labored long enough in the counting
room and possessed driving ability, you could eventually control the paper and become a director in all sorts of enterprises
bulging with prestige. It was an honest ambition. I could
appreciate the fact that Conland, a man of strict commercial
integrity, got as much of a thrill from a new full-page advertisement as I did by staying up all night to distill the last ounce
from a new story. The woods were full of news stories, but
advertising contracts did not fall from trees in a glen. I knew
that the advertisements which produced our dividends had not
been served to Conland on a silver platter. He had gone out
and fought for them. The stockholders could not have found
a better man to make the paper pay. I admired him for his
competency but I resented any interference from the business
office. Sloane and Sherman had pounded that viewpoint into
my head. They believed that what a newspaper had to say
was more important than the goods it sold for department
stores. But on the other hand, if it didn't sell the goods, the
editor often found himself in the unblest position of a man
who couldn't say anything. His paper curled up and died
under him. I was to discover that later.

I felt that Conland and I saw the newspaper business from
radically different viewpoints. I believed that a paper of the
Courant's prestige should have engaged in crusades for the
public good. The business manager adhered to the tradition
of printing the news after it had happened. He surprised me
one evening at a dinner conference by telling me that the

Hearst management had offered him a salary of $30,000 a year
to become the business manager of a Boston paper. He had
turned down the offer but he admitted it had been a temptation. He was satisfied to "grow with Hartford," as he put it
and to manage a paper which reflected its conservatism.

I was losing a battle with myself in an effort to adhere to
this policy. Ignoring labor news, which affected vast sections
of Connecticut, went against my grain. Cutting down to two
sticks a story which involved thousands of Democrats was
almost a daily occurrence which added to my annoyance. Clark
had warmly criticized me for using a two-column headline over
the news that the House of Representatives had voted favor-
ably on the woman suffrage bill, an idea which he had denounced for years as pernicious. What we said, editorially,
in those days about Carrie Chapman Catt who organized the
woman suffrage party would seem incredible now.

I could not understand why a woman should be prevented
from voting. I had received my first blistering criticism from
Clark as a legislative reporter when I included three paragraphs
in my report of the appeal of a mother who had appeared
before the lawmakers and made a brilliant speech for suffrage.
She held by the hand her little daughter, who stood by bravely,
wide-eyed, her little mouth firmly set as the representatives
greeted her mother's remarks with laughter. The little girl,
with red bloomers under winter clothes, was Katharine Hep-
burn, later to become a celebrated actress.

I still clung to the idea that an editor's job was to search
for merit in distress and be most eager to relieve it. I knew
of evils in Connecticut that should have been exposed, but
revelations of any kind that stir the community are sensational,
and the *Courant* was not that type of paper. It would have
been easy for me, in a different state of mind, to grow old as a
conservative editor, join the Hartford Club, curse unionism,
and flourish with no revenue except for prosperity. My early
upbringing had much to do, undoubtedly, with my rebellious
streak. The *Courant,* in its own smug way, was quite correct,
but I felt it did not interpret the democratic conception of human life. The cold despotism of tradition disturbed me. I
hated to think that Connecticut was satisfied to be corrupt and
content. By inclination and temperament I was no longer
suited to the managing editorship of a paper whose peculiari-

ties, nevertheless, did not prevent it from being one of the great journalistic institutions of the country.

I never told Clark my real feelings one day when John T. Flynn, who was later to be widely known as a political economist and interpreter of the liberal trends of the nation, became the leader of a strike of New Haven newspaper men. The *Courant* looked upon the affair with horror. Clark was informed that newspaper men from many parts of the country sent money contributions to support the strikers, who had been working for a pittance, as I well knew by experience. Flynn's rebellion probably was the first step toward the organization of the Newspaper Guild. I was called into a conference with Clark in which Editor Osborn appeared from the *Journal-Courier*.

"Watch out for this, Charlie," Osborn said. "There's Bolshevism in it and if it ever forces open the sacred portals of journalism, the freedom of the press which you and I have defended will be gone forever."

Papers were becoming standardized. If you wanted circulation you bought features which rewarded you with new readers as, in the same manner, they had repaid the *South Bend Tribune* or the *Youngstown Vindicator*. Clark, reconciled, left such matters to Conland, in whose office these transactions were concluded. Syndicate salesmen flocked to Hartford to storm the last fort of the old journalism.

What happened to me on the *Courant,* in my frame of mind, was inevitable, because I believed in the exclusive news story and I was constantly on the search for it. Being beaten on a yarn actually made my heart ache. No one could have prevented me from putting to press a piece of news which I had obtained ahead of my competitors. That I included J. Henry Roraback, Connecticut's political boss, among those who couldn't stop me, was a matter of my own choice. I had inherited my strong feelings against him from Sherman, who had told the politician's satraps where to head in on several occasions.

One evening in January of 1924, a reporter from the *St. Louis Star* came to my office with a story that was to become a nation-wide sensation. He was a handsome, courageous newshound named Harry Brundidge, whose managing editor, Frank S. Taylor, was one of the keenest men that ever gauged the daily waterfall of news. He had assigned Brundidge to enter as a student, a quack medical college in St. Louis and in five months' time the reporter had been graduated with a diploma and a complete surgical outfit. Brundidge had been told by his fraudulent professors that he would not find it difficult to "practice" in Connecticut whose dangerous laxities in its medical laws made it possible for impostors to make money and endanger the lives of workers, upon whom they preyed in factory districts. Brundidge had traced an entire graduating class of his diploma mill to the "Nutmeg State" and he gave me the names of these potential murderers. He was seeking the cooperation of an influential newspaper to help him finish his job. He had been turned down by two other important newspapers of the state and, as he arrived in Hartford in the evening, he chose to visit the *Courant*, the only morning newspaper in the city. I knew that if I hesitated to help him he would visit the *Hartford Times*, where Sherman, I felt certain, would grab the sensation like a poker player scooping in a pot with four aces. I slammed the story under three eight-column headlines on my front page, and shocked the state.

The revelations carried sinister political implications and almost immediately I was in a bitter turmoil. The story became known as the "national diploma mill" scandal and brought reporters to Hartford from all important papers of the East. Dapper metropolitan newspaper men invaded the Western Union offices in a body and settled down to report the daily developments.

Brundidge and I worked like beavers, rooting out quacks and exposing them in print. Shyster lawyers rushed in with libel suits. A special grand jury was summoned and indictments were handed down while the investigation progressed to its climax. I pressed into the service our political writer, Theodore Wallen, who, as a result of this upheaval, was to transfer his services to the *Herald Tribune* and become the chief reporter of its Washington bureau. He informed me on the third day of the cannonading that Boss Roraback was deeply agitated by the commotion and intended to consult Clark about it. As Wallen was the liaison officer between the editor and the political baron, I knew his information carried significance.

One of the first of the rogues to go to prison as a result of our crusade was a typical graduate of the diploma mill, a fraudulent surgeon who had undertaken to treat the injury of a factory worker, the head of a family, who had caught the tip of his finger in a machine. While the patient lay senseless under a can of chloroform, the "doctor" attempted unsuccessfully to sew up the wound. Making no progress he gave his helpless victim another can of chloroform, cut off the finger below the second joint and managed to sew the stump. When the operation was completed the workman was dead.

I had not forgotten my factory-driven family and this outrage infuriated me. There were other cases on our list of a closely similar nature, some involving babies whose little lives had been risked in the hands of these invading charlatans. I printed on the front page of the *Courant* a picture of the operating chair in which the innocent worker had been fatally betrayed by an ignoramus permitted to practice his butchery under the laws of the state.

Roraback telephoned me personally on the day this issue appeared and told me I was giving Connecticut a "black-eye." He said the state would never live down the disgrace heaped upon it by the scandal I had spread in all parts of the country. He asked me if I had consulted Clark about my actions. When I informed him that I had used my own initiative, he replied:

"See him at once and find out where you stand. You have endangered yourself. Your job is at stake, you damned fool! Clark will tell you so himself!"

I thought it was singular that during the early part of this agitation Clark had made no comment to me about it. The facts were sensational and I had used spectacular means to reach the public. Roraback felt that the scandal would be construed as a reflection upon his political leadership. I had seen him snap his fingers to put bills through the Legislature to suit the conveniences of his followers. The *Hartford Times* for years had excoriated him for his dictatorship.

Conland ordered me to treat the sensation in a subordinate manner and to drop it as soon as possible. The big headlines clashed with his idea of the *Courant's* traditions. He was in close consultation with Clark about the situation. But it was too late for me to retreat. The *World* was leading the metropolitan field with the revelations which had become a part of the nation's daily reading. The responsibility was mine. I continued to print all of the facts of the case, including a congratulatory letter addressed to me by the grand jury.

I knew my actions would have serious repercussions for me. Now I understood why Sherman, after twenty-five years, had left in the night. I did not inform Conland of Roraback's threatening telephone call to me. I thought this information would be useful if I were forced to go to court and fight for what I thought would be a fair price for my *Courant* stock which I would have to sell back to the company, if I had to leave. I was working for a private corporation and the stock was restricted and I felt that my energies had helped to push it up a few pegs.

As I fought on I waited for the blow. There was a tradition that nobody on the editorial side of the *Courant* had ever incurred the wrath of J. Henry Roraback and remained on the paper. His power in national Republican politics was considerable. He was the head of vast utility projects in Connecticut, a director in great insurance companies, Republican National Committeeman, close friend of all high priests of the Grand Old Party and political ruler of "the land of steady habits."

Conland, meanwhile, sat in his home at night, trying to see both sides of the situation. He had climbed rapidly. He had toiled too long on the *Courant* to make an issue in favor of a more liberal news policy at this stage of his career. This was no time to disagree with an aged editor who controlled the paper and who, obviously, had but a short time to live. Conland undoubtedly would be his successor in control. He had struggled hard to reach that vantage point and he deserved that recognition. He hated Roraback as much as I did but Clark admired Roraback as a great politician. Conland came to the only conclusions that a man in his position could reach during his exemplary climb up the ladder. He was a success in his forties, his hair had turned white during his labors for the *Courant* and his temperament fitted into the fibre of the old paper. He conformed and I did not. At the height of the victory of my crusade he asked me to hand in my resignation.

The business manager gave me time to "throw my lines out," as he put it, and seek employment elsewhere, preferably outside of the state. I received from him a signed letter informing me that Clark had confirmed the decision to remove me. I understood the situation completely and did not blame Conland. Success, at times, requires tough decisions.

Wallen, a capable newspaper man, whose stories interpreted the local conservative viewpoint held by Roraback, told me that the political baron felt that the medical revelations had gravely embarrassed his prestige. The reporter himself was now nervous over the whole affair. He knew he could not remain on the paper after Clark died. Roraback's influence over the *Courant* would then be over. "You'll have to get out first," Wallen wrote to me, while on an out-of-town assignment. "You're up against the wall. Eventually I'm going to land myself something on a New York paper. From what I have heard I think it would be advisable for you to leave the state. I like Roraback and he doesn't blame me for what I have written about the crusade. I took your orders and he holds you responsible for smearing it all over the country. He never forgets."

Reflecting upon this episode, which was to whirl me into some of the maddest years of New York journalism, I can be charitable about Roraback. The time was to come when he would be swept out of power in "the land of steady habits." The Democrats, whom he hated, were to remove from him all the privileges of patronage that had been his life. Finally, he would look over the nation and stand bewildered before incomprehensible changes. And then he would leave the luxurious home of his estate, gaze for the last time at his Connecticut hills and put a bullet through his brain.

Wallen, who believed we were entitled to a Pulitzer prize for our campaign, induced me to go to New York with him to present the details of our work to John William Cunliffe, then Director of the School of Journalism of Columbia University. Brundidge told me later that the crusade had been considered as a possibility for a journalistic award in the year of 1924, but the judges were unable to decide between the St. Louis reporter and the *Courant*. While this matter lay in abeyance Wallen informed me sheepishly that Clark had told him the *Courant* would not accept the prize under any circumstances, considering such publicity a form of cheap advertising.

I decided to work out the few days I had left on the paper

and the recommendations I made regarding promotions of my assistants were accepted by the management.

I did not inform Sarah immediately of the turn which affairs had taken at the office. There had been serious sickness at home and the best-known child specialist in Hartford was in almost constant attendance. Alphonse and Henry were badly ill of influenza and little Peter had been stricken by pneumonia. Sarah stood anxiously beside the baby's bed at night, with the physician, when I left. I could not add to her burden by telling her that I had lost my job and that her home behind the hedge had become nothing but a sorry dream.

On my last evening as managing editor of the *Courant*, Woodrow Wilson died. It was on February 3, 1924, the eve of my birthday. The news was of grave importance to the world and I toiled far into the night, through vast amounts of copy to cover each phase of the great ex-President's significant life. Now he was a good dead Democrat and the *Courant*, which had heaped him with abuse for years, would bury him under shouting headings and columns of type. Thinking people in Connecticut might remember the attacks upon him as "hypocritical acts by gentlemen superlatively honorable."

I was sipping a mug of steaming coffee at my desk long after midnight when Sarah telephoned me. When I had left home, Peter, although very ill, appeared to be holding his own, as the doctor had informed me. Later reports had been of the same nature. Now the baby had taken a sudden turn for the worse and the specialist was trying to save his life. I was preparing the eight-column headlines for the front page on Wilson's death and making up the "dummy," a meticulous task. Immersed in the news I had forgotten it was my last night on the paper. I turned everything over to my assistants, jumped into a cab and raced home. When I arrived, Peter was dead.

After I left the death chamber I sat near a telephone stand at the bottom of our staircase, trying to realize what had happened. A special messenger rang the bell to give me a copy of the *Courant's* first edition. I always had written the eight-column headlines as managing editor and I wanted to make sure that in its news treatment of the national tragedy the old paper would live up to its reputation. I was dissatisfied with a word in one of the lines and I telephoned a correction. It was a mechanical act that had become a part of me.

I sensed the presence of someone on the second landing of the stairs. I glanced up and found Sarah looking down at me with an expression of suffering which comes only to a woman's face when she has lost her baby.

"You're worse than a soulless gambler!" she said. "All you can think of, day and night, is the paper. Even now! A gambler stops when his den closes up. You NEVER stop!"

Her sobbing voice tore at my heart. The words of her anguish reminded me of the soft, melting flute notes which drop brief tears of music in *La Bohème* before Mimi dies.

I turned my face away. I stumbled to the fireplace where I tried to poke remnants of wood into a glow. The kindlings fell into powder and rubies of tiny coals flickered and disappeared into the blackness. The fire was dead and I stood looking into the ashes.

"You won't have to worry any more about my passion for the paper," I said,—with all of the kindness I could find in my crushed soul.

"What do you mean?" The question trembled on her lips.

"I've been fired," I said.

BOOK III

MUSCLING IN

CHAPTER I

At midnight, in March of 1924, I was in New York on Times Square, reading with some uncertainty in my mind a recommendation from a great managing editor to the reigning chief of the best type of journalism in America. If something came of it I would be again on a morning paper, and Sarah believed that my night work had reduced me to the status of a boarder at home. The loss of Peter had almost estranged us.

I had said farewell to Sherman before leaving Hartford. I sat in his living room as he paced about, glancing at me with an ironical smile which I remembered when I did something he liked but of which he could not officially approve.

"I worked with Carr Van Anda on the old *Sun*," he said. "He's the greatest newspaper boss alive. I think he can do something with you."

When I left for New York I carried the following letter to Van Anda, managing editor of the *New York Times:*

My dear Mr. Van Anda:

Most recommendations of newspaper men are routine but I want to call your special attention, both as a newspaper man and as a friend, to Emile Gauvreau. Mr. Gauvreau has been managing editor of the *Hartford Courant* for five years but is now looking for an opportunity elsewhere. With the exception of your own, his news sense is the most highly developed of that of any newspaper man I ever knew. He follows the scent of a story like a hound and is an indefatigable worker. He is devoted to the news end of a newspaper and wants to get into a wider field. He has no bad habits. The newspaper that secures his services will get a tremendous worker. I should be glad if you could give him consideration.

Sincerely yours,
C. L. Sherman.

The letter got me to Van Anda's office where he was engaged with preoccupied editors in selecting news for the front page of his paper. He sat at his desk making decisions, studying proofs and taking sips from a huge mug of coffee, much as I had done in Hartford. I realized I had selected an inopportune time to consult the greatest managing editor in the country about a job. A polite assistant read my letter and referred me to the city editor whom I was to see on the next day. Matters then would be taken up through regular channels with Van Anda, he said. This busy subordinate probably was the innocent cause of the most violent turning point in my life.

I walked up Broadway reflecting upon my new prospects until I reached the Hotel Empire which had honored me with a "due bill," a courtesy which entitles a visiting newspaper man to a room and food without charge, if he doesn't take too much advantage of the privilege.

In the morning I saw from my hotel window the building of the Macfadden Publications, practically across the street. Large flags, carrying the name of the publisher, were flying from the roof. Perhaps if I had put up elsewhere for the night my mind would have operated in a different direction and it is likely that Van Anda would have hired me. Sherman's recommendations were not cast aside. They were rare notes.

I had a kindly feeling for a Macfadden magazine known as *Physical Culture*. As a boy I had followed tenaciously some of its suggested exercises and as a result my right leg had developed sufficiently to permit me to ride a bicycle. Furthermore, I had written two or three love stories for *True Story*, a monthly of the Macfadden group. For each story I had received $150, a remuneration which seemed incredible to me. The payment for each one of these harmless confessions, which required but the work of my day off from the paper, had exceeded my week's salary on the *Courant*, as managing editor, by $60. What Van Anda would have said, had he known that I wrote love stories for Macfadden, becomes a matter for literary speculation.

I was concerned with the situation at home. The tragedy of the baby remained in my mind and I felt that newspaper work on morning papers eventually would prove disastrous to my marriage. As I looked out of my hotel window I thought of writing for magazines, including Macfadden's, and buying an old farm my mother-in-law had abandoned in Colebrook,

Connecticut. There, I hoped to live on the earnings of short
stories and work on a novel which I already had entitled *The
Land of Steady Habits.*

I had been forced to engage lawyers to obtain for my
Courant stock a price higher than Conland had been willing
to concede but I won my point following some unmelodious
shenanigans typical of the sculduggery which generally results
from an argument about money between people born in Connecticut or Vermont. Conland was a Vermonter with a New
England alertness in any deal about money when he believed he
was right. I had developed my own Connecticut technique in
such matters, having learned from others who were more
prosperous than I was. I had made it a habit to put money
aside for years in readiness for emergencies and when I left
Hartford, after a bitter fight over the stock, I possessed
$18,000. The money from the securities accounted for a con-
siderable part of this sum and most of it was to be put aside
for the education of my sons.

Introducing myself at the Macfadden offices I was surprised
to be taken immediately to the editor in chief, Fulton Oursler,
a tall dark intensive man with penetrating eyes and a long
nose, an executive of staggering energies who drained quarts
of milk in his office and smoked cigarettes until he was
shrouded in smoke. In a few moments he introduced me to
Bernarr Macfadden. I was astonished to discover that the
physical culturist, whom I had imagined to be a giant with
bulging muscles was of medium height. He looked even
smaller as he reclined behind his desk. He possessed sharp
features, a rapid glance and was endowed with a certain quick
intelligence, an ability to reach the core of a problem without
wasting time.

My departure from the *Courant,* as a result of the medical-
diploma-mill revelations had injected my name into newspaper
stories of the investigation. A number of these accounts pictured me as some sort of martyr. Macfadden, who had no use
for doctors, quack or legitimate, was keenly interested in the
fight I had been waging. As a result of our conference I was
engaged to organize an afternoon tabloid newspaper to be
published in New York under the name of *The Truth.* The
publisher was not interested in my original idea of retiring to
the woods to write love stories. He spoke of his projected

newspaper as a crusading daily, which would tell the truth under all circumstances, and I listened to him with enthusiasm.

I hoped that Sarah would be satisfied with my new employment. I was laboring under the whimsical delusion that my work on an afternoon tabloid would free me from my desk for evenings at home. Sarah, however, decided to remain in Hartford with the children until I had launched the paper; and I quartered myself on Morningside Heights with a group of professors from Columbia University, one of whom I had met during my campaign to save Mark Twain's home. They expressed interest in my new enterprise, whose details I did not outline to them. They were under the impression that I was to produce a publication of the type of the *Nation*, or the *New Republic* and gave me, nightly, a number of suggestions which might have been quite useful to those periodicals. Later, when the first issue of my paper appeared on the newsstands, they were petrified with astonishment and shunned me as a pariah in a cafeteria where we had been gathering at breakfast for intellectual discourses.

In the beginning I had no privacy in the vast Broadway office where I planned my paper. I worked in a wilderness of desks where copy was prepared for the publisher's magazines, which seemed to be innumerable. As my task was a deep secret I could talk to no one about it and became known among the milling copyreaders and editors as a mysterious stranger. My face has always had a somewhat lugubrious cast and I wore, at the time, the type of collar later to be made famous by President Hoover. My New England solemnity was still with me and it got about that I was an imported vicar who had been engaged to guide the magazines into channels which would not offend the church. During this period I walked into a nearby speakeasy for a rye highball and one of the editors of *True Ghost Stories* standing at the bar peered at me until he lost his self-control and dropped his glass to the floor.

During the second day at my desk in the large office, a cold afternoon in April, janitors appeared and opened all the windows, letting in an icy wind. While I was turning up my coat collar, a tanned, athletic creature attired in sandals and a leopard skin sprang from somewhere and in one leap landed on a desk and commanded everybody to rise. A large number of the workers, male and female, climbed up on their own desks with surprising agility. Others stood up in the aisles. The entire department was set off into violent calisthenics, swimming in the air, inhaling, exhaling and legs kicking back while the leopard man, his voice reflecting a lust for life, exerted the limb swingers into a furious tempo. Hardly daring to look up at skirt lines which were above my head, I hunched my way to a fire escape where I found kindred souls inhaling cigarettes. They told me the exercises were not compulsory.

All the stationery for *The Truth* had been printed when the business manager was hired for the enterprise. He was a gray-haired executive, past middle life, formerly of the old *Globe,* named John Cook. The new paper's title seemed to leave him in a stupor. The bold intention to stalk the truth and publish it every day, he said, would result in nothing but disaster. As I had a number of crusades in mind for the public good I was disappointed when Cook, after weeks of agitation, prevailed upon the management to abandon the name. It was decided to call the paper the *Evening Graphic.*

I worked incessantly for more than five months to gather a large organization. Macfadden bought the old *Evening Mail* building on what was then City Hall Place, a depressing street, hardly more than an alley, and when I went to inspect the premises my heart sank. All machinery was covered with rust, and in the forsaken city room lay a coffin covered with an American flag. The coffin had been borrowed from an adjoining undertaker shop to play its melancholy role at a newspaper wake when the old paper, in whose columns I had met Franklin P. Adams and the noted cartoonist, Rollin Kirby, had been sold down the river. I sat on the coffin in the gloom of the abandoned place, reflecting upon the uncertainties of journalism.

The plant, by commendable courage, was put into working order and after two rehearsals of putting the new publication to press I was ordered to launch it on September 15, 1924. I often wondered later why I failed to consult the astrologer on my staff before this date was selected. Macfadden announced the forthcoming *Graphic* in page advertisements in New York papers as the most unique daily that would ever be seen since Johannes Gutenberg did his first printing. This claim was not exaggerated.

Behind his venture the publisher had a definitely new idea.

If it had been possible to apply it to daily journalism, in all of its editorial branches, the *Graphic* might well have reached a million circulation in a comparatively short time. The plan was a revolutionary treatment of the news, influenced directly by *True Story,* which had been Macfadden's inspiration, and already had produced for him a great fortune. The magazine devoted itself entirely to stories of human experiences told in the first person, by those who had undergone them and eventually had a wide influence on important publications which copied the technique. As applied to the *Graphic,* the account of a man who had killed his wife was not to be written in the third person from a police report. The prisoner was to be interviewed and his confession printed under his own signature. The headline over such a story might have been:

I MURDERED MY WIFE
BECAUSE SHE COOKED
FISHBALLS FOR DINNER

———

I Told Her I Would Never
Eat Them Again But She
Defied Me to the End

———

By Jonathan Peters

———

After three days of blood-sweating to apply this treatment to all the news that came in the *Graphic* staff was on the borderline of hysteria, myself included. The project would have required an enormous number of men trained for the purpose. The formula was abandoned while I was attempting to use my acquaintance with President Coolidge to obtain from him a story to justify the heading:

I CAN GET ALONG
BY USING ONLY 10
WORDS EACH DAY!

The circulation, meanwhile, had climbed on a curiosity sale to 400,000. At the end of the second week it was down to 83,000, a figure which the circulation manager, an old Frank Munsey man named O. O. Scattergood, assured me was "solid." The solidity of this readership, however, disturbed Macfadden who wanted 500,000 at the earliest possible moment.

"With that number of readers," he said, "people will listen to us, and we can carry on our campaigns effectively for public health."

The *Graphic* might have been a flash in the pan but for a mysterious army of followers of the physical culturist's principles. In New York there were thousands of them, all loyal subscribers of *Physical Culture*. They bought Macfadden's daily paper religiously and soon came down in droves to help me run it. The spectacle of powerful gentlemen, sleeves rolled up to bare bulging muscles, while they tore my telephone books in half with one sweep of the hands, was not uncommon when I entered my office. I remember a terrifying red-headed person, weighing at least 275 pounds, who waited until I was settled at my desk before he chinned himself outside of my high, closed door, his straining pop-eyed face glaring at me through the transom.

One morning I found a man hanging by his long black hair from the water pipes across the ceiling. He said he had the strongest hair in the world. Those who performed feats of strength wanted members of the staff to attempt to duplicate them. To reach the city room I had to pass a corridor along which were gathered healthy specimens with arms flexed, and, as the editor, I had to feel a number of muscles before I got to my destination. Most of the strong men carried their own tape measures and encircled themselves with the ribbons while my secretary, Elita Sheasby, an astute young woman who always had an old telephone book to spare, pacified the visitors by noting down figures of increasing chest expansion. One man drove a spike through a plank with his bare hand. The most disturbing of these Titans was a member of the International Weight Lifters' Association who, one morning, picked me up, chair and all, and deposited me on the top of my desk. He felt my muscles and left in disgust.

"How did Barney happen to pick you out for editor?" he asked.

CHAPTER II

THE *Graphic* advocated Macfadden's physical-culture principles and his sudden crusades for health led me into extraordinary bypaths. The publisher often came to my office with new
ideas after a brisk thirty-mile walk from his home in Nyack.
At times he had walked the full distance to his headquarters at
1926 Broadway in bare feet, leaving far behind him younger
enthusiasts who fell moaning by the wayside with stubbed
toes and sour faces. He was the most vigorous man I ever
knew, full of unbounded energy and he used much of it to write
page editorials for his tabloid and magazines in which he fired
broadsides at the medical profession. He believed the marriage state was best for man in general and had a large family
of handsome daughters who grew up under his strict health
regime. Finally he had a son and wrote an editorial in which
he announced the discovery that parents, through his principle,
could produce a male child without the possibility of being disappointed. Although the secret was later revealed to me by
Mrs. Macfadden I could not explain it to our readers. The
publisher believed it would be of untold value to crowned
heads and for some time I negotiated with Japanese dignitaries
who expressed marked interest in the theory, as the Emperor
of Japan had been undergoing some difficulties in bringing
forth a male heir. The secret remains locked up in the inner
recesses of my mind, its worth negligible to royalty during
these evil days.

Our basic policy was implacably opposed to doctors and
their ilk. On my staff was a health adviser who, in his own
columns, told any of our readers who felt badly, perhaps after
having read our paper, to "drink orange juice" or "paint it
with iodine," as the case might be. Undoubtedly, the advice
prevented many people from forming the habit of stuffing their
bodies with medicines and often I was visited by subscribers
who reported decided improvement after using our remedies.

In my own case I have no doubt that orange juice would have been much better for me than other liquids which have flowed through my system.

Our editorial proclamations that right was on the scaffold and wrong was on the throne in medical affairs brought added resistance to the *Graphic's* progress but Macfadden clung to his principles. His beliefs, as they affected his newspaper venture, were to cost him several million dollars. I had to form a certain alertness to grasp quickly the purpose of his projects.

During the Christmas season of 1924, under the publisher's orders, I borrowed the entire soup kitchen equipment from the Army at Governors Island and established the affair in a large lot in front of our office. Macfadden asked me to announce in the paper that a warm soup, prepared from one of his recipes, would be served day and night to the hungry of New York. I chased half of my staff out to buy the ingredients; fat soup bones, countless bags of flour, corn meal, onions, peas, spinach, salt and such. By the time my reporters had the fires going under the cauldrons, incredible numbers of bearded human derelicts had arrived, impatient to be served although the peas had hardly simmered. The substance was thickening, however as I stirred one of the huge pots while my rewrite battery rushed up with boilers of water from an adjoining undertaking establishment, which was also engaged in a speak-easy enterprise, as my helpers had obviously discovered. Our project assumed staggering proportions and I harangued the crowd, calling for men who knew something about cooking and announcing, also, that we had to get out a newspaper.

Late that night, from my office window, I watched the fires burning while thousands of starving and lousy wrecks of life wolfed Macfadden's soup, whose peas went down like hot bullets. Bob McNamara, an old *World* man, who stood beside me, saw a replica of Lambert's bust of Napoleon on my desk and turning back to the glare and the shadowy squatting figures he said:

"Sire, we are gazing at the camp fires of Austerlitz!"

Somehow, I never forgot McNamara's remark. The *Graphic,* which has since had no historic duplicate, was to have its Austerlitz in circulation but its Waterloo was inevitable. I should have seen it in the flames crackling under the cauldrons.

In launching the *Graphic,* its most ambitious project had to be abandoned. We hoped to revive the Hall-Mills murder case of 1922, reconstruct the crime, accuse certain people of it in our first issue and bring about a trial. I had visited the scene at New Brunswick with a special investigator and we had talked to Jane Gibson, the "pig woman," and other characters familiar with the circumstances. The slaying of Rev. Edward Wheeler Hall and the choir singer, Mrs. Eleanor R. Mills, still remained in public memory and a solution of the mystery would have attracted tremendous attention to our new paper. But using assumption as evidence is a dangerous matter and in an eleventh-hour talk with Fulton Oursler, Macfadden's supervising editor, I voted against the story as something which, I was certain, would lead to disaster. Oursler, though disappointed in our preparation in this enterprise, agreed with me and Macfadden concurred.

My activities in the Hall-Mills affair finally leaked out, and Phillip Payne, later as managing editor of the *Mirror,* a morning tabloid which Hearst had launched three months before our appearance, picked up the cold trail I had dropped and, in a series of sensational stories, caused the arrest of Mrs. Hall and some of her relatives. All were declared innocent by a jury. The *Mirror* was sued for a tremendous amount for libel damages and forced to settle for a sum running into six figures. Payne had acquired much circulation but, apparently, to recapture his prestige he attempted to fly to Rome and lost his life in the Atlantic Ocean. His death, of which I may have been the innocent cause, was to bring about a more turbulent turn in my life.

The *Graphic's* circulation skyrocketed to 200,000 when some genius in the organization conceived the idea of offering $5,000 in cash prizes for the correct solution of a month's series of crossword puzzles. Thousands of people in New York had been working out the puzzles in the subways and when the news spread that money might be earned by such labor, our presses hardly could keep up with the demands. Macfadden, who told me to make the puzzles easy, ordered me to start a second contest, this time with prizes totaling $25,000. The names of the winners were announced in the old Madison Square Garden and I spent an hour forcing my way through the largest crowd I had ever seen, to reach the building. Hundreds of policemen had to be called out to handle dense masses of people. The tabloid had accumulated 300,000 readers by that time but was meeting vicious opposition from the *New York Journal*. Hearst, thoroughly aroused by the competition, had offered $30,000 in crossword puzzle prizes.

With the *Mirror* in the field and the *Daily News* well established, I became involved in a three-cornered tabloid struggle for circulation, which was to be one of the bitterest of my experience. I had, by this time, moved my family to New York, but again my home life degenerated into limited hours of sleep before I hurried to the office. The battle into which I had been drawn required all of my time and concentration. The details of this experience I included in an autobiographical novel a few years later in which I foresaw my separation from Sarah.

I paid no attention to the years flying by and drove myself to reach a million circulation to establish the *Graphic* as a paying proposition. I was on the books of Macfadden Publications for $50,000 of stock in the corporation, on which I had made a down payment of $10,000. I was paying off the balance with dividends and my own money and in my headlong plunge for security, I had to sink or swim.

Looking back I am forced to the conclusion that Macfadden was the only sincere publisher with whom I was ever associated. Regardless of the criticism drawn by the *Graphic's* desperate methods to seek a footing, the physical culturist never forgot the original principles of his health campaigns. My dealings with him were trying when the question of advertising came up for discussion. He attacked high-heeled shoes as a menace to a woman's anatomy in his editorials after we had obtained a valuable series of advertisements from a well-known shoe company. I have known publishers who would have walked around on stilts to secure that form of revenue. Advertisements for men's hats in the *Graphic* provoked Macfadden to write an editorial urging men to go about hatless to "air their hair." He loathed cigarette smoking as an insidious habit and fought us to a standstill during our efforts to wear him down to the point of accepting tobacco advertising. His attitude toward liquor advertising would have been as adamant, had prohibition not been in force. He refused to accept money as advertising revenue from products in which he did not believe. I have never worked for another publisher who permitted his personal convictions to interfere with the money his paper could bring in.

Clement Wood, in his authorized biography of Macfadden, lifts the curtain from the early struggles of the advocate of healthful exercise and explains much of the physical culturist's uncompromising stand in his struggles to make the nation health-conscious. The publisher's father was a drunkard who died of alcoholism. His mother died of tuberculosis when Macfadden was ten years old, and at fifteen he, himself, was threatened with the disease. By his own methods he struck off the shackles of weakness and became a remarkable athlete. At sixty years of age, in 1928, he was the liveliest man I had ever seen on a tennis court. At seventy he drove his own airplane. He once told me that by his method of dieting, proper exercise and eating carefully selected foods, he saw no reason why he should not live to be 125 years old. He had an uncanny faculty of predicting a man's life span merely by looking at him. He knew the body and its first signs of deterioration. I remember four or five of his prophecies with a shudder because they came true.

The publisher, at one time, had an ambition to head a new post in the Cabinet, to be called "Secretary for Health" and, as he outlined the idea, I saw some reasons to justify it. He contributed large sums to the Republican party although I do not believe his mind would have been confined to strict party lines, had he entered politics. Finally, he developed definite longings for the nomination for the Presidency and those close to him received the impression that he would have accepted the honor from either of the major parties. He appeared at the national conventions where he established headquarters but, somehow, no "Macfadden for President" boom ever got under way. He believed in a strict "pay as you go" policy for the nation and plenty of exercise. His cabinet undoubtedly would have been muscular. On one of my missions for him I consulted Judge George W. Olvany, chief of Tammany Hall, about the possibility of obtaining the nomination of Macfadden for Governor of New York at the time Alfred E. Smith ran for the Presidency. Olvany said:

"Macfadden would be a popular candidate but the propaganda that would be brought against him by the medical profession of the nation would prevent his chance of election. The doctors will never forgive him."

During the *Graphic's* desperate efforts to increase mass readership I became responsible for a pictorial creation known as the "composograph." It was a device finally perfected by Harry Grogin, our assistant art director, and through its process scenes could be recreated without the necessity of photographing them. These pictures have since become museum pieces.

The circulation of the *Graphic* increased by 100,000 copies when, after the death of Rudolph Valentino, whose biography I was publishing, I produced an illustration, by our new method, showing the motion-picture actor entering the spirit world and meeting a number of celebrities who had passed on before him. No particular attention would have been paid by the legal authorities to our "composographs," an invention which still hounds me, and provokes bursts of sardonic laughter from those who remember it, but for the fact that I decided to illustrate the buffoonery of an eccentric millionaire who was to go down in newspaper history as "Daddy" Browning. He had married a young woman known as Peaches Heenan and their squabbles became the talk of Broadway. Such papers as the *New York Times* and the *World* considered the matter of enough social importance to let their conservative readers in on it. But the *Graphic* was pounced upon, and John S. Sumner, who had inherited Anthony Comstock's post as agent for the Society for the Suppression of Vice, caused the arrest of all executives on the paper, including Macfadden. As I considered myself responsible as editor, I arranged to free my associates and face the consequences in Special Sessions Court.

Macfadden wanted me to be defended by a good lawyer but the only one he could remember as a resourceful legalist was William Travers Jerome who, many years ago, had become a national figure as the prosecutor of Harry K. Thaw. We visited Jerome and explained the case to him. He was then an aging man, living in the past. He had never heard of "Daddy" Browning or the *Graphic* but he nodded his head patiently while he tried to absorb the details of the commotion. Finally he asked:

"Let me see the newspaper which carried this material."

We produced a copy of our journal, which may have been

the first tabloid Jerome had ever seen. He adjusted his glasses, looked at it intently for a moment and quickly returned it to us.

"Plead guilty," he said.

We then visited Max Steuer, a millionaire barrister in closer touch with modern events, and the case was thrown out of court.

The newsstands of the country, by this time, were swamped with sensational magazines, a large number of them of the art and sex variety. *Physical Culture,* which observed the definite purpose of improving health, had 400,000 readers. *True Story* sold more than 2,000,000 copies a month. Sex magazines of other publishers had a total combined circulation in the country of 55,560,000 a year. As the average copy is read by four persons this meant no less than 222,240,000 yearly readers.

Newspapers edited chiefly for entertainment left their conservative competitors behind. The *Graphic's* circulation finally soared to 700,000, running neck-and-neck with the readership of the *Journal,* whose staff had trained its guns on our tabloid in a merciless warfare. We had unhorsed three of Hearst's managing editors on his afternoon paper. I was held at my post practically day and night. Macfadden was convinced we could reach a million and launched the Sunday *Graphic* which acquired 350,000 readers after the first few weeks of a mysterious engagement with my Hearst competitors. For a time my Sunday papers seldom reached the newsstands and interested observers reported huge bundles of them gliding down the East River. These guerrilla tactics came to a sudden end when we began to reprint, under sinister-looking type, from one of Macfadden's magazines about the films, some harmless installments of the life of Marion Davies, a motion-picture star of recognized talent, whose career had been aided by Hearst. His circulation chief, at the time, was Moses L. Annenberg, whom I was to meet some years later. My triumph in this struggle, however, was short-lived. Macfadden decided to increase the price of the Sunday paper from five cents to ten cents, and that was the end of our Sabbath publication.

My days became kaleidoscopic, my nights uncertain. Macfadden often awakened me at three o'clock in the morning with a circulation idea. One night he called me up with a suggestion which added 30,000 to our next day's run.

"Some convict was executed at Sing Sing last night," he said. "Run a full-page picture of his face on the front page and over it use a two-word headline, two inches high: 'ROASTED ALIVE!'"

The publisher became stirred by the choice of contenders in the Atlantic City Beauty Contest. The girls selected to appear before the judges who crowned "Miss America" each year, were anaemic, he said. He believed it was a bad omen for the future mothers of the nation. I found a number of irregularities in the competition, exposed them, and this heaven of beauty was closed up for a few years. Fay Lanphier was recorded in the history of national beauty as the last "Miss America" of the time and the *Graphic* was sued for $4,000,000 in libel damages. Earl Carroll, one of the contest judges, a spectacular theatrical producer, telephoned me that he was suing the paper for damages of $500,000. I informed him I would pay no attention to the threat unless he raised the sum to $1,000,000. He did. The other libel suits resulted in a detestable struggle during which I was "framed," as this embarrassment is described, by a chorus girl, evidently friendly with the plaintiffs, while I was looking for evidence. Judge Olvany, then ruler of Tammany Hall, rescued me by persuading District Attorney Joab Banton to discharge one of his assistants, involved in the conspiracy, and who was about to have me indicted on the false charge of subornation of perjury. Banton, who was entirely ignorant of the matter and totally innocent of its complications, fired the assistant district attorney in my presence. I was beginning to discover the importance of having some friends at Tammany Hall.

I was now under a bombardment of libel suits. Adding up the damages demanded of the *Graphic* one evening, I found the sum amounted to $12,000,000. I quieted the agitated treasurer of the publication by telling him to take the money out of my salary. There was a tendency among certain lawyers, most of them without principles, to attempt to exact money from publishers of sensational news publications. One batch of libel suits, amounting to $7,000,000 cost the company only $5,290 in judgments and settlements, a tribute to Joseph Schultz, our tiny little lawyer, thin as a rail but of rugged courage, constantly fighting. Whenever I visited his office his face blanched.

I suppressed the details of a tragedy of interest to Connecticut because of my attachment for the man who was its central figure. Senator Frank Brandegee, who had become the motivating force of the Senate Committee on Foreign Relations, committed suicide in Washington by inhaling gas, an act which shocked Washington political circles. At the end of his successful campaign of 1920, which I had helped to promote, he had asked me to become his secretary, an offer which I had declined. One evening at the Hartford Club, during an intimate conversation, he told me he had remained a bachelor because of a hopeless affection which he had conceived as a young member of the House of Representatives, for a daughter of a former President of the United States.

"I'm supposed to be a hard-boiled politician," he said, "but sometimes when I think of what might have been I find no happiness in success. Every time I see her in the Senate galleries it all comes back. Her father told her I'd never be anything but an obscure Congressman. Years have gone by and I still have that pain in my heart about it."

We ran a story about a mysterious, veiled woman who threw flowers on his grave. She remained unidentified.

Circulation now had to be kept up by making news. We could no longer wait for calamities to happen. Characters were built up and paraded. Hot news became the wild, blazing, delirious symptom of the time. Peggy Hopkins Joyce was always good for a banner line. Payne scooped the town whenever she appeared with a new husband. Through the cooperation of Terry Turner, a theatrical press agent whose audacity I have never seen equalled, I met competition by moving into a hospital girl Siamese twins who announced they were to be cut apart to enable one of them to marry. To Turner's relief The American Medical Association took prompt steps to stop the operation and while circulation soared from this excitement I took advantage of a breathing spell by making an impulsive and hazardous trip to Honduras, to forget my surroundings.

Charles Phillips of my staff, an old reporter who had worked for the *Times* when Adolph Ochs was establishing it into the great paper it finally became, had been talking about an expedition to interview General Sandino, the Nicaraguan rebel. Ryan Walker, my art director, a widely known liberal, obtained a letter of introduction to the revolutionist from his brother, Socrates, who lived in Brooklyn. Phillips, Walker and I landed in Honduras from a fruit steamer in the summer of 1926 after surviving a tropical hurricane which threw the ship four times on its beam's end and caused a heavy loss of life on the east coast of Florida. One night, when it appeared that we were going down, I crawled on my hands and knees to Phillips' cabin where he was engaged in praying in front of an upset dresser on which he was trying to hold plaster statues of Saint Joseph and the Virgin Mary in an upright position.

"If these statues don't stand up we're gone!" he shouted.

We licked our wounds for three days at Puerto Cortez and made our way, in the hands of rebel guides, into Nicaragua through banana jungles to Sandino's outposts, although American Marines were in the region looking for him. The trip was accomplished in the face of hardships which, somehow, I enjoyed as a novelty. The rebels, who referred to Sandino as the "Washington of Nicaragua," and who hated American promoters in the banana business, gave us a message to the American people and we crawled back to a safer climate. In the jungles, Walker was bitten on the face by a tarantula, a large hairy spider, which I had brushed off my temple in the darkness and evidently swept to his cheek while I was beside him. I could not recognize the artist's swollen features at a plantation where we had staggered through swarms of gnats to spend the night. He was cured by native homeopathy. A parasite had gotten under my epidermis and seemed to race about my body beneath my skin. I had to sit in an almost scalding sulphur bath up to my neck to get rid of it.

Leaving Honduras, during our first night out on the same boat which had brought us to the tropics, a steamer of the Cuyamel Fruit Company, I was horrified when Phillips announced at the captain's table that he had appropriated an altar cloth from a venerable Spanish church as a souvenir of our adventures. He produced the embroidery, whose great age had not dimmed its exquisite design of heavy gold threads. The captain, a superstitious Norwegian still shaken by the hurricane, pushed his dinner of tripe aside and turned white. The desecration, he said, would result in three deaths, including himself as the navigator of the boat. He looked at us significantly. Phillips, now almost out of his mind, wanted to throw the altar cloth overboard, but the captain told him it was too late. He urged us to take the next boat out of New York and return it.

Four days after our arrival Phillips was found dead in his room at the Brevoort Hotel. Two days later, the captain followed him. I wrote a story of the coincidence which I can only explain by the fact that Phillips had collapsed from a heart attack during our hardships. The captain, who was an enormous eater, may have dug his grave with his teeth. Walker was stricken by a brain hemorrhage almost immediately, but pulled through and died five years later.

I took charge of the altar cloth, reverently, and placed it on my mantelpiece, not being able to recall the house of worship from which it had been appropriated. Some day, during a future pilgrimage, I hope to find that church, far inside Honduras, deposit the embroidery on the altar rail and say a prayer for newspaper men who are not always accountable for their actions.

CHAPTER III

FIVE years of tabloidia turned my hair iron gray before I reached my middle thirties. Each day brought a new adventure, which I grew to expect as an opiate. The mainstay of my original staff still was with me, though some had left for wider fields of recognition. Charles Macauley, noted cartoonist of Pulitzer's *World,* was drawing for the *Graphic* and was to be with me until his pen should fall from his hand. I had advertised him to such an extent that his first wife had thrown him into the "Alimony Jail" for certain arrears. In Hartford I had bought from a New York feature writer a story which described the "Alimony Club" as a place where jolly fellows gathered about a great oaken table, banging tankards. Now the jail took on new meaning for me. I discussed cartoons with Macauley while we sat on his prison cot in a ghastly cell lighted by a swaying bulb. And the aging artist, one of the last of the noble line of Thomas Nast, Sir John Tenniel and Bernard Partridge of *Punch,* drew with his board propped up on his knees, oblivious of the bars. Producing pictures from his own honest impulses represented the only freedom he wanted.

Lester Cohen, my contest editor, had become the author of *Sweepings,* a widely discussed novel. He had married Eden Grey, an actress of rare beauty, and their happiness brushed my heart with the feather touch of envy. They went to Hollywood to enjoy Lester's first taste of financial success. John W. Vandercook, who had followed Cohen in my contest corner, soon rose to higher intellectual vibrations and was hailed as the brilliant writer of *Black Majesty.* He grew a beard, became dignified, and when I saw him years later I avoided tabloidia in our conversation. Ed Sullivan, my sports editor, finally sought richer pastures, where he became an authoritative Hollywood historian, his words printed simultaneously in 500 newspapers. Louis Sobol was quietly preparing to become "The Voice of Broadway." There were others, future money-making playwrights and fine newspaper specialists such as Sutherland Denlinger. Leo Casey, an intrepid Irishman whom I had brought down from Hartford as a reporter, was to become Wendell Willkie's publicity adviser. Herbert Ekins, pounding one of my typewriters, would not have believed that later he would win a passenger race around the world in an airplane for publisher Roy Howard and become a noted war correspondent. Jack Miley, a violent anti-physical culturist, was in training on my staff to develop into a recognized sports authority.

And, in a corner, sat a hunched figure with a white lean face of deceptive humility, looking up occasionally, startled. He pecked a typewriter, nervously, with a frenzied determination, but from the machine, a form of gossip was beginning to appear which he himself never dreamed could be accorded the benediction of print in a daily paper. When his column, "Your Broadway and Mine," became the talk of the town, no vestige of humility remained in him.

He was known as Walter Winchell, a vaudeville "hoofer" who had been introduced to me by Fulton Oursler as a possibility and I had put him on the payroll at one hundred dollars a week, as I recall it, and fifteen percent in commissions on any theatrical advertising he could obtain. No stranger phenomenon has yet appeared in the newspaper business. Gossip acquired such a tangibility, such a grip on his life, chiefly from the bare nucleus of a slim fact that, many times, he was more often cleverly wrong than monotonously correct. The *New Yorker* has said that he was wrong at least forty per cent of the time, but he was never dull. That he could convey as much implication in a line as could be safely expressed in a column, undoubtedly accounted for the fact that, some fifteen years later, he boasted that his technique had helped him to "salt away two million smackers." His income tax indicates that this statement might well approach at least sixty percent in accuracy.

His lack of newspaper experience, when I began to handle his copy; his refreshing *insouciance* about the difference between a subject and a predicate, became an ironical asset which preserved his personality and may have had the virtue of saving him years of learning to be like everybody else. In his pate rattled more than a grain of genius which was to produce a "slanguage" often too puzzling for the venerable gentlemen of the courts who were not permitted to go beyond old man Webster.

"Blessed events" were no longer confined to official bulletins from royal households, and disintegrating marriages appeared in print long before the judges heard their painful details. Making an innocent interrogation serve the purpose, at times, of damning affirmation, had as much to do with the rash of intimate columns now spread over the land, as Winchell's diaper drolleries. For more than a decade I was to be held to the task of "legalizing" his output. Our mutual relationship was never boring. No paper but Macfadden's tabloid could have nursed such a prodigy who, by some form of self-hypnosis, came to feel himself the center of his time.

Such were the newcomers cutting their eyeteeth on the old floundering *Graphic,* in its rattle-trap building. Other metropolitan papers were glad to hire these men when they leaped for safety from my crazy sheet.

One man helped to satisfy my passion for music at that time. He was a retired bank burglar, now on good terms with society, and wrote stories of his experiences for a living; a tall, prematurely gray-haired Irishman with twinkling eyes in a sensitive face. He was known as Jack Grey and became the *Graphic's* crime expert. He was the first person I met in New York who enjoyed the opera, where he appeared regularly in evening dress and top hat. His long serial, *The Confessions of a Bank Burglar* for *True Story* had much to do with the magazine's climb to its first million mark. Returning from an execution at Sing Sing, Grey would dash off his story and pick up an interrupted argument as to whether Bach was a typically diatonic composer as opposed to César Franck.

When the notorious Gerald Chapman was arrested in Connecticut I assigned Grey to visit him at Wethersfield Prison where he obtained the prisoner's life story. The two, no doubt, revived recollections of the time when the imagination of the professional petermen was recognized by the police as something which challenged the intellect. Grey's visit to the prison caused a mild sensation later when Prosecuting Attorney Hugh Alcorn discovered that my reporter had once been one of the most expert safe blowers in the East. It is an adopted rule in penal institutions that a former inmate is not to be admitted in prisons unless properly escorted to a cell for a prescribed period. Grey, however, verified my conviction of the theory of reformation and justified my belief through the years by his complete honesty of purpose.

Life went on for me as a series of explosive episodes. People who had stories of injustices, which no other paper wanted to print, came to see me. A young mother visited me one night, holding by the hand a little girl of tender beauty. She introduced herself as Nan Britton and her child as the daughter of President Harding. Miss Britton had written a book called *The President's Daughter* and wanted me to print a story about it. She had interviewed other editors unsuccessfully. I looked into her daughter's innocent face and saw that it was all true. Her eyes, unforgettable, serene and unafraid, told it all. I had looked into Harding's face, too. I remembered his eyes. I sprang the story under a large headline, and Nan Britton's book became a nation-wide best seller, its climb recorded weekly in the conservative press.

Miss Britton had some trouble when her book appeared, and she inserted the following on a flyleaf of future printings as demands came from all parts of the country for her tragic story:

"The first edition of *The President's Daughter* was hindered and trodden upon by interests which do not want to see this mother's true story given to the world. On June 10, 1927, six burly New York policemen and John S. Sumner, agent for the Society for the Suppression of Vice, armed with a 'warrant of search and seizure,' entered the printing plant where the making of the book was in process. They seized and carried off the plates and printed sheets. On June 29, in a magistrate's court, the case was dismissed. The seized plates and printed sheets were returned to the publishers."

The President's Daughter resulted in the organization of the Elizabeth Ann Guild, the decisive factor in a humane movement which brought about legislation in New York State to recognize the legitimacy of the children of unwedded mothers. Sensational treatment is sometimes required to destroy our inherited barbarisms.

At times I was filled with a desire to leave on blind ventures, after the manner of my gropings through tropical jungles. I saw no permanency in anything. This feeling is well explained by W. Somerset Maugham in *The Summing*

Up: "Perhaps the only thing of which I was certain was that I was certain of nothing else."

Something, with an element of the fantastic, happened at this time to produce a temptation which I finally fought down. While the *Graphic* was being held up by the intelligentsia as an example of the Great American Menace, it had, somehow, got into the hands of King Prajadhipok of Siam who was struck by the originality of my "composographs." He wanted to support a tabloid paper of entertaining features in Bangkok, and through Francis Bowes Sayre, adviser in foreign affairs to the Siamese Government, the *Graphic* was approached to produce an editor to fulfill the King's desires. I was informed that Queen Rambaibarni disagreed with the King and wouldn't have the *Graphic* in her boudoir. Arguing with a king and queen about the *Graphic* would, at that time, have been a matter of satisfaction to me. I had argued about it with everybody but royalty.

There was no time to turn the problem over in my mind. The King expected quick action. Don Garden, one of my copyreaders, an imaginative newspaper man, decided to take the job and embarked for Siam while I throttled my feelings of envy. From what I heard of Garden's adventures I came to the conclusion that he deserved the highest honor the King could bestow, the Grand Cross of the White Elephant, a decoration peculiarly applicable to some tabloid newspapers.

Some of the city's best people were now helping to run the *Graphic*. Congressman Fiorello La Guardia had his own little department in the paper in which he took solid cracks at those who opposed his liberalism. He wrote vigorous words without pay and hoped to launch a magazine of his own to be called *La Guardia's Weekly*. He had taken me to his home in a noisy district full of Portuguese and rolled up his sleeves and cooked spaghetti which we washed down with chianti.

"Journalism and politics make a great combination," he said.

Rev. John Roach Stratton, the most vigorous churchman that had ever ransacked a Bible, came to see me and questioned me about my readers. He was convinced that tabloidia attracted the sinners of New York and furnished a new field of salvation. His spectacular sermons decrying the degradation of humanity drew great crowds and he believed that his fervency had made the Holy Ghost reach his flock through the roof of his church.   I prepared a "composograph" of this phenomenon according to his description.   After studying it carefully he agreed it was a good representation of the way it had happened and I printed it on the front page.

Nicky Arnstein entered my door one night with two ominous looking gentleman who appeared to be bodyguards.   He wanted to sell his life story.   I refused to buy it until he had included in its chapters his recollections of Arnold Rothstein, a sinister power in the political underworld.   Arnstein complied reluctantly with my request and I paid him $4,000 of the company's cash, hoping to syndicate the revelations, and get the money back while printing them in my own paper.   Newspapers around the country were not interested in the noted gambler's experiences and I was criticized by the business office for wastefulness.   Months went by and one Sunday evening Arnold Rothstein was shot.   The police scandal which ensued rocked New York, and I began to print Arnstein's manuscript in installments under the headline:

ARNSTEIN'S OWN STORY
OF ARNOLD ROTHSTEIN!

Before I could print the details referring to Rothstein, Nicky Arnstein appeared again with his companions and informed me that the next published installment would result in his death and that mine would inevitably follow.   This was confirmed by a friend on whom I relied at Tammany Hall. He urged me over the telephone to sell the story back to Arnstein if I cared to live.   Arnstein put a large down payment on my desk and walked off with his narrative.   He was a man of his word and as time went on he saw to it that every cent I had paid him was returned.   Arnstein had not been connected with Rothstein in any way but he knew much about him.   I had gambled with my visitor to print a story which may never be revealed, unless Nicky dies before I do.

Macfadden and I had a somewhat difficult time agreeing on the subject of humor for the paper.   He wanted me to revive *Peck's Bad Boy,* which had made an impression on him in his early days.   Winchell's column, to the publisher, was a mass of unintelligible jargon.   I caused to be created, at the publisher's suggestion, a number of comic strips which emphasized physical culture. "Little Samson," one of his ideas, showed a tiny man with bulging muscles who invariably appeared to catch a massive safe falling from a tenth-story window. Occasionally he found four men struggling to move a grand piano out of a moving van and solved the problem by lifting the large instrument up on the palm of one hand, like a tray. Macfadden roared with laughter over the antics of "Little Samson" but the small creature finally disappeared with his brothers of the flesh who used to tear up my telephone books.

One man on our staff came to benefit from this type of humor. He was a slight, worried and pale artist named Gus Edson who, every day, had to draw a muscular girl character attired in jersey and shorts. She had a mean left jab and went around delivering knockout blows to tough customers who took advantage of the weaker sex. Edson pushed through my door regularly to find out if his work was satisfactory. One day he caught me in the act of taking a drink of Scotch for a toothache and never recovered from his embarrassment. Finally, when the creator of "Andy Gump" was killed Edson slipped into the dead man's shoes and drew the widely syndicated "Andy" in such a manner that he looked more like himself than at any time since he had popped out of an ink bottle.

The *Graphic* was forced to depend on stunts and sensations to hold its readers who consumed considerable time over the tabloid's concoctions, very little, no doubt, to their improvement. Meanwhile, the daily historians of the era reported the news of importance for papers of less circulation. I received many letters from sympathetic followers who urged improvements in our comics after the manner of the *Daily News* which held the masses spellbound with its strips drawn with an element of suspense and continuity. Its "Gasoline Alley" had produced a lady who had a baby after nine months of excitement, every day of which had been studied by hundreds of thousands of loyal subway readers. People could tell you the whole history of "Skeezix" for years back without knowing anything about news of the slightest importance. More and more I saw muscular people reading my pink *Graphic* in the subways but they were outnumbered five to one by the intent faces behind the *Daily News*.

Defying this underground readership, Macfadden launched

an editorial campaign which was almost a body-blow to our circulation. He advocated an increase in the five-cent subway fare on the theory that real estate taxes thereby would be reduced. We soon had to abandon this appalling crusade. He had another idea which involved the millions transported daily under the streets of New York. He engaged an engineer to draw plans for a double-deck subway car to lessen the crowding of passengers. The tunnels were not high enough for this invention, and when we discovered that riders in the upper deck would have had to sit head down in a tortured position and probably develop into a permanently hunchbacked generation we dropped the project and started an agitation for "Walk to Work" clubs.

We more than regained the losses we had suffered through our editorials advocating an increase in subway fare by buying the memoirs of Mayor John F. Hylan, a zealous champion of the five-cent rate whose election was due largely to his views on this subject. An increase of 76,000 readers amply rewarded us for the $20,000 we paid for his autobiography which had to be deleted in certain sizzling spots to protect the reputation of some of New York's best-known citizens.

We supported the experiments of a professor of "brain breathing," a series of exercises which involved inhaling through one nostril, with certain neck movements which were supposed to induce more active cerebration and quicken the wits. Some members of our staff went through the performance without noticeable results although Bill Plummer, our night editor, whom we called the "Iron Duke," reported that it dispersed the hangovers of a number of his reporters.

The publisher brought to me one day a man who had been cured of the drug habit by physical-culture methods and told me to announce in the paper that the emancipated victim would explain the process of his salvation free of charge to all slaves of drugs who cared to visit him at the *Graphic* office. That evening our editorial rooms were turned into a raving asylum by all manner of terrifying, shaking creatures who crawled with pawing hands over shuddering copyreaders, climbed on chairs and finally had complete possession of the place. The "Iron Duke" saved his edition by calling the police.

When Frank Munsey died, as owner of the *Sun*, Macfadden asked me to find out if the property was for sale. An executive of the celebrated paper listened to me with a kindly tolerance, gave me an expensive cigar, patted me gently on the back and showed me how to get out to the street. Later I saw him at a banquet and he gave me a questioning, uncertain look.

A member of our organization taught me how to forget the cares of tabloidia by taking me off on flying jaunts. He was Jimmy Williamson, Macfadden's brother-in-law, a happy-go-lucky Englishman and *bon vivant* who had become an air enthusiast and who had the use of the publisher's airplane during weekends. Williamson owned a small, collapsible bar which he secretly installed behind the pilot's seat and shook cocktails for me 2,000 feet over the Woolworth Building before we swooped down to Atlantic City for lunch. One Sunday we induced Payne, editor of Hearst's *Mirror,* to join us. Less than a year later he was to lose his life in his plane, *Old Glory,* in the Atlantic. Payne settled back in his seat after his cocktail, watched the flying, golden clouds below us, wiped tears from his eyes and began to sing:

> *"Jesus lover of my soul,*
> *Let me to Thy bosom fly."*

The editor told us he was suffering from some disappointment of a personally tragic nature, the knowledge of which, he told us, would die with him. Later, Hearst, who deplored his death, informed me that he had made every effort to dissuade Payne from taking the flight.

The *Graphic* became the rendezvous of frustrated artists and battered idealists who were always sure of a hearing in our sanctum. Many trailed in to tell their troubles to Ryan Walker, our art director, whom I have already mentioned: a little man of bushy hair, with a smile of sympathy and eyes of deep understanding and communicative humor. He wore the garb of the artist, including a wide-brimmed hat and flowing black tie. I saw him give away, many times, all but two or three dollars of his salary to the poor of the tenements on our street. He talked of a kindly Communism as the only remedy for the evils of mankind. Finally, he went to Russia, after marrying Marjorie Smith, a New Haven girl on my staff, and died in Moscow. Upton Sinclair came to see him in our art department and waited while Walker pushed all other work aside to prepare gigantic fig leaves on colored cardboard which Sinclair took to Boston to use in a protest parade against literary censorship.

The bearded Carlo Tresca, then a vigorous liberal agitator, often dropped in to discuss the day of judgment against capitalism. He finally got $150 from me during an impassioned appeal for his flaming newspaper, *Il Martello,* which was defending birth control, a crusade which sent him to prison for a time. He induced me to launch a campaign to save two obscure Italians, named Greco and Carillo, who were falsely accused of having shot two men in a Fascist parade in the Bronx. While we were floundering in this fight the noted lawyer, Clarence Darrow, came to our rescue and without any fee saved the prisoners from the electric chair and restored them to liberty. During this struggle for justice we accidentally used a picture of Leo Carillo, the motion-picture actor, as one of the men facing execution and he sued us for $150,000 damages for anguish of mind. This was a minor matter of the *Graphic* which was the most-sued paper in American journalism.

Hans Stengel, an accomplished German artist, a master caricaturist who was determined to draw for a purpose, visited us despondently with batches of his sketches of the life of the twirling twenties. His sardonic drawings which reflected his fine genius gave him no living and he was forced to obtain temporary work imitating the love and marriage pictures of Nell Brinkley for the *Journal,* while Miss Brinkley was on a leave of absence. When I saw him for the last time he threw a portfolio of ten drawings on my desk.

"Save them," he said dryly, "they may come in handy."

One of my assistants, Joseph Appelgate, discovered that in some of the drawings Stengel had pictured himself as suspended from a rope with a leer on his face. Before I could communicate with the artist he had committed suicide by hanging himself during a party in Greenwich Village. We used his drawings with the account of his death.

The last Christmas promotion party for our readers was an occasion I was to remember. The *Graphic* distributed toys to the poor from the bandstand in Central Park and had obtained permission from Mayor Jimmy Walker to land an audacious Santa Claus in an airplane in the sheep meadows, a short distance away, where thousands of children had been attracted to the scene. In clear weather, the venture would have been hazardous but the sky became overcast in the afternoon and soon the Park was swept by an icy, howling wind. Three hours went by while the children set up a clamor for the delayed Santa whose part was to be played by Will Mahoney, a popular Broadway comedian. He was to be flown from Long Island by a barnstorming aviator known as Swanee Taylor who would have attempted a rocket flight to the moon for any imaginative editor ready to put up the money for it. After two dangerous forced landings on the way, Taylor, who believed his reputation was at stake, actually brought Mahoney down in the Park following some desperate maneuvering 500 feet above us. As the screaming children crowded about the plane, Mahoney, a mass of icicles, rose angrily in his red suit in the open cockpit, yanked off what was left of his white whiskers and wig, and shouted:

"To hell with Santa Claus! I'll never ride in these damned things again!"

CHAPTER IV

THE *Graphic* left its shaking building on City Hall Place, to my relief, and installed itself in an ample structure on Hudson Street. Before we moved I had invited Walter Wanger, the motion-picture producer, to discuss some business at my office after lunching with him. The passenger elevator was stalled in the upper regions and I rang for the freight elevator, with Wanger at my side. As I pressed the button, the large, groaning car, loaded with tons of lead, fell through the shaft from the fourth floor and crashed into the pit in our faces. I thought the building had come down at last. Wanger looked at me blankly, leaped for the pavement and dashed madly up the street. That was the last time I saw him.

Our presses in the new building were started with a glowing celebration. Mayor Walker arrived, in striped trousers, braided coat, ascot tie and top hat, to push the button. A strike was impending in the subway and the Mayor became the "slot man" of our copy desk, dictated the news of the crisis and wrote the headlines, which I engraved in his handwriting for an extra while reporters of the city's press were clamoring outside to interview him. A large room had been reserved for a buffet luncheon for guests, including motion-picture stars of grace and beauty. The Mayor drank champagne with us to the long life of the tabloid and we chatted with bright-eyed sirens and threw care away.

Walker was the Pied Piper of tabloidia, the night mayor of the town, leaving behind him a trail of glamorous news. No picture editor could ever be sure his day's work was done until the merry Mayor had retired. I lived a few doors away from him, then, on St. Luke's Place, and the cheers and huzzas of his escorts who paraded him home got me out of bed regularly in time to go to work.

The city reflected his spirit with gay abandon. All sang his praise from the bar-room bouncers to the Park Avenue Bourbons who had turned the Central Park Casino into a Petit

Trianon. We printed a report that Walker, by special dispensation, would permit Harry Hershfield to move into the Swiss chalet in the Park to induce more concentration on his comic strip, "Abie the Agent." Marshal Henri Phillipe Pétain, hero of Verdun, landed in New York to make a triumphal tour and reporters followed the great soldier and the Mayor who, as the official host, insisted that the municipality would pay for the wine at every oasis. Both were to go through vicissitudes before the expenses of that party could be written off the books. Walker resigned as Mayor, and years later the city mailed the impressive wine bill to Pétain in Paris. The Marshal never forgot the episode, as indicated by news dispatches. In 1941, after the Maginot Line had cracked, France had fallen and what was left of its government was shuddering in Vichy, Pétain called in the foreign correspondents, described the memorable celebration and then with a shake of his hoary head, announced that New York had asked him to settle for every toast he drank to the glory of France and American freedom. Any Frenchman would have admitted that this was the last straw.

I found interesting companions when I had time to cultivate them and I was often invited to the National Arts Club and the Players Club where the illuminati questioned me as to the *Graphic's* purpose. Luce and Hadden, who were putting *Time Magazine* on its feet, quizzed me in an emporium, apparently suspecting some unrevealed subtlety behind our publishing methods. "What the hell is it all about?" Luce asked. I wished that I could have explained it all to him. His own venture was the only one I was really interested in.

I remember long talks with Mary Austin, the most gifted woman writer I ever knew. She spoke from a rich background of association with Mae Sinclair, George Sterling, Jack London, Willa Cather and D. H. Lawrence. She could reconcile diverse elements and call out the best thoughts of those who came within her radius. Her advice had a salutary influence on my personal life.

Gilbert Patten, known to millions of boys in the early 1900's as Burt L. Standish, the author of 208 books on the life of Frank Merriwell, came to my office looking for something to do. During my boyhood I imagined him to be a millionaire, writing on his yacht at the dictation of Merriwell, himself.

Patten discussed the changes that had come upon the new generation. "Dime novels were pretty tame after all," he said. His efforts to revive his two-fisted hero proved discouraging. A kiss to Frank Merriwell symbolized love and marriage. The author who had held his character to this old-fashioned virtue finally found himself in such reduced circumstances that he faced eviction from his home.

Macfadden appointed a board of editorial advisers who induced him to retain Edward L. Bernays, a celebrated counsel of public relations who met with us regularly, for an attractive fee, to give our organization a new sense of direction. Bernays ruled out Macfadden's barefoot walks to his office and his physical culture showmanship, which the publisher abandoned with reluctance. The country, by that time, was beginning to forget his bold campaigns against social diseases, his health crusades which had freed women from steel corsets and finally permitted them to swim without the old-fashioned bathing attire. Under the direction of Bernays, the publisher was sent on a precipitous trip to London to address the House of Commons as the Father of Physical Culture. I was instructed to prepare a four-page history of the event, and in my research I discovered that Daniel Webster had taken a trip to England to be accorded similar honors. I printed pictures of Macfadden and Webster, side by side, in a unique treatise which was mailed by the thousands to members of every legislature in the country, countless clergymen and Washington lawmakers.

George Sylvester Viereck, an able journalist and poet of unusual merit, was employed at that time as an advisory editor of Macfadden's publications and gave some time to a study of the *Graphic* although he seemed more interested in my own case history which he held largely responsible for the tabloid hysteria of the day. His personal conclusions about me I considered of sufficient interest to include in my first novel, *Hot News*. I might have heard the same sermon from a psychoanalyst for a high fee.

"You need the courage to extirpate your conscience if you want to be a success in your business," Viereck said. "It still remains with you as a sort of atavistic survival of your childhood. I am not telling you to bury your prudence in the same tomb with your conscience. In the first place you will never be happy with any woman. You are pouring out all your passion,

tenderness, all you have to give, all your love, vitality and libido
into jazz journalism to escape from the realities of life. This
enables you to give vent to all the base instincts—lust and
savagery and crime—which dwell like Apaches in the subcellars
of your mind, without assuming responsibility for your es-
capades."

This may not have been a fantastic analysis during that
period of my life although I have suspected that the frustrated
poet in my adviser may have accounted for much of his satanic
school of thought. Years later, when the University of Okla-
homa Press asked for nominations for the world's worst book,
a project obviously aimed at Hitler's *Mein Kampf*, Viereck
rose to the defense of the scorned artist, turned dictator, in a
eulogistic letter which included the following:

"Millions of flowers must grow in the garden to achieve
one matchless rose, and billions of men must be born to produce
one superman like Goethe, Napoleon, da Vinci or Hitler!"

The staff intellectuals never told me how to keep up the
circulation. This problem was left to my own resources although Macfadden was not lacking in ideas. Nothing, perhaps, equalled in mass interest in New York in several decades
a project for human happiness which the *Graphic* announced as
the "Guild of the Lonely Hearts." Friendless people were invited to describe their mode of life and the companions they
hoped to meet, and soon this affair, which became a medium
through which yearning letters were printed and exchanged,
grew to such proportions that it required a separate staff to
keep abreast of it. We hired Madison Square Garden for a
"Lonely Hearts Ball" which jammed the place with thousands
of forlorn, inhibited creatures, maiden ladies aroused from
despair, bashful bachelors and prancing widows. Many, doubtless, were made happy, as indicated by the marriages we recorded when these friendships bloomed into warmer affections.

This enterprise was brought to an end less than a year
after it had been launched by two gravely disturbing events.
A woman who represented herself as a guest of our "Lonely
Hearts Ball" deposited a baby on my desk and asked me what
I proposed to do about it. It had happened after the ball, she
said. While negotiations were proceeding to settle the matter
I was notified that the New Jersey Police had identified the
victim of a torch murder as another "lonely heart." As the

"Iron Duke" remarked, we were not to blame for snakes in the grass which had crept into our garden of love but we drew a quiet curtain over this sociological experiment.

Meanwhile, resistance to our advertising salesmanship had become almost insurmountable. Advertising managers appeared and disappeared. John Cook, our old business manager was gone. When the *Graphic's* first issue had come off the press, he reached for a copy, gazed at it wide-eyed, gasped and clutched at his heart in stunned surprise. Later he was taken ill and died.

Macfadden's tabloid was in a hopeless competition with the *Journal* which roared its sensations. The slightest deviation from the shouting headlines would have cost thousands of readers. For a time the new paper was ahead of all of its unfriendly standard-size neighbors in the metropolis. Yet, selling such circulation to an advertiser was a task which might have taken years to accomplish. The paper I had launched was bleeding to death. In addition to original investments in the *Mail* plant and in other necessaries, Macfadden had reported deficits of $519,018 in 1924, $1,579,470 in 1925, $1,459,645 in 1926, $1,074,888 in 1927 and $563,796 in 1928. *True Story*, a highly successful publication, whose business management was under the direction of O. J. Elder, a competent executive, was pouring much of its money into the *Graphic's* losses.

As a stockholder, probably the third largest single owner of securities in Macfadden Publications, I was interested in the *Graphic's* prospects. I talked about it with Macfadden who was becoming concerned about the drain on the treasury but still believed in the paper's future.

"If we can get the losses down to $10,000 a week," he said, "we'll be sitting pretty."

In March of 1929, the situation seemed to be improving and I received a reassuring note from Elder, for whom I had a high respect, and who was in close touch with the corporation's intricate details. The losses were coming down. One evening Macfadden telephoned me to call upon Albert J. Kobler, advertising executive of the *American Weekly*, Hearst's Sunday supplement which was distributed to his papers about the country, a fabulously successful publication. Kobler had become publisher of the *Mirror* and wanted to confer with

Macfadden who appointed me as an emissary. Kobler invited me to attend a formal dinner party at his Park Avenue residence, where business would be discussed after the other guests had left. Later, while I reclined in his ornate study, the master salesman informed me that Hearst wanted to buy the *Graphic* for $2,000,000.

Macfadden, upon hearing the news of my conference, ordered me to see Kobler again and report that the *Graphic* could be bought for $4,000,000. Hearst, then in California, had to be informed of these negotiations, and my meetings with Kobler trailed along until they reached a condition of stalemate. Macfadden refused to give in and Hearst would not increase his price.

Serious changes which had taken place in the business department of the *Graphic* had become irksome to me. For some time Macfadden had been operating, as a majority stockholder, the tabloid *Daily News* in Philadelphia, a paper launched by William S. Vare who hoped that it would help his ambition to become a United States Senator. With Macfadden's help and Vare's power, the paper had climbed out of a deficit in 1928. Its backers had met losses of $445,588 in 1926 and $212,194 in 1927. Lee Ellmaker, the paper's chief executive, had been asked by Macfadden to come to New York to cut the *Graphic's* losses. I could not agree with the Philadelphian's method of operation. I believed that a high-powered New York business executive could have saved the *Graphic* whose editorial policies, in 1929, were no longer drawing criticism. Ellmaker's idea was to cut expenses "to the bone." One of his plans involved the use of discarded engravings of old crossword puzzles, to save money. Puzzle addicts never forgave the *Graphic* for this economy. I found myself in a completely unhappy frame of mind in what I now felt was a hopeless battle. I did not blame Macfadden, whose courage I admired. I could no longer summon the enthusiasm nor the resourcefulness necessary to hold the circulation I had accumulated. My work for five years had required an infinite capacity for excavating excitement and I needed a rest. I was alarmed by the fact that good literature no longer held my interest. I remember trying to read Goethe's *Wilhelm Meister's Apprenticeship* and the words held nothing for me but a jumble of meaningless thoughts.

I had turned my common shares in Macfadden Publications

into preferred stock, and one morning I sold my holdings which brought me considerably more than $60,000. Macfadden had treated me fairly and I had been able to save considerable money aside from my investments in his business. His securities had always paid regular dividends. I was becoming independent.

One of my last battles on the paper involved Winchell, with whom I had been clashing continually. Held to the *Graphic* by contract, he was adopting every conceivable means to be discharged so that he might obtain more money from Hearst. I had endured his abuse with tight lips and when he found he could not budge me he got into the habit of irritating Macfadden by telephoning him at three o'clock in the morning and shouting imprecations. One forenoon the publisher ordered me to discharge the columnist by releasing him from his contract. According to a report which I never verified, Winchell, in one of his telephone tirades, at four A.M., accused the physical culturist of having eaten a planked steak floating in Worcestershire sauce while he was supposed to have been on a diet.

I fired Winchell and the gossiper made a flying leap for the exit with a shout. I threw Louis Sobol into the columnist's job and he soon caught on to Winchell's formula but wrote in less heated vein. He was a slight, sensitive person with trustful eyes, a baldish head and long nose. He had escaped from Connecticut, somewhat after my fashion, and had found rough going in New York as a playwright. He was to live up to my expectations and never have to worry about money for years to come, landing, eventually, in Hearst's lap.

Weeks followed during which I debated with myself about my resignation. Macfadden at that time made large profits from some of his magazines but I knew that Hearst, in his old conflict with Joseph Pulitzer had spent $8,000,000 before the *Journal* had brought him any return. Our competition was even more intense than the battle Don C. Seitz had so well described in his biography of Pulitzer. All I could see ahead for the *Graphic* was a long period of financial drain. When to tone down its sensationalism with the assurance that the paper still would hold a half-million readers and appease the advertisers was a problem I was no longer able to judge. Pulitzer had accomplished it although he had never aroused the wrath which had come down upon us. The old Sunday *World* under Brisbane had reached the high watermark of 623,000 until it had become too offensive for Pulitzer, and Brisbane had gone over to Hearst. The history of this hectic journalism seemed to have developed into an endless cycle.

Memories would remain of the tabloid's feverish struggle, the attacks it had survived and the men and women who, in the beginning, had joined me and who knew how much harder it was to hold the attention of hundreds of thousands of low-brows than to please 30,000 highbrows. One practically starved to death pleasing highbrows. Most of my writers had tried both policies.

I would miss the tireless Father of Physical Culture with his eagerness for right living, his visits to my office in the winter in his frontier attire, his coonskin cap and moccasins, the little Chinese stoves he carried in his pockets to keep him warm while he swung his arms in the cold. He would bring in a big bag of cracked walnuts which he spread out on my desk and we ate them as we talked circulation. The country had received and digested his message of health and had profited by it. Now physical culture was no longer a novelty.

One afternoon in the Spring of 1929, I went to Macfadden's office and saw for the last time the silver trophies recognizing his physical prowess, pictures of his daughters in athletic uniforms, his wife in a bathing suit in which she had won a hard swimming race on the Thames near London. I liked the Macfaddens but I had to tell the fighting publisher that I was through and I left with regret because I understood him. His muscles did not permit him to pull his punches in the newspaper business.

CHAPTER V

I SHOULD have gone back to Carlyle with my savings in my pocket and read: "The wealth of man is the number of things which he loves and blesses, which he is loved and blessed by." I knew money could not make me happy but I wanted enough of it to be secure. I was soon part of those who were pursuing the same object in a lunatic dance. I invested every cent I had into the Stock Market, and dense fumes of finance filled my brain.

The calloused money-mad of the summer of 1929 might well have been a living novel, too rapid of movement for even a Zola to absorb. Rich New York was merry, drunken and debauched. Now I did not have to report the cruel waylayings, the predictions of Evangeline Adams, whose astrological charts guided a number of important gentlemen, including Presidential aspirants, whose names may as well be left out here. The headlines of the midnight revelries, the night-club jewel robberies, the "heart balm" suits of unscrupulous lawyers, the crooked decisions of crafty and subservient judges, no longer kept my pencil busy.

The kept harlots of this society could tell you more of what was happening in town than people who had been elected to conduct its affairs. Mistresses lived on the fabulous gains of Wall Street tips amid tears and laughter. The perfumes of these women, supported by gentlemen who kept the pictures of their wives and children on their business desks, could never be expensive enough to eliminate the aroma of the gutter which reeked under their Louis XIV beds. Actresses, night club wenches, doctors playing the market with the money they raked in from venereal treatments, underworld politicians, racketeers interested in the collection of high art, gamblers, the occasional virgins who were considered among the underprivileged—all of them were woven into this metropolitan tapestry of a dying era. My tabloid headlines had exaggerated nothing.

I watched my stocks go up with the usual emotions. At

the rate they were rising, I felt I could sell out eventually for $300,000. Some of my conservative friends were going to get out at the first million. I remember one Wall Street tip which brought me a profit of $1,500 in twenty-four hours.

Kobler, the new publisher of the *Mirror*, lunched with me frequently, talking in panoramic generalities. We strolled into a collector's shop and he offered to buy me a lock of Napoleon's hair. Later, from a secret compartment in his Park Avenue study, he produced a letter which Napoleon had written to Fouché while Moscow was burning. My hands trembled with eagerness as I read it. He possessed the finest collection in the country of George Bernard Shaw's manuscripts and while I studied them, the publisher would leave me in his huge Gothic rooms, with knights in armor at the doors and Madonnas in niches. The atmosphere of the place and its treasures fascinated me, and he knew it.

One sparkling Sunday morning Kobler appeared at my door in his Minerva limousine with a stiff chauffeur in front.

"I'm taking you for a ride," he laughed.

We drove through Long Island while he talked of the value of sixteenth-century Italian majolica plates and the sculpture of Giovanni della Robbia. The publisher was of medium height, inclined to paunchiness. He had penetrating but moist gray eyes, a high forehead, florid complexion, white hair, thin lips and a dominating Semitic nose. His clothes were of expensive English tailoring. He poked a yellow cane with a snakeskin handle into the rich upholstery of the car while he described the wonders of the art world. Suddenly he tapped his stick against the front window, motioned to the left and we turned into an exclusive estate and got out under a porte-cochere. Kobler hurried me through vast rooms decorated with some of the art objects he had described and in the middle of a corridor he opened a door and pushed me through it.

"Here he is, Mr. Hearst," he said.

Sitting at a large breakfast table, and facing me, a big man rolled about restlessly in a massive chair, his head thrust out on a thick neck. His frame seemed to be made of loose, clumsy bones and as he looked at me his heavy hands reached out, here and there, for opened tins of imported delicacies from which he speared choice bits and ate them in a nibbling fashion.

Some have described the face of William Randolph Hearst

as long, like a horse, with ice-cold blue eyes. Somehow I received a different impression of him. He might have been a
creature of many eyes, taking me in completely and yet being
able to see before him all the tins he reached out for, without
looking at them. The two eyes I saw in his head never left
me, as though I had disturbed the edge of a web, of which the
queer shape of this man, formed somehow by the fluid material
of life, was the center.

The eyes I looked into may have been cold for a fleeting
moment but were filled immediately with merriment.

"So YOU'RE the *Graphic*," Hearst laughed. "You have
created an awful nuisance. It may not be an indictable nuisance, but it is irritating to the *Journal*." He spoke in a high-
pitched voice, tinged with friendly raillery. "Sit down," he
said, pushing some of the tins toward me. "Try some of these
things. They have come a long way and I find them delicious."

Kobler sat down with me and I bowed slightly to Mrs.
Hearst at my right, a little person who was perched on a chair,
looking at me somewhat after the manner of a suspicious spar-
row. Hearst discussed the *Graphic's* career at length and insisted that Macfadden had made a serious blunder by refusing
to sell his tabloid. He was well acquainted with my circulation enterprises and questioned me about my methods of operation. He spoke in high praise of the work Captain J. M.
Patterson had done with the *Daily News* but believed something could be accomplished to catch up with him.

"It will have to be a battle of brains," Hearst said. "Papers
are no longer put over by rough and tumble fighting. When I
think of what we had to go through in Chicago, I'm glad those
days are over."

He got up with surprising quickness. "I'm uncrating some
furniture for my lighthouse," he said. "Perhaps you might
help me and we could talk while we work."

He called a servant who provided us with hatchets and we
proceeded to the lighthouse, a white tower overlooking Long
Island Sound. The publisher's estate, one of his many properties, was on the shore at Sands Point. The large rambling
house he occupied was of stone, rather Gothic flamboyant in
style, reflecting his baronial whims.

While we talked, Hearst and I hacked away at crates, pulling excelsior from early American pieces such as highboys,

benches and chests. Various periods were represented in card tables, candlestands, wing chairs, love seats and what not. I admired the flat surface decorations and wood inlay work of some of the furniture and my remarks seemed to please the publisher who felt the lacquered areas with a certain fondness.

Somehow, this man's conversation, colored with flights of humor, as our hands touched while pulling the excelsior from the crates, made me forget that he had the prerogatives of a king, that he was worth $220,000,000, represented by twenty-eight newspapers, thirteen magazines, eight radio stations, two motion picture companies, $41,000,000 in New York real estate, 14,000 shares in the fabulous Homestake Mine and 2,000,-000 acres of land with cattle, chicle and forest. Someone has said that Hearst did not care about anything except the thing he was looking at, and now I was occupying his attention because my work had checked the progress of the *Journal*, which had the largest circulation of his twenty-eight newspapers. I was aware that this man of power and immense wealth had taken me to the summit of a mountain where no man can sit without an uneasy feeling about his future.

We discussed all manner of subjects, from comic strips and motion-picture stars to the possible fate of the League of Nations. The talk was prompted largely by his questions to draw my opinions and pry into my general knowledge. He was quick in comprehension, positive in conclusion, strong in his likes and dislikes, emphatic in his utterances. Once or twice he disagreed with me rather harshly but I felt that his manner covered an affectionate nature for those to whom he became attached. Up to that time I had never met a man of more diversified interests. He was endowed with a fascinating charm. The conversation went on for a long time, apparently because I held my end up.

The publisher asked me a question or two about the sudden ascent of Walter Winchell and told me that the gossiper had been placed on the *Mirror's* payroll at a salary of $1,000 a week.

"Winchell seems to satisfy the whims of the younger degeneration," he said. "It is typical of the times."

I found that Hearst did not hold much hope for the new "degeneration." Young people, he said, rather sadly, really didn't care whether truth was or was not true. The process of teaching them anything would have to be new and amusing to hold their attention. He spoke of the great bores he had met and told of a friend who had bought a trained parrot to subdue a bragging banker, who, for important reasons, should not be insulted.

"When the banker visited my friend and began to brag," Hearst said, "the parrot preened in its cage and in a skeptical voice said:

" 'Aw, Chri-i-i-st! Aw, Chri-i-i-st!' The banker finally caught on."

Our conversation was interrupted by Mrs. Hearst who peered in and remonstrated with the publisher for wasting time.

"What in the world are you doing, Willy?" she twittered. "A lot of people can uncrate that furniture and you know very well you'll never look at this lighthouse again. Many visitors are waiting."

The multi-millionaire took a vicious swipe at a crate with his hatchet, leaving it imbedded in the wood and we marched back to the Gothic towers.

A gay set was milling around an immense hall dominated by a tremendous fireplace and Mrs. Hearst flitted about as hostess. I gathered that the house had not yet been completely furnished. An impressed gentleman told me that more art objects were to arrive during the following week. Hearst left me and met a young lady with whom he danced little steps in a pirou-ette. Kobler had disappeared and I was in the middle of a crowd whose minds were stuffed beyond hope in some opium dream of money making. Wall Street tips were passed about, one or two of which I noted mentally.

Kobler emerged from a portal, sought me out and dragged me to a corner.

"You've made a hit with Mr. Hearst," he said. "He's invited both of us to drive in his limousine to 57th Street. He's going to spend the rest of the afternoon buying art objects. I'll tell my chauffeur to go home. This is very important."

Soon we were hurrying to New York. Hearst was humming a popular tune of the day from the motion-picture success, *Broadway,* and drummed with his fingernails on the window of the car. He was bubbling with humor. Kobler called his attention to a column of editorial paragraphs and news comments which I had written daily for the *Graphic* for three years, and Hearst recalled it to mind.

"He writes like Brisbane," Kobler said.

"That's a good idea," Hearst replied. "I believe that would help the *Mirror*. Why not start it right away?" He tapped me on the shoulder, "Ape Arthur," he laughed. "It may do him good to know that someone else can do this."

The *Mirror* entered the discussion, some references being made to the losses it was undergoing, but Kobler was enthusiastic about its future prospects. Hearst ended this part of the conversation with a few words which seemed to convey a cautionary meaning.

"Remember, Albert," the publisher said, "that you are in the position of a man who has moved into a house after buying it under a mortgage. And I'm the man who holds the mortgage. You're running the house and paying off on the mortgage."

At the 57th Street art gallery Kobler left me, after a pat on the back and I was immersed with Hearst in hundreds of photographs of medieval fireplaces, castles in Scotland, interiors of paneled rooms, paintings and statuary. He bought that afternoon, apparently by looking at pictures, the rooms of an entire French cloister of the seventeenth century and asked my opinion of a sixteenth-century fireplace, every stone of which was to be transported from abroad. He spoke of a complete twelfth-century Cistercian monastery which he was importing from Spain in 14,000 packing cases. At this time the millionaire's warehouses in various parts of the country were stuffed with such purchases, most of which he never saw.

I admired the photograph of a painting of a blonde woman reclining on a divan but he cast it aside.

"Blondes come high," he laughed. "Old masters last longer."

Mrs Hearst who accompanied us to the door of the gallery in the limousine had left with the car, and the publisher asked me to drive with him in a taxicab as far as his Riverside Drive apartment. On the way he talked about a number of his executives and their capabilities. He referred several times to Joseph Connolly as an energetic young man with a brilliant future in the Hearst organization. Joe, my competitor as a reporter in the New Haven days, now was the head of Hearst's newspaper syndicate known as King Features and was approaching a salary of $50,000 a year.

Hearst said good-bye to me in a cordial fashion and I drove home, my mind in a whirl. Before I retired I received a telephone call from Kobler, who wanted to see me the next day for luncheon at the Ritz-Carlton. His voice carried a warm friendliness. "I never knew what a diplomat you could be," he said.

The *Mirror* publisher reserved a special table for us at the Ritz on the following day and ordered a colossal repast. It was my first twenty-five dollar luncheon. When I was reposing comfortably smoking a dollar cigar he produced a document which in legal terms appointed me editor of the *Mirror* for a period of five years on a sliding-scale salary beginning with $25,000 a year. I declined to sign the contract and for a moment Kobler showed his irritation. I thought the time specified was too long and he cut the length of service to three years after a business argument during which he promised me freedom of action in all editorial policies. I was chiefly interested in the daily column I wanted to write and I told him frankly that executive work did not appeal to me. It was no longer a part of my natural inclinations. While I hesitated over the dotted line he produced a check for $10,000 which he stuffed into my pocket.

"That's just a bonus," he said. "We're going to be happy together. We're going to get out a great tabloid and do splendid things."

I put my name down on the contract.

CHAPTER VI

I ABSORBED my first lesson in Hearst office politics as soon as
I crossed the threshold of the old *Mirror* building on Frankfort
Street, near the Brooklyn Bridge. Walter Howey, almost a
legendary figure in the sensational journalism of Chicago and
New York, later the mythical hero of the spectacular Broadway
play, *The Front Page*, had not been informed that I was to
succeed him as editor of the tabloid. For several days nothing
was done by the management to clear this situation and Kobler
advised me temporarily to treat as an "associate editor" the
man I was to supplant. I knew that Howey, as one of Hearst's
favorites, would not leave without a duel on the staircase. He
sparred for time by dividing editorial responsibilities with me.
I worked during the day, preparing the first edition which he
invariably disemboweled in rampageous fashion when he
reached the office in the evening. We sat in the same cubbyhole
at adjoining desks, smiling placidly at each other. Meanwhile,
Kobler reflected upon the situation with a bland expression.

"This matter," he said, "requires the tactics of a Talley-
rand. It is part of the office routine of all Hearst enterprises,
which you will understand as you become a part of the family.
It will work itself into an explosion and when the fireworks
are over Mr. Howey will no longer be around."

My column of editorial paragraphs had begun to appear
daily, following an alluring announcement in the *Mirror* about
my news analysis. King Features Syndicate had prepared
about my fulminations great broadsides which might have done
credit to the arrival of a circus. I was endorsed as one of the
most astute editors in America by United States Senators, Governors, Congressmen, theatrical producers, nationally known
entertainers such as Rudy Vallée, authors and churchmen,
whom I had not met and who, I assume, had never heard of
me. This promotion staggered me. Later I was to discover
all sorts of shortcuts to fame in the Hearst empire.

Howey and Kobler were soon at daggers drawn, flying into

rages when they referred to each other. I inhaled their poison after the manner of a peaceful citizen who has forgotten his gas mask in an air raid. Arriving at the office on my first day in this unpredictable vineyard, I found Howey and other editorial executives engaged in the operation of bouncing red tops attached to long elastics. I was given one of them by Howey who attempted to teach me the principle of catching the top when it bounced back. George Clarke, the little roly-poly city editor, was quite good at it, but after an hour of bouncing and watching the others I had made no progress. I noticed that sob sisters on the staff had mastered the art.

The editor finally solved the bouncing mystery by explaining that it was a new game called "Yo-Yo" and that he proposed to make New York "Yo-Yo conscious" by giving the tops away to thousands of people who clipped coupons from the *Mirror*. The city editor was certain that Jimmy Walker would lend a hand by demonstrating the Yo-Yo on the City Hall steps in front of photographers. Before this enterprise could be achieved Kobler, in a furious temper, ordered the cargo of Yo-Yos sent to the paper's warehouse.

Howey, a resourceful man, produced another idea which he described as a "sure fire" circulation builder. It was based on daily cash prizes to be awarded for the most individual designs sent in by readers who squirted blobs of ink on a piece of paper and then folded it in half with the smear on the inside. When it was opened, incredible creations appeared. This endeavor was called "Blotto" and I found members of the staff experimenting with it, their hands and noses black with ink. Kobler threw the invention into the wastebasket before it could be announced to the public.

The fireworks predicted by the publisher came unexpectedly when he asked me to launch a crusade against Larry Fay, a West Side gangster, who was running a racket in the milk business under the protection of Tammany leaders. I prepared this campaign with enthusiasm and had it all in type with pictures in the forms when Howey arrived. Inspecting the proofs he rushed to the composing room, and livid with anger, threw the type to the floor by handfuls.

"This was Kobler's idea, I suppose," he shouted, amid the clatter of machinery. "As the publisher he'll have to stay upstairs and publish."

I put on my coat and hat and went home. Later in the evening Kobler telephoned me to express his surprise that the story had failed to appear. I told him what had happened. He asked me to visit his apartment where I met Colonel Frank Knox, who was then the general manager of Hearst's publications. The Colonel, a muscular, reddish man of steady eye and strong jaw, a fearless journalist who was later to acquire the Chicago *Daily News* and become Secretary of the Navy, listened with unconcealed disgust to Kobler's recital of the affair.

"This is nonsensical," he said as he turned to me bruskly. "Place your name on the city room's bulletin board as the editor in charge immediately and go after Larry Fay and put him out of business. It's about time for some newspaper to summon up the courage to clean up New York. It can be done by any editor who is not afraid to try it."

I obeyed his orders on the following morning, and Howey left with a look in his eye which needed no words to inform me that he had a long memory. My stories blasted Fay out of his milk racket. He sued the *Mirror* for damages of $200,000 but was murdered before I could debate the matter with him in court. Knox resigned as general manager about a year later and I regretted it. I had lost a powerful supporter to whom I could have appealed in a crisis.

Tammany, meanwhile, inadvertently furnished us with some news which boosted our circulation. City Magistrate Andrew Macrery, who had been reappointed to the bench, was beaten to death when the installment payments for his job to political racketeers fell into arrears. Reputable report had it in those days that the price quoted for certain City Magistracies was $35,000. It was believed that more than one Tammany Supreme Court Justiceship sold for a matter of $75,000. I kept this in mind when our staff, some time later, investigated the disappearance of Justice Joseph Force Crater who, undoubtedly, was done to death. I was informed at that time by a Tammany leader, whose confidences I had to respect to save my own neck, that powerful gangsters operated their own private crematories where bodies were disposed of. Their location, in an adjoining state, was never revealed to me.

My clash with Howey had been unavoidable. Our silent feud was to go on for six years. He was not only a newspaper man of wide experience but an inventive genius. He spent much time working on the problems of so-called telephone wire photographs and frequency modulation in picture transmission and later his experiments helped the progress of a machine to transmit illustrations by the radio process. I had to dismantle one of his inventions in my cubbyhole after he left, a loud speaker arrangement which was turned on full blast when Herbert Kaufman, widely known editor and author, telephoned the office from his home at Tarrytown to dictate certain meticulous corrections for his daily full-page editorials. A brilliant conversationalist, he invariably found himself in a talkative mood when his confining work was done, and launched into long discourses about the state of the nation. Howey's invention made it unnecessary to hold the receiver to one's ear for a half-hour or forty-five minutes while the essayist was expounding. Occasionally, when Kaufman asked for approval of some remark between ten-minute periods, Howey, noticing a pause from the loud speaker, would shout into the transmitter: "You're perfectly right," or "It goes without saying."

The *Mirror* had led a precarious existence since the death of Payne whose stories of the Hall-Mills mystery had almost ruined the paper's prestige as an advertising medium. Hearst had tried various methods to pump life into the tabloid. For a time Victor Watson, a crusading editor regarded as Hearst's confidant, had conducted its affairs. Hearst, in a fanfare of promotional advertising at last announced that the paper had been sold to Alexander Pollock Moore, formerly Ambassador to Spain. While struggling for mass readership the diplomat printed daily, at the top of the tabloid's front page, the slogan: "A Clean Tabloid Newspaper." This proclamation was looked upon as a confession of past sins by business men and not only failed to attract advertisers but repelled whatever readers the *Mirror* had possessed.

I had met Moore while I was editor of the *Graphic* and found him despondent about the *Mirror's* plight. I had printed a report, current in society at the time, that he might marry the widow of Enrico Caruso and he asked me to deny it.

"I was the husband of Lillian Russell," he said, "and when she died I knew I could never look at another woman again. She will always be my Lillian of sainted memory."

While matters grew worse on the *Mirror*, President Coolidge suddenly appointed Moore as Ambassador to Peru. The sale of the tabloid back to Hearst again must have been one of the quickest business transactions in journalism. Before anybody on the paper could realize what had happened the diplomat was on a boat bound for South America. The publication's business manager, in bewilderment, radioed the Ambassador:

"Have you forgotten your obligations to the *Mirror* as its owner and publisher?"

And the diplomat, now far out at sea, radioed back:

"Don't be silly!"

The *Mirror's* books, which Kobler produced for me, told plainly the story of the murderous losses the paper had suffered during its first five years. Macfadden's deficits on the *Graphic* were small in comparison. When I took the editorial helm of Hearst's tabloid it was still losing $15,000 to $20,000 a week and its circulation was far below 300,000 readers. Kobler, however, was the first purposeful business man that had become responsible for its management. The stupendous advertising success of the *American Weekly* had been due entirely to his ingenuity. He had convinced Hearst that the vast circulation of the syndicated Sunday supplement could be sold as a unit to advertisers and had proceeded to do this without any salary. He was satisfied with the commissions, which had brought him in as much as $450,000 a year and had made him a millionaire. His resourcefulness turned the tide on the *Mirror* which, in less than three years' time, hauled itself out of a sea of red ink and doubled its circulation.

The publisher had supervised the erection of a tall building on East 45th Street, where the paper was installed and began to thrive. I was often with Kobler as he watched the structure go up. He was at times excitable and impulsive and one day, brandishing his cane, he berated a bricklayer for wearing a silk shirt and accused him of gambling in the stock market. The new quarters seemed to be finished with almost incredible speed, and, once moved in, the *Mirror* appeared to take on a new impulse.

Kobler, with success within his reach as a newspaper publisher, had over-extended himself financially, and the Wall Street depression of 1929 hit him a body blow from which he was not to recover. When the crash occurred I was too busy handling the news of its disastrous effects, including the suicides of some of my acquaintances who were jumping from windows, to pay any attention to my own holdings which I had permitted to soar without selling.   In three weeks' time I lost $150,000 but I saved myself from being wiped out of the market by obtaining a loan from the Chase National Bank which enabled me to free my remaining stocks and pledge them as security.   Part of my salary for a long period to follow, was used weekly to reduce my note.

Although my speculating friends, a few of whom lost less than I did, were depressed into a state of hopelessness, I learned that quick profits led inevitably to a bottomless pit and that money not earned by hard work is a shadowy inheritance. While rescuing part of my securities at the house of Samuel Ungerleider & Co., at a time when the market was continuing its headlong plunge, the head of the brokerage firm directed my attention to a man who stood as a frozen staring corpse before the blackboards which told a story in no need of explanation.

"That man has just lost a million dollars."

I watched the victim curiously and saw that the agony in his face was mingled with a covetous love of money, an avaricious lust for gain, which gave him a most curious inhuman expression.   It seemed to mark the faces of all those suffering from his disease.

My transactions at the Chase National Bank were in the hands of G. W. Dusenbury, an assistant cashier, a man of kindly sympathy and one whose heart was torn by the accounts he had to close.   My remaining securities, he said, were as good as the country itself.   If they reached bottom the nation would go with them.   It was an accepted philosophy which I had then begun to doubt.   Finally, Dusenbury, overcome by the pressure of his work, crushed by the misery he had to witness daily, fell ill.   And one day, he died.   Many fine, honest bankers went the way he did during that period.

Watching his paper's progress constantly, Kobler became too engrossed in it to pay much attention to his personal affairs. The tabloid became his life.   His dream was to fill it with choice advertising.   Mine was to give it a million readers through smashing crusades and murder-mystery solutions. We worked together day and night, and at times, in exhaustion, he dragged me to a theater where he promptly fell asleep.

We attended the Metropolitan Opera where, to my horror, Kobler was soon composed in slumber, his snores rising when the shepherd's pipes began playing the message of despair to the dying Tristan. I could have shot in cold blood any other man guilty of such an act.

Often Kobler soliloquized at the Ritz where we gathered in the luxurious suite of Paul Block, the newspaper publisher. Herbert Kaufman, the editorialist had left the *Mirror*, and among my additional duties I had to write pieces in defense of Jimmy Walker, whose stewardship of the metropolis was undergoing a terrible raking-over by Judge Samuel Seabury. Once, at one of these conferences, Grover A. Whalen had appeared—a breath-taking fashion plate punctuated by a gardenia. Earlier, while he was police commissioner, public interest in the Rothstein murder, which was impossible to solve, had been lulled by his great traffic campaigns and far-seeing anti-Communist demonstrations. I took notes amid the cross-fire of advice which Mayor Walker received. He seemed less concerned than his friends about the fate ahead of him. He was more interested in a remarkably trained bird that sang several bars of *Ich Liebe Dich*. It had come in a cage from Vienna, a lively present for Betty Compton, Jimmy's charming friend, whom he was soon to marry after a romance which kept the tabloids in feverish excitement.

I attended a boisterous party given by Ray Long, brilliant Hearst editor of *Cosmopolitan*, who had scooped all competitors by obtaining Coolidge's memoirs. Long's servant poured a Prohibition drink for him and for me, during the hubbub, and spilled some of it on a lacquered table. The liquid ate into the wood like an acid and left a corroded, green scar on the finished surface which began to smoke.

"Damn it," Long shouted at the servitor, "why can't you be more careful? This is a choice piece of furniture. That stuff will ruin it." And then, lifting his glass: "Down the hatch, boys! Here's to success!"

Victor Watson, editor of the *American*, and uncertain of his job, sat gloomily in a corner. A few years were to fly by for him before he leaped from the 11th floor of the Abbey Hotel. Life was to be even shorter for Ray Long who would put a bullet through his head. But before that he was to go to the land of the Soviets and write a book praising the Russians as hard-drinking people that knew how to carry their liquor. His dedication comes back to me with irony:

To my son,
RAY LONG, Jr.,
with envy for the fact that he will live to see so much more of what will happen in Russia than I possibly can.

I read the book and I wanted to go to Russia to find out for myself whether the Communists really had a solution to the problems of existence.   I knew that the life I witnessed, the life I lived, was headed for an abyss.   That conviction probably saved me.   Many of those whom I watched in this witches' dance are dead, and it all took place in less than a decade.   They looked into the pit and fell in.   Somehow, I managed to scramble back.

Kobler invited me, one evening, to his cloistered Park Avenue study where I met Walter Lippmann.   The publisher was attempting to sign the noted analyst under a contract to write for Hearst.   Lippmann listened politely and with an amused smile and a certain delicacy he turned the offer down. Kobler told me Brisbane had said:

"If we could get Lippmann and Broun over to our camp to write according to our viewpoint, we would HAVE something.   These damned idealists ought to know that they could have a larger audience, and make more money, too, if they would only be practical."

Brisbane invited Heywood Broun to his palatial Fifth Avenue residence and offered him a Hearst contract with a salary and syndication rights which would have increased Broun's income at least three times over.   Broun, with a disarming laugh, waved it aside.   As Broun told the story later, he stood before a huge fireplace, looking up at a painting of Brisbane's father.   He turned to the editor and said:

"What a marvelous face your father had.   It reflects the calm outlook of a man who is right with himself."

"Yes," Brisbane said.   "He looked that way because he never had to work for Hearst."

I had started a series of biographies of the "Big Shot" racketeers, former pimps, pickpockets and porch climbers now riding about in limousines with their "molls" adorned with

jewels bought from "fences." I obtained the early police records, fingerprints and photographs of these gangsters which I
reproduced to illustrate sardonic "success stories" of their
careers. I did not get very far with this series. The late
Lester Jones, Vice-President of the New York Newspaper
Publishers Association paid me a visit to give me certain reasons why the names of three racketeers, and particularly of
one, Morris (Little Ziggy) Zeig, should not appear under any
circumstances. "Ziggy" participated in many enterprises, including rumrunning and beer distribution. Jones, who was a
man of integrity, told me frankly that certain newspapers, particularly of the sensational type in New York, depended on
"Ziggy" and others of his gangster influence to settle labor dis-
putes and gang wars which developed among the tough workers
employed in certain circulation departments. The racketeers,
Jones feared, had become powerful enough actually to cripple
the newspaper distribution systems. The police kept out of
such scraps.

"You're morally right," Jones said, "but you won't get anywhere because gangsters are politically protected. They can
reach as high up as they can reach down. That's the way this
town is run and every publisher knows it. It's hopeless and we
have to do the best we can with it."

In my own mind I reflected that Jones had exaggerated the
situation insofar as circulation racketeering was concerned as
I knew that organized circulation gangs had never operated as
such in New York City as they had in Chicago, although at
various times hoodlums had been hired by different newspapers
to harass the circulation departments of their competitors. I
did not doubt however, that many managements of newspapers, conservative as well as sensational, were under obligations
to organized gangsters, who had been hired to "protect" their
plants and operations during the "outlaw" pressmen's strike
of 1923.

I felt that gangsters might threaten our distribution but
beyond upsetting a few news-stands little would come of it.
Peter Bloom, head of the *Mirror's* circulation force was ready
to fight it out. He was big, two fisted and honest, and sold
the paper regardless of the editor's idiosyncrasies. But Kobler
swallowed Jones' tale whole and was fearful of bloodshed. I
was forced to call off the campaign. At about this time our

watchman in the distributing department had fatally shot an intruder while papers were being loaded for delivery. By dint of the efforts of expensive defense counsel hired by the newspaper, although an ex-convict, the employee was acquitted of homicide.

After my gang crusade was abandoned I met James J. Hines, Tammany leader, in what seemed to me an accidental encounter. Tall, powerful, with pale blue eyes, a strong jaw and inquisitive nose set in a wide, rugged face, Hines could mask his expression in a split second. He still possessed the muscles he had developed as a blacksmith in his youth. I knew of him as a politician of far-reaching influence and I had no knowledge then of his connections with the notorious racketeer, "Dutch" Schultz, who was operating a policy lottery. An important executive of the *Mirror*, an old New Yorker, advised me to cultivate Hines' acquaintance for my own protection. The Tammany leader never mentioned my editorial trends and invited me on several occasions to attend prize fights with him. Occasionally he asked me to use items about Tammany benefits, donations of turkeys to the poor, and similar philanthropies.

Kobler became involved in a furious quarrel with Winchell who pounded out his revelations in a corner of the city room behind a glass cage. The night clubs, which were controlled by protected racketeers, fed the gossip columns of the period and all sorts of one-line implications floated through the syndicates to be reprinted by provincial editors. Senational news of the metropolis came from Broadway.

Winchell held his readers for months in readiness to rejoice over blessed events which often failed to happen. The reckless, midnight women who believed themselves pregnant after reading his column occasionally telephoned in pleasant surprise to have him guess again. Gangsters ruled the town and were disposed to fight and embarrass any attempt to scrutinize their operations. It was considered smart by gay, well-to-do people to hobnob with infamy. Debutantes who took part in this life looked like hags five years later. Everywhere in this glittering jungle, men and women seized the cup of poisoned pleasure which the town offered. You were known by how much money you spent. Night-club proprietors distributed, with precision, the exact proportion of attention measured out according to the amounts paid for the drinks.

Breach of promise suits had become a racket of shyster lawyers. Damages demanded by broken-hearted women were rarely less than $200,000. When these "heart balm" shells began to fall rather close to influential friends of the Hearst organization I was asked to launch a campaign for new legislation to rule out this amorous technique from New York's social life. My editorials received wide endorsement from harassed quarters, the agitation was taken up with enthusiasm and the Albany Legislature finally passed a bill which became a law and protected all gentlemen of gallant disposition which inclined them to expensive knight-errantry.

Tabloid circulation thrived on the doings of Wall Street gamblers of shallow capacities, on the cheating knavishness of the temporary rich, reflecting the psychology of the vice-ridden, in whom all faith in virtue and all sympathy with purity and nobility of character had disappeared.

Certain principles were laid down by the mad, Broadway crowd as invariable rules to follow. One should always pay a cardsharp gambler, but could make a tailor or a grocer wait. A man should not lie to another man but could lie to a woman. An insult in a night club had to be met with a fist. Some women lived great passions, each one as though they had never lived any others and sold the stories of their experiences for $500. Divorces were so common that Winchell announced them long before they reached the courts. At this time he told me that the "code of the mob" would not have countenanced any item describing a husband as cheating on his wife. When his gossip resulted in legal threats, he inserted a line in his column, such as: "Smith: excuse it please." But as the offender, the gossiper rarely pardoned.

Transom chronicling produced some whimsical twists. It was a common thing for columnists of this type to use items presumably based on communications they received from their secretaries to give the impression that their gossip was of extreme importance to people of consequence. Often, whole columns were filled with such information as: "That banker called. Wants you to wait until he sees Secretary of the Treasury"; "Senator C—— says he will see the President about your suggestion" or "White House would like to have you hold off; too startling for the public mind." The gullible swallowed these items as proof that the snoopers were behind the scenes with the leaders of the nation. Westbrook Pegler, in his own column, labeled these activities for all time as "gents' room journalism."

"Big Shots" ambled in and out of our offices to hear some of the gossip before it got into print and often to offer kindly suggestions. Charles (Lucky) Luciano, later to be convicted as an operator of a wide-spread vice racket frequently sounded the keynote for smart Broadway reading. A familiar caller in the *Mirror* city room was Owney Madden, the leading racketeer of New York whom I had not met socially and who conferred with people on my staff who were in closer touch with his affairs.

Winchell was now protected with bodyguards and went about with a loaded automatic in his suit coat and a second loaded automatic in his overcoat pocket. At that time he included in his column a department entitled, "Recommendations to Diversion Seekers" and Kobler had ordered me to kill it as it gave free publicity to night club entertainers who got into the paper without paying a penny for the advertising. The columnist had an ingenious way of nullifying my blue penciling, and his recommendations soon appeared in the form of one line items called "orchids and scallions" which he presented in type to those who qualified according to his ideas of success, or who, worn by care and dissipation, had disintegrated in the realm of entertainment.

Printed gossip often referred to political racketeers with the respect usually accorded to judges. Criminals had become public characters, and were made into heroes. Any crook who beat the law could find a mob cheering him when he left the courthouse in triumph. The "mob" ruled the town. If it did not rule some of its newspapers it had little to fear from them.

Winchell astounded the police one evening by practically predicting in his column the assassination of Vincent Coll, a racketeer who had broken with the "Dutch" Schultz gang. Less than an hour after our paper had gone to press, a gangster found Coll in the telephone booth of a drugstore and pumped a stream of bullets into him from a Thompson sub-machine gun. While the columnist was crowing over the accuracy of his prophecy he was summoned before the authorities and apparently satisfied them with the story that he had received advance news of the murder on a slip of paper, anonymously mailed to him, and which he had destroyed. Years later, after Texas Guinan the night club entertainer had died, he said she had given him the information.

Killing Winchell's "recommendations" had brought me into an open battle with him. We had not been on good terms for a number of years. While on the *Graphic* I had presented a map of Europe to him when he announced in his column that a party of Broadway friends had stepped off from an ocean liner "at the port of Paris, France." On another occasion he had referred to Émile Zola as a famous woman writer. When these samples of ignorance got by he seemed to think I should have caught them. The items I lassoed, however, were of a more important nature. Libel suits which occasionally cracked over my head as a result of his vagaries had taught me to be vigilant.

Our news treatment of gangster activities had not pleased the "mob" whose leaders now read the *Mirror* with avidity. In my own signed column I had minced no words about their affairs. My interrupted series on the pickpockets who had become "Big Shots" resulted in a number of warnings which had to do with my welfare. One of them, a boldly written threat sent through the mails threw Kobler into such a pitch of alarm that he called the police and a detective was assigned to sit at my desk while I edited the *Mirror*. This excitement I considered as all a part of the job although I had not forgotten what had happened to Justice Crater, who was rated of more importance to the community than a tabloid editor.

My crime crusades finally came to a climax which did not overwhelm me with surprise. The facts of the matter, now recorded in the office of District Attorney Thomas E. Dewey, and received as my testimony under oath by a grand jury which forced the "mob" to the wall, might seem incredible today, but during the double-crossing times of prohibition, my experience, had it become public, would not have struck many people with amazement.

One night, after I had retired, I was informed over the telephone by James Hurley, assistant sporting editor of the *Mirror*, and Alfred Daniels, assistant night editor, that I was to be "put on the spot," as it was then realistically described. A loyal telephone operator at our switchboard, had connected

in my two informants with a long distance call which had been
put through to Florida. According to notes, which were carefully taken down by Hurley and Daniels, the party on the New
York end of the wire told a listener in Miami that the "mob"
had stood enough of my interference and that Owney Madden
would put me in a position where I could no longer annoy
anybody.

Hurley and Daniels were reliable and trustworthy. The
former had been a lieutenant colonel in the World War and
the latter was a trained New England editor of years of experience. I listened to their report, at first with some indifference
and tried to get back to sleep. Within a half hour they called
me again to tell me that Owney Madden and six of his notorious gorillas, readily recognized by our reporters, were in
the *Mirror* office discussing matters with a member of my staff
who had put in the Florida call. I jumped into my clothes and
dashed for my office and from the partly opened door of a
corridor I saw Madden and his gangsters in what appeared to
be an argument with an individual whose identity I was to
reveal later to the grand jury.

Hurley and Daniels urged me to abandon all thought of
consulting the police, many of whom were then under the
domination of Tammany Hall's political buccaneers. From a
near-by speak-easy I telephoned Jimmy Hines, getting him out
of bed at his home. He listened to my information calmly
and said he would produce Owney Madden at any time I
wished in the morning at a place of my convenience where I
could appear with my own witnesses. Madden was then a
fugitive from justice, having been ordered back to Sing Sing
by the State Board of Parole while he was supplying thousands
of speak-easies with beer.

"Listen here," said Hines. "I can promise you that I will
straighten this out. Go back to bed. Nothing will happen to
you. I'll see to that. Madden is not in the bumping-off racket.
He's running beer, and that keeps him pretty busy."

In the forenoon I arrived at my place of appointment with
my witnesses, including Kobler, who showed his apprehension.
Others of my entourage included Jack Sheehan, my political
reporter and close friend, and Otto Fein, a brawny member of
our circulation department, who had brought a revolver. The
meeting was in a speak-easy known as the "Fish Inn," on the

second floor of a small building on 44th Street, around the corner from Lexington Avenue. Hines entered with us and stood looking nervously out of the window. Soon a large limousine crowded with men stopped in front of the place. It was a car of bullet-proof glass which Madden constantly used and familiar to the Broadway crowd. The racketeer stepped out briskly, followed by four or five of his bodyguards, in plain view of three policemen, and led his gunmen up the stairs. We sat down around a large table while the doors of the place were barred and the speak-easy's business suspended during the conference.

Before the discussion began, Hines consulted Madden openly about the Parole Board's order which was being speculated upon in newspapers lying before us.

"I think you'd better wind up your affairs for a while, Owney," the Tammany leader said. "Take your time at it and get everything straightened out. I'll tell you when to give yourself up."

Somebody asked Madden if he wanted a drink before the parley, and he replied:

"Give me a glass of sink water. That's all I drink in these places."

The gangster was a small-sized, wiry, nattily dressed individual of thirty-nine, and his eyes had the cold stare of the trigger man. He had come to New York as a child from Liverpool, where he was born in 1892. On the West Side, before he was old enough to vote, he had become known as "The Killer." When he was nineteen, the police had credited him with two murders and suspected there might have been more but could not prove them. He had served time in State prison for second-degree murder. During his career he had been arrested fifty-seven times and convicted twice. One conviction had to do with a traffic violation. Now he was immune from the law under powerful political backing and controlled the beer-running of New York. He was supplying as many of the city's 50,000 speak-easies as his illegal brewery's capacity would permit.

I sat at one end of the table facing Madden who evidently knew what I was going to say. His face was expressionless but for his eyes which displayed a certain eagerness as he twitched about in his chair.

Hines turned to me and said:

"Boss, tell Owney the story you told me."

I described the circumstances in detail to the racketeer who listened attentively and met my gaze steadily, as if to impart some message of friendliness. When I finished my account he admitted everything.

"In the first place," he said, "get the idea out of your head that I'm responsible for this. It started in your own office. I was called up to come over to the *Mirror* with my staff. The guy who called me up is O. K. with the mob. A friend is a friend. But when he told me what he wanted me to do I washed my hands of it and I can prove it by my own men. I'm running beer, and that's all. I'm not taking nobody for any ride. And I'm not putting no editors on the spot. I told the guy so. You was as safe last night as you are today."

"Shake hands with the editor on that, Owney," Hines broke in.

The racketeer extended his hand across the table and I grasped it.

"That goes!" said Owney Madden. "You can peddle your papers without worryin'."

CHAPTER VII

I HAD learned from my newspaper experience that the best enjoyment is half disappointment compared to what we intend, or would have, in this existence. Living in the half-world of tabloidia I could appreciate this philosophy even more. I soon found to my chagrin, that my editorial crusades could not always be of my own making and often had to be directed against those with whom I sympathized.

One day, Kobler asked me to turn our batteries on Mae West, hard-working motion-picture star, and rake her fore and aft. The order resulted in one of the many arguments we had when I wanted to know the reason behind our sudden declarations of war upon people who were minding their own business. The publisher and I generally fought across my desk, the engagements consisting of fists pounded on its plate-glass surface, sudden outcries and whistling whacks which he took at an old Queen Anne chair with his cane. This piece of furniture, which he had presented to me, and in which he said I might relax between editions, somehow withstood a merciless beating for five years. Once, during one of our business discussions, I threw an aluminum desk lighter through a glass bookcase. This destruction brought about a mutual agreement that gave reasonable protection to office property thereafter.

During these explosions of temper, Kobler, a well-read, intelligent man, talked after the manner of Sam Goldwyn of Hollywood. He would accuse me of "eating the hand that bites you" or "going all around Robert Hood's bush." He said the tabloid business was not all "rag, tag and cocktail," which is what I was afraid it was. On one memorable occasion Goldwyn had visited Kobler to obtain publicity for a new star named Anna Sten. If I could have noted the conversation between these two keen and excitable men of commerce I would have had a piece fully as funny as anything Mark Twain or Finley Peter Dunne ever wrote. At one heated point Kobler charged that Goldwyn was "hood-winging" him by offering him Miss Sten "on a silver bladder."

We turned our guns reluctantly on good old Mae West who had become *persona non grata* in the realm dominated by San Simeon. Kobler was vague about the cause of the warfare. He said it was reported that the buxom actress had used a few jocose bon mots which had offended Marion Davies. Hearst newspapers were printing a number of pictures of Miss Davies at the time and Hollywood reported that she hoped to revive her talents on the screen. Hearst had been interested for years in the film industry. A long article about his multifarious activities in the *Saturday Evening Post* had referred to the actress as follows: "Among the girls who found parts in Hearst pictures was Marion Davies, born Douras, a beautiful blonde from the Ziegfeld Follies choruses with wideset grave eyes." Hearst had starred her in a succession of films. She made a notable hit in *Little Old New York*, and other productions. According to the *Post's* information, the publisher lost $7,000,-000 in picture-making.

Although I was invited to one or two receptions where Miss Davies greeted friends when she came to New York I never met the actress. Kobler often listened to the star's ideas about the *Mirror* while I paid attention to Mrs. Hearst's suggestions. Comparing notes, we found that the recommendations we absorbed never seemed to agree. During one of her visits at my office Mrs. Hearst said the tabloid should be filled with little, ten-line items of information to give the paper a newsy appearance. At that time she disagreed with her husband who had launched a campaign to abolish all American ambassadorships.

"Willy feels very strongly about it," she commented, "but it would certainly be an awful blow to social life."

Miss Davies seemed to look upon the *Mirror* with realistic appreciation. Through her cooperation Kobler arranged an appointment for our reporters to meet Alma Rubens, widely known star of the silent films. Miss Rubens dictated her confessions which had added 65,000 new readers to our tabloid. I began to suspect that Miss Davies knew something about circulation.

The pommeling we gave Mae West revived some of my recollections about her. As editor of the *Graphic* I had attended one of her plays which had to do with the vicissitudes of a number of ladies who were in an unfortunate position in

Shanghai. During the second act a British admiral, in full uniform, visited them with his staff of officers who proceeded to remove more than their epaulets. As naval men of such rank were not usually to be found in the place depicted by Miss West I described the play to Congressman La Guardia who considered it an insult to the British Navy. He urged me to send a protest to the British Embassy and permitted me to quote him in our front-page display article which described the affair as an outrage. The British Embassy replied that it would give the matter grave consideration and I heard no more from its diplomats. Meanwhile, Miss West announced that tickets for her performance would have to be ordered weeks in advance. She telephoned me to thank me warmly for the "fine publicity" and added:

"Come up and see me sometime, and bring La Guardia."

This was a remark in which no impropriety might be assumed. The playwright intended it as an invitation to us to visit the rehearsal of one of her new productions uptown. She not only wrote her own plays, but rehearsed them under her direction and appeared in them. She was the most hard working girl I ever met, with no time for nonsense. I attended a rehearsal of one of her performances, *The Virgin Man*, where I saw, for the first time, Alan Campbell, a capable young actor who later married Dorothy Parker.

The attacks on Mae West were carried on sporadically, and eight months after I had left the *Mirror* the Hearst newspapers were still engaged in warfare against her, as indicated by the following memorandum which the publisher sent to his chain of newspapers:

Los Angeles, Cal., Feb. 23, 1936

Attention of all Hearst newspapers, publishers and managing editors:

The Mae West picture, *Klondike Annie,* is a filthy picture. I think we should have editorials roasting the picture and Mae West and the Paramount Company for producing such a picture—the producer and director and everybody concerned.

We should say it is an affront to the decency of the public and to the intelligence of the motion-picture profession.

Will Hays must be asleep to allow such a thing to come out, but it is to be hoped that the churches of the country are awake to the necessity of boycotting such a picture and denouncing its producers. After you have had a couple of good editorials ROASTING the indecency of this picture, then DO NOT MENTION MAE WEST IN OUR PAPERS AGAIN WHILE SHE IS ON THE SCREEN. AND DO NOT ACCEPT ANY ADVERTISING OF THIS PICTURE.

It is astounding that the Paramount people should have had the stupidity to produce such a picture, when it has been demonstrated to what a degree the screen has benefitted by the clean pictures that have been made since the public uprising against screen filth. It goes to show that some screen producers are not influenced by any moral consideration, but only by fear of public indignation. And the only way of influencing such producers is by the people showing that *pandering to the lewd elements of the community is not profitable.*

WILLIAM RANDOLPH HEARST

While I was managing editor, Hearst paid his first visit to the *Mirror* since it had been launched seven years previously. When the tabloid had first appeared, Howey, one of its original editors, had taken a copy to the publisher at his apartment. Hearst, sitting on a pile of cushions in a lounging robe and in his bare feet, studied it while it was on the floor, turning the pages of the tabloid over with his toes which he could manipulate with a certain prehensile agility.

Before the Lord of San Simeon arrived at the *Mirror* office, Kobler, in considerable excitement, ordered the city room floor to be swept of all traces of paper. Members of the staff had to put on their coats and adjust their collars until finally the establishment took on the appearance of J. P. Morgan's banking house. Hearst chatted with me in my private office, expressing his pleasure over the *Mirror's* progress. "It's what you leave out of a newspaper that keeps the dullness from it," he said. "The more you leave out, the brighter the paper becomes."

The millionaire journalist then stepped through my door to inspect the city room and seemed startled for a moment. He looked at me and remarked:

"This place looks too damned clean for a newspaper office!"

I managed during these times to write my first novel, *Hot News,* which had a lucrative sale. The reviews across the country were encouraging to me. The story appeared serially in the *Saturday Evening Post* and I sold it to the motion pictures for a large sum of money. I wrote the book after midnight in my office when my main editions had rolled off the press and the drumfire of outside typewriters had been reduced to the sound of pattering rain. I loathed carbon copies and dashed off the tale as though writing for a deadline. It was imaginative fiction but strongly influenced by my experiences up to that time, which was 1931. When personal affairs depressed me I forgot them by writing 4,000 words at one sitting. Early one morning the job was done and I stuffed the story into a large envelope. Ray Doyle of my staff, a massive Irishman of unfailing humor, invited me to the "Fish Inn" for a "nightcap." I accompanied him with the envelope under my arm. The reporter introduced me to a concoction of applejack in which he specialized at the time to avoid the occasionally disastrous effects of ordinary prohibition alcohol.

Whatever may be said about applejack, it had not dulled Doyle's memory. Several blocks away from the speak-easy, after we left it, he recalled that I had been carrying a parcel. My manuscript of 100,000 words was gone and I had made no copy of it. We retraced our steps to the taproom which was closing up. My novel was not to be found. A roustabout was sweeping the debris of the night into a large ash can. From the middle of it I rescued *Hot News*.

The novel, which told of the idiosyncrasies of tabloidia with thinly veiled characters, one of them being Winchell whom I had changed into a female gossip writer, disturbed Hearst who communicated his displeasure to Kobler, who in turn, ordered me never to write another book. To dampen my enthusiasm he remained at my desk, to keep me on the job, brandishing his cane and watching me work on the night that my movie opened on Broadway as *Scandal for Sale*, with my name in the lights. I had dedicated the book to Payne, whom I described as having sacrificed his life for circulation. Hollywood pounced upon the episode of his death in my story and featured Pat O'Brien in the role of a newspaper man who plunged into the Atlantic in an airplane while reciting the Lord's prayer. I saw the picture once and could never see it again.

I lived with my family in an expensive apartment near the *Mirror* office and got home each morning at four A.M., when my nervous frame ached for sleep. I left at noon after a hurried breakfast. At times, when extras had to be rushed off, I did not get to my own supper table. It was the old story.

Sarah wanted to buy a house and I agreed to the purchase in New Rochelle of an elaborate home which, including a mortgage, was valued at $50,000. I bought the place while standing in front of its wide lawns. I remember vaguely the real estate dealer's descriptions of its commodious quarters and the master's bedroom but I did not go in to look at them and he undoubtedly thought I was a queer person.

"I understand writers," he said. "They don't want to be bothered with details."

The curtain which had fallen between Sarah and me after Peter's death had desolated both of us. But a man plunging into his work can forget much. A wife, staying at home, remembers. A woman marries to make a beginning and a man often marries to make an end. Perhaps a newspaper man of my type should never have married. I knew that real happiness would not come to Sarah and me. We had become too irreconcilably different in our attitudes toward life. A separation was inevitable because I could not change myself. I moved into bachelor quarters.

Kobler after battling with the Hearst organization for many months, finally obtained Hearst's permission to launch a Sunday edition of the *Mirror*. He was bitterly opposed by a group which believed the project would injure the Sunday *American*. The Sunday *Mirror's* chief asset was a colored rotogravure magazine, the first of its kind in the New York Sunday field and as soon as the new issue was published it won such wide approval that within a few months it had obtained more than a million readers. Kobler had clung to the printing theory that color was a thing meant to be appreciated and not ignored and I had fanned his enthusiasm to the limit. It was my first clean-cut million in circulation and I was proud of it although, as I sat in my office on Saturday nights, I failed to notice any higher pitch of key in the sound from the pressroom. It failed, somehow, to put new music to the magic of a million buyers. It was the same dead rumble but it lasted longer.

In organizing the paper Kobler became entangled in a new argument with Winchell. The publisher handled all verbal negotiations with the columnist as I no longer spoke to him.

The gossiper wanted an additional $1,000 a week to write his column for the Sunday issue but we launched the new paper without him and got a million readers, much to his surprise and apprehension. From our new army of followers I did not receive a letter asking for the publication of Winchell's column on Sunday. Kobler had become increasingly fearful of his latitude and was even more rigid with me in his instructions, many of which came from Hearst, to watch the babbler's morsels which I slashed whenever they were dangerous.

The gossiper included at that time a department in his daily columns entitled "Things I Never Knew Till Now" in which, one day, he printed an item about Joan of Arc that might not have appeared in the Broadway pillar had Winchell been aware that she was a saint. The comment, undoubtedly unintentional, had a murderous effect on our circulation and immediately the Catholic pulpits rang with denunciations of the *Mirror*. Father Charles Edward Coughlin turned the affair into a national scandal in a radio sermon which was followed by a withering boycott of our tabloid by Catholic readers. Kobler reached Father Coughlin and attempted to hire him as a columnist to appease him. The priest rejected the proposal. Meanwhile, through the mediation of high Catholic dignitaries I appealed to Cardinal Hayes in abject fashion, to intercede in behalf of the paper with the Catholic clergy and its followers and the great prelate undoubtedly saved the *Mirror* from deplorable consequences. Winchell printed an apology to our Catholic followers.

Kobler and I became involved in a number of unexplainable episodes which he blamed on my campaigns against the political racketeers. One Sunday afternoon the entire water supply of the *Mirror* plant was suddenly cut off. As the engravers and photographers could not function without water in their vats they were unable to prepare pictures for reproduction. A tabloid without pictures would have been no tabloid at all and the crisis increased as the hour hand crept around the clock. No city official of Tammany Hall's water department could be found to remedy the mysterious condition. Kobler was away in his Minerva, speeding along some purple horizon. An ordinary plumber would have been useless. Heads of departments burst into my office in alarm. It began to appear that the *Mirror* would not come out. I locked myself in to think while I streamed with perspiration and suddenly I had the flash of an idea. I broke the glass of our private fire-alarm box and sent in two alarms. In a short time our street was crowded with every piece of fire apparatus that could get into it. Amid the turmoil I told the firemen I wanted water and in a few minutes I had tons of it. The firemen discovered that the main choke valve controlling the building's water supply had been cut off.

This excitement had hardly been forgotten when Kobler received a death threat with a ransom note demanding $10,000 in cash to be deposited in a white shoebox under a tree in Long Island City on a certain midnight. I appeared in the Minerva at the appointed place with the shoe box which was stuffed with copies of my own editorial columns, a collection of Winchell's "blessed events" and the comic strips of "Mickey Mouse," a little character whom I had adopted as a good-luck charm. As the bells in a church steeple struck twelve I put the box under a branching elm in a lot while headquarters detectives with drawn revolvers hid in the underbrush and behind billboards. This interesting adventure had to be recorded among my unsolved mysteries.

Kobler had not forgotten the Owney Madden affair, nor had I. We preserved affidavits which described its details but the publisher would not permit me to make an issue of it before the authorities, being in dread of the notoriety which would have attached itself to the paper as a result of any official complaint. I kept the matter in mind, however, and at that time met Milton Diamond, an influential lawyer, a man of enviable standing in his profession who guided me through my labyrinthian matters, including threats on my life, and became my best friend and adviser.

I gravely agitated night-life members of the community by exposing the activities of Irving Wexler, better known as "Waxey Gordon," a nickname bestowed upon him early in his pursuits as a symbol of the smoothness with which he could extract a victim's wallet from his pocket. Waxey now was a "Big Shot," with heavy investments in rum-running operations and interested in antiques, as Arnold Rothstein had been in Rembrandt etchings and Whistler paintings. I was not sufficiently acquainted with Gordon's social circle when I began to print his history. He was then the chief financial support of a

Broadway musical comedy in which a popular dancer was to be starred. Her set smile still lingers in my memory. I made the painful discovery that the Gordon story, which was appearing as a serial, had prostrated a wealthy gentleman whose hospitality I had occasionally enjoyed and who was tenderly interested in the dancer's career. Such pressure was brought to bear on me by mutual friends that I listened to the suitor's tearful plea who told me that my revelations would cause the dancer to lose her job and bring to an end a romance that had prolonged his life. Love prevailed and the charmer's aging patron, a renowned bridge player, came to my office thereafter to consult me about rapturous missives which he wrote to her and howled agonized protests while I reduced them to prosaic language, keeping in mind that the hunting season for breach of promise suits was still open. I was happily freed from this role when Prosecutor Dewey packed Gordon off to prison. My Don Juan friend had been roped in to such an extent that he had to contribute to the racketeer's defense.

CHAPTER VIII

I HAD a vague notion in the winter of 1932 that time was passing but I forgot about it on March 1 when the infant son of Colonel Charles A. Lindbergh was kidnaped. Kobler saw in the case a chance of forcing the daily readership of the *Mirror* to the million mark of our Sunday issue. The tragedy held the interest of the public completely and he watched our mounting figures in feverish excitement.

"If we could find the baby," he said, "that would make us the most popular paper in the country. Where's your ability as a Shylock Holmes?"

A few days later I was in Canada with Arthur Mefford, one of my trusted staff men who had accompanied me on brief notice with a convict who had been recently released from Leavenworth Prison and who said he knew the leaders of a gang of rumrunners who could produce the baby for $50,000 ransom. Mefford and I were confined as hostages in Montreal during a paralyzing snowstorm while mysterious negotiations went on between groups of racketeers. I had been authorized by one of Lindbergh's lawyers to act as an intermediary.

Edward Doherty, a crack *Mirror* reporter, meanwhile had been sent to ask the Governor of Michigan to release four racketeers from his State prison as part of the deal included with the ransom demands, a request which the Governor said he would comply with if the baby could be produced. I have often wondered how much of this wild adventure had to do with the final developments of this shocking drama. The sum demanded by the gangsters was the exact amount that was paid later by John F. Condon, as Lindbergh's agent, and which brought about the arrest of Bruno Richard Hauptmann who possessed the money.

In a guarded room with Mefford I was permitted to telephone Kobler who assumed I was about to return with the infant and wanted to meet me at the Canadian border. According to plans which he described as having been devised by "executives higher up" the baby was to be presented to Jimmy Walker on the New York City Hall steps and after necessary photographs had been taken an official party would be organized to transport Lindbergh's rescued son to its mother in New Jersey. Though I failed in my mission I became so incensed over the projected exploitation of the crime that I paid the entire expenses of the expedition (a matter of about $800), during which Mefford and I assumed considerable risks.

I made the interesting discovery during our incarceration that society columns are not read exclusively by the elite. Gangsters with whom we conferred were engaged in clipping from New York newspapers a list of names of wealthy people who had gone to Florida for the winter where the porch-climbers flocked annually to make their usual hauls of jewelry at Miami and Palm Beach.

Sensational newspapers spent small fortunes for exclusive news developments of the kidnaping, in many cases being betrayed by rogues who demanded advance payment for information which led to nothing. Lindbergh agents engaged the services of two New York racketeers, Irving Bitz and Salvatore Spitale, who, it was hoped, might establish some contact with gang overlords, and uncover a clue. Arthur Brisbane became a reporter himself and met Al Capone in his cell in Chicago only to learn that the czar of crime knew less than the police working on the case.

I decided to get the viewpoint of one of the most prosperous racketeers in New York about the crime. One night, before the Lindbergh baby's body was found I visited Frank Costello who controlled the speak-easy slot machine monopoly. He lived in a sumptuous pent-house apartment on Central Park West and received me in ornate Japanese silk pajamas, the most expensive raiment of its kind I had ever seen. We held our discussion in his music room, in the corner of which stood a gold-plated piano. Behind the iron grill work of a fancy portal, two of Costello's henchmen, tailored in blue serge, served as bartenders at a bar of modernistic design with an immense mirror of blue glass. Among the gentlemen to whom I was introduced later at the bar were two New York magistrates in a mellow mood.

Costello was positive in his conclusions about the Lindbergh tragedy and made a prophecy which was soon to be verified. It was based on his own deductions as the slot machine baron was not engaged in the more brutal phases of the rackets.

"That kidnaping is no underworld job," he said. "You fellows in the 'legit' fail to realize that we don't have to do such things to make money. We have our own rackets and observe our own laws. We have a world of our own and there are some things we don't do. 'Big Shot' operators wouldn't steal a baby for money. The kidnaping is the work of a lone wolf who may have had help from cheap crooks. That baby is now a 'hot package,' as we call it in our language. Somebody got nervous and dropped it while it was being stolen and it was buried. That's why all your clues lead nowhere. Look for a cheap crook who worked the thing out and you'll be nearer a solution. Soon, he'll be trying to spend the dough. Don't waste your time trying to pin this on the mob."

Our conversation came to an end when Costello's wife appeared in evening dress, flashing with jewels. She had returned with friends from a theater party and deposited herself at the gold-plated piano. Amid applause she slowly played *The Farmer In The Dell* with one finger. Costello took me to the ornate barroom in each corner of which was a slot machine.

"Try your luck," the racketeer said, amiably.

I inserted a twenty-five-cent piece in one of the contraptions, pulled its lever and four dollars in quarters jingled into my hands. Pressed by Costello, I tried a machine in another corner with the same results. The magistrates, pulling other levers, were enjoying similar good fortune. The racketeer became incensed when I pulled two heaping handfuls of quarters from my pockets and offered to return them to him.

"What the hell do you think I am?" he stormed, "a punk? Nobody loses in my house! I won't say this will happen to you when you try these things in the liquor joints. Better get your money back now, while you can."

Turning down the eccentric hospitality of an underworld success would have been mildly described as imprudent. Costello would have considered it as an insult. I observed the tactfulness of the magistrates and when we left, each of us had been supplied with a bottle of genuine Benedictine while our pockets were loaded down with our host's speak-easy booty.

In the spring of 1932, before the Democratic convention was held, I became vitally interested in Franklin D. Roosevelt's

addresses. I had seen enough of graft, corruption and political
hypocrisy to believe that a new trend of thought was needed
to save the nation.   I had a strong feeling that the end of
Prohibition would wipe out racketeering, and I admired Roosevelt's determination to legalize alcoholic beverages.   I wanted
to meet him.   I knew James A. Farley when he had been a
boxing solon on the New York State Athletic Commission and
through him, my political reporter, Jack Sheehan, arranged the
meeting and accompanied me to Albany where we had a long
luncheon with the Governor of New York, who was to be the
next President of the United States.

I was struck by Roosevelt's assurance of his own destiny.
He had a flashing mind and I never saw, before or since, anything to equal the confidence that shone in his aristocratic face.
His "Forgotten Man" speech had, by that time, struck an
inspiring note.   Much of our conversation I recorded in my
third book, *What So Proudly We Hailed* when I returned from
a trip to Russia.   Roosevelt outlined his entire program to me,
including his intention to recognize the Soviet Union, which
was to influence me in my decision to visit the people under
Stalin.

The following from *What So Proudly We Hailed* may be
of some significance now:

> "We will help the people yet," Roosevelt said, but his face
> clouded with momentary apprehension. "It will have to be
> soon.   They are getting restless.   Coming back from the
> West last week, I talked to an old friend who runs a great
> Western railroad. 'Fred,' I asked him, 'what are the people
> talking about out here?'
>
> "I can hear his answer even now. 'Frank,' he replied,
> 'I'm sorry to say that the men out here are talking revo-
> lution.' "

At the luncheon table with us were two charming women of
high intelligence.   One of them was Miss Marguerite LeHand,
the Governor's secretary, who was to devote her life to the New
Deal President.   She recalled the campaign of 1920 when
Roosevelt, as candidate for the Vice-Presidency, had gone
down to defeat with James M. Cox.

"That will not happen this time," she said, her chin firmly
set.

Throughout the conversation I noticed that Roosevelt, while discussing his plans, never used the expression, "If I am elected." He talked as a man certain of his future and punctuated his remarks with "When I am in the White House."

The Governor was interested in the details of my Fourth of July accident and the effect it had had upon me and invited me to go to Warm Springs where he said he had been benefited while fighting off the ravages of his own illness.

"But those things do not really matter," he said. "I once knew a disabled football coach who directed his team from his wheel chair in which he was wrapped up in blankets. And that team was unbeatable because his mind won the games!"

I returned to New York convinced that Roosevelt would be nominated and elected although none of the high executives I knew in the Hearst organization agreed with me. A number of them thought I was slightly unbalanced on the subject.

While the *Mirror* was progressing, Kobler's financial affairs were reaching a crisis. One evening he told me that the crash of The Bank of United States, the largest financial catastrophe of its kind in American history, had involved him to such an extent that the paper would be taken from him unless he were given time to produce a sum approaching $900,000, as he informed me, to cover thousands of shares of the bank's stock which he had used as collateral for the purpose of borrowing money. His obligations held by The Bank of United States alone, amounted to a half a million dollars. This bank was closed, and while it was collapsing Kobler had taken me to a feverish midnight conference of its executives. One of them wanted me to write, for the New York press, pull-page advertisements announcing that the institution's alleged resources of $300,000,000 were slightly frozen assets which soon would thaw out. If I had put my name to such essays it is quite likely that I would have gone to Sing Sing where some of the bank's chief officers eventually landed.

Kobler's news was devastating to me. I cared little about the effect his removal might have on my personal fortunes but I admired the publisher's tenacity and I hoped some reward would come to him for the trials he had endured to switch the paper from the red side of the ledger. He had salvaged it from the junk heap. I had been approached twice by executives who wanted me to betray him when they discovered the tabloid was no longer a financial drag. Hearst could not have been aware of the conspiracies that went on among the captains of his empire who fought constantly to push each other out.

I saw no hope in consulting other Hearst executives about the situation Kobler was facing. Those whom I had met were not Kobler's friends, but the type of people, pompously professional, who refuse to learn anything more for fear that in acquiring fresh knowledge they might let it be seen that they had not known everything in the first place.

I outlined a plan which seemed more staggering to Kobler than the crisis which was upon him. I proposed to launch a campaign for the nomination of Roosevelt and announce the *Mirror* as the first New Deal paper in New York. I suggested that we offer this proclamation to Edward J. Flynn, then Secretary of the State, in hope that he would use his influence to soften the pressure for immediate payment of Kobler's notes. The publisher's largest note, for $499,915, was to be called in three days. There was little time left. Flynn was a close friend of Roosevelt, eager to advance all plans for his Presidential nomination. Under the circumstances I felt that the Secretary might offer a helping hand to a substantial business man found in a familiar distress whose sufferings were now fairly well distributed about the community. I had experienced the pain acutely, myself.

A few days later, while I prepared to launch my campaign for Roosevelt, Kobler remarked:

"What do you suppose Hearst is going to say to this? He favors Garner for the nomination. There will be hell to pay. Will you take the responsibility for this as the editor?"

The publisher listened to my last tirade in respectful awe. The *Mirror* came out for Roosevelt with cartoons, editorials, pictures and stories and I received two pleasant notes from the New Deal candidate. Kobler told me laughingly, of the upheaval that followed among the policymakers of our organization, and at San Simeon, when we came out for the more abundant life. And, as Winchell might have described it, I "took the rap."

CHAPTER IX

IT seemed incredible to me, when I considered the brevity
of life and the important things there are to do during its
course, that I should be earning a salary approaching $30,000
a year in a pursuit in which I had come to see nothing but a
waste of one's time. I had accumulated circulation by pushing into the back of my mind all that I had learned about the
value of constructive news. I had no time to indulge my
tastes for good literature which, years ago, I looked upon as a
means of life. Those with whom I associated were too busy
stalking the dollar to read anything worth while. Outsmart-
ing a competitor in a deal involving a comic strip was of greater
consequence to mass readership than years of training in
interpreting significant happenings. Signing up the exclusive
services of "Mickey Mouse" in New York was considered a
master stroke—incidentally one of the accomplishments of
my *Mirror* regime. But "Mickey" wasn't such a bad sort.

My left-wing friends who used to discuss the coming
world catastrophe at the *Graphic* office had dropped me as a
hopeless capitalist. I was unable to hire Ryan Walker on
the *Mirror,* whose art department was competently handled
and when he learned he could not join me he began a series
of cartoons in the Communist *Daily Worker* in which I was
depicted as a pathetic figure carrying a can of garbage on my
back labeled "tabloid trash," while I trailed a parade of pluto-
crats in high hats with dollar signs on their bellies. Walker
finally abandoned these bewildering attacks and packed off for
Moscow to end his days in some Utopian nightmare.

I bought my last comic strip one New Year's eve when
Ham Fisher, known in New York art circles as the "pride of
Wilkes-Barre, Pa.," an enthusiastic cartoonist who sought to
introduce his wares to the metropolis, befuddled me with a
rare bottle of Burgundy during a hilarious celebration. When
I woke up the next day I found I was the sponsor of "Joe
Palooka," an exemplary character who never drank or smoked

174

and was good to his mother. Strangely enough "Palooka" became one of the most successful ventures in the comic field and soon had Fisher living in affluence and riding an Arabian horse in Central Park.

Occasionally, in the evening, when James Montgomery Flagg relaxed after his grind of illustrating magazine stories I dropped into his studio to absorb his amiable cynicism as a tonic. Through him I could recall my early ambitions to be a musician and cartoonist. One night he pulled a curtain from a painting of Lincoln who stood in a worn dressing gown looking anxiously from a White House window across the Potomac. All the agony of his struggle to save the Union appeared in his gaunt face. It was a conception of high order, superb in its execution.

"That's the sort of thing I should love to do," he said.

"Who painted it?" I asked.

"I did. But it took time. People today want everything in a hurry. Let's not talk about it."

On the other hand, George B. Luks, famous as a painter of the first rank, talked mostly, whenever I saw him, of the happy time he had when he drew "Hogan's Alley" and the "Yellow Kid" for the *World* after the creator of the comics, R. F. Outcault, left Pulitzer for Hearst. Luks despised the ostentation of irresponsible wealth and during his last days often invited editors of sensational newspapers to his studio where he insulted vapid social climbers who had been lured to see his paintings and who fled in horror from his remarks.

"There's a headline for you," the artist would shout: " 'Noted painter tells society to go to hell!' "

Restlessness and boredom seemed to characterize those who had reached the top. They described their success with mirthless laughter. Business luncheons were held in speak-easies, some of which occupied old, palatial residences. Brisbane visited one of them and devoted half of his column to the experience as something unique in our civilization. Every executive I knew had a bar in his desk, myself included. Salesmen signing contracts demanded drinks, which had to be something "right off the boat." In our own building I discovered an electrical expert who managed to find time in the cellar to manufacture "Irish whisky" which he sold for $1.50 a bottle. Some members of our organization reported it wasn't bad.

Each newspaper staff had adopted its own drinking establishment and supported it handsomely by imbibing with abandon. Policemen on the blocks were paid two dollars for every beer keg moved in. The "Fish Inn" had become a tavern of renown, word having spread that it was endorsed by Owney Madden, Tammany Leader Hines, editors and writers. Soon, its owner, Frank Thompson, a genial Irishman of booming laughter, had more trade than he could handle. The crowded bar was held up one night by apprentices of the "Dutch" Schultz gang, and customers cheerfully complied with all requests made by youngsters holding automatics in shaking hands. In a thriving French restaurant near the waterfront, Garet Garrett, editorial feature writer for the *Saturday Evening Post,* defied gunmen who had come in for loot on a busy evening and was shot three times through the stomach. He recovered by some miracle.

A good portion of my hard-driven reporters had been drinking at the "Fish Inn" on credit at seventy-five cents a swallow and as months went by the debt reached an imposing amount. Their rescue from this bondage became a prohibition legend. The *Mirror* had as its advertising manager a veteran of Park Row named Bill Crompton who held in years gone by an unofficial record as the sleepless survivor of the longest poker session in New York. He engaged the proprietor of the "Fish Inn" in a game of hearts and after seventy-two hours of continuous play Crompton won the saloon and all it contained. Thereupon he called for the bills outstanding, crossed off every cent owed by *Mirror* men and graciously returned the speak-easy to its distracted owner.

It became unpopular to attack "Big Shots" who were involved in all manner of Tammany Hall philanthropies and were praised by the poor. I became engaged in exposing public menaces with the help of Cornelius Vanderbilt, Jr., once a tabloid publisher in his own right and an instinctive reporter who was always good for a banner line whenever he saw me. Crusades were his hobby. Often we were up all night tracking down sensations which had to do with the drug evil. Social life seemed to be appalling to him and he expressed his feelings in books which his set looked upon as heresy. It reminded me of the evenings I had spent, while editor of the *Graphic,* with Houdini the magician, whose passion was to unmask spiritualistic seances. The story of these expeditions had brought about a libel suit which the judge dismissed when the plaintiffs were unable to produce their ghosts in court.

One episode of these fantastic times I recall with remorse. The owner of a bird shop, specializing in canaries, wanted a picture of his establishment to appear in the paper. Cameramen took their photographs at that time by igniting powder in a pan and the young shutter man on the bird shop assignment must have used an extra amount of it. Peering through the smoke after a staggering flashlight explosion the proprietor fainted when he discovered that every canary in his shop had dropped dead.

No paper of mass appeal could afford to be without a staff astrologist or a palmist who could tell you how to improve your fortune. Vanderbilt, himself, often read palms to amuse social gatherings where we found ourselves together, although he did not believe in this sorcery. The young millionaire must have possessed a psychic sense which I remembered five years later when I recalled that he had predicted I would be living on a farm, feeding chickens.

The *Mirror's* official astrologist was a small, gray man of middle age who spent endless hours studying charts of his calling with a burning faith. He perused the charts of the *Mirror* and predicted terrifying upheavals. I saw him for the last time when he came in with a chart which involved his own existence. He had discovered that all signs had combined against him and that death would catch up with him in three months. He discussed the turn of affairs with a half-comic, philosophic calm, declined to tell me about the direction in which I was heading, drew two weeks' pay and vanished.

There was a report at the time that Evangeline Adams, the city's most popular astrologist, had predicted her own death. A year before she died a lawyer gave me the news of a suit which one of her assistants had prepared to file against her for certain claims and accountings. Each time Miss Adams selected a date for her appearance in court, the plaintiff, naturally familiar with the stars which influenced Miss Adams' life, insisted upon waiting until the heavens would be of complete disadvantage to her and, incidentally, most propitious for him. Miss Adams, of course, sparred for a delay whenever she found that the planets were ganging up on her. The lawyers and the judge finally threw up their hands and the trial was never held.

Readers of papers of mass circulation turned first to the astrological predictions of their daily activities, according to their birthdates, before reading anything else. The promotion of any form of superstition rarely failed to increase circulation. Later I encountered many Americans, otherwise intelligent, who were convinced that Adolf Hitler's military and diplomatic successes in the months of March and September were due to his acceptance of astrology as an exact science. An editor, inclined to scoff at such conclusions, had to beat a retreat from the inevitable question: "If there's nothing to it why do you hire astrologists to tell these things to the people?"

I had brought over from the *Graphic* my friend Macauley, the cartoonist, whose fine pictures graced our editorial page and were often reprinted in periodicals of importance. He was devoted to Roosevelt and his drawings and the *Mirror's* political policies preceding the Presidential nomination of 1932 brought me into Tammany circles campaigning for the New Deal. I was thrown into friendly contact with James W. Brown, Public Administrator of Bronx County who asked me if I might not be interested in going to Washington as a Congressman. A nomination was open in the Bronx, where I would have had to move and establish residence. I went around with Brown to visit district clubs and meet some of "the boys." His sponsorship, I have no doubt, would have assured my election. He had been responsible in great measure for the political career of Edward J. Flynn who had become a close adviser of Roosevelt. But my inclinations rebelled at the thought of the perpetual handshaking, the everlasting smile the office-seeker has to freeze into his face, the deadly speeches, the endless promises to be "regular." I had seen too much of it. I was not a "good mixer," due, probably, to the social isolation of my early boyhood. Yet, I sought an escape from a way of life that at times impressed me as being slightly above the crustacean order.

I visited Flynn about a vague plan of going to South America to do diplomatic work in some country full of intrigue and rebellion. He told me Roosevelt was seriously considering him for the post of Ambassador to Germany. The appointment did not seem to interest him. He preferred to perform his services closer to the throne. While waiting for some turn of affairs to grip my interest I went back to the monotony of my murders, Sally Rand's fan dance and the twilight of Clara Bow.

My companions now were often musicians of fine training who played in night-club orchestras with a cold cynicism. The symptoms of the era had created a tempo of madness which smothered everything that remained of the melody of the period. Percussionists set the pace of the new broken rhythm by talking to themselves while they hammered until dawn. One celebrated drummer had begun the vogue by bringing down his drumsticks with each syllable of a verbal expression. Talking, he found, was necessary to hold the mind to the new jungle beat. While he played he repeated one phrase continually: "Pork chops and lyonnaise potatoes." To master a different tempo, another professor of the sticks shouted steadily above the din: "Chopped liver and pickled herring."

Broadway became a rash of trumped up bands, led by oily haired gigolos with fixed smiles and pictured as the nation's most irresistible lovers, log-rolled into lights and featured in various cities by tabloid accounts of their fake romances. Their acquaintance with music was probably less than a drunken bassoonist's knowledge of Bulfinch's *Mythology*. No longer were the tunes of the night exulting and orgiastic. Dancers responded with a hangover sway to regurgitating brass, a lunatic pounding, an obscene neigh from a muted horn.

Soon the jitterbugs would be "shagging" in the theater aisles. "Swing" was coming in. Tabloidia had to keep up with these trends. But bank panics and unemployment were giving the shouting type a new complexion. "Playboys" were not worth a line of gossip. They couldn't play without money. The threadbare thirties were making it tougher for people to buy the apparatus of revelry. The art of glamorous long-drawn love-making had died in the banner lines. Pent-house Pompadours were walking the streets.

CHAPTER X

In the summer of 1933 I wrung a leave of absence from Kobler, quit my desk upon brief notice and left on a pilgrimage to Russia. My decision apparently stunned the publisher who reached me by radio telephone for two or three days while I was aboard the S.S. *Rex*, bound for Naples. I had worked four years without a vacation and he had picked out a place where I was to rest in the Catskill Mountains where he could keep in touch with me. Over the waves his voice grew fainter and fainter until finally he resorted to radiograms, the last of which gave me an account of Winchell's first experience in having his nose flattened in public by a prominent victim of his gibes. Al Jolson had let go a rugged left at the gossiper, setting somewhat of a vogue. "I hope this will make you feel better," Kobler had added.

My trip to the Soviet Union reflected no significance of my views although I was interested in studying living conditions among the Communists. In my frame of mind, perhaps I would have joined a polar expedition with eagerness. My flight had not been entirely unpremeditated. Dr. William I. Sirovich, a member of Congress, whom I had met as a newspaper man, had organized an unofficial mission of Senators and Congressmen to travel through Russia and I was invited to go along as an observer. I recalled that in my interview with Roosevelt he had told me he intended to advocate the recognition of the Soviets.

Sirovich, whose impulsive decisions were to have bewildering effects on my routine almost up to the time of his death, was a dapper, gray-haired man of slight stature, stern look, set lips and high forehead. A red carnation was as much a part of his attire as his Phi Beta Kappa key. His activities included the writing of plays, and escaping his play-readings was a problem that began to tax my ingenuity as soon as the Statue of Liberty had vanished in the mist.

Lying in a deck chair I tried to put together the Chinese puzzle of my existence. The only satisfaction I got out of living came from sporadic attempts to write. I had produced another novel, *The Scandal Monger*, the story of a Broadway columnist who had changed his name from Willie Goldfarb to Roddy Ratcliffe and whose superficial qualities had struck a popular note and made him rich. Winchell threatened to resign unless the book were suppressed. Kobler was in a towering rage during the tumult until he discovered I had dedicated the volume to him. He cooled down, grasped my hand in appreciation and asked me for ten autographed copies. There had been much eyebrow raising among the reviewers over this venture. It had been called to Hearst's attention and had displeased him. One comment about the story which impressed me came from Lewis Gannett of the *Herald Tribune:* "If Mr. Gauvreau is a realist, the book should become an important document for the pathological history of our age." One could not reason in the atmosphere of our workshop without being a realist. Solicitous members of my photographic staff had presented to me a heavy Luger automatic, expecting that I might suddenly need it. Winchell and I went about the city room exchanging malevolent glares.

Tabloidia had other matters to occupy my attention. I had been exposing the regime of President Machado of Cuba, having been provided with the facts by Miguel Mariano Gomez, wealthy mayor of Havana, who was in exile with his entourage in New York. Gomez wanted to organize a revolution in Cuba, and Sheehan and I conferred with the prominent Cuban and his staff. My stories had been picked up by the Hearst newspaper chain and the wide publicity's effect on future events in Cuba was to be considerable. Gomez was a slight, pale man with dark eyebrows and wet black hair. He had the look of a French duelist who feels he has accepted a fatal challenge. He talked of a private expedition to capture the Havana police stations and late at night in the Ansonia Hotel we pored over dotted maps of the Cuban capital. Sheehan believed Gomez could obtain machine guns for the fight for freedom from Waxey Gordon. The racketeer was never too busy with his antiques to explore more exciting sidelines. Gomez was under the impression that Waxey was a manufacturer of firearms and wanted to meet him, but by that time Waxey was on his way to a place where such discussions were not permitted.

On July 2, 1932, I had attended the wake of the *Evening Graphic* which, after eight years, rolled off its last copies. My successor as editor, Louis Weitzenkorn, staggered out of the experience with an idea for a play, *Five Star Final,* which became a Broadway success. He turned his play into a motion picture and remained in Hollywood for a number of years, surrounded with money and pleasant company.

One of my campaigns had not added to the security of my position. With the cooperation of the *Mirror's* literary reviewer, Charles A. Wagner, a courageous Jew who had the appearance of a German, and who had joined a leading Nazi Bund organization in New York, I obtained information of the subversive activities of Hitler's followers. While we were printing these revelations Wagner and I were summoned to Washington to testify before a Congressional committee investigating the underground movement. At the capital, a Hearst paper, whose editor must have felt the impulse of cutting his throat later, publicized my testimony under a large headline and printed my picture two columns wide, assuming, apparently, that my stories had been authorized by the Hearst organization. I got back to my office to discover that Hearst was conferring with high Nazi officials in Berlin about matters which he has recently revealed in answer to charges, later withdrawn, in the original publication of Ambassador Dodd's *Diary.* I was ordered by an important executive of the Hearst Management to stop my crusade. It is extremely likely that Hearst in Berlin knew nothing about this. Considering present-day events his well-paid subordinate may have reason to be ashamed of himself. He was typical of Hearst's advisers, known as the "little Turks," who surrounded themselves with mystery, apparently believing they would seem less great if everybody understood them.

Kobler, whose fate hung with mine, had renewed my contract until January 1, 1936 with an increase in salary. Hearst, who, within limits set by the corporation laws, tapped the till of his organization whenever he liked, needed more money for his four palaces at San Simeon, the importation of additional Madonnas, and stones of the architecture of the Spanish Renaissance. These unsuppressed desires, in conjunction with other more practical matters, resulted in slashes in our payroll. Within a short period my staff members had to undergo twenty per cent cuts in their salaries. Men under contract were protected from these slashes, but as I had to do the cutting I would not have been able to look my underpaid subordinates in the face without accepting the reduction myself. In my own case it was a heavy one. For this reason Kobler had extended my agreement with the organization to permit me to get back some of my money. Certain other men under contract refused to accept reduced pay. Winchell, whose income from various sources was then more than $5,000 a week, laughed at the suggestions.

For a number of years Hearst's castles had been a drain on his newspaper empire. The amounts levied in the years before the sale of Hearst securities to the public reached a vast figure. Forrest Davis, in an article for the *Saturday Evening Post,* pictured Hearst as scooping out all of a publisher's cash reserves between trains. For a long period of time the millionaire's personal luxuries were never curbed. At San Simeon, he slept in a celestial suite beneath his towers in a priceless bed that had once held the restless, fitful form of Cardinal Richelieu.

Mark Hellinger, one of my columnists, offered a unique solution to help the newspaper owner during our salary reductions. Refusing to permit any changes in his contract, the writer proposed to mail Hearst $50 each week out of his own pocket until affairs at San Simeon had been stabilized. The Broadway observer, of whom I was quite fond, had married Gladys Glad, a Ziegfeld Follies beauty whom we advertised as "the most beautiful girl in the world" when she became the editor of a *Mirror* column which scattered joy to women who wanted to enhance their charms. Mark and Gladys had a disagreement for a brief period but were happily reconciled and during the estrangement he decided to take a trip to encircle the earth and produce a daily department to be called "Broadways Around the World." The project was launched after much trumpeting from our horns of promotion, blown lustily every day by Donald Williams, a man of gentlemanly reserve who finally fled from the business and became a successful New York lawyer.

Mark prepared a number of daily columns in advance and

we received additional essays from him until he reached Vienna. From this city of merriment and *gaieté de coeur* he sent us a glowing account of his impressions and then disappeared, and his columns ran out. As they were widely sold by King Features Syndicate this became a serious matter. Arthur James Pegler, my chief soothsayer, a celebrated Hearst war horse, was certain that Mark had been enticed by the Turkish bazaars in Istanbul. James Whittaker, an imaginative rewrite man, who happened to be familiar with Ottoman literature and customs, saturated our traveler with the atmosphere of the East and maneuvered him into Russia, then dropping the matter in exhaustion. Pegler took over the task and every day the veteran wrote, under Hellinger's name, an entertaining and sometimes dumfounding travelogue of the Broadway bard's experiences in the land of the Soviet, through the Punjab of India and across the mountains of Tibet. By the time Pegler had pushed him into the Orient I was frankly worried about my absent columnist from whom I had received no word.

One afternoon, while Pegler was propelling our Broadway philosopher along the Great Wall of China for the next morning's issue, Mark called me in a bland voice from his apartment. He had come home unannounced and had been recapturing lost sleep for five days. Vienna had stopped him. We kept Hellinger in hiding until Pegler managed to haul the columnist, under feverish pressure, across the Pacific and fly him home for a world's globe-trotting record of which we made no official claim. A number of editors who bought the syndicated column wrote to us that it had broadened the minds of many readers.

But now I was on the high seas with nothing to concern me but the plays of Dr. Sirovich. Our delegation soon reached Naples and we stormed the crater of Vesuvius, dashed down to Pompeii and slept in Sorrento, where I hardly had begun to absorb its breathtaking enchantment before we were off to Rome. Members of Congress waste no time in their sightseeing. We flew over the Alps to Vienna and continued our pace to Warsaw where I found refuge in a wine cellar near the tomb of the author of *Quo Vadis*. But on a train to Moscow,

Sirovich trapped me with his manuscripts, and through the dreary Russian landscape I listened to two plays, each of five acts and innumerable scenes, entitled *Tin Boxes* and *The Plotters.* When we got off I welcomed my first tumbler of vodka.

We met many of the Soviet leaders, including Mikhail I. Kalinin, one of the chairmen of the Communist Central Executive Committee and Presidential figurehead, a grinning, shuffling figure with a cap over one ear reminding me of the creatures who accost people in New York for the price of a cup of coffee. He thought America was "O. K." V. I. Mezhlauk, then vice-chairman of the State Planning Commission, who wore the attire of a modern business executive, contrasting strangely with the raiments of his staff, expressed some opinions which may be of significance in the distraught present.

"We are not building up a great army to conquer people outside," he said. "It is to keep them out. The insults we have stood from Japan would have started a war long ago if another nation had been involved. We were so trustful of Japan that we left our Far Eastern border almost without any defense. She had assured us officially that she would not go beyond a definite line in Manchuria. These assurances were repeated right up to the complete occupation of the whole of Manchuria and to the occupation of what is called Manchukuo. That is a bit of Japanese humor too dangerous to laugh at. But we are determined to avoid war."

This statement I included in my book, *What So Proudly We Hailed,* which I wrote when I returned but I was not permitted then to add the following remarks by Mezhlauk which may throw some light on Russia's present position:

"Even if Japan decides to take Vladivostok, we would not fight, because we are not ready. When we are prepared we will seize what we believe is necessary for our own protection. The diplomatic moves we may make in the future will not change the fact that Germany will remain our chief potential enemy, with Japan as the second foe to consider. As long as Germany is at our front door we will avoid a fight with Japan. We may have to make a deal with both. Hitler knows this already. He will start the trouble."

It may be assumed in the light of these views, which were authoritative, that Russia's advance into the Baltic States and

Finland, was inspired by a distrust of Germany although Stalin, by that time, had signed an agreement with Nazi Germany to supply some of her needs, a pact which I believe was sealed with less enthusiasm on the part of the Russians than Hitler proclaimed it to be.

Stalin would not receive us at the Kremlin, although we were permitted to wander freely through the historic place. Constantin A. Oumansky, who was to become Soviet Ambassador to the United States, a trained and resourceful careerist under Stalin, informed me in Moscow that the Russian ruler wanted to avoid the impression that he was seeking American recognition. The Dictator enclosed himself in his rooms while we stood outside in a corridor of brooding gloom.

Oumansky, with whom I talked on several occasions, was small of stature, boyish in appearance and seemed to convey the impression that he was capable of greater things than those which he performed. His personal convictions, one felt, would never embarrass him to the extremity of a purge. The smartest of Stalin's puppets was the chief of the Soviet Bureau of Press Relations, a smooth, suave appeaser, carrying out to the best of his ability the orders of a man utterly devoid of moral scruples. This schooling made it an easy matter for him six years later, as ambassador, to explain as perfectly justifiable the pact with Hitler who had called the men of Moscow "the scum of humanity." When Germany's hellhound leaped upon the Russian people it was even easier for Oumansky, who professed to hate capitalism as much as Viscount Halifax cherished it, to greet the British Ambassador in Washington as a comrade fighting for civilization. *Columbia the Gem of the Ocean,* blared from Moscow's radio in 1941 as a compliment to the nation which up to the moment of Hitler's invasion of Russia had been described by Communist diplomats as decadent, imperialist and bourgeois, was a piece of humor which could only have been appreciated by the grim toilers outside of the Kremlin who knew in the first place which side they would have chosen in the world's struggle with Berlin's creeping anti-Christ. The pen stroke of 1939 which freed Hitler to devastate Europe did not come from the Russian people, intelligent enough to foresee that when the Germans started their war, it was to be with the hope, when it was over, of looking upon the earth and seeing nobody of any consequence but themselves, as George Santayana has ably expressed it.

The idealistic Russians I met in Moscow and Leningrad were shot within three years, following sensational trials. Karl Radek, a journalist whose following in the Soviet was of great proportions, dissipated some of our illusions following a dinner in Leningrad at the Hotel Europa whose luxuries could hardly have been imagined by the lines of people I saw daily waiting in the streets for cucumbers and black bread. Radek, who became a sensational breast-beating figure in the subsequent purge trials, is either in prison now, or the victim of a firing squad, and I may quote what he told me and Dr. Sirovich.

"Russia trusts no one," he said. "For its own protection it will engage in a partnership with its worst enemy if it can worm an advantage out of it. It is more realistic than hypocritical. We are all of a piece with our so-called civilization. Russia's alliances will never be permanent with any nation. It would not lift a finger to discourage Hitler from launching a war on the continent. Russia then would watch all contenders until they became so weakened that all the peoples concerned would be at the mercy of revolution. Then we would step in. We will let the others fight and ruin themselves. We will not discourage their inclinations. Then the Russian hand will reach out. There is no idealism about it."

Coming from Stalin's editorial adviser this statement was a shock to Sirovich who, at a lavish banquet of the international fur traders in Leningrad, had compared Lenin with Jesus Christ. He attributed Radek's words to the champagne that had been streaming through the proceedings. The Congressman did not touch spirits of any kind. I believe Radek had become drunk enough to tell the truth about the Red inner circle.

My favorable impression of the patient men and women in the factories, in the airplane plants, on the great dams and in the fields remains, however. They wanted to improve their own conditions and recoiled at the thought of war with any nation. I spent many weeks among them, and with reliable interpreters and my knowledge of French I gathered much of their thoughts and aspirations. The workers talked freely of their hope for a better world and accepted their regimentation as a temporary annoyance which would lead to a more abundant life. They were totally ignorant of the undermining propaganda their leaders were spreading outside of Russia. But here one heard nothing of liberty as a prime necessity or desirable means of existence. These masses did not miss it because they had never had it. Of America they inquired: "Are the people comfortable and do they have enough to eat?" Not once was I asked: "Are they free to think for themselves and do as they please?" That question was not in the catechism of the planned society. I heard so much of the planned society that, today, I cannot read the word "plan," appearing with increasing frequency in Washington dispatches without some vague apprehension.

I felt then that the rigid regime of the Soviets was necessary to discipline 170,000,000 people and bring about some semblance of order after the revolution. France had lived through the same experience. I was hopeful that something of good might come of it for the Russian people and I said so in the book about my journey. That there were many other sincere but bug-eyed pilgrims aside from myself who saw eventually that the Communist purpose under Stalin was as empty as the sloughed off skin of a snake in the summer, affords me some consolation. My Congressional companions were fellow travelers only in the sense that they paid for their transportation to go on a picnic about which they have long since reached my conclusions.

Honest thinkers in Russia, among them Maxim Gorky (who was later poisoned), told me they looked to the United States to give the world a balanced and peaceful civilization. Those who sought to reconcile the ideals of pure Communism with the freedom of Democracy were soon executed. The "practical" revolutionists remained, well supplied with money drained from the toil of those in servitude, to ferret their way into America under orders to undermine our form of government.

Thoughts entered my mind of my old co-worker of *Graphic* days, Ryan Walker, who had died in Moscow after a disheartening pursuit of the Communist mirage. I wanted to visit his last resting place, and a sanitation official, to whom my requests may have become annoying, drove me with an interpreter to a crematorium, and from rows of shelves selected a little fluted urn of dark green ashes, bearing a Russian label, and which he handed to me with some irritation.

"There," he said, "if I'm not mistaken, is your friend."

Perhaps it was Walker, his forgotten days of struggle for the downtrodden, his hopes of a system of living too perfect for human nature, all reduced to bottled dust.

With a resentful official of government printing, who had not been expecting me, I transacted a little piece of incomprehensible business. My novel, *Hot News*, had been published in Russia to the extent of 300,000 copies and had been reviewed as an example of capitalistic journalism. My royalties amounted to $215 in American money which I was ordered to spend within the confines of the Soviet Union before I went back to a less enlightened world. In Finland the book was published as a short magazine serial and the Finns paid me slightly less than the Russians who had produced my story by the tens of thousands of copies.

On my way back across the continent all the talk was of approaching war. I had been quoted in the Moscow *Daily News* as having described Hitler as a maniac and as a result I was advised to make my way around Germany to avoid inconveniences. Warsaw, to be a shambles six years later, paraded its aimless troops and camouflaged cannon while Polish officers, later to abandon their men on the battlefield, roistered in luxurious night clubs.

The Czecho-Slovakians seemed to be closer to the realization that forces were acting to direct events which might decide history for generations. They clung to the belief that France and Russia would help them. I hurried to Austria to make preparations for our group while Sirovich remained in Prague for a talk with President Thomas G. Masaryk.

Nazi planes were dropping paper swastikas over Vienna when I saw Sirovich again. Masaryk had told him that the peoples of Europe would rise up to defend their faith in Democracy when the time came. Czecho-Slovakia would be the Gibraltar of freedom in Europe. The only talk I heard about liberty was within its borders.

The manager of Vienna's Hotel Bristol, our place of abode on the Ringstrasse, often listened to Sirovich's conversations and suggested a visit to Chancellor Engelbert Dollfuss at the Cabinet building. The Congressman saw no importance in the proposal. But the manager said he could "fix it up" for us easily. He reached for a telephone.

"Give me Dollfuss," he said.

Our conversations with the tiny round man whose feet could not reach the floor from a sofa where, a year later, he was to be butchered by the Nazis, left no impression on us. I asked the Chancellor about the swastikas, the talk of trouble. Austria, he replied in German to Sirovich, who put my question to him, was too small a country to be harmed.

"And furthermore," he said, "Mussolini would stand for no nonsense."

In Switzerland, at Zurich, I encountered practical people ready to fight. Many of them felt that Hitler might make a thrust into France through their venerable republic. Near Belfort I was permitted to inspect part of the Maginot Line. Hundreds of feet down, under tons of steel and concrete an assurance came over me, with a wine glass in my hand, that France was safe from invasion. It would have seemed preposterous then to believe that the French would be stabbed in the back by their own leaders, debauched by Hitler's ideas and money.

In Paris I should have seen the significant signs of approaching disintegration. A free people may be represented by the character of its press. The journalists I met on some of the recognized papers were a hopelessly cynical lot. Later, many were revealed as bribe takers. The truth to them was something to be perverted for a price. The downfall of France, I believe, had much to do with the rottenness of its newspapers where traitors were bred. An American tabloid, in comparison, would have appeared as a torch of honesty.

I recall one small experience, which may, or may not have indicated the prevailing trend as I went about with French newspaper writers and editors. *Hot News* had been published in Paris under the title of *Scandale Avant Tout* by the thriving printing house of Au Sans Pareil of 17, Rue Froidevaux. The book had been widely sold according to the figures I saw in the books of the publisher who invited me to attend a dinner where I was introduced to the reviewers who had given me good notices. There must have been a regiment of them. I insisted on settling for the dinner. When this merry occasion was over the publisher imparted to me the information that all favorable reviews had to be paid for from the author's royalties. Such matters were placed on a cash basis by the French newspapers. You escaped bad notices by paying for good ones. The money that remained from my literary emoluments after the reviews had been bought and the publisher had raked in his share, turned out to be the exact amount demanded by the translator of my story.

French conversations, wherever I went in Paris, reflected all of the avarice of the period. A society, diverted from praiseworthy employment to an idle class without prospects or honor, was preparing a cemetery for the laborers, miners, shopmen and peasants who were the only people of the population who talked of fraternity and patriotism. Instead of promoting to places of prominence the worthiest specimens of the nation, the French had elevated their grafting and traitorous politicians who used their power to sell their countrymen out. Perhaps it is the best known characteristic of Democracy that its greatest men are always examples of fame made by bitter opposition. I had never forgotten what my father had read me out of Bodley's studies of France:

"It is to the French that Frenchmen display animosity more savage, more incessant, and more inequitable than to the people of any other race."

The *tricoteuses* who took their infants to see men and women losing their heads on the guillotine might have viewed with the same complacence the spectacle of a ruling class rushing to its doom because it believed that the pursuit of money was the chief privilege of Democracy. France was enjoying the few remaining years of her careless, laughing liberty. In America we had already been jolted out of our laughter. We were learning rapidly. Looking back on my old French ancestry I was glad I had never been brought up to think of a hyphen. I rejoiced in the feeling that I was an American. No better lesson could be absorbed from a trip to Europe.

CHAPTER XI

BACK at my desk I looked at the tabloid turmoil with increasing detachment. I broadcast my Russian observations from Hearst's radio station, whose management insisted upon the talk which I based on the notes that, later, produced my book. This episode was to add to the irony of the consequences which immediately followed its publication.

I was informed that the United States would recognize the Soviet Union in November of 1933, and Kobler, interested in the news, asked me to introduce him to officials of the Amtorg, the Moscow government's trading corporation in New York. He planned to devote a special edition of the *Mirror* to the prospects of increased commerce with Russia and expected the issue to produce $75,000 in advertising revenue by the use of color pages to be sold for a high price. Matters were discussed at a plutocratic luncheon in which our Communist conferees wallowed with proletarian appreciation. Hardly four days had passed when in the middle of preparations for the project, the publisher, obviously disturbed, canceled it abruptly without explanation.

I was invited as observer of our Congressional group to attend a banquet at the Waldorf-Astoria where the event of recognition was lavishly celebrated. Maksim Litvinov, Stalin's Commissar of Foreign Affairs, soon to be reduced to a puppet, rejoiced with prosperous American industrialists who saw vast fortunes ahead in exports to the Soviets and who cheered and toasted the hammer and sickle on a huge red banner hanging over their heads. Some well-known capitalists were hailed as comrades that night and didn't seem to mind it.

I kept up my bachelor life although my family saw me regularly at my office while I was immersed in business, and talked to me after the manner of visitors conversing with a prisoner behind a screen. My sons were preparing to enter college and lived with Sarah in the New Rochelle home whose maintenance absorbed much of my earnings. My existence again became the shadow of a life whose dubious pleasures I would have renounced but for my obligations which had geared themselves up to higher standards of living as rapidly as my salary rose. As Sarah had pointed out, one could not afford to live on the wrong side of the railroad tracks on $30,000 a year.

It was all of a piece of modern financial success and held me in an environment of mental stagnation and in which, as it appeared to outsiders, I continued of my own volition. I was now definitely a part of that strange race of people, aptly described in an editorial in the *Herald Tribune,* as spending their lives doing work they detest to make money they don't want to buy things they don't need in order to impress people they dislike.

The two books I had written which described the aimlessness of the work I was engaged in had been accepted in some quarters as a tongue-in-the-cheek performance, though extensively reviewed, while Hollywood had poured money into my lap for one of them and called for more. Both novels were being published in England and had received favorable notices in the *Times* of London.

My journey had made me more conscious of the significant affairs which took place beyond the confines of our side show. I contemplated with mounting irritation my scrambling racket to lure readers. At times, in this struggle for headlines, the world of sensations did not seem to be big enough for us. Yet I knew we could not stand flat-footed upon the ground by merely printing the news. Now there were wrangling conferences about circulation in the offices of the general management, occasionally attended by John Hearst, son of our monarch, who was learning the business, and who wanted to know why the *Daily News* was so far ahead of us. During one of these gatherings at the wailing wall, Solomon Solis Carvalho, aged chieftain of Hearst's editorial tribe, assigned three men to read the *News* from the time it was first published to find out how it had acquired its leadership, a matter of studying fifteen years of type. One could survive such autopsies by playing the office politician, the smirking courtier and listen to tirades with an angelic smile. Editors endowed with this stamina moved up from $30,000 a year to $40,000 or $50,000. It required a strong stomach.

I found some interest in La Guardia's campaign for the mayoralty and I plumped for him, although this was not an orthodox policy with Hearst. His *American* later cartooned the little Congressman as a wild figure waving a flag which had been printed in red ink to drive home its implications. I was ordered to stop boosting his candidacy although the best citizens in New York recognized him as a public servant who was honest to the point of viciousness and whose courage they relied upon to pull the city out of the worst state of political corruption since the days of Tweed. He hated the prohibition law and no man had done more in Washington to bring about its repeal. He often planned his strategy at a dinner table of the "Little Venice," a lively Italian speak-easy restaurant on West 13th Street, where we discussed his prospects. He had promised to buy me the "best drink in town" if he were elected and he made good his word in a place I had never heard of but which lived up to his recommendations. There his friends drank to his health and toasted him as the next President of the United States, an office which many insisted would not have been beyond his equipment.

Kobler had become a man who was containing himself under grave financial difficulties. The State Supreme Court had permitted him to settle his obligations of $499,915 held by the closed Bank of United States for $150,000 in cash and possibly $25,000 more, in addition to Kobler's $100,000 insurance on his life. Four years previously he had been rated as one of New York's millionaires with a constantly growing income.

He leaned more upon me for advice. We had been conducting a $40,000 prize contest involving daily picture puzzles and much later when I doled out large sums to the winners I remembered that he had hoped the money would help subscribers in need. An attractive little blonde of eighteen, a salesgirl in a ten-cent store, won $5,000 in cash as the main award. She looked at the check incredulously; then, with a cry of astonished triumph, embraced me and fainted dead away in my arms. When she had been revived I gave her the advice which I thought Kobler would have imparted to her with a pat on the head:

"Blondie, put it all in a good savings bank and keep away from the stock market."

One night the publisher and I attended a banquet where I was formally introduced to Arthur Brisbane. While on the *Mirror* I had never come into contact with him. The famous editor seemed like some chopped-off trunk of oak, his profile almost a straight line, extending into a double forehead. He had a face which might have been of flint, a firmly mortised jaw manipulated from thin, unsmiling lips. His steady eyes had the metallic blue of steel but as I studied him he impressed me as an old man who was trying to preserve his strength.

He greeted Kobler gruffly, almost with a touch of animosity and gave me a piercing glance.

"I know all about you," he said. "I told Mr. Hearst to hire you."

When we were back at our table, Kobler, who had flushed at the remark, whispered loudly in my ear:

"Watch him. He would like to take the *Mirror* away from me and push us both out, now that we have made a go of it."

I became interested again in the affairs of Cuba. I felt, through one of those hunches which seem to be a part of my nature, that it would be the landing place of my next "moon and sixpence" flight. Sergeant Fulgencio Batista was in control of the island Republic following a revolution which had forced President Machado into exile. Carlos Henriquez, a Cuban-American who had introduced me to Gomez, kept in touch with me. While I was in Russia he had covered the Cuban revolution for the *Mirror* and was now back in New York. One evening he telephoned me at my office in an excited and tearful voice. His cousin, Dr. Luis Henriquez had been imprisoned in a fort in Havana and was to be executed early on the following morning. He begged me to use whatever authority I had in an attempt to save the physician's life. The man under sentence of death had studied to be a doctor in New York and was known for his charitable activities among the Cuban poor.

I made a note of the emergency on the back of an envelope which I tore apart and stuffed the remaining paper with its scribbled words in my pocket. A change in editions then occupied my attention. Soon I had forgotten about the doctor who was waiting to die. Later Kobler called me to join a party at a tavern off Broadway. He sought some futile merriment to clear his mind from a growing depression. I sat down with a merry group of mixed company and had some wine. Possibly two hours went by. The publisher, as we were preparing to leave, asked me to take down a telephone number where I was to reach him. I yanked some papers from my pocket and a little white slip fell out and sailed about until it landed in a girl's lap. Before returning it to me she read the words on it with feminine curiosity.

"Luis Henriquez to be shot at sunrise," she laughed. "How quaint, these days!"

I snatched the paper from her and reached a telephone booth from which I dictated a cable to Sumner Welles, then American Ambassador to Cuba. I described the plight of the physician and urged the diplomat to intervene on the grounds that the *Mirror* was personally interested in the prisoner's welfare. The memories of this episode were later to lash me as a whip.

*   *   *   *   *

Editors described 1934 as a great circulation year, marked by disasters and bloody purges by Hitler. I wrote a large headline about the butchery by the Nazis of my little acquaintance, Dollfuss, in the Cabinet building in Vienna. Across my desk swept accounts of hurricanes, strikes, the assassination of the King of Yugoslavia and French Foreign Minister Barthou; the murder of Sergei Kirov, close friend of Stalin, which provoked the slaughter of a number of the Russians whom I had met. Now we were keeping pace with events. There was a certain satisfaction in covering news instead of uncovering it.

In the early Fall my routine was jarred by an office episode which filled me with horror until it came to a desirable conclusion. It had to do with the part Winchell played in the circumstances of Richard Bruno Hauptmann's arrest as the slayer of the Lindbergh baby and it involved me as editor of the *Mirror* in a journalistic scandal which was suppressed with difficulty through friendly authorities. Official records, which I was permitted to study, through the courtesy of the New York Police, make it possible, now, for the story to be told for the first time.

On September 10, 1934, headquarters police reporters were

confidentially informed by officers high in authority, that several of the gold certificates which were included in the Lindbergh ransom payment, had appeared in circulation in a specific territory and that an arrest might be imminent. Responsible editors in the city were told that publication of this development might drive away the man who was spending the money. Thereupon a rigid covenant was entered into by all newspapers to withhold the information in order that it might not interfere with the course of justice. The mere appearance of an item telling of such an occurrence, as Sidney B. Whipple pointed out in his authoritative book, *The Lindbergh Crime,* would have produced a stoppage in the flow of "hot" money.

After several days had passed, Winchell, in some manner, got wind of what was going on. It would have been comparatively easy for anyone working on a newspaper staff to have heard about it. Perhaps the former vaudeville hoofer felt that his gossip corner was absolved from any consideration of office pledges.

On Sunday, September 16, while the promise made to the authorities by the press was being faithfully kept, Winchell announced the facts exultingly in his radio broadcast, which happened to be on my evening off. An editor of a competitive newspaper who had tuned in on him telephoned me immediately in furious anger. I called the *Mirror* to discover that Winchell had slipped the same account into his column. I heard for the rest of the night from police officials and federal agents who were incensed over the outrage and accused me, as the editor of Winchell's outpourings, of having prevented the solution of a heinous crime. Lieutenant James Finn of the Bureau of Criminal Investigation and Inspector John A. Lyons of headquarters were appalled by the act. Finn had been working patiently on the case, guided by a map studded with pins showing the spots where the ransom gold notes were appearing. The pins were slowly forming a circle in the Bronx about the focal point from which the criminal was operating.

It happened, however, on Saturday, September 15, the day before Winchell's broadcast, that Walter Lyle, a gas station attendant, had become suspicious of a ten-dollar gold note which the driver of a Dodge sedan had passed to him to be changed and he had jotted down on the certificate itself the license number of the automobile.   This piece of vigilance was to send the murderer to his doom.

As the banks were then closed, Lyle did not deposit the bill until the following Monday, September 17, when a bank teller verified the fact that the certificate was part of the ransom money.   It was fortunate for justice that Hauptmann was not one of Winchell's radio listeners, nor a reader of his column which appeared on that day.   Otherwise the murderer, who had been resourceful enough to creep into this country illegally, would have been driven to cover and might have escaped.

I was so distraught over this affair that I had no sleep for forty-eight hours.   To my relief, on September 18, the slayer was trapped with $13,750 of the Lindbergh gold notes through his license number.

In the face of these facts Winchell attempted to claim full credit for solving the crime.   He went to the station house where the prisoner was being questioned and was roughly ejected by police officers.   He was then attempting to obtain, according to detectives who stopped his operations, an admission from the gas station attendant that the Sunday night broadcast and the item in the Monday column had made him suspicious of the gold certificate to the point of taking down the license numbers of Hauptmann's car.   The salesman, of course, could not make such a statement, as he had received the incriminating bill and had noted down the vital license clue the day before Winchell had blurted out his gossip.

The Broadway peeper had almost destroyed our most valuable news source, which was the police department.   The matter was patched up but not forgotten by the authorities and but for the diplomacy of Robert Barke, the dean of police reporters who had covered headquarters for twenty years the *Mirror* would have been barred from any further official information on the Lindbergh tragedy.   I received from J. Edgar Hoover, chief of the Federal Bureau of Investigation, a letter thanking me for having withheld from print information which might have interfered with the course of justice in the case.

Kobler seemed to be strangely indifferent over this upheaval about which I wrote a detailed report for the management.   Joe Connolly, whose power was increasing in the Hearst organization, consulted with us and pointed out that it would soon have to be decided whether Winchell's actions were beyond the control of the *Mirror,* itself. After Connolly had left, the publisher put his face in his hands and slumped over his desk.

"There are greater troubles than this," he mumbled.

Late in October of that year the cause of Kobler's dejection suddenly became clear. One evening he entered my office with a dragging step and sank heavily in my dilapidated Queen Anne chair. His cane clattered to the floor from nerveless hands. There was an expression of agony in his face which made me stop my work. He was fifty-eight but he might have been taken for a man of three score and ten.

"I've lost the paper," he said. His eyes, sometimes rheumy, were now moist with tears. "Hearst has turned the *Mirror* over to Brisbane and he's taking charge of it tomorrow. He will pull all the plants of our little garden out by the roots. That's our reward for hard work. Life is a game of marked cards."

He explained some of the circumstances of his troubles. Upon becoming publisher and ostensibly owner, he had given Hearst a note for $1,300,000 in part payment for the *Mirror's* stock and assumed liabilities of $1,000,000 of the corporation formerly owning the paper.

"It's the mortgage that Hearst talked about at Sands Point," he continued. "I was too optimistic about the future. I really thought at one time that a man's safety depended upon his borrowing capacity. A lot of people thought that way. We were all millionaires on paper. But the money was there to borrow. The banks were pushing it in your face. I put up a Park Avenue building of fifteen stories with apartments to be rented for $25,000 and $40,000 a year. Those days are over for everybody. We didn't know when to stop. You know what happened to me. There were plenty in this organization who saw to it that the paper's mortgage was called when my troubles began. Past performances mean nothing. I've lost the paper—but I'm not through yet."

He gave me a check as part of a considerable sum he owed me. Before the Wall Street crash he had asked me for $5,000 of my $10,000 Hearst bonus which, he said, would install me on the ground floor of a project whose aim was to confine the vitamins of cod liver oil into tablets. When the ground floor went down and I landed in the cellar of this proposition, Kobler, who had descended with me, told me my money would be returned.

He braced himself to go through my door for the last time. He would not shake hands. "This is no parting," he said, his voice choking. "We're going to be closer than ever on some other paper, maybe. We might give Hearst a good fight."

He waited until his eyes were dry, put his chin up and walked into the city room to say good-by to the employees.

"Good luck to you all," he called out, "and don't work too hard. It doesn't always pay."

BOOK IV

THE GREAT ILLUMINIST

CHAPTER I

THE news of Brisbane's invasion of the *Mirror* created among
its toilers an atmosphere of consternation and drove some of
the old timers on the staff to more than their usual potations.
We were steeped in the legends of this Man of Momentum,
of his dictaphones in the staterooms of his trains, in airplanes,
in his motor cars, on ferryboats, even by the side of his bed,
his thoughts constantly flowing. In half an hour he could
dictate two columns of editorials. Before starting a vacation
he dictated thirty-nine editorials in three hours. His words
reached 30,000,000 readers daily. His brain, if examined, a
member of the National Academy of Science had reported,
might reveal six separate dynamos of mental impulse in his
cerebral cortex. This, one professor had said, was indicated
by the editor's capacity for work.

Some of us had heard of the editor's father, Albert Brisbane, a man of unusual integrity and decided ideas; a disciple
of Charles Fourier, famous Utopian Socialist of the time of
Ralph Waldo Emerson. The elder Brisbane had even led,
with a sort of delicate Communism, a band of followers in a
movement which launched a settlement for the pursuit of
civilized happiness. It was known as the Brook Farm Colony
and was one of the first Fourier experiments in socialized living. Albert Brisbane had met Karl Marx and Fourier and
most of the famous radicals of Europe and pondered the
thoughts which were later to shake the world to its foundations.

This background became interesting when compared with
the philosophies of Brisbane the Younger. In his twenties
he had promised to become an independent leader of American
liberal thought. Some remembered crusades of an almost
radical nature which he had conducted. But this was in the
back alleys of time, and discussion of such history was frowned
upon. Now, the famous editor said of his father: "I am paid
for doing badly what he did well. I am paid the largest salary
of any editor in the world!"

Arthur Brisbane's secretaries had no time for thoughts on socialized living, assuming that such vagaries crossed their minds. The editor did the thinking. Each modicum, each granule of his reflections had to be transferred to paper immediately from the wax cylinders of his dictaphones. This anxious routine in the *Mirror* office was supervised by Mrs. Sylvia Jerman, a tall, light-haired, angular person of questioning eyes in a long but attractive face with an emphatic chin. Sometimes she flashed a disarming smile. She spoke in a low-pitched voice and went about silently on flat heels. Her awe-struck loyalty to Brisbane amounted to Oriental fanaticism. Her husband, Paul, who joined this caravansary soon afterward, was more contemplative. He was an unemployed architect and had taken the job of assistant secretary, not only in a spirit of adventure under the great man but because money was need at home for the children. He was small and spare, his eyes alert in a thin, Roman-nosed countenance. He had a tender manner and a delicate discrimination of social and artistic values. Later when he tried to reconcile the Fourier philosophies of Brisbane's father with the sweat-shop hum of the wax records we would go out together to a near-by bar for a long drink.

Mrs. Jerman had been about our building before Brisbane moved in, presumably to give him a report of the prevailing atmosphere. I received a reassuring little letter from her.

"I never saw a paper so exciting as yours," she wrote. "Now I see what they should be like. The place positively reeks of enthusiasm and progress. You have made a permanent convert."

For some reason our art department seemed to reflect the greatest concern of the establishment over Brisbane's arrival. Macauley, coming in with his daily cartoon, was full of melancholy predictions. These had pushed John Governale, the art director, a Latin of sad demeanor, into a state of nervousness close to panic, and while the rumors of shake-ups were reaching a climax he hurried to my office with a piece of strategy.

"From what I hear," Governale said, wiping his forehead, "he's a holy terror; one of the holiest. Macauley says the first thing Brisbane is going to do is to call for two full pages of prehistoric monsters, like the stegosaurus that romped around millions of years ago. There isn't a stegosaurus in the shop. We've got to get a cargo of those things."

I lost no time in acting on this suggestion, and within a few minutes, half of the day office staff, led by Macauley, was rushed out by Clarke, the city editor, to forage the libraries, the Museum of Natural History, and universities for photographs of mounted specimens and drawings of these forgotten creatures. Clarke indicated a comforting familiarity with the crisis by shouting an injunction to his men as he herded them to the elevators.

"If you want to hang on to your jobs," he cried, "don't come back without a brontosaurus. It was eighty feet long, weighed fifteen tons and its brain only weighed two ounces. That's the first thing Brisbane will go for!"

The little city editor was equal to almost any emergency on a Hearst paper. He was typical of the tabloid city-room boss of the period. He directed a staff of human shock-absorbers who went through their work like anti-aircraft gunners under a bombing raid. Newspaper work to him was something like a game of "cops and robbers" and he knew the history, from coast to coast, of every racketeer whose name appeared in print. Clarke never hesitated to carry out my crusades against the "mob." I had sent him to Philadelphia to interview Al Capone, when the gang leader was imprisoned there and he had no trouble in obtaining an audience. He returned with an amazing story of the gang czar's activities in jail, from which he operated his enterprises over five telephones by long-distance calls.

Brisbane lost no time in calling a conference in my office with my nervous field marshals. My desk, by that time, was covered with the trophies of Clarke's raids on the museums. Nothing herpetological, mammalogical, ichthyological, amphibiological or even ornithological had been ignored. Topping the pictorial pile was the brontosaurus which in its day, a librarian had assured us, was visible for thirty-five miles in all directions. Then came the duckbill trachodon and the *tyrannosaurus rex* which was about to tangle tooth and claw with his pet hate, the armored tricerotops, apparently both fast on their feet. The thunder reptile was next in line, with its vast family of dinosaurs; the diplodocus and others too numerous to mention.

In assembling this deposit a photograph of a disk-mouthed beauty from the Lake Chad tribes, her lips stretched as big as pie plates, had slipped in by error and it was the first to catch Brisbane's eye. He snatched it up and burrowed into the mound.

"Quite a collection," he said. "How did you happen to round it all up?"

"Some of the boys thought it might come in handy," I replied, dryly.

He grunted and continued a minute examination, selecting many specimens. Governale's stegosaurus was flung contemptuously into the waste basket, being, unfortunately, just a little fellow, only the size of an overgrown elephant with a double row of bony plates along his back. Clarke, meanwhile, watched with satisfaction as Brisbane grabbed the brontosaurus.

"Those things would certainly add to our traffic problem today," Clarke commented, as the separation came to an end.

"No levity," Brisbane said testily. "I'll see you all tomorrow." And with an armful of specimens he hurried out and slammed the door.

"Well, I guess we can safely go to press without the brontosaurus tonight," Clarke added. "But it's begun, boys; it's begun!"

We were left in no uncertainty as to what Brisbania was all about. The new master announced to the press associations that he had taken the paper over, and hinted at a strange alchemy which would draw new readers by the hundreds of thousands. "This paper appeals to an age of condensation and hurry," he wrote, "and, published within reach of twenty million population, it intends to include among its readers a fair share of that population."

Brisbane's entourage included his own cartoonists, and two of them, known as Bressler and Packer, seized a corner of Governale's parapet and cartoons began to flow from their slanting tables as though produced on a conveyor belt. These feverish penmen, rubbing elbows in a state of mutual jealousy, had reduced the famous editor's formula to the science of the assembly line. Rough sketches were dashed off and placed in a pile for inspection. A sure-fire subject would be finished in ink, to which Brisbane added his aphorisms. When I visited the artists during their first day of the new regime each was finishing strikingly similar drawings showing a worried Uncle Sam sitting in a little rowboat, carrying the legend, "U. S. Navy" over which, bristling with guns, towered a huge battleship labeled "Japan."

"He'll grab that one," said Bressler. He was a jumpy little man of aggressive countenance. "Packer is making his battleship bigger. We don't take any chances. We've been running out of stock on this subject lately. They're always good this time of year. We're through with the rich dowagers riding with poodles in their limousines at Palm Beach while starving mothers shiver in the North."

Macauley's drawings of solid craftsmanship were shunted along the rusty spur track of oblivion. Brisbane had selected one or two which were too good to dismiss and virtually created a scene when he rejected a drawing of Columbia, pictured as a tall female reassuring Uncle Sam. "This," he said, "looks rather as though Columbia were arresting an old man for disorderly conduct." The remark had mortified the veteran cartoonist who was putting into his product a final flare of brilliancy.

"Brisbane never forgave me for a drawing I made of Hearst years ago when I was working for Pulitzer," Macauley said. "My slogan will have to be, 'resign or be resigned,' but I'll take it standing up. I'll keep at it until they count me out."

The vast output of editorial ideas known as Brisbania which was fed to 30,000,000 readers a day did not entirely gush from the editor's brain. He had his own system of *aide memoire* which speeded his mind. He scanned scores of foreign periodicals, ripping out pages of pictures: Charles Laughton as a Cornish Jekyll and Hyde from the London *Sketch;* Tutankhamen's 3,000-year-old trumpets, from the *Illustrated London News;* birds and mammals from Netherlands Guiana. These were appropriated bodily and rushed to the photoengraving shop for such editorials as "Study This Face!" or, (referring to the trumpets) "How Would *This* Sound on the Radio?" Meanwhile, artists working in a polished, familiar groove, deluged the dictaphone orator with platitudinous ideas of their own. All this spurred the wax cylinders.

Occasionally, a cartoonist such as Winsor McCay, noted for his *Dreams of the Rarebit Fiend* of years gone by, drew, with unerring impulse, a half-page picture of a ball of fire labeled "The Sun," which stretched huge hairy paws grasping little white pills over which appeared the names of the planets, and their distances in millions of miles from the flaming furnace. To this creation would be added a half page of words after being poured in Brisbane's rasping voice from the wax cylinders into the numbed ears of weary typists who conveyed the intelligence to paper. Never in the history of journalism had the dictaphone taken such a beating.

"Children and other primitive minds do not grasp abstract ideas," said the Voice. "Tell your children: 'The big light that you see in the picture is the sun. It is one million times as big as the earth on which you live. The sun turns round and round, like a wheel, and you go around the sun like a whirling ball.'

"It will stimulate the imagination of your children to know that the earth whirls around the sun more than one million five hundred thousand miles a day. This will make a child think about something more important than baseball. Read to your children *The Universe Around Us* by Sir James Jeans and remember that if the earth and the planets should fall into the sun all would melt and disappear, *and you with it!*"

After a sufficient amount of these dismal speculations had been added to frighten the average child into idiocy, Brisbane wrote the headline:

"Here We Live! Whither Are We Going With the Sun?"

If this concoction did not fill the page, canned material which Brisbane was constantly preserving would be inserted in the remaining space, such as, "Why Hindus Wiggle the Big Toe." Then the whole matter was locked up in the front-page form of the "educational section" of the Sunday *American* and printed by the millions.

To those unfamiliar with Brisbane's dictation, listening for the first time to the wax records repeating his words may have simulated the thrill of hearing an unintelligible language in an African jungle. Stenographers who could not get used to it were packed off. He indicated explicitly in each sentence all punctuation marks, capital letters, full stops and go ahead signals. He would shout "Caps," before a capital letter.

"Uncaps" was the warning to decapitalize and proceed with small letters.

For instance, it was an ordinary experience for a stenographer to attach the earphones to her head, sit before her typewriter and hear:

"All caps what if every church uncaps next caps Sunday uncaps should post a placard on its doors saying colon quotes caps these doors will be closed uncaps and our way of worshipping caps God uncaps will be forbidden question mark uncaps unquote."

After a hard day at this sort of thing Brisbane had been asked to address a banquet of utility magnates. In preoccupied fashion he talked as though he were dictating into his machine. Those not acquainted with his office manners were left speechless when he began to address them as follows:

"All caps gentlemen uncaps colon a great writer named caps Sir James Barrie uncaps has said that quotes life is a lesson in humility unquotes period."

A secretary jerked the editor's sleeve, reminding him he was not dictating and the speech reverted to understandable English.

At times, with the irritability of advancing years, Brisbane would launch into a defense of old men. When Vice-President Garner, who was Speaker of the House, handed over the gavel of the Speakership to the late Henry T. Rainey, Brisbane's dictaphones rasped as follows:

"The interesting fact about these individuals is that they are TWO OLD MEN. Mr. Garner is past sixty. Mr. Rainey is past seventy. The men that won the World War—Clemenceau and Lloyd George—were old men. Clemenceau was past eighty. Marshal Foch who led the Allies to victory was an old man. Von Hindenburg became President of the German Republic when past eighty. Hitler is a youngster, confident of his power to dictate to the people of Germany. Perhaps he will succeed. Let that encourage men that have passed fifty without losing ambition."

Brisbane pigeonholed his editorials about the Sermon on the Mount and the blessings of Christianity when the European dictators asserted themselves. He praised Mussolini for his massacre of the Ethiopians. Power, no matter how attained, fascinated him. In one of these Ethiopian fulminations, he added the following, perhaps for his own personal consolation: "Wise is he who knows the winning side, if his conscience keeps quiet."

Although he gave Hitler an occasional dusting of the jacket, Brisbane's opinions of the Dictator were written with interesting private reservations. He admired the upstart's audacity and believed that history justified cruelty, although, as he pointed out at the luncheon table, "such thoughts in print would not be popular with our Jewish population." He was impressed with the murderous Nazi purge of the previous summer. "On this occasion," he wrote to me in a memorandum, "Hitler did some shooting that needed to be done. There is something admirably decisive about the man. He shot men who were indulging in practices that were just as well interrupted. That was the way to handle it."

Younger members of the staff remained in a state of hypnotized wonderment in the presence of the editor who boasted openly that from a cub reporter he had risen to $260,000 a year. He had formed the habit of telling his fabulous salary to strangers within a few minutes of their introduction. As a young editor he had written: "A man wastes his soul who devotes its forces only to accumulating wealth." Now he wrote that "it is wise to accumulate money. If money were divided among many hands you couldn't have the magnificent things that Mr. Rockefeller has built."

He loved money and made no bones of the fact, glorified it; and no personal anecdotes of his repertoire were told with greater gusto than those which dealt with his real-estate profits. He regaled me with one of them after we had published a story and picture of an art exhibit held at the Ritz Tower apartment hotel which, when he had built it in 1926, was the tallest residential building in Manhattan. Clarke, in his effort to please the Great Mind had overreached his *savoir-faire* in announcing to our readers that this stony spear of achievement was the property of the new head of the *Mirror*. The bombshell broke over my head as soon as Brisbane saw the paper but he cooled off to tell me the story of the Tower deal with a certain physical pleasure.

"In the first place," he said, "we will not help our circulation by chasing art exhibits. We'll leave those things to your friend Kobler who now has more time to be a connoisseur of

the artistic refinements of life. I'm not too old to appreciate
the purpose behind your story. You thought it would please
me because you think I own the Ritz Tower."

He uttered an incredulous laugh and slapped his thigh.

"Well," he shouted, "I don't own the Ritz Tower. I knew
the crash was coming two years after I had put that building up
and I advised Mr. Hearst by letters and telegrams to dispose
of his properties before the catastrophe. He would wire back:
'Arthur, don't frighten me; Arthur don't scare me! Things
will never be as bad as that. Real estate is the best thing to
own.' "

He laughed again, this time with an approach to real mirth.

"So I went to see Mr. Hearst and I said, 'If you think real
estate is so good, I'll sell you the Ritz Tower,' and by God,
he bought it, and you know what happened after that! He
had to keep that thing going for a time at a loss of damned
near $125,000 a month!"

We never mentioned his real-estate transactions again, but
they occupied many of his waking hours. It was about this
time that Hearst, laughingly discussing his chief editor's business ventures, had remarked: "Arthur comes to me all the
time with some wonderful plan to make money, but when I
examine it, I find the profits are to be divided ninety percent
for Arthur and ten percent for me."

Brisbane still had on his hands a number of metropolitan
buildings which he had not disposed of and they began to have
a serious effect on our routine. During a strike of elevator
operators I listened to his tirades as if I had been personally
responsible for the walkout. He asked me to interview the
District Attorney and the Mayor as to the rights of owners of
buildings.

"These strikers will stop at nothing," he raged. "I have
in mind the sabotage that will follow, the cutting off of heat
from apartment houses and office buildings forcibly; the
dangerous interference with the workings of all elevators.
Have the Mayor and the District Attorney tell us that if these
people invade our premises we can have them arrested for
burglary. We can send them to Sing Sing!"

One of his innovations, soon after moving into the *Mirror*
was a long block of type which he boxed over the masthead of
the front page, starting off with two words: "Editor Speak-

ing." This gave him an opportunity for some singular last-
minute blasts before we went to press. Here he hammered
away at his pet prejudices, high real-estate taxes, his hatred of
dogs. Here he flashed his nostrums and social antidotes, constantly absorbed by new theories which he often adopted and
set forth as his own. One which caught the Mayor's eye and
made him wonder whether a campaign was about to be launched
against him ran as follows:

"Dear Mayor La Guardia: Would you like to buy for
$50,000 a good building and lot in New York's business
centre, two doors from Fifth Avenue, assessed and taxed by
the city at $135,000? That sounds like a bargain, doesn't it?
The *Mirror* can offer you many such in Manhattan real estate.
How long can that last without New York taking over half of
Manhattan Island's real estate? This is a friendly question.
But it *IS* your problem."

One day, the editor stopped all operations in the "wax
works," as Clarke now described Brisbane's sanctum, by chasing out two secretaries to verify the fact that brooms in one of
his buildings had been worn down to stumps before the apartment superintendent could buy more. Waste was his chief
abomination. He would trim a photograph down with a
pair of scissors until legs, and sometimes ears, were snipped
off, to reduce the size of an engraving and save on its costs.
He preached on the subject of waste. The *Herald Tribune,*
in reviewing his life later, described his office at the *American*
as an example of this tendency to hoard. It was packed full
of old chairs, tables, desks, stoves, wastepaper baskets, book-
cases and bird cages which he had accumulated during fifty
years in the newspaper business. At meal times, this hatred
of waste manifested itself curiously, according to his obituaries.
When dining at fine restaurants and hotels he often found himself unable to finish all the food on his plate. On such occasions he summoned the waiter and asked him if the left-over
morsels would be wasted. If the waiter said that the odds
and ends of food would be given to the dog pound or some
other worthy charity, Brisbane would permit his plate to
be removed. But if the waiter replied that the food was headed
for the garbage pail Brisbane cleaned his plate to the last drip
of gravy.

The editor's abhorrence of waste had not helped matters

financial in the *Mirror's* affairs. Upon his arrival he had put himself down on our payroll for an additional $1,000 a week and a bonus of ten percent of the net revenue. This self-crowning act was accepted as a last straw of affliction by our counting room from which, at times, moans of anguish were heard. A clamor immediately was set up for a reduction in general expenses, led by Brisbane himself who was all over the building like a beagle stirring up "hell-knows-what-all," a descriptive phrase used by Robert H. Johnson, our gray-haired, harassed efficiency expert. Johnson was the typical cost-cutter of modern business. Such valuable men may be found in every organization, engrossed in the magic of subtraction to turn a loss into a profit. Ideas, such as red stickers which remind you to turn out your light when you leave your desk, come from their brains. One of them even had invented a toilet-paper machine which sliced off what was conservatively considered the right proportion of paper, and probably would have clipped your fingers right off, if you had taken advantage of it. Johnson had the distinction of being one of the first efficiency men to make use of the "perpetual office memo envelope" which had to be used over and over again until, finally, it lay in your hand like a dead fish, but it saved money.

The dreaded plagues of cost-cutting which swept over the Hearst empire struck the editorial departments periodically with devastating effects. In these crises I admired Johnson's fairness. Under the present onslaught I was ordered to trim the payroll by $1,500 a week, which meant the decapitation of many loyal heads. Postponement of this slaughter involved days of interminable arguments, recriminations, acid conferences from which one emerged in poisoned exhaustion. The American Newspaper Guild was not then in operation, although there were rumblings of such a protective movement which was looked upon by Brisbane as a symptom of anarchy.

For days the editor read our daily fiction stories, then criticized them brutally. He wanted to know how many persons I employed to grind them out. He was amazed when I informed him that they were written entirely by one individual, a tireless little man named Lewis Allen Browne, about sixty years of age, whom I had brought over from the *Graphic*. He performed the incredible task of turning out for the *Mirror* a daily short story of 2,500 words, a daily detective mystery of

1,000 words, and daily installments of 3,500 words for a monthly serial certain to leave the reader in suspense each morning, and which he described as "cliff-hangers." He threw in, for good measure, a complete novelette for the Sunday edition. He wrote incessantly on three typewriters, jumping desperately from one to the other, his list of characters pasted up on the wall in front of him. This enslavement brought him $150 a week. He died two years later.

"That's an output of about 60,000 words a week," Brisbane grunted. "I've done better than that at times. But I'll let him alone. I think he's earning his money."

The editor now poked into every corner, stirring workers into maddening eruptions. The burden of his lamentations seemed to be that a tabloid did not require so many people because it was a small paper.

"When I look into the city room," he grumbled, "during the few hours when we are busy I see thirty or forty persons trying to do something. What are they all doing? Although this may not mean anything to you, I only see a handful with blue eyes. The rest look like a lot of white-collared butterballs. It annoys many when I talk about blue eyes but any man who ever amounted to a damn in history had them, or gray eyes, even men from dark races, like Napoleon from Corsica, Caesar from Rome. Here is a short list: Washington, Jefferson, Lincoln, Roosevelt, Edison, Henry Ford. Look up the others."

Winchell, during these days of excitement, emerged from his rabbit warren, now somewhere in the bowels of the building where he stirred his brew of gossip, and tagged Brisbane around the floor. It was difficult to decide which of the two bragged the most about his salary. In this respect, the Broadway bard whose thin hair was turning gray, had something to talk about. The *Mirror* was paying him $1,200 a week and fifty per cent of the money from the syndication of his column, amounting to some $750 a week. He was reported to be making $5,000 a week from his weekly radio talk. Out of this he paid the state and federal governments in taxes around fifty percent which left him an income of approximately $185,000 a year. "Even two Presidents of the United States couldn't earn that working at the same time," he said.

He saw an advantage in trying to become familiar with

Brisbane and although he had no importance in the editor's life he soon became an authority on the subject. Brisbane read Winchell's column as a painful duty and pink slips dropped on my desk daily warning me to watch the pitiless pillar more closely. My secretary had to start a separate file of these complaints.

"I don't understand a word of his jargon," Brisbane told me. "It is something that has caught hold of our modern degeneration, as Mr. Hearst calls it, and Winchell is cashing in on it while it lasts. I'm always worried for fear he will land us into a pile of trouble. He annoys me. There's that feverish restlessness of an excited mind about him that interrupts my work when he pops into my office. Yesterday he pulled out a bagful of clippings from his pockets, things people were writing about him and he wanted me to read them! Does he think we're working for him?"

Winchell and I carried on our business intercourse by crackling notes whose contents had long since ceased to shock the frozen-faced secretaries who exchanged them from our offices. Brisbane called this hostility regrettable and blamed my French ancestry. He had occasion, almost immediately, to taste some of the vitriol I had diluted for eleven years from Winchell's pen when the gossiper, piqued by a remark Mrs. Roosevelt had made about his type of journalism, slipped into his column a gibe about her teeth. Between Brisbane, Winchell and the new cartoonists, added cares besieged me and the thrust at the First Lady had gone by my nose. Brisbane was in a rage about the incident as the secretary of the Brewers' Board of Trade had telephoned that the brewers, who believed that Roosevelt had put them back into business, were incensed at the insult, demanded an apology and planned to act upon the slur at their next meeting. There were many repercussions from this item as Winchell's column was widely syndicated.

"We'll get four alert editors and two lawyers to read his column, if necessary," Brisbane bellowed. "How can we tell what he's going to do next? What will Roosevelt say the next time I see him at the White House, with that unpardonable ridicule printed all over the country? That fellow Winchell is a barrel of copperheads. But I notice his eyes are blue."

"Blue and hard," I added.

Explosive incidents now occurred with progressive inten-

sity as Brisbane included Winchell's column as part of his reading of the day. Unfortunately he read it after it was in print
when it was too late to do anything about it but roar at me
over the telephone. Those in authority who opened the paper
in fear and trembling, when Winchell's deposit of hot lava appeared from the press, recoiled from the extremity of editing
his copy personally. That was my job and after more than a
decade of it these shells of wrath bounced from my dugout
like blunted missiles on armorplate and left me in a state of
Hindu composure. Editing Winchell had developed in me a
philosophical imperturbability which, otherwise, my nervous
make-up might never have acquired. After the task was done,
one washed one's hands of it, with a feeling of renunciation, a
quietude of the soul. All the mean-spirited distractions of life
glided away in the face of serenity.

Some of these Winchell episodes, constantly adding to Brisbane's paroxysms of fury, were side-splitting to the rest of us.
But one had to keep a solemn face. The Baron always cracked
the jokes. Clarke frequently climbed to the roof of the building where he could recover from recurring convulsions of
laughter. Like an imp, the perverse Winchell, at this time,
seemed to go out of his way to take pot shots at our advertisers. This sharp-shooting was so subtly done that it got by.
As the result of some private argument with the I. Miller Shoe
Company, a popular store, he had penned an item that described its salesmen as having invented the slogan: "The Shoe
Must Go On!" Brisbane himself had caught that one, like a
shortstop grabbing a sizzling line drive out of the air, as we
were closing the last form.

The next day Winchell had announced that the motion picture *Becky Sharpe* was not technicolor. This cost us a full
page of advertising. He had also printed the fact that his wife
was to have a baby; and Macy's department store advertisements, which appeared regularly next to his column had pointed
a bargain display directly at him in the line of necessities for
"blessed events." Winchell imperiously notified a high Macy
executive, that a suit would follow a repetition of such shenanigans which were beneath the dignity of the gossip columnist.

Brisbane's anger was beyond description. "Who in hell
does he think he is?" he demanded. "I'll fix his wagon for

him! I'll send him to cover an execution! I understand his stomach can't stand it!"

Such resolutions, however, were never served on Winchell over my head. High executives of the Hearst management whose incomes were below Winchell's, squirmed at his items, and read everything he wrote with apprehension but lacked the courage to restrain him. I received many subterranean orders to curb him from the tremulous who made sure their names would not be known to him. Brisbane had adopted that attitude, as Kobler had before him. There was something about Winchell that people feared. By implication, without even the use of a name, he could make the gullible quake and writhe and even suffer. All this he justified as fearless duty. "I let him have it today," he remarked. "He had it coming to him." To those who were stupefied by his outpourings, occasional hints in his column of his Ogpu index summoned to memory forgotten peccadillos, early deviations from rectitude. The bland, hypocritical appeasers who held me to the task of keeping Winchell in leash pulled his stinging barbs from their hides and saw to it that he would never identify their hands, ever ready to plant the knives in his back. Such thoughts may have turned over in his mind as he cruised homeward cautiously with his automatics and his armed bodyguards in his car whose special radio set was tuned in on police calls.

Brisbane secretly admired Winchell because of the money he was raking in from Hearst. The gossiper's bombast at times made the editor snicker. But most of what he read from Winchell's pen, aside from pea-shooter darts at advertisers, on which he pounced readily, was meaningless scrabble, gibberish claptrap that he feared might reduce the person who read it to some form of imbecility. "Shakespeare described it," he said. " 'A tale told by an idiot, full of sound and fury, signifying nothing.' " He said he read Swift as an antidote after reading Winchell's column.

To Brisbane, Broadway seemed to be an unexplored jungle where roisterers wasted their substance. His ignorance of that thoroughfare was illustrated in a memorandum in which he inquired whether the French Casino was really located in Paris or New York. The place was a brash Broadway night club whose pictures of partly nude females were being exploited by press agents and appeared in the papers.

From the time of my association with Brisbane until our relations were severed, the idea of using the mind to pile up money, and power with it, dominated him. Men who acquired fortunes fascinated him. How had they accumulated it? On two occasions he had asked me to tell him the story of Winchell's beginnings and his salary of one hundred dollars a week and commissions when I had put him on his first newspaper payroll in 1924. "That money came fast to him," he said, anxiously shaking his head. "Maybe too fast."

Coming into my office one afternoon with a sheaf of editorials he found me sitting at a desk piled high with work.

"Do you ever sit back and put your feet up on the desk?" he asked. I steeled myself for some caustic dictum, which only the hidden humors of his mind could reveal. The setting sun playing on his chiseled face produced shadows that looked like those on a negative held up to the light.

As usual he answered his own question.

"John D. Rockefeller once walked in on Walter Teagle. I assume you know who he is—head of Standard Oil of New Jersey. He found Teagle swamped the way you are. And Rockefeller said: 'I want to see my managers, their desks cleared, and their feet on the desks, studying how to make more money for Standard Oil.' Teagle took the hint."

He added his fistful of editorials to my growing mountain of toil, twinkled a boiled eye and wheeled out.

Brisbane interested me as some sort of fictional character in a strange world. Men who worked with him called him the Great Anachronism. I tried to understand him. I knew that on the Hearst papers a man was certainly not expected to write always what he believed, but rather to produce, even with enthusiasm, what he knew to be futile, perhaps harmless and, on some occasions, false. Hearst paid well for this type of weather-vane thinking. You changed your editorial mind as Hearst changed his, like throwing off an old hat. Brisbane had done it for a long time for $260,000 a year. No other faculty than the memory seemed to be necessary for this type of success. Least of all was any use made of reason, either analytic or synthetic.

The editor was beginning to remark to me, with growing irritation:

"You reason too damn much."

One day I told him I reasoned because I had read some of the greatest books ever written through his recommendation in his early columns. He looked at me silently and then invited me to lunch. At the table I felt that he apprehended the growing rebellion in my mind. We had, at that time, a memorable talk at Pietro's which was a few doors from the *Mirror* building. I noted down the conversation later at my office.

"Exactly what is your ancestry?" he asked, pouring out for each of us a glass of claret.

I told him I came from old French-Canadian stock and that my grandmother was Irish from County Cork.

"That may account for it," he said. "One side wants to drink and the other side wants to argue!"

He burst into a high laugh and drank part of his claret. "Let's have a good argument," he said.

"There is nothing wrong in a sincere conflict of thought," I countered. "You have often advocated it in your own editorials. I learned through you years ago Plato's description of the men in a cave and the trial and death of Socrates. I argue for a thing when I believe in it and I can also respect a sincere opponent."

He seemed to study me with a growing interest and his face screwed up as though he suddenly remembered a mean action which had not tortured him when he committed it but which bit into him now. The remembrance of such an act never dies, as I have found out.

He began to thrust and parry, to sound me out.

"Who in your opinion was the greatest man that ever lived?"

"Jesus Christ," I replied.

His face softened. "That's where we disagree," he said, pushing aside his glass. "The greatest man that ever lived was Nero. He had the courage of his convictions and used the ignorant rabble to achieve his own ends. I know you are bursting to tell me that he had a criminal mind and that he trampled under foot all respect for natural law and human obligations, but who hasn't in this world, to accomplish anything to make him dominate in history? Even Plato urged his wise men to abandon the serene life of contemplation for the turmoil of practical affairs. Where would this world be if we had all followed Christ's teachings to the letter? 'Sell what thou hast and give to the poor,' for instance. You will find

out, if you want to make any money, that it is not always wise
to be disturbed by what we call evil, though its existence must
be admitted. Without using some of it some of our great
people would never have gotten ahead. That's why I think
Nero was a misunderstood man.

"And as for Christ, let me tell you something about HIM.
I don't profess to know what it is like to believe in something
to the point of being prepared to be killed for it. That must
be quite an experience. Such martyrs are the trouble makers
of this world.

"Christ was an agitator. The Roman provinces were becoming increasingly disturbed by men of His type but they
treated them for a while as we do here, letting them shout to a
rabble from a soap box, so long as they do not upset the Government. The Roman power was stern but permitted a good
deal of liberty. The governors allowed everything up to the
point where they thought it necessary to be severe. It was
Pilate's misfortune that he had Christ on his hands and if he
had not turned Him over to the mob he would have lost his job
as governor for failing to maintain order."

He made a movement of his large, square, thick-fingered
hands, rubbing them together, washing them, then shaking off
imaginary drops.

"Pilate had to set an example. He held duty above the
desires of his own conscience. He knew that conscience was
cowardice, and we've been clawing each other about that ever
since. I think it was one of your own race, who wasn't dominated by the church who said that the sufferings of the innocent
atone for nothing and only add one evil to another."

He spoke nervously, apparently irritated by his own words,
almost alarmed, as if the sentences had mysteriously wrapped
themselves around a talking cylinder to slip into millions of
Sunday pages and mock the innumerable pictures he had printed
of Christ on Christmas Days.

There had been similar conversations between us but this
time I sensed a warning, more than a pointed implication, more
than vaguely threatening language. I was to think as he did,
so long as I had charge of the printed word going through a
Hearst press.

The editor lumbered into my office later with a question
which seemed like a personal accusation:

"What do you propose to do about circulation?"

CHAPTER II

THE *Mirror* was then selling more than 600,000 copies a day. This was unsatisfactory to Brisbane who believed that New York was the hub of a wheel whose spokes reached out to 20,000,000 people. Our paper, he felt, was entitled to the pennies of one and a half million of that population at least. He referred to the success of Captain Patterson and his *Daily News*. What did he have in brains that we did not possess? Hearst's rejection of the tabloid idea when it was presented to him by George de Utassy, years before Patterson had stormed the field with his new journalism, was dead history now. And the shrewd Patterson had hemmed us into a pocket from which we would never fight our way to our first daily million. This I knew from bitter, hard-headed experience and I bore with Brisbane, the *vieux lion fatigué*, when he went back to the Spanish War to recall the circulation records he had broken on the *Journal*. His eyes would flash as he stormed up and down the room, like a destroyer at sea, belching a broadside. "By God, sir, where the hell were we getting the war news in 1898? I read it off the bulletin boards of the papers that could pay for it, with my binoculars and then dished it up to the people in better fashion than my competitors could present it! People were sitting on the curbstones reading it! A million was nothing. We can do it again!" He smashed a massive fist on my desk. "By God, if they want slush today, they're going to get it!"

It was inevitable that the "slush" should come down on my head like a fallen plaster ceiling from such fireworks of desperation. This time, the idea was love and marriage. That had never failed. The *Journal* had imprisoned hundreds of thousands into its camp with love and marriage after the Spanish War had unfortunately come to an end. Brisbane said he would bring Mrs. Marie Manning Gasch, the original Beatrice Fairfax, to New York to do what she did for the *Journal* at the turn of the century. Love and marriage worked then, and, by God, it would now. Nell Brinkley, of bygone fame, was cruelly routed out of well-earned retirement with a young husband to do a half-page drawing a day. Beatrice Fairfax required a full page for the love project which I was ordered to set aside immediately. Brisbane himself sounded the keynote: "Get married, have a baby and buy a car!"

Mrs. Gasch bounced in from Washington within twenty-four hours, entering my office with the step of a grenadier. She was a big-boned massive woman with an assertive jaw, an ageless sort of person, who thought she knew the younger "degeneration," and with more humor in the twinkle of her flashing eyes than Brisbane had acquired in seventy years.

The gathering took place before my desk where the editor and I were untangling ourselves from a wrestling conference of futile ideas.

"Well, here I am, Nero," said Beatrice Fairfax. "Where do I sit and when do I start?"

Brisbane peered at her, spanning almost forty years in a flash of thought, when love confessions, suborned in the daily print, had fevered the circulation barometer. "You know what your job is," he said kindly. "I don't have to tell *you* anything. Let's do it over again."

They embraced, two old warriors of circulation, forty years falling from their shoulders, today's problems forgotten, their aged triumphs flaming up again like Greek fire. The editor turned and left abruptly. It was the first time I had seen him in an effort to mask an emotion. Beatrice Fairfax, now approaching seventy, turned her back on me and blew a stentorian blast into an ample handkerchief and dabbed her eyes.

"O. K., Boss," she said, her voice choked, "let's get going." She was rolling up the sleeves of a dress which still had the Victorian touch.

Upstairs, bellowing into his dictaphone, after sidetracking a full-page editorial for the Sunday *American* on "Civilization and the Wheel," the wheel which ruled our destinies, from the little prayer wheel of the superstitious Asiatic, to the giant wheel of the dynamo, Brisbane's voice droned:

"Young ladies and gentlemen, don't fail to read the love and marriage page in tomorrow's *Mirror*, and daily thereafter. Nothing is important but (capitals, quote) LOVE (uncaps, unquote) nothing is important but true (no quotes, no caps)

love, nothing makes it worth while but (full capitals) LAW-
FUL MARRIAGE (uncaps) Stop So read the *Mirror's*
(quote) Love and Marriage (unquote) page Stop Get married
as soon as you can. (Caps) Have a baby."

Nell Brinkley's pictures passed before me as though flashed
on a screen, the young couple facing the world, the girl of
exuberant breasts in the abbreviated bathing suit, sitting forward in a canoe labeled "Marriage," the husband in the rear,
guiding the craft over an incessant flood of words:

"Marriage is the foundation of civilization. Study this
picture! The boy and the girl in the canoe, beauty at the bow,
manly strength in the stern, typify the adventure of marriage.
We address the question to young and old that are single:
WHY DON'T YOU GET MARRIED? Have children.
Buy a car. Buy one big enough for MANY children."

The rejuvenated Beatrice Fairfax soon discovered, to her
discomfiture, and to Brisbane's mortification, that our young
Americans, interested in the married state, wanted a car before
they had babies and also wanted to know how they could avoid
a baby until they were sure of being able to support one. They
knew all about cars. Babies, they had heard, could be
postponed.

Brisbane left for Hearst's ranch with his caravansary of
secretaries, stenographers and his chief attendant, Big Emil
Steinheuser, who lugged the dictating machine as if it had been
a portable arc of Mosaic times containing the sacred Thora.
From various parts of the country telegrams poured in on me
from the editor. A wire from the alfalfa fields of Nevada,
through which he was traveling, was typical:

"Perhaps love and marriage page needs a discussion. Is
man or woman more intensely affectionate? Keep away from
anything dealing too closely with sex. Find out whether impulse toward other sex and toward marriage and children is
stronger in women or in men. I think it ten times stronger in
women, more insatiable for biological reasons. Get important
person, preferably clergyman, to say that. Put question to
well-known men and women, actors and actresses, motion-
picture people. Perhaps some movie lady, divorced several
times, could be considered an authority. Perhaps a better
authority would be somebody who married and stayed married.
Keep this on high plane. Use pictures of those interviewed

but for God's sake don't use photographs of horrible looking men like Rev. Dr. Cadman or the long-nosed Mr. Durante. This applies to all similarly repulsive individuals."

Telegrams and memoranda from the dictaphone settled over me like a plague of locusts. During the nine months of my constant association with Brisbane, his output directed to me alone could have compared in size with the two volumes of Buckle's *Introduction to the History of Civilization in England* which he recommended as good reading. One became a philosopher under this storm of paper. The only lesson I could gather from it was that a man who learns or acquires all he knows from others must be full of contradictions.

As I came to work in the afternoon I noticed that Fall had spent itself. Autumn leaves, scurrying before the wind, reminded me of the cyclone of messages which engulfed me when I opened my office door. Brisbane's innovations had made no marked improvement in our circulation nor had his love and marriage campaign influenced the vital statistics. He became increasingly irritable and I began to enjoy the caustic humor of his memoranda which lashed and flayed what he described as the staff's supine imbecility. Office boys, quick to sense injustice from on high referred to the editor as "Old Doubledome."

Soon he had another idea which was to add a new inmate to our institution. The Great Illuminist was to assume the title of director general; I was to sit on the lower step of his throne as editor in chief and relinquish the reins of managing editor to a successor who, it was hinted mysteriously, would galvanize us all into the great charge to capture a million and a half readers. Brisbane had pried Stanley Walker from the city editor's desk of the *Herald Tribune* by offering him some $200 more a week and Walker, a venturesome soul, walked into the web. He was tired from a pardonable celebration of his departure from his old newspaper when Brisbane piloted him into my office.

The noted city editor, a newspaper man of brilliant attainments, was a slight, sharp-featured Texan with a nose leading to a quick point and surmounted by Brisbanian blue eyes. The editor introduced him to me with undisguised satisfaction.

"This is our new managing editor, who has already informed me that he finds our city editor just hard-boiled enough. Show him the ropes. He'll learn quickly enough."

Walker greeted me heartily. He was still being warmed by the sunny notices of his best seller, *City Editor*, a creditable addition to any newspaper man's bookshelf. He grinned when I told him I had read it with personal interest. Journalism he termed a noble calling, too great to be damaged by the depravity of tabloidia. His book pictured the *Mirror* as a hopeless sheet full of half-baked features, handicapped by lack of news service, inaccurate in its stories and surviving solely through the flabbergasting information of Walter Winchell, a conclusion with which Winchell heartily agreed.

Walker asked Brisbane in my presence for a formal announcement of his appointment to be tacked up on the bulletin board. The old man hurried him out of the door, pointing to the city desk with a shaking finger. His face was stormy as he turned on me:

"What the hell did he expect? To be taken out there in a sedan chair? By God Almighty! The first thing a real managing editor does when he's hired is to jump in and raise hell— and he'd better start raising it damned soon!"

As press time approached I found Walker sitting at the horse-shoe copy desk in Buddhistic calm, studying operations while copy whirled by his pointed nose. No doubt he had already concluded that the *Herald Tribune* handled matters in a fashion more to his liking. The shouts of Clarke had taken on a new fortissimo as he riffled through a batch of photographs with the dexterity of a faro dealer. Our first edition went to press with added din and clamor. Walker left his chair that night with no illusions about our formula. Hearst's tabloidia was not for him. In his book he had called it by its right name.

Editor and Publisher, the newspaper trade journal, interviewed Walker regarding his curious change of position. He was referred to as iconoclastic. The new tabloid editor announced he had left the *Herald Tribune* for "fun and money." He preferred the word "said" to "stated," "exclaimed" or "declared," a reform he proposed to institute. Removing the word "exclaimed" from our columns might have been disastrous, and Clarke saw to it that it remained in our vocabulary.

Walker's sense of humor helped to smooth his brow while weeks hurried into the limited months of his nightmare on the *Mirror*. He had a number of constructive ideas to submit but

Brisbane's editorial duties, holding him hunched to a dictaphone, were now crowded more and more into spare moments
between conferences on real estate and he became almost inaccessible. Walker made a final effort to see him to recommend
the appointment of a clergyman who was to write a daily
column on spiritual topics.

"I couldn't get to first base because of his secretaries," the
new managing editor told me that evening at Dinty Moore's.
"His satraps let me peer at him as he mumbled into his electric
douche-bag, and then they led me quietly away."

Walker solved his office problem by establishing himself in
a glass cubicle with several briar pipes, a huge container of
aromatic tobacco and a smart brunette secretary. "Let me be
the consulting editor," he said, twinkling a humorous eye amid
the confusing din. Between working moments, through clouds
of smoke from his burning briars, came the inspiration for his
next best seller, *Mrs. Astor's Horse* which left me out of its
clinical studies. In *City Editor* I had been described as a "peculiar genius," but without the required ability to threaten
Patterson's leadership. Walker referred to me as having been
the brains of Bernarr Macfadden's *Graphic*, that fabulous sheet
"founded by the great muscle-flexer and carrot-eater." As the
author put it, the *Graphic* had lasted to the amazement of all
(myself included) for eight years and, "for a time the circulation mounted alarmingly." During those days, according to
Walker's book, I had written the following memorandum for
the office bulletin board:

"The circulation of the *Graphic* has reached the point where
it is tearing the guts out of the presses. This has resulted from
my policy of sensationalism. Any man who cannot be yellow
has no place on the staff."

As the staff of the *Graphic* had never needed such admonition it is highly improbable that I would have wasted my time
writing it. However, it was good speak-easy gossip, and many
had compared it with Brisbane's own introduction in an after-
dinner speech in 1910 when he shouted proudly, in defying the
rebukes of the pulpit, "I am the editor of the *Journal* and I
hope it is the yellowest of them all."

Brisbane appeared at times from his upper world, descend-
ing on a cloud of dictated fulminations which kept our editorial
page going for days, sometimes weeks, while he hibernated to

Florida or Hearst's California ranch. Winter was coming and
he followed the sun as much as he could. He hated the rigors
of cold weather and muffled himself in a flaming red scarf,
beating his arms about his stout body to restore his circulation,
as Macfadden had done in coonskin cap, moccasins and sensible
clothes. The arm-beating was an atavistic gesture which the
physical culturist understood, but the editor resorted to it instinctively, perceiving perhaps, that his years were numbered.

I found him one afternoon in a small corridor leading from
my office which gave an unobstructed view of Walker's cubicle.
Stanley, at that moment was sitting back, smoking his pipe, his
feet upon his desk.

"What is he doing in there?" Brisbane asked.

"It appears," I replied, "that he has his desk cleared and,
like Mr. Teagle of Standard Oil, he may be studying how to
make more money for all of us, and maybe for himself."

Such sallies, instead of provoking his displeasure, usually
drew from him cackles of laughter, which sounded far away,
as though his mouth were the cavernous outlet for the humorous channels of one of his ornithological creatures.

The editor squinted at Walker in his glass box. "Now he's
writing something. Is he writing for us?" he asked.

His hand clamped over my shoulder like a vice. "Has he
got another book on his mind?" he asked. In grave agitation
he maneuvered me into my office, as if to verify some horrible
suspicion.

"There's nothing worse for this business than a man affected with literary hives," he stormed. "We're throwing our
money away on people who want to write books. They think
only about their own best-selling glory. You will never know
the hell I went through with Frank Wilson and Richard
Harding Davis when I was managing editor of the *Sun*. They
were garbaging for material for books, and I knew it. But I
got my money's worth out of them! What do these aliens
care about the paper? They think they're better than I am
because they try to describe the soul!" His face seemed to
have taken on the mask of some disembodied spirit, terrifying,
unreal; his voice was a hoarse rasp. He was revealing himself.

"I told David Graham Phillips where he could head in,"
he continued. "They were all arrested when they tried to
serialize his *Grain of Dust*. He wound up being shot in

Gramercy Park. Keats Speed was one of my men. He never tried to father a literary abortion. He stuck to his paper work. His *Sun* is read in all the best clubs today. The book writers laugh at me because I talk to millions in words of one syllable for $260,000 a year! Who ever made that much writing a book? We don't want book writers here. The thing to do is to shoot them down before they poke their noses into this business, studying life at our expense. Books—books written on Mr. Hearst's money, and mine too! Smell 'em out," he roared, "and don't let me catch you hiring any more of that breed !"

That evening marked the next to the last literary discussion I ever had with Brisbane. At the time, I was working after office hours on my third book, which had to do with my adventures in Russia and my typewriter keys seemed to turn into little saws whose strokes cut through the bars of a prison. My contract with the *Mirror* was copper-riveted and stretched through more than twelve unpredictable months. I had no illusions about what would happen when my volume appeared.

CHAPTER III

BRISBANE returned in an agitated mood, a few days later, from a chat at the White House with President Roosevelt. The New Deal's sociological reforms were disturbing Hearst into open editorial denunciation on the front pages of his chain newspapers. Brisbane, in his syndicated column, presumably read by millions of the masses which had swept Roosevelt into office, had to confine his signed criticism to pin pricks. He had years ago educated his readers to the reforms he now privately deplored. The heads of large corporations, whom he had subjected to almost constant assaults for a generation, were now, in his private estimation, the helpless victims of a tyrant more rapacious than his own Nero.

"Roosevelt is a stick of dynamite," the editor said, pacing the floor of my office. "In the first place he has ideas, and ideas are dynamite for a Democracy. When that man gets out of the White House we won't recognize this country. He thinks that the proper duty of man is to arrange an easy way of life. We're all going to pay for this through the nose. The taxes to come will make what we pay today look like chicken-feed, and with my money I know what taxes are. The income tax is an *exceedingly painful thing*, let me tell you. Roosevelt won't let anybody tell him anything about money. I don't believe his man Morgenthau knows the difference between one dollar and two dollars. What was he—a dilettante farmer or something?"

An additional office problem had developed from the New Deal's political economy. Hearst, in his exasperation, wanted to throw out from his papers all of the NRA Blue Eagle labels which announced daily from his mastheads that we were doing our part on the road to a more abundant life.

"When Mr. Hearst looks at that Eagle," said Brisbane, "he has to postpone his dinner. I've told him it would be too obvious to throw it out all at once. Roosevelt has got the people with him by promising them everything, and it has got so that you can't take a crack at him without bringing our own readers

down on us. The thing to do is to gradually reduce the size of
the Blue Eagle in our engravings until it croaks from anaemic
shrinkage."

We proceeded to strangle the Eagle. The *Mirror* carried
two of them, a fairly large one in the left ear of the front page
in a box announcing the weather, and a smaller but none the
less vigorous bird over our editorials. The latter was promptly
decapitated. Its brother on the front page suffered a fate worse
than death. Brisbane studied the Eagle's painful reductions
daily with impatient dissatisfaction.

"I can still recognize him," he grumbled. "He's beginning
to look more and more like a moth-eaten Soviet duck. But
he's still visible."

The word "member" in the feeble NRA label could no
longer be read by the naked eye and the slogan, "we do our
part," had assumed the appearance of microscopical Chinese.
Our engraver was losing his temper over these tortures. "Why
don't you let that poor turkey alone?" he asked, when he
brought down his last effort, smaller than the head of a ten-
penny nail. It looked like the silhouette of "Mickey Mouse."
Brisbane ordered a tiny circle drawn around it and watched
the diminishing duck relentlessly as it faded into an obliterated
dingbat.

During this period Brisbane literally shouted himself hoarse
about mounting taxes. He thundered the following blast into
his dictating machine while I waited for it to be typed:

"A convict is found in prison receiving his 'relief' check
regularly and a Communist gentleman held by the Government
for deportation also gets his relief check regularly. The Government was supporting the convict in the prison and the 'Red'
man in the detention department, and the relief checks came
regularly. These facts interest taxpayers that must provide
everything."

No tax crisis, however, could swerve the Great Illuminist
from his first journalistic passion, the perfect headline. He
pounced upon the tired craftsmen of a carelessly written heading like a monster gadfly on an unprotected truck horse. "I'll
wear the hair off my legs until I can pound some fundamentals
into these overpaid groundhogs," he shouted. "Here's a caption over a picture: 'Strike Fight Flares!' Where is the im-
becile who wrote that? The picture shows painfully enough

what is going on: policemen swinging their clubs at the heads of scurrying strikers. If somebody asked you to describe this would you answer with, 'Strike Fight Flares'? No! If you had any brains you would say: 'Cops Swing Their Clubs on Strikers' Skulls!' Tell the news exactly as it is in the plainest kind of English. This struggle to grab something apart from the news ruins a heading every time."

In headline writing he had reached the zenith of his newspaper knowledge. His short, abrupt way of stating what he thought, what he saw; a way that appealed to a gigantic mass of readers made him unrivaled as the master of that technique. He was untiring in his attacks on the long-spun caption. Those who could stand his abuse learned enough from him to become the best headline craftsmen of the day. One had to remember to reduce to the utmost of simplicity the choice of words that drew the reader's eye to the column of type. A heading was transformed from a label into a shock of information.

His eyes glowed when he reviewed great headlines of the past, chiefly his own.

"I remember one which was good," he chortled, "but it wasn't ours: 'Peeping Dowager Names Actress.' That told everything. All you have to do is to make it exciting. Force people to shout to read headlines. Tell it in conversational American. If Mrs. Roosevelt falls downstairs, and doesn't break her neck, the headline should be: 'Mrs. Roosevelt Falls Downstairs,' and not, 'Eleanor Tripped Her Little Toe.' The best headline I ever wrote was: 'The Bull That Butted the Train Off the Tracks!' Let's begin where the action begins and stop where the action ceases."

In those days I learned much from Brisbane although I could not agree with his views. Meanwhile holidays sped by as though we were in a Roman galley, rowing with strained backs, seeing nothing but what was already behind us, wincing under a lash of words sharper than whips. This was no regatta. The Galley Drum Master fixed the tempo faster every day, swinging his hammers with the beat of a metronome.

All I could remember of Thanksgiving in 1934 was a last-minute editorial about the Puritans and the fate they had carved out for us, accompanied by a drawing of conical hats, blunderbusses, buckled shoes, pumpkins and a horizon full of skyscrapers and airplanes.

"Holidays are important," Brisbane told me. "Watch them on a big calendar. Keep looking ahead. Christmas is coming, New Year's, then the days of the great Americans, born in February, followed by March with St. Patrick's Day. Green paper! And never make fun of the Irish. Their Patron Saint drove the snakes out of Erin. What about the snakes of Communism? There's a cartoon!"

Charles Macauley had reminded me that Christmas was coming. He was preparing a half-page picture of the Christ stretching his hands in benediction over a world garlanded with holly leaves. The artist's drawing hand was in a paralyzed twist of neuritis and he gripped it with his left to guide the trembling fingers holding the pen over his board. He was on the sidelines, wasting away. Few of his cartoons were printed. Most of them were flung in the wastebasket by Brisbane who called them archaic.

Soon the cartoonist was bed-stricken, a telephone by his side, his knees propped up to hold his drawing board, his brave wife, Elaine, encouraging every faltering stroke of his agonized pen. Brisbane, patrolling the city room like a roundsman, noticed his disappearance. "He's through," he said. "Take him off the payroll. He never had the Hearst touch."

Macauley bent at his work and it probably kept him alive for the few weeks he remained among the quick. I did not fire him but lied to him mercifully when he talked to me about ideas from his bedside telephone. I told him his drawings were scheduled for many days ahead.

"I know what Brisbane wants," he said. "I could never bring myself to do it before. It's too easy; and the style he wants, without depth, without background, is not Charles Macauley. That's not the art which worth-while magazines have reprinted over my name. I didn't get the Pulitzer prize for that. But I'll try."

Weeks passed and Macauley held to his drawing board as a wrecked mariner clings to a water-logged plank.

"Am I still on the staff? For God's sake, don't let them fire me. I see my checks are still coming in. Am I still in harness?"

"Yes, you're still one of us."

As the end approached, he telephoned me for the approval of a cartoon that would show the NRA Blue Eagle choked to death by the righteous hand of Business. He loathed the idea of it, having advocated Roosevelt's policies from the beginning. He had already started the drawing and was putting in his strokes every agony that the bird could suffer. His voice was weak but the electric impulse of the telephone carried his fighting spark.

"That ought to please the old Buzzard!" he added, with pain-checked hilarity.

He finished the drawing down to the last cross-hatch, sent it in and died under an oxygen tent, an uncorked India-ink bottle and a pen within his reach, a smile imprinted on his pain-twisted face. He was still in harness, still the fine craftsman who had won the Pulitzer prize. Death had been kind. When I took him off the payroll he was in his coffin.

I stood in Brisbane's doorway a few days later while his secretaries attempted to catch his eye. I had been summoned by memorandum for a specific time but he had apparently forgotten about it. He was dictating Christmas editorials and for a moment listened impatiently to a quotation from Charles Lamb which Mrs. Jerman was trying to read to him above the grind of the "wax works."

"Let not work bind the free and holiday-rejoicing spirit down," she repeated raising her voice unnaturally over the clatter.

"That's not the way he wrote it," he snapped. "Look it up again—on second thought, never mind. It's no good anyhow." Suddenly he saw me. "Did you want anything?" he asked, in the tone in which he might have addressed an importunate Broadway beggar. "Oh, yes, I sent for you."

He came immediately to the subject. Frank Farley, a well-meaning Irishman on my staff, had been writing a political column for the paper. The chatter and gossip had helped to entice political advertising. Now the column was to be discontinued immediately and Farley fired without explanation. I stood inside the portals uncertainly as Brisbane abruptly closed the conversation by hunching himself over his dictating machine into which Paul Jerman clamped a new wax record, like loading a cannon in battle. The tireless voice was off again.

"It is not merely the birthday of One Noble Spirit; it is a birthday for all, a day of hope for all the human race. . . . The beautiful character of Christ stands apart from all theology, all discussion or question. . . . His is a character of pure good, self-sacrifice. . . . His mother that attended Him in the manger. . . ."

On Christmas Eve Brisbane entered my office with a port-folio of advance editorial material, photographs of our old friends, the jungle beauties of Lake Chad with their extended lips, the Thunder Reptile, the dinosaur eggs of the Gobi Des-ert. He was off to Florida for the holidays.

"Have you fired that Farley, the political man, yet?" he asked.

"No. He has worked here since the paper was started, more than ten years ago. I think we can find some other rou-tine for him."

"Fire him!" he thundered, losing his temper. "Fire him today! Don't you understand an order when I take my valu-able time to issue one? That man has offended people who can add even more to my real estate taxes. I won't have it, I tell you! They've got to know that I had nothing to do with what he wrote. They've got to know that he was fired out on his neck!"

"But it's Christmas eve," I protested. I hoped he would forget it all while sunning himself on Biscayne Bay and I was sparring for time.

The reference to Christmas Eve left him stunned but sud-denly touched him off into peals of laughter until his face was distorted.

"You mean you can't fire him on Christmas Eve!" he roared, wiping tears of Brontosaurian mirth from his eyes with a large bandana handkerchief. "Say—say," he choked, "this is the funniest thing since 'The Old Homestead'!"

He came to my desk and protruded his granite face, now shorn of all traces of laughter. He peered at me as if he had just made the painful discovery of coming across traces of virtue in a person in whom he had never suspected its exist-ence. "Fire him now," he murmured, his lips a narrow line. "You're not married to him, are you?"

I called Farley in and managed to mumble the fateful words, more dreaded in a newspaper office than in any other business. I bowed my head for the inevitable comment.

"On Christmas Eve?"

He was a middle-aged man, sombrely dressed, tall and thin,

with graying hair and a long, pensive face whose pale eyes saw little of humor in life. He had worked for the paper from its beginning, a matter of eleven years. He stood turning his hat in his hands. Around the block church bells were ringing, and in the street homeward bound workers were calling out the usual greetings.

"Jesus," he said, "not on Christmas Eve! I've got to go home and trim a Christmas tree. We've spent a lot of money for the dinner. How can I tell the wife on Christmas Eve?"

He stumbled out of the door. "Jesus," he kept mumbling, "on Christmas Eve. Jesus!"

CHAPTER IV

KOBLER, watching our chimerical performances from his Park avenue cenotaph, was doing more than licking his wounds. He had in the Hearst empire a group of sympathizers who were as hopeful as he was that Brisbane's nostrums would soon result in restoring the *Mirror* to its old regime. The former publisher had let the bars down so far as his diplomacy toward the veteran editor was concerned. The verbal venom that came from the lips of the deposed advertising genius exceeded all of his previous outcries when he invited me at night to his library of first editions for a doch-an-dorrach. He swore oaths of eternal vengeance at the mention of Brisbane's name. He was ready to write the oaths in his own blood and bared his arm from which the blood would come.

The cruel turn of affairs on the *Mirror* had not only broken Kobler's heart but reduced his span of life. By a strange irony, in this bitter struggle for power, Brisbane and Kobler were to die within a few days of each other not much more than a year from the time of which I write. The editor now referred to the former publisher with contempt while the latter, who had once promoted Brisbane as the world's greatest commentator described him as an empty barrel with the staves falling off.

Brisbane was not unconscious of the shrouded candle-holders who watched his weakening blows. The old man in his final effort to storm the parapet of the *News* was tireless in his strategy. Even though his ammunition was old, it had worked once. He dragged out of his past all the outworn jugglery of his trade, the journalistic slack-rope-walking of 1898. Hearst now prodded him with satirical notes, telegrams of sarcastic railleries. He sent him one message which said: "Dear Arthur, you are now getting out the worst newspaper in the United States!" But for the Hauptmann trial which was getting under way we would have slumped below the 600,000 mark we were barely holding. When this news sent us up again, Beatrice Fairfax received less than fifty letters a

day from her page on Buicks and bassinets.   Love and marriage could not compete with murder.

The editor had taken time out to celebrate his seventieth
anniversary. He sat before a tremendous cake at the Hotel
Warwick, and Joseph Connolly, fat and chubby, reclining
closely at his left, laughed benevolently as the old man tried
to blow out the candles. Joe was beginning to sustain a higher
relationship to Hearst than other men. The Medicean gangs
of the organization watched him furtively but he accepted his
office politics with an Irish smile. It was rumored that he
would soon be general manager of the newspaper empire. Joe
was followed by sycophants, members of defeated cliques who
had sheathed their knives and joined his group as favorable reports about him grew apace.

Brisbane asked me to collect clippings from the account of
his birthday party in the *New York Times*.

"They're becoming mellow about me," he said. "Time was
when such an event would have been ignored."

Said the *Times*:

> Arthur Brisbane will be seventy today. Not seventy
> years old. Just seventy. . . . He seems fifty. . . . He says
> it is a great responsibility to have 30,000,000 readers daily.
> That is more than voted for Franklin D. Roosevelt. On the
> other hand, Mr. Hearst pays Mr. Brisbane $260,000 a year
> for writing his daily column, and that is almost four times
> more than Mr. Roosevelt gets. He says his purpose is to
> make readers think. . . . Others have imitated his style.
> Why haven't they succeeded? Mr. Brisbane grinned and
> said: *"Le style, c'est l'homme."*

Such recognition had a singular effect on the editor's tabloid
activities. The next morning I received the following memorandum from him:

"Will you inform the editor of the pink edition that we
would make a better impression on business people if we had
left out last night's picture of the lady who keeps a 'gay house'
in Chicago. At least off the front page. Also she is hellishly
ugly. Let us print photographs of as FEW prostitutes as possible unless they commit an interesting murder, or otherwise
force themselves into the news, as they are bound to do. I see
also that the *News* used the word ADULTERER in a headline.

Let them have it. That sort of thing will swing the church over to us. Stories of vice we want to tell coldly. By that I don't mean that we have to leave out the interesting facts, but we shouldn't tell the reader about it as though we were *enjoying* it. Also I notice we speak of 'Dutch' Schultz as 'the fat boy,' but on page two we print a picture of him looking thin. Dig up a recent picture of this racketeer immediately."

No details were now too trivial for the editor to mouse over. As in the old days he wanted to show by drawings what the camera could not reveal. He spent much time instructing artists and sub-editors in this accomplishment.

"Here's a story," he would say, "involving the problem of whether a woman should ever tell her husband of her slips from the straight road before her marriage."

We would gather about him like medical students at an autopsy conducted by a famous surgeon.

" 'Should a Woman Tell?' That is the obvious headline. Now for the drawings. In the first panel wife admits to husband her relations with former lover before marriage. Woman is in bed with newborn baby. Husband glares. In the second panel, husband is jealous and she offers to bring old lover to house to convince him their relations have stopped. Third: husband comes from behind curtain. Confronts lover. Fourth: the murder according to the wife; husband fighting lover with penknife. Fifth: big question mark with words 'Which One Killed Him?' "

He developed a passion for large photographs splashed across the page. In this way he wanted to depict the muscles of Joe Louis. He sent for Louis, interviewed him and then announced in his column that a gorilla could lick a heavyweight prizefighter or three prizefighters at one time. He chased out Dan Parker, our sports editor, with instructions to sound out Jack Dempsey on the theory. Parker was incredulous when I verified the assignment and spent the afternoon with the former champion discussing gorillas, returning in a state of hypnosis. Discovering that Dempsey agreed passionately with Brisbane, he devoted his entire column to the subject. Dempsey clung to the idea that a gorilla could bowl over a whole platoon of heavyweights. "But," added Dempsey, "why bring this up now? There are enough gorillas in the fight game already." This provoked an animated debate in fistic circles.

Gene Tunney, retired heavyweight champion and Shake-spearean lecturer, closed the argument with an intellectual coup by looking up the matter in his Encyclopaedia and discovering that man has twenty-four ribs while a gorilla has but thirteen. "The gorilla," he announced, "grabs something and tries to crush the life out of it. A Dempsey left hook landing on the stomach would tear the animal in two." Later *Time Magazine*, pursuing the subject in the *Encyclopaedia Britannica*, found to everybody's surprise that a gorilla has thirteen PAIRS of ribs, one pair more than man.

All this was attracting attention to Brisbane but left the *Mirror* in the shadows. Even the dead King of the Hejaz, lying in state across a whole page, failed to move the populace. The editor called for double-page pictures of cataclysmic disasters, volcanic eruptions, which were not then available, and finally, earthquakes. The latter he hurriedly canceled because of their possible effect on California real estate. He fought shy of earthquakes. One had occurred in Southern California during his *safari* and from Detroit he had characterized it in his column as mild shocks and that a few people had been frightened by falling bricks. This description had appeared on several front pages adjoining photographs of four and five story California structures torn to pieces, with headlines of loss of life.

He pounced on the story of a sensational murder in the Knights of Columbus Hotel. A young Presbyterian novice had blundered drunkenly into a room and shot to death his seventeen-year-old bride and a priest. It was the sort of news from which editors recoil because of its religious ramifications. Here Brisbane displayed his technique. All details were printed but attention was called to the editorial page where, under the title, "A Dreadful Tragedy" it was authoritatively announced that "no good cause, religious or other, can be smirched or injured by the action of an individual."

Said Brisbane, behind the gory details of the scandal: "One traitor can not disgrace, or in any way affect the honor of a great army. One traitor to faith and decency cannot disgrace a church or a profession."

He showed us many letters from Catholic readers, including priests, praising him for these words of charity.

"Catholics," he said, "must be treated like bank presidents. When these people get together they can ruin anything."

Editorial attitudes on foreign policy were governed by Hearst's prejudices. After the Paris Government had asked him to leave France, with more speed than dignity, the wealthy publisher saw nothing of any good in that country and it is reasonable to suppose that he aired his views later on this subject during his dinner with Nazi leaders in Berlin. Thereafter, Napoleon was always referred to in Brisbane's editorials as an Italian genius who had the misfortune to be licked by a second-rater known as Wellington. Hearst had no love for England.

Brisbane was closely guided by his chief's whims on international affairs and would burst without warning upon some unsuspecting nation with an attack that might last for days. Uncle Sam was pictured as a pathetic dotard suffering from an inability to discriminate, and forever playing into the hands of smart British diplomats.

At the moment, the Hearst papers were attacking Russia on the premise, or so it seemed to me, that Hitler had saved Europe from Bolshevism. The *Journal* carried in 96-point type such eight-column headings as "Bayonets Prod Russian Mothers to Work!" The *American* would follow with, "Soviet-German Break Looms" and "Moscow, Assailed by Nazis, May Recall Envoy." When such stories were sent to me by the Hearst high command I threw them into my wastebasket. They did not conform with what I had seen or heard in Russia and were revealed later for what they were worth by the pact between Stalin and Hitler.

Brisbane in his column, dodged the Communist-Nazi issue with subtle pills of comment. Cartoons were more to the point, however, and behind the scenes, orders from him were direct enough. "Please ask Chamberlain (a Hearst cartoonist) to map out Sunday *American* cartoon," he wired me from Kansas City, "showing Russia under the Czars, long line going to Siberia, and under Stalin, millions dying of famine. Divide cartoon in two halves. Make not too gruesome for Sunday readers."

Yet the editor, in his editorials, had hailed the Russian revolution as the greatest event in a progressive civilization since the tumbrils. Now he wrote: "For the time being, 'kings are out' of the picture of government and social organization.

Man may become dictator if he has enough power of will and mind. If somebody could write a true and prophetic book on 'The Government of Tomorrow,' telling just how men will be managed by dictators, fifty or a hundred years from now, it would be an interesting book and would probably surprise everybody."

Half-page broadsides in 12-point type appeared in Hearst's *American*, surrounding the Star-Spangled Banner in full colors under the heading: "The RED Insult to the American Flag." This usually referred to Communist meetings. Norman Thomas, perennial Socialist candidate, an innocent bystander of these affairs, was generally included as one of the culprits tearing down the pillars of civilization.

"They are the mouthpieces of proletarian dictatorship," the editorial shouted, never mentioning the Bund camps sprouting up all around us. "They stand for tyranny, for the rigid regimentation of American life, for the subjugation of the individual by forceful repression."

Soon I recognized those words, almost in identical fashion in a Hearst tirade against Roosevelt. Growing taxes, it seemed, had driven our high command to furious onslaughts. We were instructed to carry such headlines in big type as "Soak the Rich," in an effort to promote sympathy for those possessed of much of this world's goods. This, unfortunately, was misinterpreted by Brisbane's 30,000,000 readers who, presumably, did not have millions salted away. "Soak the Rich" was so widely applauded that it was immediately changed to "Soak the Thrifty." As this had no appeal to millions who couldn't save anything it was finally changed to "Soak Success." This at last was unanimously endorsed by all Hearst executives earning $50,000 or more a year. It was finally decided to depict the nation as made up of 130,000,000 stockholders unable to obtain dividends from a vast corporation which was being driven to ruin by traitorous directors taking orders from Moscow.

Hearst now had his own pen in hand and produced such front-page diatribes against Roosevelt as "Promises and Laughs," for his newspaper chain:

Candidate Roosevelt, laughing gaily, in 1932, promised to reduce bureaus and commissions, PLEDGED himself to

balance the budget and REMIT EXCESSIVE TAXATION.
Now we know what he was laughing at. Under the guidance
of *his Communistic advisers* he began an onslaught on "big-
ness in business." This is a laughing Administration. From
the top down everybody laughs. American factories are
closed. And the Administration laughs. Ten million are
still out of work. And the Administration laughs.

These editorials worried Brisbane, who felt that the millions who had elected Roosevelt were still with him. "And
they'll stick to him until he's tired of the White House," he
said, shaking his head, ominously. "They'll never vote him
out. He knows what he's done. He's dynamite." His attacks
in his syndicated column were more subtle, and in January,
1935, when Hearst reached a climax of bitterness about the
New Deal, he prevailed upon him to devote much space to the
President's birthday ball, an event which was celebrated all over
the country and whose proceeds were distributed to the welfare of infantile paralysis victims. This sop, it was hoped,
would prevent the complete alienation of vast groups of Roosevelt supporters who read Hearst papers.

The pressure for more spectacular sensations to attract
another million readers was felt by this time from the master
minds to the office boys. The editor admitted he had promised
Hearst almost immediate results. Now under the lash himself in a grim urgency of his own creation, he was ready to try
anything. These predicaments, usually the result of jealousy,
greed or vaulting ambition in the organization inevitably forked
one off to the road of desperation to make a showing. Circulation came first when Hearst demanded it; anything to flash
a row of figures under his nose to pacify him, to turn his mind
away from immediate problems to a castle in Scotland or the
importation of medieval fireplaces, stone by stone, from France.

The Hearst papers and the tabloids had been prowling
around Englewood, N. J., trying to snap, without permission,
the first photograph of the second-born son of Anne Lindbergh. She had shunned reporters since the murder of her first
baby and lived in dread of the ordeal she would have to face
during the Hauptmann trial. Colonel Lindbergh's attitude
toward newspapermen was one of loathing and repugnance.
His aloofness made him even more vulnerable as a public tar-

get. Clarke, our city editor, who could be as hard-boiled as a
Cuban garrotter, had set a trap for Mrs. Lindbergh and her
baby by sending Dick Sarno, a resourceful staff photographer,
disguised as a butter and egg man to follow them around in a
black wagon with side curtains, and "shoot them" during the
split second they were in focus. Anticipating repercussions I
explained the situation to Brisbane.

"Get the picture," he said, "and get it first! We will be
blamed more for not printing it and letting somebody else get
ahead of us. This is no time for squeamishness. The *News*
has been getting away with these stunts long enough. They
showed Mrs. Snyder roasting alive in the electric chair and
look where they are today!"

The black-wagon maneuvering was typical of the Hearst
methods of obtaining pictures. Photographs, which might
have been had by the innocent process of asking for them, had
to be taken by a mysterious now-you-see-me-now-you-don't
hocus-pocus. Nothing could be done without strange creep-
ings in the forest.

The *Mirror* office still talked of Editor Payne's astonishment one night when a gawky, new reporter walked in with a
photograph which the staff had been trying to get for days by
all sorts of *escamoterie*, such as crawling up drain pipes, shad-
owings after nightfall and petty bribery, but accomplishing
nothing. When asked to explain, the simple-minded beginner
said he had telephoned the owner of the picture, asked him for
it politely and was told to come over and get it. This was so
flabbergasting that the apprentice, henceforth, was looked upon
as not wholly in his right mind and he was soon let out as a
naïve incompetent.

Our man in the black wagon, peering through his curtains,
snapped little Jon Morrow Lindbergh walking happily from his
private schoolroom in a bright blue jumper suit, holding his
mother's hand. Mrs. Lindbergh was totally unaware that the
picture was being taken, a piece of enterprise which was carefully explained to the reader. When this little boy came into
the world, something more than two years back, his mother
was still weeping over the murder of her first-born. The black-
wagon photograph was widely sold by Hearst's International
News Photos to other newspapers.

This picture covered the front page of the *Mirror*, and Brisbane approved the headline which appeared over it:

FIRST PUBLISHED PHOTO
OF 2ND LINDY BABY!

It was widely reported that Colonel Lindbergh considered this publicity a final, unpardonable assault on his privacy. Later, when he left with his family on a tramp steamer in what was accepted by the public as self-exile, Brisbane carried the following comment in his column:

"The departure of Colonel Lindbergh and his family for England is not a good advertisement for this country, its police and its system of justice, but it is the advertisement that the country deserves. If you had a small boy constantly threatened with anonymous letters, and had already lost your only other child, kidnaped and murdered, you also might move out."

CHAPTER V

THE "Thunderer," his derby hat pushed back, was rattling the keys of a typewriter in a small alcove which flanked the city room, his eyes turned upward as though he might have been in an animated trance. Returning from the news desk I had to interrupt him for a decision affecting our work for the evening, which was to be one of goading pressure. It was Wednesday, February 13, 1935, in the late afternoon, a date which lingers in newspaper memory. A jury had been out all day to decide the fate of Richard Bruno Hauptmann, murderer of the Lindbergh baby and we were to stand by for the verdict no matter at what hour.

Brisbane swung about, returning apparently from a detached world. He pulled a sheet out of the machine and crumpled it up, then carefully unrolled it. Sentence after sentence, he had written: "The quick brown fox jumps over the lazy dog" and "Now is the time for all good men to come to the aid of their party." He flung the yellow wad away.

"I'll bet you a dollar you don't know what I was doing," he said, almost sheepishly.

What he was doing appeared obvious to me.

"You were playing reporter because you feel this jury excitement. Perhaps you thought you were back on the *Sun* as a cub, dashing off a story about an old lady who broke her leg in a potato race at the church picnic."

I had scratched an emotion in him. At times I felt that this man, always externally aggressive, withheld his inner self to a degree approaching the abnormal.

He held my arm. "Yes," he said, "I was looking back. Maybe I've missed something in this life; I don't know. I have everything I want, and I'm over seventy, and I still get a thrill out of this business. It keeps me going. But the keenest thrill is the reporter's. The man who will risk his neck to reach the telephone with the verdict will get more out of it than you and I. Those fellows in the field don't know when they're happy. It will come back to them when they're old. When you're old you look back and say, 'God, have I made mistakes!' But let's stop being sentimental. This verdict should push our circulation to 800,000 at least. If we can only hold it and then get that damned million!"

Brisbane had done a characteristic job of preparation for the extra. Here he was the master of Hearst journalism, planning editions which came out a minute after the news was flashed. More conservative competitors who clung to the ethics of writing a story after it had happened tagged along behind these enterprises bewildered and stupefied. I remembered ruefully my Hartford experience with the Dempsey-Carpentier extra as I examined once more the editor's cunningly conceived strategy for the coming night's work.

He had ordered three different stories written in advance to cover each highly probable outcome of the verdict. These had been set up into type, cast into plates and locked on three separate presses with a profusion of photographs. All I needed to do was to push the right button when the flash came. Harakiri would not have been considered sufficient punishment for the man who pressed the wrong one.

Brisbane had dictated the headlines, their size and display treatment and the opening paragraphs of the accounts for each alternative. This was a day's work in itself but had not interfered with his regular column, his outside editorials, for daily and Sunday papers, his cartoon inspirations and his real estate business. He had asked for headline type four and a half inches high and as nothing of this sort could be found an artist had to draw the letters and turn them into specially engraved plates so that the size required could be produced.

For the advanced page on the possible verdict of guilty, Brisbane had dictated: "At last the Lindbergh child is avenged, justice is done, and Hauptmann will go to the electric chair. He could not escape. The FACTS were there. The MONEY was in his pocket."

If on the other hand, Hauptmann should be acquitted, Brisbane ordered the same size of type used with, of course, a different account, with pictures of the Lindbergh family, a picture of Hauptmann, his wife and baby, instead of the electric chair, with captions appropriate to the occasion. Preparations had also been made for the contingencies of a disagreement of the jury.

So eager was the editor to make a "killing," that he wanted 100,000 copies of the "guilty" extra and 50,000 with "acquitted," printed in advance and distributed to far points, making sure, as he pointed out, that "such papers be placed in absolutely reliable hands so that none would be stolen or peddled viciously or accidentally, if events did not occur according to expectations, as had happened occasionally in the past with sad repercussions." This idea he finally abandoned.

After the printing of our tens of thousands of prepared extras when the verdict should come in, the presses were to be stripped and "replated" for additional tens of thousands of rewritten issues to give the multitude a less harassed account of what really had happened. Brisbane went into the details of captions for the pictures, preparing for instance, in the event of a guilty verdict, the following line to be used over a photograph of Colonel Lindbergh and his wife: "Vengeance is theirs, but it gives them no comfort."

The editor went home for dinner, and due to the demands of the day upon his energies fell asleep. At times, in the office, he would slump heavily into a chair berating himself for a slowly weakening vitality which he had believed indomitable. His type would not quit. Death reached these men in bed, catching them unawares. In the alcove Brisbane had a sort of pallet, a temporary resting place, on which he threw himself after an exhausting day. One evening I found Sylvia Jerman stroking his forehead like a nurse. His countenance was unguarded, shorn for the moment of all protective aggression. The presses were humming for the first edition and he was mumbling: "That noise is not disturbing; it's a kind of music." After these spells he would go home and dictate in bed, wearing a skull cap and shawl.

The slightest unbending on Brisbane's part which gave him the semblance of possessing human feelings usually recalled the admiration I had for him when I was a reporter. I wanted this night to produce the 200,000 or more extra circulation he hoped to get and possibly open the way for his million, and I inspected the pressroom under these reflections. Here, press crews, covered with oil and the smear of ink, some of the men stripped to the waist, were gathered about their machines, infected as much with the excitement as the editors above. The crews were betting on the fate of Hauptmann, depending on which of the three presses first rolled off the verdict. The men around the press geared with the plates of "acquittal" were asking odds of the toilers ready to start the press whose label was "guilty." The "disagreement" gang was lively with wagers. These grimy toilers roared out news of death and destruction, convinced that no paper could last long without devoting itself to the evils of mankind.

The sensational press had covered the Hauptmann trial by storming the bench of Justice Thomas W. Trenchard, a tired gentleman bewildered by an insatiable journalism which danced in a circulation carnival about his robes. Drummed-up headlines had gorged a public which waited with impatience for the prisoner to be hurried to the gibbet. Even Brisbane believed the business had reached the limits of a Roman holiday. He had returned in disgust from the affair, and issued a warning to the Hearst chain:

"We may be accused of railroading Hauptmann. Let us give the public the impression that the judge is handling the case. We are constantly referring to the prisoner as 'the German.' If he were Irish we should not drag in the Irish, and if he were Jewish we should not drag in the Jews. *THE GERMANS ARE THE LEAST MURDEROUS OF ALL RACES.* Their average in murder is much lower than ours, on the average by about ten to one. Emphasizing that Hauptmann is a German is an insult to the German people, and Mr. Hearst wants these insults stopped at once."

The insults, however, were flung at the freedom of the press, whose loss, if it ever comes, will have been accomplished by such debaucheries of its integrity.

No trained journalistic seal in captivity had been kept away from the quaint courthouse at Flemington, N. J. Brisbane himself guided the hand-picked sob sisters of the Hearst circus, calloused, berouged creatures who wrote "How the criminal impresses a woman."

They convicted him in type long before the judge's charge. Winchell had fled Broadway for the trial's spotlight. His dread of falling into obscurity had landed him into Row A, Seat 5 in the courtroom where, daily, he contributed his own voodooism to the performance. Each piece of incriminating evidence he claimed to have predicted months ago but he was not crowing about the part he had played in the episode of the ransom certificates. Tattlers of his type devoted their columns to their profane ambitions and lost themselves in a maze of self-exploitation. The technique of it was to let out a yelp of triumph if one of their mad guesses came true. Three days before the verdict was reached, Winchell, whose daily items were fashioned to create the impression that he was behind the scenes, announced in his Sunday night broadcast that the jury would bring in a recommendation for mercy. *Time Magazine* pounced on him for this when the trial was over. Court officials were under the impression he was in charge of *Mirror* operations on the scene and he had appropriated all but one of the press passes intended for our working staff, hoping, probably, to distribute the balance to Broadway cronies. Brisbane had forced the gossiper to disgorge, being interested in two of the tickets which went to the editor's friend, Bernard Gimbel. Credentials were passed around from person to person, as though they entitled their holders to box seats for a bull fight.

Sitting at the city desk, waiting for the verdict on the night that was to push Hauptmann into the death house, I felt for the last time in a newspaper office the hunch of instinct, that strange presentiment, beyond reasoning, which seems to turn a newspaper man's backbone into a divining rod. A fixed belief came over me that the stoical German would go to the chair. Under pressure, when that old feeling became powerful, I was always tempted to gamble with the news. I had played it on the *Graphic* by actually printing and distributing 50,000 copies announcing that Lindbergh had landed in Paris before the aviator on his famous flight was reported to have been sighted over Ireland. In those days I met the *Journal's* competition by a passionate intuition. Hearst, the master of this poker publishing, had been a pretty good guesser, himself, in his time.

Now I knew that the minutes ticking off the blood-sweating moments between the return of the jury and the seating of the judge meant a national scoop for the first reporter who could get the right news out of the courtroom to his press association. My hand guarded a telephone which connected me with the pressroom. A crowd of excited hangers-on, most of them holding wagers on the outcome, had swarmed into the city room. These people, theatrical managers who wangled newspaper items with free tickets, sleek Broadway press agents, advertisers and their wives in evening gowns, who wanted to see how a tabloid got out, and almost prevented it from doing so, popped up on so-called "big nights." An editor, whose paper had to beg for advertising, generally gave up his office to space buyers on these occasions.

Below these Daumier faces, the workers, tense and drawn, sat about me in a semicircle. Stanley Walker, his eyes sparkling, watched me intently, drumming a tattoo with a pencil. Clarke was lighting one cigarette from another. He lived for these nights. Hinson Stiles, assistant managing editor, of classic countenance and Byronic collar, the example of patience and fortitude when I had to risk the decisions, stood at my right, his hands in his double-breasted vest pockets. He was repeating the Hearst slogan: "Get it first, but first, get it right." It often happened that we got it first but got it wrong. It recalled to Clarke a famous Hearst battle with the old *Sun*. The *Sun* had said: "If you see it in the *Sun* it's so!" Hearst had replied: "If you see it in the *Sun* you're lucky."

On the wall a big clock with a remorseless face masticated the minutes like a gum-chewing reader. An office boy sprang from the teletype machines which were grinding out behind me the reports from the courtroom. He trembled as he handed me a yellow sheet. It was a flash. The jury was in! A bulletin followed: The foreman was nervous and ready to speak. Another bulletin: Justice Trenchard was on his way from his chambers! Somebody had aroused him from a sound nap which he had taken after a good dinner.

Now was the time to obey my hunch and release the press which would roar out the news that Hauptmann was to die! For the first time in my tabloid experience, something stopped me. Perhaps it was the influence of Walker, the only man on our staff, except myself, who had been trained in the old tradition that required an editor to wait to print the truth. I wondered what the celebrated city editor would have done in my spot, now that he was one of us. He was known for his hunches. We exchanged grins and he watched me sweat as I sat tight.

Suddenly, Peter Bloom, the circulation manager, broke through the crowd with a maddened glare. "The *American* is out with the verdict! Hauptmann got life!" he shouted. "What the hell is the matter with you? We're licked already!" A blasting voice came from the pressroom telephone: "Are you God-damned fools asleep? Trucks are rushing up the street! Bruno is acquitted! Let's go, for Christ's sake!" Outside, leather-lunged news vendors were already bawling their extras.

Again, the hunch said: "Sit tight; he's going to die!"

I depended on one man, Ray Doyle, my tough Irish reporter. I was to hear from him through a direct line from Flemington and I gripped that telephone until the knuckles stood white on my hand. By now the crowd believed we had been hopelessly beaten. Amid Bloom's curses and the general raging I held out. Five minutes had gone by during this pandemonium. Was Doyle waiting for the real verdict after panic-stricken reporters had guessed wrong? Obviously, the contradictory extras strengthened that assumption. Behind me the teletypes were at it with their foundry clatter: "Justice Trenchard calls the court to order." Bloom almost wrecked the machine. "That's past history!" he yelled. "What the hell are we getting out? A quarterly?" Two more minutes of frenzied agony and my Flemington telephone rang.

It was Doyle, cool, deliberate. "Guilty!" he said. "Guilty as the devil. It's the chair! I'm going out for a powder!"

I released the right press and called a blessing upon a good reporter. The *Mirror* was the first paper on the streets with the correct verdict. Even the Associated Press had sent out a false flash, committing one of the few great blunders in its long history of accuracy.

We approached Brisbane's million that night working for hours, changing the paper over for details and late photographs. Gordon Kahn, a rewrite genius, spun the running account. He was a peppery little man with the stern face of a Prussian officer and wore a monocle. Before opening a paragraph he wound himself up until he looked like a human pretzel, then he released his first sentence after the manner of a pitcher putting a curved ball over the plate. Mrs. Hauptmann's deathly smile he described as one which could be seen only on the faces of martyred women in the paintings of Italian masters. Later he went to Hollywood where such imagination brought more money.

Brisbane, pulling himself out of a sound sleep, telephoned me after midnight and grunted his pleasure over the result. He called up Hearst in California, claiming full personal credit for the entire performance, as I was informed later. It was pardonable. It was his last extra.

CHAPTER VI

BRISBANE now had to divert his energies from our circulation problems to counteract the public resentment which Hearst's "red-baiting" policies was arousing in intellectual circles. The Hearst papers had been attacking leaders in American education, such men as Professor Charles H. Judd and President Hutchins, of Chicago University, President Chase, of New York University, and President Graham of North Carolina University. Hearst had been calling them Communists and enemies of the nation. He advocated legislation branding teachers as unfaithful and compelling them to take oaths of loyalty. "Red scares" had been fostered and campaigns conducted against colleges and public schools, alleging they were centers of sedition. These assaults had been made upon sincere people who were trying to work for a genuinely better social order.

One thousand noted educators convening for the annual convention of the Department of Superintendence of the National Education Association, denounced the publisher as a national menace. The proceedings, reported in detail in the *New York Times* of February 25, 1935, and the press in general, had been brought to a boiling pitch by a virulent public attack upon Hearst by Professor Charles A. Beard.

This was not a denunciation to be ignored. The educators had addressed a resolution to the United States Senate demanding an investigation of "Hearst's spurious anti-red campaign, creating high emotional tensions and threatening to result in strained international relations and even war."

Brisbane admitted to me that the situation was serious.

"It has been Mr. Hearst's policy," he explained, "to go on sublimely during these affairs and let them die down. Later, when the enemy is asleep, he wipes them out. But something will have to be done about this. We will recruit students from schools and colleges, bring them to New York, show them through our plants and talk to them about our sound American principles. This will be my job. I shall have to talk to those boys and girls."

I met many of the youngsters while they were visiting Hearst's establishments. They were interested in the gigantic mechanism which produced the papers but expressed a complete boredom over the printed matter. Some of them laughed openly at Brisbane's campaign to "get married, have a baby and buy a car." The young women looked upon Beatrice Fairfax as a well-meaning grandmother, who shouldn't be expected to know what was going on. As a matter of fact I think Beatrice was becoming fed up with the whole business. The young men, I noticed, had something of old wisdom in them. There was nothing of the complacent self-conceit which characterized the youth of the early 1920's. These young people of 1935 wanted to know what was ahead without any bunk. They wanted to do their own thinking and must have looked upon our editorial policies as created by a pack of fools.

Brisbane encountered humiliation while trying to teach Hearst Americanism to his young visitors. Addressing them at a banquet he was openly jeered. One boy, head of a college paper in the Middle West, after hearing him praise American business, wanted to know why, a few weeks before, the Sunday *American* had printed a long article by Oswald Spengler charging that America was "a boundless field of unscrupulous dissolute dollar-hunters." The editor was left speechless. This was not the generation he had addressed after the turn of the century when, in praise of yellow journalism, he shouted: "What's the rainbow got that we haven't got?" This young crowd could not be pacified by "Alphonse and Gaston," the "Katzenjammer Kids" and "Happy Hooligan." They were interested in the economic crisis and what it was going to do to them. Brisbane, to them, was just one of the multi-millionaires whom they blamed for prevailing conditions.

The "Children's Crusade," as the editor called it, was abandoned. Youth had angered him because he could not control it with his column of 30,000,000 circulation. "The only word these young scamps understand is 'proletariat,' " he raged. "They're only fit for the goose step. That's what they're all going to be doing soon."

* * * * *

High society had become the fiery cross of our office. In the Hearst organization there were several interpretations of the *haut-monde*. A dowager might be recognized as omnipotent by the *Times,* treated as a Hindu deity by the *Sun* and land in our wastebasket because she had snubbed Mrs. Hearst. I had been provided with a long scroll naming the people who "belonged," and those who didn't, their good deeds and bad deeds; and I sat at night like Vishnu's avatar, comparing my Brahmanic laws with the interpolations in our society column. Privately, Brisbane had a loathing for what he still called the "four hundred" but he possessed a high respect for Mrs. Hearst's changing list.

The editor carefully studied the pictures of society ladies which appeared in our paper. Those on Mrs. Hearst's fluctuating record were no longer maidens dancing to the music of flutes, and printed photographs of those who were not pleasing to look upon provoked loud outcries. Our art department was ordered to retouch wrinkles and restore sagging chins until illustrations of the elite, passing through this sorcery, became unrecognizable. Governale, our art director, moaned continually, during this crisis.

"Look at this dame," he would say, holding up a photograph. "She began to run to bones and angles during the Rutherford B. Hayes administration. Pipe those bags under the eyes. How the hell are we going to fix her up? She's hopeless."

I commiserated regularly with Howard Shelley, who was our chronicler of social affairs. He was an impressive, slightly rotund gentleman, reflecting the glass of fashion, an amiable middle-aged bachelor of fine character to whom I had given a pseudonym to add to the dignity of his rounds. While we were selecting a pen name for him, old Pegler, whose imagination had helped to transport Hellinger around the world, wanted us to introduce the society writer to the public as Ravenwood Huntsbottom, a suggestion which was spurned by the management. I finally brought about a compromise by baptizing Shelley after two of the oldest streets of New York and he went down to tabloid fame as Barclay Beekman.

Pegler, whose recommendations I often adopted, was an extraordinary individual approaching seventy, the proud father of Westbrook Pegler, widely known columnist. The elder

Pegler had the appearance of a member of the House of Lords and was invaluable on assignments which required the uncovering of art frauds—a typical Hearst story—and used to obtain amazing information from the galleries by first offering to buy a $75,000 painting. When he had gathered his facts he would point with his cane at some mysterious flaw in the artist's work and depart. Later he described me in an interview with *Time Magazine* as "that fantastic Frenchman" but, apparently conscience-stricken, he wrote me that the boys of Editor Luce had exaggerated the remark.

Late society stories were often handled by Pegler, when Barclay Beekman had retired for the night. Whether the irrepressible veteran introduced himself on these occasions as Mr. Huntsbottom is a matter for his own memoirs. Pegler could write a whole column on a parvenu who juggled peas on his knife. But dowagers were his relish. He never refrained from describing a certain Park Avenue duchess as the old-time clipper *Hornet,* the pride of a great fleet, sailing into a room, her prow well up and her long pedigree flying from her spanker gaff, small barques of commoners passing her on the port side. A vigilant copy desk destroyed his salty word-picture several times. He loved the sea and when he finally managed to get this description into the paper he was happily shifted from society soirees to ship-news reports which came by telephone from the boys bobbing around at Quarantine.

Brisbane was interested in Pegler's changing activities and asked me to treat him with consideration. The reason for this politeness was revealed in a memorandum to me from the editor:

. . . He is the father of Westbrook Pegler who writes with the kick of a mule. Every time that boy lands on Mrs. Hearst's prize-fighting philanthropies my day is wasted. He has an unpleasant memory for things we're endeavoring to forget. There's no use trying to talk to anybody about stopping him. His column is a dose of prussic acid. Treat his father right and maybe his son will become human.

Our society problems eventually reached a fearful climax. Brisbane had informed me that Mrs. Hearst looked with solicitude upon the marriage of Mrs. John Jacob Astor Dick and Enzo Fiermonte, an Italian prize fighter. The alliance

was deplored by the Astor family, he said, and society hoped
that headlines about the romance would not be prolonged.
References to this affinity in the Hearst papers, which dredged
up the last details of it, had become poisonously offensive to
all Astors. To soothe matters we were instructed to pay respectful attention to the charitable activities of Mrs. Vincent
Astor. We leaped upon one of her benefits for unemployed
girls and grouped all photographs of the philanthropists present, which included Mrs. Astor, the Hon. James W. Gerard,
former American ambassador to Germany; Mrs. Franklin D.
Roosevelt and Mrs. William Randolph Hearst among others.

By now the impression prevailed in our art department that
all photographs had to be improved on general principles by
Brisbane's beauty treatments and when the Astor layout appeared it was disheartening to behold. A young artist, who
had labored over the ambassador had spiked his moustache
until the diplomat had taken on the resemblance of the Kaiser.
Mrs. Roosevelt appeared to have swallowed persimmons.

Brisbane, who was visiting Hearst's ranch at San Simeon
received a copy of the paper and sent me the following message:

"Somebody must have deliberately gone out to insult Mrs.
Astor in your layout of unemployed girls. In our paper she
appears as a hideous hag and cross-eyed, which she is not.
Gerard can sue us for what we did to him. As for Mrs. Roosevelt nothing worse could have happened. Is this a Communistic plot? You will hear about this when I return."

I received an air-mail letter from the editor cautioning me
to ignore a widely printed story that Mrs. Astor Dick Fiermonte had bought her prize-fighting husband from his wife for
$17,000. The story appeared in the *News* with colorful trim-
mings. I ordered the city editor to handle the Fiermonte
matter with tongs but I was in the position of a captain who
never knew where the next break would come in the line. I
had forgotten Dan Parker, the humorous dictator of our sports
department.

Sporting editors by now had gone far afield in their editorial
research. Some of them discussed everything but sports in
their authoritative columns. Managing editors had ceased to
bother with the gentlemen who handled the doings of the box-
ers and wrestlers, and a strange evolution had come about.
Sports columnists, suffering from ennui when tied down to

mundane news of fake matches, gravitated into magazine writing or dropped sports altogether and went in for the cannonading of Westbrook Pegler or the philosophy of Heywood Broun. They made good at it because editors had let them alone in the first place. They had humor, wrote naturally and when they developed into soothsayers they were paid much money. Then their views appeared under an announcement which pointed out that they were strictly personal and did not reflect editorial policies under any circumstances, God forbid! And as a result these pulpiteers gathered great followings.

Parker often wrote for his sporting pages a whole column on the wave of liberalism sweeping the country, and the possibility of Pussyfoot Johnson coming out in favor of fan dancing and Bishop Cannon advocating pari-mutuel betting as opposed to stock-market gambling. On the day when Brisbane returned from San Simeon, Parker had selected for the text of his sermon the marriage of Mrs. Astor and her prize-fighting lover. It was a Homeric poem, set in double-column measure, running apparently without end, to be sung to Spanish music with mandola and castanets, entitled: "The Saga of Enzo the Ginzo." I felt the need of a restorative as soon as I read the first stanza:

> *"In far-off Parenzo, lived Enzo the Ginzo,*
> *Stout son of the Butcher Fiermonte,*
> *Whose masculine beauty won every patootie*
> *In the realm of the House of Piedmonte."*

The whole sad story was immortalized. A cold chill possessed me as my eye caught the line: "When he married the widow and soothed her libido." The ballad was woven into a word-tapestry which cried out over Enzo's renunciation of garlic to win love and fortune.

Brisbane had read it all. I draw the curtain on the scene of delirium which followed. When the tempest was over and I was alone I understood why Gene Fowler locked the doors of his office and pulled sepulchral tones from an accordion when he was managing editor of the *American.*

After this poetical lava had cooled off, Brisbane began a clinical study of our sports department. Parker conducted his engine of energy with a fearlessness which was refreshing in a sordid realm manipulated by characters whose reputations were not even doubtful. When sports followers wanted the truthful low-down they read Parker aloud. What he said was accepted as law in the back rooms of sporting grog shops and training quarters. His integrity, strangely enough, saved him his job half a dozen times while I was his managing editor. As often happened, a man of probity in the post of sports editor was liable to discover that he was reposing in oblivion. Parker, after several years on the tabloid, found himself in the strangely anomalous position of a man who could not be fired because he was honest. This phenomenon was accepted by the management as a singular circulation asset among the sporting fraternity. Winchell, at one time, had attempted to influence Kobler to displace Parker by hiring Ed Sullivan, my *Graphic* sports editor. I liked Sullivan, but I liked Parker better and for his protection I obtained a contract for him.

Brisbane's attitude toward the vast amount of space which the Hearst papers devoted to sporting news never ceased to puzzle me. No other papers in the country carried comparable areas of type on such subjects as horse racing and prize fighting. Yet the editor in chief of our imposing chain rarely let a day slip by without referring to the race track as the Gehenna of all amusements. He was present at championship fights, writing his whole column on the results, describing the attending wealth with contempt and deploring the spectacle as one of the dark calamities that usually preceded the downfall of a decadent race. This was even more noticeable when the bloody encounters were held in the name of the Milk Fund Charities, one of Mrs. Hearst's philanthropies. Because of the trouble between the Kingdom of Italy and the blacks of Abyssinia, Brisbane predicted an international riot before Joe Louis fought Primo Carnera. He suggested that both fighters were owned by gangsters and stirred up such moral excitement that when the fight took place the attendance was doubled and Mrs. Hearst's charitable coffers were filled to overflowing.

The editor went so far as to visit the dressing room of Paulino Uzcudun, noted fighter of the Basque race, to describe the healing ointment being rubbed into his eyebrows and the grease applied to his gloves to make them slip. On that evening Uzcudun went down in four rounds of slaughter before

Joe Louis but the aged journalist already had visited the Negro, examining his fists, noting his cool demeanor and winding up by comparing the anxiety of Joe Blackburn, his trainer, with the solicitude that Odysseus displayed for his son Telemachus. Brisbane's accounts reflected a feeling of nostalgic suffering over the fortunes that changed hands in fifteen or twenty minutes at Madison Square Garden.

Hearst sports writers absorbed these narratives with philosophical resignation and prayed to keep out of Brisbane's orbit. All of this had been anticipated by the perspicacious Parker, and when the great editor invaded the *Mirror* its sporting department was even better prepared than Clarke and his brontosaurus. The sports editor and his trained beavers had fortified themselves with books about the beginning of the human race and studies of the behavior of the anthropoid apes of Asia. They had neglected few avenues of approach to the problem of human evolution and were frequently consulted by Clarke and myself when Brisbane's mind swerved in that direction.

Parker had not completely recovered from his interview with Jack Dempsey about the gorilla when Brisbane asked me out of a clear sky to fire Fred Keats, a member of our sports staff and one of the best informed writers of race-track news in the country. At the time, Keats specialized in selections and predictions and had received a high rating from the *Sun, World-Telegram* and the *Journal.* From what Brisbane told me later, I gathered that one of Keats' selections had offended Joseph E. Widener, a highly reputable millionaire Philadelphia sportsman, who owned a string of horses. Keats' column was ripped out of an edition on the way to press.

This was a staggering blow to the sports department and telephones rang late into the night with messages from disappointed followers. Parker and I disagreed violently with Brisbane over his high-handed action and after three days wore him down to the point where he permitted us to restore Keats to the payroll. Newspaper jobs under Brisbane, during his last years, often hung on the whims of friends whose displeasure meant that some head had to come off. Money, among some of the old, bred a timorous outlook on life, an occasional baseless suspicion of disloyalty and intrigue carried to fantastic limits. Some thoughtless remark dropped by a gentleman of haunch, paunch and jowls and based on nothing but a fleeting impression provoked by a bad liver, could pack a man off jobless after ten or twenty years of service. I had seen it happen.

In the case of Keats, his circulation value had forced Brisbane to give in and he did not accept the defeat gracefully. He pored over Parker's pages looking for something to criticize and finally discovered that the sports writer specialized in the inelegant but descriptive word "burp" in his accounts of wrestling matches. In one column of type Brisbane had counted fourteen "burps" which he had patiently ringed with a red pencil. This he attached for my benefit to a page of dictated harangues against sports reporting in general and "burping" in particular. He couldn't find the word in his dictionary and was sure Shakespeare had frowned on it. If the word "regurgitate" did not suffice, he said, perhaps the whole subject had better be dropped. Even "belching" was undesirable. I suggested that the offending word might well have originated from Trimalchio's Dinner, as described by Petronius. He said he would investigate that theory but meanwhile the word had to go.

Although Keats remained with us there followed from Brisbane's dictaphones a tirade that had never been equalled by him against the race tracks. In 12-point type he used the top of the front page to shout his denunciations.

"Thousands at the track, at the 'Great' Kentucky Derby; millions in poolrooms exchanging money for experience. Insiders, including horse-dopers, *jockey bribers* will make money. Rich men and women will enjoy cheap excitement and cheaper newspaper advertising. Such is the 'sport of kings.' Show this to your gambling friends!"

Brisbane was said to have lost a neat wager years ago on a race which had turned out to be fixed and had never forgotten it. Of his friend Moses L. Annenberg, who was later to be sentenced to prison while publisher of the *Philadelphia Inquirer* in the largest income-tax scandal in the history of the country, and who had amassed millions by controlling racetrack information, Brisbane wrote:

"A man who makes more money out of horse racing than any others in the United States *never bets a dollar* on a race.

He KNOWS horse racing, and is content to supply information, on which the foolish gamble."

In reviewing the life of Annenberg in *Colliers* in 1939, John T. Flynn wrote that Brisbane was a silent partner of Annenberg in these fabulous race-track enterprises. Flynn said the information had been given to him by E. Z. Dimitman, Annenberg's executive editor. During my researches for this book I verified the fact without any possibility of doubt, that Brisbane had no financial association whatever with Annenberg in his racing-news empire. The editor was personally sincere in his abhorrence of the race track.

Betting on the races by Hearst employees, who toiled knee-deep in tempting race-track tips, reached such an alarming pitch that in 1935, Hearst, from San Simeon, personally sent to all publishers of his papers the following order of the day:

> It has come to my attention that many of our employees are spending entirely too much time perusing race-track form charts, making bets and watching results of races during business hours. I have also noticed that a number of employees leave the building during business hours to go to adjacent book-maker establishments.
>
> Will you please inform everyone in your departments to discontinue the practice of leaving the building during business hours to go to book-making establishments. Also to kindly eliminate the attention they are giving race-track betting during business hours.
>
> I do not wish to do anything drastic in this matter, but if the condition is not materially improved, it will be necessary to take decided steps.

If the "decided steps" had been taken on Hearst's papers in New York alone, perhaps a corporal's guard might have been left on each publication to carry on their work. This was evident on the *Mirror*. The elements that moved and molded the staff were bound to have an effect of unaccountable mischief on the individual. Hearst reporters gambled because they had more respect for a lashed horse than they had for the editorials in their own papers which cried out against the crooked track, a few columns removed from the racing pages which promoted it.

When Brisbane wrote that Annenberg KNEW horse racing and never bet a dollar on it he had but one implication in mind. From evidence which the editor had gathered he was convinced that those who made money from the track practically stole it from the pockets of the foolish victims whose feeble minds enslaved them to the depravity of the nation's pool-room population. It was a moral offense for which no indictment could be obtained under the American laws. A man could amass millions out of it, but could not be stopped unless he failed to share at least part of his gains with the federal income tax department. The tragic hypocrisy of the whole mess led into a labyrinth of crime, often to murder.

Brisbane hated this racket as bitterly as Billy Sunday hated the devil. Hearst's order of the day had been the result of evidence which the editor had uncovered in our own business. Race-track gambling had demoralized a number of Hearst newspaper men who got out of bed every morning with the pleasant thought of making money without working for it. Hearst hoped to halt their scramble for the new El Dorado, hence his unique command.

Brisbane in his editorials branded the sport henceforth and irrevocably as a gigantic fraud and the man who bet his money on it as a derelict of abysmal ignorance. Meanwhile, our sporting pages, and those of other Hearst papers were giving even more than usual space to the promotion of the amusement. Aside from a two-line note, Brisbane had never asked me to enforce rigidly Hearst's order against race-track betting in our department. He knew that those who indulged in it would have laughed in his face.

Readers who took their race-track betting seriously, following every tip on the *Mirror's* sports pages, and who tried to digest the editor's fiery denunciation of running horses in the same issue, were soon writing to him in large numbers, demanding an explanation of these inharmonious tones in their family organ.

The following was typical of the bushels of letters received from exasperated supporters:

Dear Editor Brisbane:

Which is it—editorial stupidity or "Joe and Asbestos" intelligence? In your editorials you say a man CANNOT make any money betting on the races. But on your sporting pages "Joe and Asbestos" PROVE a man can make money betting at the track. You say it's all wrong but your sporting pages tell us to bet our heads off. Why not pull yourself together?

"Joe and Asbestos" were mythical race-track characters created by the sporting cartoonist Ken Kling who had achieved such a success with the pair on Pulitzer's *Evening World* that he was now guiding their destinies on the *Mirror*. Kling, in his cartoon strip, would start his characters off with a five-dollar bill at an authentic race track on the day of a race, place their money on an actual horse and often pick a winner. Day after day this would go on until "Joe and Asbestos" had increased their original investment to $500 and sometimes $1,000. Kling was a preoccupied little man with gimlet eyes whose head seemed to move constantly from right to left as if on a pivot. The production of "Joe and Asbestos" was a mysterious affair. Wild horses could not have dragged the details of the business out of Kling. His strip fascinated many readers who used the two characters as financial advisers and often by aping them, rolled up the same bank roll in real life. If "Joe and Asbestos" encountered disaster their followers suffered with them but rarely complained, charging the whole matter to the uncertainties of existence.

The trail of Brisbane's persistent prowlings promptly led to Ken Kling's door. The editor asked me for a complete explanation of this magic and ordered me to throw it out of the paper. As "Joe and Asbestos" occasionally suffered heavy losses in their mythical betting I was confident that Kling was in no way connected with irregular channels leading to the race track. Kobler had taken a fling at it and lost $75. I still believe the comic strip was legitimate as far as that form of sport could be. The *Evening World* would not have countenanced it, otherwise.

Brisbane did not know that "Joe and Asbestos" helped to support the *Mirror*.

Kling produced a ten-cent booklet which contained the names of horses and future races in which they were to run. A code carried in the comic strip referred to the names of the horses in the booklet. This gave the disciples time to buy the booklet in advance and arrange their finances. Kling, on some occasions, sold as many as 50,000 booklets a week. He pocketed seven cents per booklet and defrayed the cost of its printing. The balance went into the coffers of the *Mirror,* whose chief bookkeeper handled the transaction with the eye of a lynx. The *Mirror* portion had averaged as high as $600 a week, sometimes higher in the summer.

Brisbane listened with rapt attention as I explained this new field of finance. He took in the whole matter as a piece of mesmerism. He grunted but was not surprised when I told him that Kobler had arranged the details.

"And so we're actually making money out of horse racing," he said, crestfallen. "According to those figures we're taking in at least $30,000 a year. Well, I'll be damned!"

He returned, humbled, to the "wax works," and "Joe and Asbestos" remained, impregnable, to carry on their responsibilities. This finished the great editor's campaign against the race track. He never again ridiculed the running horse.

CHAPTER VII

Episodes born of Brisbane's quixotic impulses hurried my existence to a climax inevitable as hitting bottom in sliding down a greased pole.

The army of fresh readers we had attracted through the Hauptmann trial melted as the snow now vanishing under the Spring sun. The daily million was a mirage. Bitter parting shots had been fired at us by our new followers before they retired to less bewildering literature. The editor read their letters painfully. People were tired of his gorillas, his dinosaurs, his grudging admissions that the starving should be fed but that the rich should not be called upon to do it.

Rising costs of editorial output took up my time. Brisbane's additions to the staff, his love-and-marriage opiate, his wired editorials and his own salary had added more than $5,000 a week to my budget. Before I left the *Mirror* in June, editorial expenses had climbed above $17,000 a week. This did not include demands made by other departments of the paper. Our advertising situation was doleful.

The editor was alarmed about the turn affairs were taking. His promises to Hearst of at least a million daily circulation were hopeless. He had thrown out of the paper everything that might have given it a fringe of prestige. I had been using an interesting column by Hendrik Willem Van Loon, illustrated with his unique drawings. Van Loon was sold down the river to another Hearst paper in a barter arrangement for a comic called "Betty Boop." Van Loon never knew how low down the scale he went in this transaction. We had to throw in a cartoon strip called "Pete the Tramp" with Van Loon's essays to corral the "Boop."

Brisbane showed no tendency to have the tabloid cater to anything above a prurient curiosity. Any effort on Stanley Walker's part, or mine, to prevent the paper from hitting the lowest common denominator of intelligence jeopardized our jobs. Our policy seemed to be to inflame the reader in his congenital resentment of privacy, to assure his vulgar assumption that anybody's doings are everybody's business. Under Brisbane's generalship the handling of legitimate news had become a farce.

The Great Illuminist's fanfare, when he had taken over the *Mirror* had attracted the curious attention of his rich friends, some of whom were advertisers. He urged them to buy the paper and criticize it. His blind confidence that he could drive the publication to a million circulation daily in a few months had literally put him "on the spot." The criticisms he received were brutal.

Eddy S. Brandt, President of the Brandt Advertising Company of Chicago, wrote as follows:

> After looking through every page, I can't find any reason why you call it a newspaper. Why don't you print on pages two and three a condensed report of all the important news of the day, and then follow with the thirty-six or forty-four pages of human interest stories, such as having a baby, buying a car, etc.

Brisbane replied:

> Thanks for your letter, thanks in fact TWICE. Exactly what you suggest is what I want to do, only in one column, not in two pages. The Bible describes the creation of the world in about one solid column and a tabloid newspaper ought to be able to describe the news of the day in that space. I mean the news worthwhile.

Stanley Walker was assigned to the task of boiling down the entire "worthwhile" news of the world every day to 500 words with significant editorial explanations, a burden which reduced the Bible's description of the creation to child's play.

Brisbane apparently had forgotten he had invited the criticisms of his important friends and his anger mounted with each reply. He asked me to read a letter from Kenneth Collins, then an important executive of Gimbel Brothers of New York, part of which follows:

> I was shocked at the preoccupation of the *Mirror* with nothing but cheap scandal, murder and arson. You once commented to me that you were going to ask your editor to print

only the kind of news one would want to show to a fifteen-year-old daughter. The front page of your paper has a story about a mother who has been refused custody of her own child because of her misconduct; another about two men guilty of outrageous crimes against children; the last one about a son who has just murdered his father, with the naïve editorial comment, "Gerard is Sorry." That would seem to be the genius of understatement.

On the same day the following news was reported on the front page of the *New York Times:* Hitler insists upon a plebiscite in Austria; a prominent official of the Catholic Church assails the President; the one great test of NRA in the Supreme Court is to be abandoned; Tugwell is to hear the $95,000,000 plan for Land Relief. . . .

These are matters that concern the rank and file. Yet I see practically no mention of them in the *Mirror*. . . . I have a genuine interest in the success of the *Mirror* and, incidentally, a certain concern over a number of advertising failures we have had in the past few days from the paper. I believe that ideas of cheap sensationalism are still motivating most of your writers.

The letter from Collins, widely known as an influential business executive, brought Brisbane to a low ebb of activity. He assumed the attitude of a misunderstood prophet.

"The trouble with these people," he said, "is that they don't know our problems. I should like to see THEM try to get a million readers with such news as they describe. They ought to know that when I get a million and a half more readers I'll tone the whole thing down, make room for more advertising and be smug like Captain Patterson. Pulitzer did it. He was yellower than Hearst, once, but now they're canonizing him. This is pure hypocrisy!"

The editor's interpretation of hypocrisy drove me to Pietro's where I gave my orders to the paper by telephone. Once in a while I found Walker there, sitting in a corner, masking his dolors.

"Fantastic man," he said, during one of our chats. "There never has been anybody quite like Brisbane before. What has the old Caliban done now? I rarely see him."

"I suggested to him today," I said, "to pacify the rising wrath, that we carry a Bible text across the top of our editorial page, such as appears daily in the *American*. Today, for instance, the text in the *American* was selected by Rev. Abraham Heller, a Flatbush rabbi, from *Daniel*, IV:27. Perhaps you remember it: 'Wherefore, O king, let my counsel be acceptable unto thee, and break off thy sins by righteousness, and thine iniquities by showing mercy to the poor.' "

Walker buried a grin in his snifter bowl, his blue eyes twinkling over the rim, as I poured out my own potion.

"What did he say to that?" he asked.

"He said the *Mirror* wasn't bad enough, yet."

During this period Brisbane flew into inexplicable tantrums. He conceived an antipathy for "Mickey Mouse," my favorite character in the movies and comics. He said he would endeavor to convince me that this member of the rat family had no humor and was a waste of space. "Mickey Mouse" had been on the *Mirror* with me for six years. He was the only optimist on the staff. He never bragged about his following, an immense army of happy children laughing from the heart. I decided that if I had to fire "Mickey Mouse" I would walk out with him.

During these arguments Brisbane would roar: "Children can be better occupied reading Sir James Jeans about the world we live in. *Throw that rat out!*"

I wore the editor down and won a victorious battle for my little friend. Under the gathering clouds, I felt, sometimes, a premonition that Brisbane, like an ogre, would devour all the help but myself and "Mickey Mouse," holding us together to run the ship. Then, perhaps, we might throw our oppressor overboard, swing the wheel about and set sail for a magic island resounding with young, gleeful laughter.

Winchell's column now appeared seven days a week. Daily he dressed his plank of gossip and scandal, like a wild-eyed carpenter, "the tongue of his foreplane whistling its wild ascending lisp." He had suddenly supplanted Paul Yawitz by inserting his wares into the Sunday issue. Yawitz had contributed a Broadway column in the Sunday *Mirror* from the time the edition was launched, and Winchell, pondering over the fact that the Sunday paper had acquired 1,300,000 readers without his services, more than twice the circulation of the daily in which he appeared, was becoming disturbed. His only hope was to prevent other people from imitating his gossip.

The Broadway-column formula was pretty well known. The woods were full of key-hole peepers sprouting up around the country, eager to work themselves up to $1,000 a week. Winchell expressed his disgust of these imitators. Supposing the Sunday *Mirror* attained three or four million readers? Yawitz would then be talking to a larger audience in one day than Winchell could reach in six. Columnists of the gossip type were occasionally surprised to find themselves in possession of amazing reputations, without being able to account to themselves for the facts which gave rise to these strange fancies of the multitude. Soon, it might be the Great Yawitz. Harassed by these thoughts, the originator agreed to write his Sunday contribution at a cut-rate price, much lower than he had demanded when the issue was organized. Yawitz went down unceremoniously, after the manner of a general whose horse has been shot from under him. He landed safely in Hollywood.

For some reason, the supplanting of Yawitz by Winchell amused Brisbane and he prepared a little editorial for the *Mirror* announcing that the peeper's prattle would appear every day. Winchell's business, he wrote, was to collect news after the sun went down and the bright lights came on. The gossiper's persistency reminded him whimsically of Keats' famous poem, from which he quoted:

> *"Bright star! would I were steadfast as thou art—*
> *Not in lone splendour hung aloft the night. . . ."*

The editor handed the editorial to me with a laugh. "Winchell is doing the added stint for less money than he wanted," he said. "He couldn't keep out of an issue that has more than a million readers. To please him I have written a little editorial in which I quote two famous lines from Keats. I hope Winchell will not assume they were dashed off by Fred Keats, our race-track man, while the horses were in the stables."

Brisbane's disposition changed abruptly the next evening when he was leaving for San Simeon. I had been listening to a tirade about expenses.

"Suppose Mr. Hearst should die," he said, his cold blue eyes full of alarm, "do you know what would happen? The

banks would close up all of his papers that are losing money.
You and your whole staff would be out in the street. Think
THAT over. I know there are some costs we can't control.
We shouldn't have to pay so much money to King Features.
It's outside of the combination and he can take his money out
of the syndicate any time, when he wants to build castles and
all sorts of things."

His remarks were prophetic. In less than three years' time
a number of Hearst papers were disposed of throughout the
empire, including the *American*, his editorial mouthpiece, which
almost overnight, closed its doors. This depressing development had considerable bearing upon the suicide of Victor
Watson, for years editor of the *American,* and who had spent
almost a lifetime in Hearst's employ.

I received some brutal communications from Brisbane as
soon as he had reached Hearst's sanctuary. These were addressed to Stanley Walker and myself. One of them said:

> I have been studying the *Mirror* with Mr. Hearst. It dis-
> turbs us by its *extreme quietness*. We must get another half-
> million readers at once. If we can't get them I know you and
> Walker will both agree with me that we ought to get a new set
> of editors, beginning with myself *AS A GET OUT*. With
> twenty million people around us there is no excuse for selling
> only six hundred and fifty thousand papers.
>
> Mr. Hearst expresses to me the opinion that it is a mistake
> for me to have you as the editor writing a column daily, and
> also that would apply to Mr. Walker as an editor. We have
> more columns than a Greek ruin. I am afraid it will be
> necessary to stop all column writing by those that are respon-
> sible for making the paper interesting. We must make the
> paper more EXCITING. After we get one million, five hun-
> dred thousand readers we can ALL be column writers.

Walker read this ruefully, puffing his pipe. "Why doesn't
he pop out with a million-dollar idea of his own from that
five hundred thousand candle-power brain?" he asked. "This
looks like the beginning of the end, or the end of the beginning for both of us."

Brisbane's criticism was typical of the conclusions of the
high command. The *Mirror,* including the Sunday edition, at
that moment possessed a larger circulation than that of any

other paper on Hearst's national chain. Brisbane's passion for a million, his promise to Hearst, which we could not fulfill had thrown our organization into a state bordering on chaos.

The comments about my own column nettled me. I had handled this department besides my executive work, on Hearst's orders from the time I became his managing editor in 1929. I remembered what Hearst had told me at Sands Point: "Ape Arthur. It may do him good to know that someone else can do this." My paragraphs irked Brisbane and he had told me so. He had quoted one of my comments in his "Today" column, mentioning my name and position to his 30,000,000 readers and I had been deluged with letters. I showed them to him with innocent pride and incurred his displeasure. Perhaps he had a senile fear that my jottings might eventually supplant his own, when he became too old to keep going. "How would you like it," he said, "if you created something, worked at it for years, and found somebody else doing the same thing?"

I went to the composing room where Michael Hodgins, our printing superintendent, was making up the form in which my column appeared. I ripped the cold type of my essays from the steel rules and threw it to the floor. I had been writing galleys of these paragraphs every day for ten years, beginning long before I had come to the *Mirror*. The fanfare of advertising I had received when I continued the stint as the *Mirror's* editor had been only a Hearst whim.

Traveling through the country, meanwhile, Brisbane had discovered two girl lumberjacks in Idaho, towering females who had won a chopping championship in Oregon. He wired me to arrange their transportation to New York where they were to chop down trees in Central Park. This, he felt, would have an uplifting effect on our circulation and we could print stories about what they thought of our decadent civilization. I am still trying to forget this nightmare. My neck pained me for days from throwing my head back to my backbone when I gave the axe swingers their daily instructions. They must have been about seven feet tall.

I had to obtain a permit from the City Government for this demonstration and I outlined the state of affairs to Mayor La Guardia at the Little Venice. Through mouthfuls of spaghetti he roared with laughter at my new affliction.

"So," he burst out, "Brisbane wants to chop down trees for circulation! He's not going to go around hacking at this town with an axe. The Hearst crowd hasn't buried the hatchet with me yet. But I'm always glad to help a friend in distress. I'll get Bob Moses, the Park Commissioner, to find some tree for you that's no good and would have to come down anyway. But don't start any riots in Central Park to sell newspapers or I'll put you and Brisbane in jail."

My conference with Mayor La Guardia had not been confined to spaghetti and the woodchoppers. The little reformer's years of struggle for office finally had given him the exalted position which had been his life's dream—Boss of New York. Crooked politicians did not want him in power, for obvious reasons. He visioned New York as a spotless town, and sporadic crime waves made him writhe. He knew that he could not move forcibly against the corruption, the gangster murders, and the criminals so frequently released for lack of evidence so long as the Tammany District Attorney's office was not in full sympathy with his resolves. Fiorello reviewed the situation, as he had in the past, but this time he had a plan.

He hated anything which degraded the Italian people. He had chased out of town all Italian organ grinders who used to appear in the Spring with the merry tune of *The Sidewalks of New York*. He knew that a large part of the Italian population of the city indulged in a lottery controlled by Tammany chieftains and whose numbers appeared in several daily newspapers, leading people into petty vices and small crimes which usually preceded great ones.

One form of lottery was known by the innocent title of "Italian Disbursement Figures." They were supposed to inform the people of the budgetary status of various towns under the rule of Mussolini. These financial announcements appeared, strangely enough, on the sporting pages of the *Mirror, News, American, Journal* and *Brooklyn Times*. I assumed that the figures came weekly from the United Press, although I had not investigated their source, and I told the Mayor so. He said he would get to the bottom of it if he had to indict all the editors who fathered such hypocrisy.

I was not surprised to receive the following letter from him:

My dear Emile:

You will recall that when we talked over the publication of the Italian lottery numbers published in your paper, it was stated by you that these were furnished by the United Press Association. I am in receipt of a communication from the United Press informing me that it does NOT handle any such material.

Inasmuch as it will be necessary for me to run down the source of the information, I will appreciate any assistance which you may be able to give me.

Sincerely yours,

F. H. LA GUARDIA,

Mayor.

As the Mayor apparently wanted to make the investigation an official one, it became a serious matter for all papers concerned. It struck at the heart of Tammany crookedness and led to the door of James J. Hines, impregnable manipulator of the political underworld. Murders often were committed as a result of these lottery enterprises. By this time any man in a newspaper office who did not know that "Dutch" Schultz, notorious lottery racketeer, who was to be slaughtered later with his henchmen, was under high political protection, was considered an ignoramus. It was a different matter to prove this legally, before controlled judges.

With the Mayor's letter in my hand I went to Stanley Walker's cubicle to consult him as my associate. The place was abandoned, pipe rack, tobacco, books, everything was gone including his dark-eyed secretary. Clarke, studying my astonishment as I peered into the uninhabited office, explained the mystery:

"They've moved him down to the *American*. He went out like the Arabs. It's too bad; he was a good guy. He wasn't afraid to laugh. I think they're going to give him the works to make him break his contract. It's the old Spanish Inquisition."

CHAPTER VIII

I FOUND Brisbane communing in his private office with Bainbridge Colby on the day I opened the discussion about Mayor La Guardia's letter. Colby and the editor met fairly regularly in conferences which had become known as the "stop Roosevelt huddles." Words of protest often slipped through the transom about "that man in the White House" and "the years that would have to be spent to undo the harm he was doing." Power would soon be in the hands of the ignorant and impoverished. I had been introduced to the former Secretary of State during one of these discussions. Brisbane was talking about progress. Progress! It would last if you kept at it. More motors, more babies, more advertising, more money, but if you were stopped from making a profit by Roosevelt, Democracy would end. Such talks usually were followed by blistering attacks against the New Deal in the "March of Events" section of the Sunday *American* and signed by Colby.

The editor, scanning La Guardia's letter, switched from the New Deal menace to the problems of our lottery numbers. He told me to suggest to the Mayor that all editors whose papers printed the figures should be called in to reveal the source of them. The *Mirror* should not be expected to drop them unless its competitors followed suit.

To those acquainted with the financial reports of tabloid literature, the sporting pages were a gambler's paradise. The "numbers racket," whose history was written in a trail of blood, played a sinister part in helping to keep up the circulation figures of all New York papers of the sensational type. After I became managing editor of the *Mirror* I discovered that I had inherited these gambling plagues. The paper had acquired them through a more enterprising genius than I am and they had become a part of the bone and fibre of our publication. Disturbing rumors reached me that we were the "official" lottery paper in New York. The so-called Italian Disbursement announcements came in some mysterious way to an underling in our circulation department. Other figures of gambling interest were obtained from legitimate sources, as for instance, total stock sales and bond sales, from the Stock Exchange. All of these totals had become a part of a gigantic game of chance run by racketeers

Over our wires came the Cincinnati bank clearings daily which were proofread four times with a copyholder and inserted under the news of "best bets" in the sixth race on the sports page. United States Treasury balances and customs receipts also were part of the economic information studied with bloodshot eyes by the gambling element. Wall Street furnished its figures innocently but they were used as a working medium daily by those who manipulated the numbers fraud. The buyer of a lottery ticket entered the transaction with a feeling of reassurance by the knowledge that his figures originated from gentlemen in the stock market. Papers which catered to this gambling-mad clientele published the numbers on their sporting pages to make this public service easier for their readers, who rarely read anything else, thereby making it unnecessary for them to study the financial pages of the *Times*. The *Mirror* also carried a small cartoon called "Policy Pete," which displayed cryptic numbers in the hat of a little negro who cracked jokes. This amusement was for the children in Harlem who could only afford to bet a few pennies. The *Journal* adopted a similar idea known as "Policy Joe." High-powered delivery trucks of the *Mirror*, *News* and *American* engaged in a reckless race every night, breaking speed laws under special police protection, often endangering human life, to be the first to reach thousands of newsstand customers in Harlem and the Bronx who devoured this arithmetic.

Mayor La Guardia made an appointment at the City Hall to take up these matters with me and with Frank J. Hause, then managing editor of the *News* and known widely in newspaper circles as "Colonel" Hause. He was a typical success of streamlined tabloidia. His paper had the largest circulation in America. The "Colonel's" salary, including bonuses, often reached $150,000 a year.

"Colonel" Hause listened with amused tolerance to a palaver which the Mayor launched about the spiritual duty of the press. La Guardia became more emphatic as his sermon touched upon the encouragement which the publicizing of the "racket numbers" gave to those in control of organized vice.

Morally, he believed, the editors were as guilty as the lottery bosses. He spoke of the possibility of indictments.

"You can't stop people from gambling," Hause countered. "We are not telling them to gamble. The figures you speak of have been running in the papers for seven years and are worth to us in circulation from 50,000 to 75,000 readers. I can assure you that we will not stop printing them regardless of any action taken by other newspapers."

As I was shining by a reflected light I could do nothing but inform the Mayor that I would report the results of the conference to my office. In his desperation for more readers, Brisbane told me the Mayor's request was unthinkable. If we should throw 75,000 lottery readers overboard they would go to the *News*. Papers had only recently received permission from Postmaster General Farley to print the lists of Irish Sweepstakes winners, which made circulation jump. Such publication had been illegal heretofore. Now it was part and parcel of the elastic freedom of the press.

"If the government tolerates gambling in our more abundant life," said the editor, "what are WE going to do about it? Tell the Mayor we will not be the first to throw the lottery figures out."

That closed the incident temporarily. But the situation had opened a door through which fate was to push me to face my last grave adventure on the *Mirror*.

Brisbane had developed an interesting philosophy about crime news. He had evolved it from the premise that murder was the backbone of sensational journalism. That was elementary logic. One deplored crime but printed its details when it was committed, always first, whenever possible. No murder was too horrifying to be discussed in print by a noted psychologist if he were paid $500 an article. This form of editing gave a needed dignity to a revolting duty. If matters got too bad, an occasional clergyman accepted $300 to deplore the criminal instincts of human nature. At times, an attitude could be taken that society prepared the crime and the criminal committed it. But this had a touch of radicalism to it and was abandoned. Society now needed protection from the criminal and had to be told all about him, but only in a general way.

When correctly handled, crime was the best friend any Hearst editor ever could have. This you could verify from the circulation charts. Officially, Brisbane was against crime, like the preacher in President Coolidge's familiar story. One viewed with alarm, but a Hearst editor was not expected to go out of his way to stop it altogether. Such a person would be compared with the religious fanatic who cut off his right arm.

In his ectoplasmic battles against crime, Brisbane chose a theoretical, almost etheric course. "We hate to print this ugly picture," he would write, referring to the photograph of a sanguinary encounter. "It shows three gentlemen rather unpleasantly situated. But showing three kidnapers, hands manacled, heads battered, after detectives got them, is useful—especially useful to those with kidnaping ideas."

A headline for this art was: "Hideous, BUT It Teaches a Lesson." Invariably, during crime waves, Hearst cartoons showed a huge snake labeled "Crime," curled about the form of Justice, her eyes bandaged with "red tape," politicians, criminals, perjurers and "fixers" standing about. "The racketeer has millions," Brisbane wrote, "and can pay well. He can provide the politician, the 'fixer' who acts as go-between, or guarantees to get 'the right man' on the jury."

Here, the editor struck at the core of corruption. This condition prevailed wherever political evildoing existed. It was all literally true, and Brisbane knew it, but the underworld was well aware that such editorials would never go further than mere words—it would never mention the crooks by name.

On the other hand, a convict such as Alabama Pitts, Sing Sing's star athlete, who had served his time and paid his debt to society, was hounded by Brisbane into a cringing fugitive when the former prisoner tried to reinstate himself by playing in the outfield for the Albany Baseball Club. He had been arrested as a boy for a violation of the law against concealed weapons. The parole board had reduced his term for good behavior.

"This is your parole system that encourages crime," wrote Brisbane. "You may truly say with Lovelace, 'Stone walls do not a prison make, or iron bars a cage.' The parole board knocks a hole in, on the side of the prison, to let the criminals come out, as rapidly as they go in."

Events were shaping rapidly to put our cries of righteousness to the test. A grand jury, whose foreman was Lee Thompson Smith, a business man widely respected, had been holding hearings for several weeks to obtain evidence against the political underworld. The jurymen were working under conditions of daily intimidation. Some of them had received threats against their lives. Little merchants, trying to conduct their business as American freemen were forced to pay armed racketeers for the privilege of being unmolested while earning a living. These victims knew what to expect if they testified. Such evidence was difficult to place on the record. Occasionally, a witness had been found in the gutter with a bullet in his back.

The jury's attention was attracted to the voluminous reports of crime news in the sensational press and it had heard that one Martin Mooney, a reporter for the *American,* possessed information that might be used as evidence against the "policy racket," whose numbers were played by lottery ticket buyers who saw them every day in the Hearst papers. According to the *Mirror's* account of the proceedings, Mooney had inadvertently uttered the name of Hines, the Harlem Tammany leader, while being questioned about racketeering. While Mooney's reference to Hines in itself was no strong indictment of the politician it had served to connect the leader with dozens of reports about the policy vice. The reporter refused to elaborate his testimony, was arrested on a charge of contempt, sentenced to jail for thirty days and fined $250. He had been taken from Tombs Prison to court where he was released preceding an argument on habeas corpus.

Pending Mooney's final release the Hearst papers introduced him to the multitudes as a martyr, "standing true to the ethics and traditions of his noble profession, sacrificing himself for sacredness of a confidence, the foundation stone of the freedom of the press."

Brisbane shouted, editorially: "The reporter should NOT tell. The right of a newspaperman to keep confidential sources of information secret is more important than the right of a clergyman to keep secret the statements of his parishioner, the right of a lawyer or doctor, to refuse information concerning a client or patient. In the case of clergyman, doctor, lawyer, ONE individual is concerned. In the newspaperman's case the *whole public* is concerned."

This argument was based on a great principle and should have been worthy of a better cause. I said as much when Brisbane asked me to print the editorial. He became surly and pointed out that it was not our business to help the courts or its investigators. We were observers, reporting what was going on.

On that evening the grand jury requested me to appear as a witness in its criminal investigation on the following morning. It was known that I was working closely with Brisbane. Because of that fact, my testimony and my general attitude might be considered of consequence. As the situation involved my personal integrity I did not discuss it with him.

I reasoned that if the liberty of the press could be justified in protecting a source of information which led to a den of rogues, then it betrayed justice. If criminals could intimidate the press to defraud justice, the freedom of journalism was not for long and carried within it the seeds of its own death.

I had no illusions about what might happen to those whose testimony helped to crack the ring. The danger existed in the difficulty of discovering where the political underworld ended and legitimate traffic began. One met charming gentlemen of political influence whose apparent friendship had but one object: to suppress news rather than give it the light; to get a man where they wanted him if he ran a press. They respected more their own code of ethics than the blatant journalism whose hypocrisies were so glaring they could not be hidden.

Perhaps truth could hardly be expected to adapt itself to these wily sinuosities. Translating truth into action often brings about interesting decisions. There was but one answer to my meditations. When my mind was made up I fell into my first refreshing sleep in a long time.

CHAPTER IX

A CITIZEN entering a grand-jury room to help law enforcement, while much of New York County was still controlled by Tammany, faced a unique experience. Here one saw, growling outside the doors of justice, the first consequences of political protection, the mob as a scum that rose to the top when crime reached a boil. A witness had to push his way through wide-mouthed brutes who knew that their power lay in intimidation.

Lee Thompson Smith's grand jury was aware of this, barricaded in its locked room in the Criminal Courts Building. Words dropped by the mob indicated that I had been recognized by some of those who stood menacingly before the door while I pushed and struggled to reach it. "That's a *Mirror* guy," a man exclaimed in back of me. "That's the second from that sheet that's gone in there." Evidently, my reporter, Arthur Mefford, who had testified before me, had been remembered.

I had some rather formidable help in reaching my destination. Escorting me was my occasional bodyguard, Colonel Ervin J. Smith, President of the International Secret Service Association and one of his private detectives known as "Spike" McNulty, a creature fully as menacing to look upon as those who stared at him. Smith and "Spike" shoved with me, their right hands bulging in their coat pockets, a gesture as authoritative to the mob as a Nazi salute.

A heavy door slammed and I stood facing many elderly men who sat in tiers, all attentive. Their faces were refined and purposeful. Some were quite old with white beards, who had lived hopefully through many corruptive stages of government by the people. Here one could believe that Democracy was above the rabble. In the hands of such men was the responsibilty of accomplishing the salutary universal change from the delusive to the real, and make the progress of justice irresistible.

Foreman Smith stated my purpose. I was an editor closely familiar with the machinery of organized crime and I was expected to reveal any information I had to help sweep the racketeers from New York. A suggestion was made to exclude from the room the stenographers who were Tammany appointees. For obvious reasons I agreed with that motion and other arrangements were made to take the record.

Respecting the traditionally secret nature of grand-jury procedure I may not now reveal the details of my testimony but I am permitted to disclose some of its points which have a significant bearing upon this narrative. I answered questions referring to the policy numbers appearing in my paper. I mentioned the conference with Mayor La Guardia and its results. For my own protection, now that I felt I was addressing listeners who would defy intimidation I described my experience with Owney Madden, as already related here, and identified the man in the *Mirror* office who, according to the racketeer's admission, had asked him and his gorillas to take me for a "ride." I gave the names of all corroborating witnesses who had attended the "Fish Inn" conference. Omissions would have been a violation of the truth and my evidence could be described as adequate. When I had finished one of the jurymen expressed the hope that I would get safely back to my office.

Smith, the foreman, thanked me before the grand jury and asked me to introduce him to Brisbane, to whom he proposed to express officially the jury's appreciation of what I had done. I must have smiled wryly at this polite gesture but I made the appointment.

Before his introduction to the editor, the foreman informed me that my testimony had been of importance at a critical hour and that the jury needed little more to be convinced that a special prosecutor was necessary, if organized vice was to be cleaned out of the city. Lee Thompson Smith's "runaway jury" was about to raise the curtain on a new national figure, Thomas E. Dewey, whose vigor, as it turned out, was not to be confined to the business of convicting crooks. Such is fate, and such is politics.

Brisbane controlled his astonishment when Foreman Smith thanked him profusely for my cooperation with the forces of justice. I bit my lip as I watched the editor's steel-blue eyes while he listened to the juryman. Smith described me as a credit to a noble profession with a fearlessness which I had acquired, undoubtedly, through my association with the nation's greatest editor, whose column was read by millions of honest Americans. Brisbane thanked the foreman curtly and stiffly bowed him out.

Kipling conceived the only description I know to fit Brisbane's wrath on this occasion. "He churned the foam on his tusks." For some moments he was unable to speak. He demanded the details of my testimony, which I gave him. He blinked at the Madden story, having heard it from Kobler. As a matter of fact, it had become part of the records of the Hearst management.

The editor suddenly cried out: "Now you've done it! Now you've done it!" He was like an infuriated grandmother berating a brat who has smashed an heirloom.

"Think of the untold consequences to us, and to YOU," he bellowed. "We can't afford to antagonize people who will never be indicted, who will remain in power to hound us, who will laugh at this silly attempt at reform. And YOU'LL pay for it."

"Don't worry about me," I said.

"Worry about you? Bah! You're hopeless. You're being paid to think of more circulation for Mr. Hearst, not for being a policeman. I hate crooks but I'm not a policeman. Mr. Hearst doesn't pay me $260,000 a year for being a cop. That's not your job, nor is it mine!"

He fell into a fit of swearing, mingled with a singular tirade of personal invective.

"You damn Jesuit! You KNEW better than that. An editor's job is to keep out of such things, mind his own business, print the news when it happens. You damned Simeon Stylites!"

"Simeon Stylites sat on a pole for thirty years," I said by way of widening the area of conflict and getting Simeon to share some of the shrapnel.

"I know damn well where he sat," Brisbane shouted, his voice at a breaking pitch. "You don't have to tell ME where he sat. And it wasn't a pole either; it was something else. But what the hell has that got to do with this! Can you tell me why you went there without consulting me?"

"Your own editorials had much to do with it," I replied. "You have been writing regularly about the racketeering menace I have exposed to the jury. You *knew* that what you wrote was true, didn't you?"

"The truth!" he grimaced, "the truth! Have we got to go into THAT over again? Of course I write the truth. The truth is universal, but nobody but a God-damned fool would try to localize it!"

He seemed appalled at my ignorance, his anger surging up like waves, lashing and falling back.

"I can't understand it about you, a man with your experience. You didn't see any other editor there did you? Nobody in his right mind would have done it. I can't understand it," he screamed, "I can't understand it!"

"Maybe you can't, but your father would have understood it," I said.

If I had struck him a blow in the face I could not have produced a more startling change in him. He retreated to the door, fumbling behind him for the knob, not taking his eyes from mine. He had the look of a man who was hurt.

"Keep my father out of this—if you don't mind," he said in an old, thin voice.

I had not informed Brisbane of the story I was to spring in the next morning's edition. The grand jury had received the details of an offer of a bribe of $1,000,000 in cash to the State Parole Board to permit Owney Madden to remain at liberty under parole. An influential politician had approached the Board at Albany with the proposition and the Board's answer had been to order Madden returned to Sing Sing to serve out the remainder of his sentence.

Not only had these facts been given to me by a member of the grand jury but I had been provided with a list of names signed to a round robin, pleading with the Parole Board to free Madden and the signatures included several Hearst editorial employees, a number in the higher-salary brackets. Among those were some of the columnist persuasion.

I called in Arthur Mefford, my companion of the Lindbergh adventure and gave him the facts to prepare for our main story of the night. I wrote the front-page headlines, selecting type more than two inches high:

$1,000,000

MADDEN BRIBE

Jury Gets Parole Board Evidence

Mefford prepared the story with a satisfied smile. He specialized in crime accounts, hated criminals, and now published, occasionally, a magazine of horrifying annals. He had appeared before the grand jury, accepting his summons as the privilege of a good, average American. It was all in a day's work for him, as it had been when he had gone over the top in the first World War.

For diplomacy's sake I left out of the account of the attempted Madden bribe the names of the gentlemen of the round robin. The news the next day jolted some quarters of the town into a sense of realism as to what was going on. The *World-Telegram* followed it up in the afternoon with a scare heading on its front page, giving it more space than that of our own report.

Brisbane displayed the interest of a keen journalist in the affair. Our conference of the previous afternoon was apparently off his mind. I gave him the source of my information, which he demanded, and which he said would be respected. He prepared an editorial for the next issue about the facts. He expressed no surprise when I told him of the round robin. He copied down in a little book the names of Madden's friends, including those on the Hearst payroll. About that phase of it, he made one comment.

"When you moved in here," he said firmly, "you didn't think you were entering a monastery, did you?"

Plain Citizen Smith's grand jury needed but the will to ask for a special prosecutor to end protected knavery. Governor Lehman appointed Dewey as a result of the upheaval. The Governor's politics was the art of being wise for others. He was a sagacious executive, capable of acting on his own initiative. Dewey, also of that type, soon had the racketeers flying before the wrath of honest power. The courts stopped dancing as a bear with a ring through its nose for the criminal mob. Reviewing my experience I was not surprised, later, to read in the *World-Telegram* that "Dutch" Schultz, the lottery gang leader, had been slain by members of his own following because they thought he had lost his mind when he announced a plan to assassinate Dewey with the hope of ending the crusader's campaigns. As startling as it sounds, I am quite ready to believe it.

It does not seem so fantastic now that District Attorney William O'Dwyer of Brooklyn has brought to an end the operations of organized triggermen, so notorious as to become known as "Murder, Incorporated." Looking back on the whole affair I knock on wood.

New York saw gangsterism tumble to its place in the gutter with surprise, realizing at last that what it thought it had feared, it really only despised. "Lucky" Luciano, who at times ran his extortion racket from a suite in one of New York's most fashionable hotels, received a sentence of from thirty to fifty years. He made a fortune preying on women and commercializing them. He hob-nobbed with certain Broadway columnists and controlled their comments about his activities.

The trail of convictions under Dewey's hammering is newspaper history. The impregnable Jimmy Hines, a victim of his own environment, and to whom I am evidently indebted for Owney Madden's consideration, is at this writing known as No. 98719, a gardener at Sing Sing and improving steadily as a horticulturist. Much was to happen to me, however, before I could read the headlines of his conviction. When Hines was indicted on Dewey's evidence, I gave Foreman Smith the credit he deserved in a magazine article. The following letter from him about the piece reflects a rare type of modesty:

> Grand Jury Association of New York County
> 105 West 40th Street
> New York
>
> July 29, 1938
>
> *Dear Mr. Gauvreau:*
> Your flattering and encouraging letter has been received and I am very appreciative. However, I feel that you have given me a larger share of the credit than I deserve for you will recall that the balance of the jury with a few exceptions were as determined as I was that something should be done about the situation that existed.
> I can remember very clearly the splendid co-operation that you furnished and your willingness to testify regardless of

the consequences to you. Frankly, I had no idea that the Hearst organization would, or could, act toward you as it did. It just goes to show how little you can depend upon those who should be most concerned.

. . . I would have preferred your permitting me to remain anonymous as I am afraid the impression may get around that I am trying to capitalize upon the mere performance of duty. I, too, feel that Mr. Dewey has considerable work before him but if he is successful in convicting Mr. Hines, I am positive it will do more to clean up New York than anything else in generations.

Again assuring you of my gratitude and thanks, I am

Very cordially yours,

LEE THOMPSON SMITH.

CHAPTER X

THE story of my Russian travels was by this time on the book publisher's presses. I had entitled it, *What So Proudly We Hailed,* intended as a sardonic reflection on our recognition of the Soviet regime, while, in contemporary America, we maintained an attitude of indifference to crime and political hypocrisy. Photographs of the domestic scene, which passed through my hands daily, seemed to be symbolic of the Europe I had seen, which was drifting supinely into chaos. I had in mind a plan of using the book as a warning note by depicting, even brutally, the conditions which existed in this country, and which were not apparent among the masses in Russia. The articles referring to the Soviet Union in my volume had appeared in the *Mirror* under my own name and had been sold through the Hearst syndicate to 300 newspapers. The series had been well received and the syndicate pocketed its share of the profits and gave me mine.

Although I expected repercussions from the book, I was not prepared for the critical commotion that followed its appearance, and neither were Hearst nor Brisbane. So far as I was concerned I had performed a sincere task devoted to my belief in Democracy, tinged, perhaps, by a journalistic training whose headlines were far from an exaggeration of the macabre hunting ground our nation had become. I had seen crime operate under protection. I felt that the moribund needed to be shocked into a state of realism. My ambitions in this book might have appeared to be negative to some but they were not cheap.

The events which followed were more painful to Brisbane than they were to me. His attitude toward me had mellowed and we were working, apparently, with an understanding of each other. Occasionally he discussed the operations of his mind. He wrote ironical bits for his own amusement. "The world can absorb only doses of the truth; too much would kill it," he said. "Sometimes we can only attack the surface, never going deeper."

At times he accorded the church a respect full of irony. I chided him about it. His reply was that the church could expect no more from the rich. Only the poor, he said, really believed. He took up his ironic cudgel against those who would tax church property. He read the following paragraph to me with a grin:

"The religious can remember, for their comfort, and the radicals who object to the churches owning a few hundred million dollars' worth of real estate should remember with dread, that the churches are the property of the Lord, and that HE could very easily dispose of the matter by striking dead everybody suggesting, or even thinking that church property should be taxed."

Religious rites appealed to him as something touched with the barbaric and he slid his point over to satisfy himself, never giving offense to the unsuspecting. He printed a large picture of Archbishop Germanos, head of the Greek Church in Europe. "Very interesting," he wrote, "is the 'Rod of Wisdom and Power,' with the double snake's head made of solid gold, held in the left hand by this splendidly berobed creature. In the right he holds the Christian Cross, as the Greek Church presents its symbol of faith. Here we see much power in simplicity; also considerable power in gorgeousness of attire. The mind of man is dull and needs to be stimulated. The costume of the Archbishop will do it, and fill it with becoming reverence."

I felt Brisbane had a fatalistic idea of the end that was soon to come to him. He could not have driven himself harder to earn his enormous salary. He had a premonition of the death of Amelia Earhart Putnam, who was to lose her life not long after he passed on. He had met the aviatrix at a luncheon party and talked about her as "the ideal woman of the future." He believed she would be killed on a daring flight. "It would be wonderful to know," he said, "that such people live on after they die. If we only KNEW that the best of us keep on contributing to the progress of civilization after we go."

Following the custom of some other papers of the period, the *Mirror* had continued a column which gave advice on financial investments. It had recommended the purchase of

Class "A" seven percent Cumulative Preferred Shares of Hearst Consolidated Publications. A high-pressure brokerage establishment had been peddling these shares by the thousands. Hearst employees whose salaries equalled mine, or doubled it, were regularly solicited to invest in this stock.

"It is difficult to get seven percent with certainty and diversification," said the broker's literature, "yet we believe it can be done, and in our own line, namely, 'Hearst Consolidated Publications,' including therein, the largest newspaper circulation in the world. Enclosed please find data and Mr. William Randolph Hearst's personal recommendation of this issue. Send us your check and we will have the stock transferred to your name so that you will receive the June 15th dividend."

Brisbane, who did not succumb to these temptations, being immersed in real estate, feared that stockholders might hold the *Mirror* responsible for recommending Hearst's securities if the high dividend failed to materialize, and threw out all advice to investors.

"We must stop absolutely giving any advice on the purchase of securities" he wrote, in a memorandum to me. "That includes Hearst stock. The Administration is just looking for something like this to pick on. If our advice is good, the readers forget it. If it is bad, they hate us."

During this period of his life the aged editor made an attempt to recapture the long-forsaken sincerity in his thinking. Those whom he had really helped he had guided to the world's great thinkers and he returned to his early principles of referring to them in his column. I could look back to my days as a cub reporter, reading Brisbane's editorials and haunting secondhand bookstores for the great writings he had recommended.

I felt the old man enjoyed my reactions to the little arrows he shot out, tipped with irony. One day, he said: "You once asked me who I thought was the greatest man that ever lived. If you had asked me who was the most courageous, I would have said, Thomas Cranmer, Archbishop of Canterbury.

"When he was burned at the stake by order of Queen Mary, he turned to the crowd and shouted: 'This hand hath offended —this unworthy hand.' And before they burned him alive he held his right hand in the flames until it was burned off.

It was the hand with which, under compulsion, he had signed a recantation of his religious beliefs!"

The editor walked about the room in silence. "That was true courage," he said. "For having lied to himself, he made himself suffer. By God, that was something to do! My father told me about him."

At another time he was discussing with me his opinion of the trust one man could put into another. His memory was prodigious and he could fall back on what he read and repeat it.

"Swift," he said, "came as close to solving the problem as anybody. If you have read him carefully, you will remember that he said: 'I hate and detest that animal called man, although I heartily love, John, Peter, Thomas and so forth.' And he wrote to Sheridan: 'Expect no more from man than such an animal is capable of, and you will every day find my description of Yahoos more resembling. You should think and deal with every man as a villain, without calling him so, and flying from him or valuing him less.' "

*   *   *   *   *

As a tabloid editor, my so-called home routine was by this time fairly well regulated. The apartment in which I lived around the corner from Sutton Place, nestled in a neighborhood which was rarely frivolous about its etchings. Genteel inhabitants went in and out of the building, the *Times* and *Herald Tribune* under their arms. I rarely took home my own paper. One night, my elevator man, who was reading the *Nation,* had cast a side glance at a *Mirror,* which I was scanning, and had let me out on the wrong floor. I spent more time with my books, which I had managed to lug about in packing cases when I moved, with the usual travail of the bookish squatter.

Working on a morning paper, I got up at noon. White Fang appeared with my breakfast and the *Times* and *Herald Tribune.* Later I had a Scotch highball and made my way to the scene of my daily scrimmage for more readers. White Fang was a dark gentleman, silent and brooding, who might have made an excellent servant for Al Capone. While I ate he fished out a copy of the *Mirror* from his pocket, made some notations about "Policy Pete," and other financial calculations gathered from our sporting pages, imparted my orders to the housekeeper and then jumped into a subway for Harlem to give the lottery numbers a whirl.   If he had known I had anything to do with the paper which gave him the racket numbers he might have moved in with me.

I read the *Times* as a gentleman should, who makes a good salary and keeps well-informed by studying its unattractive excellence.   Then I read it for the thoroughness with which it covered divorces in little items.   These often put us on the track of society sensations with pictures.   As an obituary critic I read the accounts of the departed for professional reasons.   From the editorials I turned to the book reviews.

One morning at the end of May, 1935, I folded my *Times* to John Chamberlain's book department.   There is something magnetic in the way unusual words jump at the eyes of the slave of type.   I had often been drawn to typographical errors in the middle of a page, almost instinctively, during my years of looking for them.   The words that greeted me this morning in Chamberlain's long review, were not there by mistake, however, and they rose like a tabloid banner head:

"Hearst Upside Down"

I read on quickly and went back to the beginning.   Chamberlain had devoted his whole space to my Russian book, which had just appeared.   He recommended it as a satire on the methods of a journalism that can manufacture a perennial famine out of one year's failure in a wheat crop in Russia, or a "red" uprising on the University of Chicago campus out of the statement of a girl student that her professor believed in free love.   As a spoof, he said, my book had great therapeutic value.   He called me a tabloid Voltaire indulging in subtle take-offs on Hearst's policy while working for him.   Chamberlain said he was now almost ready to agree with the Rev. Wilbur Glenn Voliva that the earth is flat.

While White Fang poured black coffee I reached for the *Herald Tribune*.   Lewis Gannett had reviewed my book to the extent of a full column, concluding that I was still the real Hearst editor.   "He suddenly wraps himself in the flag, recites *The Star-Spangled Banner* and cries: 'Who has done this thing to us?'

"And to think," added Gannett, after comparing my work with *Mother India,* a successful travesty, "that while Mr.

Gauvreau was reading proofs on it he was editing the *Mirror.* If only the Communists would turn over to Gauvreau the editing of their *Daily Worker,* what a paper it might be!"

There were other reviews. Later they poured in. But even Harry Hansen of the *World-Telegram,* handling me kindly, was a bit baffled. No one could forget that I was a Hearst editor, although a singular one, it appeared, now that this book was out. I prepared myself to be cast out as an infidel whose profaning presence in journalistic feudalism had undoubtedly ruined Hearst's digestion.

On my way to the office I had time to think of what had happened since *What So Proudly We Hailed* had left the presses. During a hectic afternoon I had survived the experience of being "pre-lionized," a custom which required certain rites, usually alcoholic, when an author's work was produced. My publishers had looked upon my book as an event. (As indeed it turned out to be!) There had been an elaborate party at the St. Moritz Hotel and it had been advertised as "The First Literary Vodka." To my surprise, all those invited had appeared—from Mayor La Guardia, the Russian Ambassador, whose name now escapes me, former Ambassador Gerard to minor Soviet diplomats, legislators, jurists, Park Avenue nobility, liberal clergymen, poets and those of the deluded who thought that anything pertaining to the Soviet bordered on the intellectual. There had been dancing, caviar, much vodka. A wild Russian orchestra had whirled the party to Moscow and back again. Among the dancers were a number of Hearst officials, including Joe Connolly, a master of the art of heel and toe. The Hearst crowd shunned me as a leper when the reviews appeared.

Most of my staff had read the notices. A number of reporters and sub-editors, including Bernard Sobel, our dramatic critic and Gordon Kahn, the monocled wizard, shook hands with me, dubiously, as one shakes the parting hand of a man whose guilt has not quite been established but who, nevertheless is headed for the gallows. Clarke came in, dancing a new step called *Off to Buffalo.*

"Better pull your sails in," he said. "They won't pass that one up."

"What would you suggest?" I asked.

"Call up your mother, and say: 'Hello, Mom! It was a great fight! Put the coffee on!'"

There was a shrewd observation behind this clowning. Clarke knew the penalty of independent thinking as a Hearst editor. It was all bread and butter to him. The little boss of the city room was a man of brilliant imagination but rarely used it for himself. Later he was to become a gossip columnist in Boston for a Hearst newspaper.

I had a feeling that those who knew what was to happen had ducked into shelters to avoid the bullets aimed at the man against the wall. Paul Jerman, Brisbane's secretary, who kept his contact with me, as a sort of liaison officer of the sullen forces, gave me an inkling of events to come. Hearst had received a mysterious telegram from one Major Frank Pease of the "American Defenders" demanding my discharge as a menace to Hearst journalism. Paul told me my book was being studied by the general management. Copies of the Pease telegram had been received by others, including Charles Wagner, my literary reviewer.

As Ferdinand Lundberg in his excellent factual biography, *Imperial Hearst,* goes into the details of the Pease episode as a typical example of Hearst in violent anger, I may be pardoned for shedding added light on the affair.

Lundberg, in his book, reveals some facts about Pease of which I was not aware. Among other things Lundberg says:

"Major Pease, on whose solicitation Hearst discharged a trusted, highly paid employee, had a somewhat interesting history. In 1930 he campaigned against a film company when it brought Sergei Eisenstein, the Russian director, to this country. He has also carried on anti-Semitic propaganda. Although styling himself 'major,' the War Department records do not show that he is an army officer, active or retired."

The "major" was one of the many visitors who haunt editors with some form of propaganda or other. I recalled that he had come to my office a few times.

He got about with some difficulty, carrying his weight on a cane. He had lost a leg somewhere. His handicap was supposed to have been the result of a meritorious engagement.

Before Brisbane's invasion, Kobler had referred Pease to my office and had telephoned me to be careful of my conversation and to dispense with him quickly. It was Kobler's fashion of ridding himself of an unpleasant task and avoiding the making of a possible enemy. Pease at that time wanted to sell a story devoted to some supposedly inside facts about Hitler. As Hearst had met high Nazi officials in Berlin I was not in a position to pass upon any article about the Dictator and I had unceremoniously ushered out the strange visitor. Later one of his disciples made an attempt to obtain publicity for a book Pease had written, entitled *Pole to Panama*. I considered the book a dangerous piece of incendiarism and I gave it no encouragement. Looked at in the light that Hearst trusted Pease to the point of taking his word without giving me a chance to defend myself from attack, *Pole to Panama* becomes singularly interesting. If it were printed today its author would be the subject of Federal inquiry.

The book was described as "An Appeal for American Imperialism." It advocated the seizure of Canada and Mexico by the United States and left the details "to the General Staff of Capital." Pease addressed himself to the "great American crowd, to men who do not shudder at the frank display of brawn or think the heavens will fall from a *little blood spilled* on the sands of time along the way to Great Affairs; to the great host of countless Americans who, when the time comes, will PREFER action to talk; whose code is 'Nothing venture, nothing have.' "

Pease's book attacked England viciously, after the manner of Hearst's editorials. It berated Woodrow Wilson for having failed to demand, after the World War, the territory of Canada, British Honduras, Bermuda, the Bahamas and the Antilles. It whitewashed the Tea-Pot Dome affair as a politically concocted and press-exploited scandal. There were more of these heresies. The tone of this sort of talk had a familiar ring. It was thoroughly Fascist.

With further reference to Pease, Lundberg had the following to say in his book:

> Late in 1933, Hearst's *Mirror* carried a story from London about "Major" Pease and his wife. It was to the effect that they had palmed themselves off on the widow of Joseph Conrad, the novelist, as old friends of Conrad's. The *Mirror* said they took up residence with Conrad's widow, but were ejected by police when a physician came to believe they were

attempting to drug Mrs. Conrad. The Peases were then asked to leave the country and not to return.

I remembered the details of this story which had been obtained for us by Lady Rena Terrington from officials of Scotland Yard and had been printed in the London papers at the time. Reviewing this background I was not surprised by the Pease telegram to Hearst about me, which follows:

> Please consider how your organization keeps Emile Gauvreau on *Mirror* staff when absolutely contradictory your anti-Communism. Gauvreau just published filthiest anti-American pro-Soviet propaganda book ever issued in America, *What So Proudly We Hailed.* Your anti-Communism should not allow this contradiction to become a *cause célèbre.* Our patriotic duty compels opposition to book and author to limit. We are constantly working to obtain support for Hearst press from women's and other organizations. Gauvreau's employment by you besmirches and nullifies our efforts. Surely your patriotism dictates you get rid of Gauvreau at once before becoming a national scandal.

I prepared an action based on the statutes of criminal libel against the mysterious Pease but I was unable to locate him in New York. My process servers are still waiting for him.

CHAPTER XI

On the evening following the receipt of the Pease telegram by Hearst, Brisbane came into my office as though carrying a burden. He walked about, his hands behind his back, a tired old man who despised the order he had to carry out. I was correcting our first edition and looked up to find him watching me with something of pain in his face.

"You'll have to stop your work," he said. "I have something to tell you which—well, I'll tell you the way I've been TOLD to tell it to you."

"I'll try to be helpful," I said. "You want me to leave the paper."

"Yes," he sighed, "but you'll have to leave now. I've got to wire that you went right out."

It was a warm night in early June and I was working in my shirt-sleeves. I reached for my hat and coat, but there were one or two details hanging in the air.

Our Sunday magazine had printed a story to the effect that the Shah of Persia while on a trip to Paris had proposed seventeen times to an American woman, who had spurned him each time and finally jilted him for a New Jersey lawyer. There had been some threatening diplomatic correspondence, expressing the agony of His Imperial Majesty and the embarrassment of the Government of Iran. According to the Washington Legation the Shah was far from satisfied with our attitude and I had been trying to pacify that day a number of irate Persians.

Under ordinary circumstances Brisbane would have viewed this matter as pregnant with international consequences. I presented the correspondence to him and described the Shah's anguish. The editor flung the letters aside.

"To hell with the Shah of Persia," he burst out. "Why do you have to worry about him? We'll quiet him down. You've got more troubles than he has."

"My troubles are over," I said, "and I hope the Shah feels better. Good luck to you."

We shook hands and I left him standing dejectedly in the middle of the room.

I went to Pietro's and over a brandy and soda I listened through the opened windows to the roar of the presses up the street and watched loaded *Mirror* trucks rush by with my last tabloid output. Out of the night's upheaval one thought suddenly came to me, apparently unsought, but now persistent. What would happen to my secretary, Winifred Rollins? She had been closer, perhaps, to a complete comprehension of my peculiar existence than anyone I had ever known. She had been at my elbow through six years of newspaper strife, unsung, efficient, her role unapparent, self-sacrificing. Most executives accepted such loyalty by force of habit.

I telephoned her that I was through and asked her to gather my personal effects from the office and join me for a final glass of wine.

By this time the news had spread in the shop that I had been fired and several persons from the paper came to Pietro's to say good-by to me. After they had left, Winifred arrived with my private papers and belongings. Much had happened to both of us since I had hired her suddenly when she had applied for a job, fresh out of Elmira College. She was a girl of slight and graceful figure with brown hair which she wore in a straight fashion coming to a bun at the back of her neck. Her eyes were dark blue and held an eager, excited sparkle when we rushed out an extra. Laughter began in her eyes and finally wrinkled her small, slightly turned up nose over wistful lips.

Three years ago I had attended her wedding. Leaving the church I had gone with Jack Sheehan to the "Fish Inn," where we sat in silence for some time. "You've lost more than a secretary," he said. In a few weeks Winifred wanted to resume her work and I had hired her over again.

Now from our table she looked into the street, her eyes following the trucks carrying off the second edition. Her lips curled slightly as she crushed a scarcely smoked cigarette.

"I can't work over there any longer—now that this has happened," she said.

After a long moment she looked at me gravely.

"You're getting ready for another long trip, I imagine. You won't need me any more."

"If I can get the presses out of my head," I said, "I'm going to have a home of my own—a new one, and start right. 'He only is alone who lives not for another.' Brisbane dug that up, somewhere, and I'm going to find out if it applies to me."

"There's something brutal about business," she said. "A secretary can't work closely with someone for so long a time without—"

The renewed clatter of the presses and the thundering trucks rounding the corner smothered her words.

Her face was turned away and she was standing by the window, touching her nose with a little handkerchief. The din in the street died down.

"Let me know how you make out," she said.

Suddenly she was gone.

*　　*　　*　　*　　*

I retired early, but at midnight I was awakened by the telephone.

It was Brisbane.

"Would you like to have breakfast with me tomorrow at the Ritz at nine o'clock?" he asked. "That parting was rather abrupt. I have several things I want to tell you. And we can talk about books. We'll take the time."

He was at the Ritz-Carlton promptly on the following morning and guided me into a side room behind a table and flung his large black hat onto a settee. He was in a mood of almost boyish humor and for a moment studied me as if I had been an acquaintance returned from a long voyage. He ordered two tall sherry flips, giving the waiter explicit directions as to the vintage. One or two people had recognized him and watched him rather in surprise as he scaled his hat and called for the wine.

He drained his glass, ordered two more of the same and wiped the creamy flecks of the concoction from his lips with a red silk handkerchief.

"I went through your book, last night," he said. "Even though there were things in it that may infuriate Hearst, it doesn't have to cost you your job completely. Your salary has seven months to run under your contract and if you want to be another Richard Harding Davis I might arrange to send you to Ethiopia. In the meantime this miserable business might be patched up."

I was familiar with the experiences of editors who had been sent into exile by Hearst. I knew that the Lord of San Simeon never forgave what he considered an insult. I declined the offer.

"Well, then," said Brisbane, "the management will have to pay you until next January. According to your contract we can do nothing else. I've made an appointment for you to see Thomas J. White, our general manager. He won't relish the idea of paying you some fourteen or fifteen thousand dollars under these circumstances but see to it that you get it. Have them send it to you at home every week. How much money have you got, anyway?"

"I never got to my first quarter of a million," I said, "but I didn't throw it all away. And it wasn't all made from Hearst."

The conversation which followed was probably the most remarkable I have ever had with a man who has acquired millions. It was symbolic, I thought, of many things that were to happen in America, changes made inevitable by those who had vast fortunes and who were becoming fearful. It was vivid enough for me to note down, fairly completely, after Brisbane said good-by to me.

"You seem to have some sort of contempt for people who accumulate wealth," he said. "That shouts all through your book. You never knew the fun of raking in big money. I know I'll never be able to spend what I have. But it's better for the country to have money in the hands of those who know how to make it and put it away."

I recalled an episode in our composing room when he had asked me to fill out an editorial referring to the underprivileged and which required a quotation from Jesus. What I had added had made him burst into a rage and he had thrown the copy to the floor. I quoted it again:

" 'Woe unto you that are rich, for ye have received your consolation. Woe unto you that are full, for ye shall hunger. Woe unto you that laugh now, for ye shall mourn and weep.' "

"You can't make me angry," he laughed, "because this is

your day. If you want to take the paradoxes of Jesus literally, that's your business. But you can't do it and work for Hearst, or perhaps, for any other publisher."

"Morality, as interpreted by men of your power and wealth," I said, "then goes no further than a few well-expressed principles, to be compromised with."

"Principles were created for compromises," he replied. "The guiding principles of the average man are to make as much money as he can out of his job. That's his security. If he wants to be a little more idealistic, he finds eventually that he has to modify his principles to meet circumstances. Benjamin Franklin's life explains that and he was a pretty good American. The struggle for security is the problem of the individual. If he gets a footing he's got to keep going. He believes in himself and nobody else. Compare the number of people who go to the movies on Sunday with those who go to church and you will find out how many still believe there is a God who is the avenger of the poor and the weak, against the rich and the powerful. Do you still believe that?"

"Perhaps it's because I was poor, once," I said, "and my father was a factory victim. He believed in God. My main relief in losing my job is that I do not have to cut the payroll $1,500 a week more, an order which you know is still on my desk. With an income of $30,000 a year there's something that sticks in my crop when I have to call men in, reduce their pittance and watch them accept it with the accustomed liberality of the poor toward the rich."

"That's part of your job," he said. "What the hell do you suppose you were being paid that salary for—to cry over the help? Didn't you want to make any more money? You would have been in line for $10,000 more a year next January if your contract had been renewed."

"If the Hearst empire cracks up," I replied, "the avarice of high-paid executives who maintain their excessive salaries by grinding the faces of the help will largely be to blame. This system breeds the fraudulent expense accounts of the underlings who couldn't make a living wage without such mendacities. The legend that Hearst introduced high wages in journalism merely applies to his slave-drivers. Those under them have as hopeless a future as the factory hand."

"That's the basis of our whole system of industry," Brisbane said. "Those on the bottom that are worth a damn reach the top by a healthy struggle. It brings out the stuff in them. You had to struggle too, didn't you? Perhaps you struggled harder because of your lameness. Bacon explains all that. That didn't hurt you any. Do you think you would be any happier writing your conclusions for radical sheets like the *Nation* and the *New Republic* for fifty dollars a week? Try it and see how you like it, after making twice that much in a day. I notice Heywood Broun, whose Guild is trying to unionize the newspaper help, clings to his salary of several hundred dollars a week. That man is a sincere trouble-maker because he really feels sorry for the poor. Even Christ said the poor would always be with us.

"Don't you think I feel sorry for the poor?" he went on. "There are people living today who may remember some of the things I tried to do to carry on my father's ideas. But the reformer never has a chance. His bowl of lentils is his only reward. Do you know what I did once, when I was working for Pulitzer?" His eyes widened as memory recalled the act. "I came out for Henry George for mayor of New York. He was the single-tax economist and reformer. He was called a Socialist, a Communist and an Anarchist. And those who backed him were called the same names. For a long time after that people thought I was a Socialist, or worse. Maybe I was—then."

His elbow rested on the table, his thick hand massaging his tired, intelligent head.

"It wasn't helpful to be known as a Socialist in those days. But I got my Socialism from my mother's milk. I wonder what would have happened to me—if I hadn't met Hearst?"

He withdrew some clippings from a billfold. "Here," he said, "read this, if you think I haven't the courage to attack predatory wealth. Look at the date—March 4, 1934, about a year ago. I'm saving it because Mr. Hearst didn't like it and doesn't want me to write anything like this again. And now, he's killed an editorial I wrote in favor of old-age pensions. I don't see eye to eye with him all the time but I'm certainly not going to sacrifice my job because I don't always agree with him."

The clipping reflected the last spark of Brisbane's strangled liberalism. Perhaps that was the reason he had kept it. Later

I obtained a copy of it. He asked me to read it aloud and watched me narrowly as he drank his sherry flip.

" 'As men become more civilized,' " I read, " 'they move from the monster of gold and greed to the pleasantly smiling god of compromise. When really civilized they move to the shrine of benevolence and unselfishness. That shrine has plenty of room for more worshippers.'

" 'The worshippers of the Golden Calf, supposed to live in Wall Street, think only of themselves, their pocketbooks, more money FOR THE SAKE OF MONEY, and they amount to as little as the money that they get. After they get it they usually lose it trying to get more. If by chance they die while they still have it, the money ruins and makes worthless their children, nine times out of ten.'

" 'The god of compromise is good-natured, filled with self-approval. If he had a stove-pipe hat, long trousers and a black coat he could be the head of a great financial institution, as he sat, explaining how much he did for the poor, just before the institution blew up. His worshippers also enjoy self-approval. If they get a million dollars or a hundred million, they give away a little, newspapers make a noisy fuss about that, and those with the dollar mark at the front end of their names and the *philanthropist* certificate at the other end, feel proud and happy.' "

Brisbane grinned when I finished the reading. "That sounds something like your book," he said. "But you didn't know how to *do* it. You had to put in a picture of an old beggar woman sitting on a fire hydrant in front of the bank where we do our business. That thing alone would make Mr. Hearst furious and that particular item was brought out carefully by Chamberlain in the *Times* review. It was Chamberlain's analysis of your book that cost you your job. That resulted, among other things, in the Pease telegram, which, I'll admit, was a piece of viciousness. But it stirred up a lot of other things because you were never a good office politician. It's too bad the *Times* had to give you a piece as big as they might have given H. G. Wells. Your book wasn't as important as that. They simply used what you said about Russia to make Hearst squirm, because you worked for him. What possessed you to go to Russia in the first place? Those pilgrimages have done nothing but throw a mantle of suspicion over the poor saps who went there expecting to see Utopia at work."

"I have often wished," I said, "that I had lived during the French Revolution. An upheaval for freedom, as some historian has expressed it, shows the people for a brief moment all that lies undeveloped in themselves, never, probably, to find expression. The leaders whom I interviewed in Russia, those who had caviar and champagne for dinner, surveyed the scene with the cynical detachment of Tammany Hall bosses. They had the same motives. There were others, however, like our Tom Paine, who expected to be shot for their ideals and looked forward to it. I was interested in the people. Hearst can't damn a nation of 170,000,000 because their leaders have no morality."

"If Mr. Hearst decides that Russia is no good," Brisbane said, "those who work for him must write that way. That's his prerogative, for which he pays those well, who obey him. With your knowledge of French history you should have better understood him. Treat him as a modern Louis XIV and you can rationalize his actions. He is the last of his kind in the newspaper business. The days of palaces in Democracy are over. I've tried to tell him that but he's going to die like a king. If you could have detached yourself to the point where you could have understood you were working for a king, you could have made much money. A king has his whims. But you offended him which is the reason you are no longer one of his well-paid courtiers.

"So far as your views of freedom for the oppressed are concerned," he continued, "I can quote enough authorities to show that the removal of restrictions is not an indispensable preliminary to means of improvement. The rabble would not make proper use of such opportunities. A nation is happiest when the rich are safe. Perhaps we have given our downtrodden too many opportunities. Since Roosevelt came to power I have often thought that too many people are thinking of things they are not entitled to. Maybe I have guided too many of them to Voltaire and Rousseau in the millions of words I have written about self-improvement. Youth today is cynical, purposeless about life and wants none of its responsibilities. One whipper-snapper, when I was making a speech during the time Beard was attacking us, said: 'It's easy for you to talk; you have money to burn.' That young whelp didn't know how hard I had to work for my money."

"Still," I said, "Voltaire would have more to write about today than when he was packed off to the Bastille."

"He did a pretty good job on his *Letters on the English,*" Brisbane said. "He deliberately set out to see something good in England to teach the French a lesson, when France was enslaved. That was a bold thing to do and he had to flee, but Montesquieu, before that, in his *Lettres Persanes,* disguised the same thoughts in safer fashion. You should have studied Montesquieu. You can't call Russia a land of contentment and draw attention to our unemployment, racketeering, political corruption and God knows what without drawing fire on yourself. It's that damnable comparison that Chamberlain harped upon, while Hearst was trying to show it the other way around."

"I don't blame Chamberlain," I replied. "I owe him a vote of thanks."

"Better study Voltaire," Brisbane said. "He never went broke. He had his say but he got along. It's a good thing to know how to satisfy your own conscience and make the cash register ring also. Voltaire was a great man but while appearing to believe in God he never believed in anything. Rousseau said Voltaire's God was a malicious being who found no pleasure except in doing injury. Rousseau died broke. As for me I have tried to live the way Rousseau described the King of Prussia:

" 'Il pense en philosophe, et se conduit en roi.' "

The old man's elbow still rested on the table, his hand supporting his chin. His lids had narrowed, watching my face.

"Someone said," he began, "that it is not in the least likely that any life has ever been lived which was not a failure in the secret judgment of the person who lived it. Not much that I have written will be remembered for long after my obituary appears on the front pages. There will be columns about my career when I die, and nobody would hurt my feelings by telling me that will be the end of what will be written about me. I pointed out to you the conclusions that Swift reached about mankind. Don't pin your hopes too high on anyone. The idols we worship are too often of clay."

"But yet," he stroked his great forehead, "the name Brisbane should mean something to people who read. I must have taught hundreds of thousands to read the better things. My list of the greatest books is one of the best. That was service, even in the yellow press. I couldn't have reached that army of readers otherwise. Let's start a magazine and call it *Brisbane's Journal,* full of things worth while written by those who were brave enough to risk their lives for their thoughts. That sort of thing would help my son and I'll back it. Perhaps you could train him to run the magazine, bring him up to it."

I declined the offer politely. I knew what would happen to such a periodical if Brisbane wanted to have a hand in it. He could never resist the appeal he knew so well, calculated for all ages to amass a million readers. *Brisbane's Journal* would mean nothing. It might have meant something when Brisbane wrote sincerely, but it was too late to go back to Henry George. The old editor's death would be reported as that of a certain rich man. That would be the end of his works. Perhaps he understood the barbed satire of his success, typical of the age which crept back to great truths when there was little time left to nestle under their protection.

He seemed to read the reproach in my mind. He knew that I thought he had failed—perhaps that, at one time, he had just missed the goal his father had sought. Arthur Brisbane made his written words dance for money and the money they made would outlive him. His words would be buried with him.

We fell into a moody silence and I was filled with a weight of sadness. When I was a reporter, I had idolized him. Nothing much more was said until he pushed the table from him and got up heavily.

"You're not interested in *Brisbane's Journal,*" he mumbled.

"No."

"You're not interested in me."

"No."

"Good-by," he said. We did not shake hands and I never saw him again, nor his bitch-goddess, Success.

BOOK V

THE MORE ABUNDANT LIFE

CHAPTER I

CAST loose from a press after twenty-five years I discovered that habit is one of the cruelest laws of nature. My watch had been broken after I left the *Mirror* and during late afternoons I reached into my pocket for it several times before convincing myself that I was empty-handed and did not need it. This occurred as the minutes approached the first edition deadline of the tabloid I wanted to forget.

Perhaps habit is the child of impulse. The morning after my conversation with Brisbane, I had found an item in the *Times,* and had called up an underling of the early shift at the paper to have it developed for a story before I remembered I was no longer the editor.

It soon got about among my train of parasitic acquaintances that I had been fired. These were the people who slapped me on the back and relieved me of free passes to theaters, prize fights and race tracks. Now that I had no tickets to give away my telephone became an instrument of silence.

Hearst had agreed to pay me the balance of my salary which I was to receive in weekly installments for the remainder of the year. Thomas J. White, the publisher's general manager, made the arrangements with a sour smile. He found the subject of my sudden retirement painful to discuss and spent the time of my visit in his office recalling the writings of Finley Peter Dunne who had created "Mr. Dooley," whose humorous philosophy he fell upon whenever business became unpleasant.

J. David Stern, new owner of the *New York Post* had sent for me to discuss a proposed series of signed articles describing my impressions of the Hearst regime. We sat in a luxurious office dominated by a large steel engraving of William Cullen Bryant, whose poetic face seemed to frown sadly over the proposal and finally drove me out into the street. It reminded me that Julian Mason, when he was editor of the *Post,* had suggested my name to his publisher, the aging Cyrus K. Curtis, as a managing editor possessing circulation ideas and had described my New England training to discount my tabloid activities. Mason told me Curtis had shuddered slightly and turned pale.

Walter Howey had succeeded me on the *Mirror* whose first run in the evening was now boldly labeled as the "Pay-off Edition," a gambler's round-up of lottery numbers, race-track dope and sex scandals. The "pay-off" made Kobler groan.

I was notified to appear in a libel suit which had been filed against the *Mirror* by a police captain whose bank accounts we had commented upon editorially during the Seabury investigation. The officer demanded $150,000 in damages. Hearst's lawyers, in impassioned pleas, introduced me as a $30,000 a year editor who wrote nothing but the truth. They passed around to the jury and to the judge my book about Russia, *What So Proudly We Hailed* as evidence of my character and sincerity. No mention was made of the fact that I had been fired for writing it. Hearst won the case.

I encountered Stanley Walker while I watched the world slip by from the sidewalk café of the old Brevoort Hotel on lower Fifth Avenue. He seemed rejuvenated and disclosed the last chapter of his tabloid venture. The Hearst organization had shifted him to the *American* obviously to nullify his contract of $400 a week by a time-honored inquisition. He had been appointed "firing editor" and men whom he had seen grow old in journalism were brought before him to be decapitated. Faced with the brutal responsibility of packing friends off to unemployment he had torn up his agreement, flung the pieces in the face of the management and walked out.

My telephone began to ring again, not quite continuously. Ed Sullivan in his column in the *Daily News* had announced that I had "salted away" $350,000 before the "ax fell." This item carried the hilarious treatment of the truth which often characterized such printed gossip but it was a cheerful revelation to those who had enjoyed my free tickets. Now I knew how it felt to be the victim of a journalistic racket which I had nursed into being. I spent a week explaining the false announcement to income-tax collectors. A correction of such irresponsible gab rarely catches up with the error which necessitates a denial. It got about that I was throwing money

away.   In restaurants headwaiters dragged me to the best
tables and ordered expensive wines before I was hardly seated.
Having time to last out the whole ritual of Christopher
Morley's "Three Hours for Lunch Club" I no longer appreciated its Parnassian freedom.   One had to have an office
from which to escape to really enjoy the guilt of such leisure.

I was planning a trip to Europe when Congressman
Sirovich asked me to see him at the Fifth Avenue Hotel.   He
was shocked when I told him what had happened to me as a
result of our Russian picnic but the development gave him a
sudden idea.   Before I left him I had been turned into a dollar-
a-year man with the title of Director in Chief of Investigations,
of the Committee on Patents of the House of Representatives.
Almost immediately I was on my way by airplane to Washington, studying confidential Government papers with which the
doctor had loaded me down as an explanation of what I was
to do as a New Deal patriot.

Statesmen of the period were searching the Constitution
for a broader interpretation of its powers to add further contributions to the more abundant life.   Sirovich sought to
promote the progress of science and the arts, and as the Constitution dealt specifically with the protection of the writings
and discoveries of authors and inventors he had come to the
conclusion that, as head of the Committee on Patents, he could
revolutionize art in America.

The good doctor's plan, for which a long resolution had
been drawn, called for the appointment of a new member of
the Cabinet, to be known as Secretary of Science, Art and
Literature, to be installed in a new building "preferably on
Capitol Hill, to balance the new building of the Supreme Court,
and that such building architecturally shall be in keeping with
the beauty of art, the dignity of science and the visions of
literature."

My job in this staggering project was to stir up the poets,
all men of arts and letters and science, to come to Washington
to testify that this was just what the country needed.   Being
more or less familiar with the lavishness with which money was
being spent by the Administration I should not have been surprised to find men already digging for the foundations of
Sirovich's temple.

My new activities involved me in a second project about

which I was less dubious. I was to gather a mass of information necessary to bring about legislation to end all patent-pooling arrangements as they affected the aircraft industry. The Congress charged that a patent monopoly kept the Government in the dark of the progress of American aviation, gouged it of vast sums when airplanes were required for its defense arms and permitted manufacturers to sell abroad inventions of which our War Department was in ignorance.

For several days I had to pigeonhole my plans for the investigation of patent pooling and concentrate on Sirovich's project for the department of art which kept him up day and night and drove him to such extremities of exhaustion that he required help to carry him to bed. I found myself milling most of the time in an assemblage of excited poets, exuberant artists, playwrights, jobless architects, mural painters and other inspired folk whose economic condition had much to do with their clamor for official patronage.

Sirovich actually believed that a popular intellectual force would pry open the public coffers and release the millions of dollars required for his inspiration. Thousands of letters received at his office, a large number of them from men of attainment added daily to his convictions. All that remains of this turmoil, which had Washington by the ears in the summer of 1935, is a heavy Government pamphlet of many thousands of words reaching from the sublime to the ridiculous.

One side issue of this vast pipelaying to the sources of art included plans for the building of a National Theater in Washington where, as Sirovich pointed out, plays of all geniuses spurned by insensible Broadway producers would be received with sympathy. I was reminded of the plays of Sirovich which he had read to me from Warsaw to Moscow. Playwrights were already on the scene, their works ready for casting. Unemployed architects flocked in and out of the Congressman's office, some carrying blueprints six feet long, showing the theater as it would appear, one great drawing flowering into the lines of the Parthenon, another as a medieval cathedral upon which men could work for 200 years. Other architects were preparing plans for the temple of science and art. I had emerged from the churning stream of tabloidia into a raging sea of culture.

Perhaps not until this project is revived again by some

heroic statesman will the troubadours of the macaronics ever receive the attention they enjoyed when Sirovich bowed them through the doors of Congress. Poets dived from Parnassus, coming to the surface with the sweet food of the roundelay, the ode, the sonnet and the ballad. Sirovich reveled in this holiday of his creation and gave the poets at the hearings all the time they required for their explosive fancies. He recited part of Gray's *Elegy,* emphasizing the lines:

> *"Full many a flower is born to blush unseen,*
> *And waste its sweetness on the desert air."*

Not all of the geniuses were able to demonstrate their accomplishments with the ease of the poets. There was Gutzon Borglum who worked with sticks of dynamite, great chisels and electric-power drills to make huge faces out of mountains. The sculptor described to the Congressmen the task in which he had been engaged for eight years. He was carving heads sixty feet high of Washington, Jefferson, Lincoln and Theodore Roosevelt on the perpendicular surface of Mount Rushmore, in South Dakota. Until he died six years later, in 1941, at the age of seventy, Borglum, his work unfinished, remained at it, leaping about scaffolding on the mountainside, or hacking at Lincoln's long nose from a swing-seat 400 feet above the Black Hills valley.

"Granite," he said with satisfaction, "erodes very slowly—perhaps at the rate of one inch in 100,000 years. The figures are in ninety-foot relief. Perhaps in a hundred million years the mountainside will be smooth again."

"Who knows how many civilizations will come and go while Borglum's mountains look down upon them?" said Sirovich.

Borglum propelled himself into an oration, in which he supported to the hilt of his last drill the art plan of Sirovich.

"Our gods," he said, "money, power, government, war—all fall away, and with their votaries disappear, ages before time destroys the record man makes of the experiences of his soul."

Congressman Sirovich had insisted that I address one of the hearings with a description of my crusade to save Mark Twain's home. Although I recoiled from the "official type

of art" which occasionally resulted from government patronage, and which always seemed to fall below the best national
paintings of the epoch, I believed there were some good points
in Sirovich's resolution.   At least, it encouraged artistic endeavors, and I spoke in favor of his plan from that standpoint.
I criticized openly the effect of Hearst journalism on the cultural progress of the people, confessing my brief part in it.
For personal reasons I entered on the record the activities of
Major Pease who had sent to Hearst the telegram already
quoted.   Sirovich ordered my remarks printed as a special
Government pamphlet which resulted in several repercussions.
When I returned to New York I found that *Editor and Pub-
lisher,* the newspaper trade publication, then edited by Marlen
E. Pew, had devoted several columns to it in a poisonous vein.
It had also been referred to in news items around the country.
My references to Hearst seriously displeased Kobler who had
been informed that Brisbane was soon to leave the *Mirror.*
The exiled publisher hoped to resume the helm himself and
restore me to my old post as editor.   I had burned that bridge.

The gossip about my Russian book had been accelerated by
front-page articles in the *Daily Worker,* New York's Communist newspaper, which displayed my picture and described
me to the proletariat as a singular creature who had made
money out of the capitalistic system but insisted upon telling
the truth about it.   Clarence A. Hathaway edited the *Worker*
with the confidence of Peter the Hermit.   It was produced
on an old press of the *Wall Street Journal* at 50 East 13th
Street, in the atmosphere of a sweat-shop and was being attacked in the editorial pages of conservative organs, including
the *Times,* to the jubilation of the radical editors who saw
in this recognition early signs of the downfall of the upper
class.

Hathaway, at that time, was warning his readers of the
growing menace of Hitler, a party-line policy whose reversal
later forced him to swallow his own words and eventually
drove him off the paper after Moscow had made common cause
with the Nazis.   He told me he obtained his "inside news" of
the nation's capital from pipelines leading to offices of Washington correspondents of liberal views and various Government
bureaus.   This statement, by personal observation I found to
be exaggerated but there is no doubt that the *Worker* con-

trived to take advantage of leaks from sympathizers enjoying the benefits of Uncle Sam's payroll.

My trip to Moscow and its aftermath had resulted in ostracizing me from New England people of long acquaintance who had already labeled me as a "Socialist" when I had exposed the medical charlatans who were preying on the factory workers of Connecticut. I discovered that Russia had its drawbacks as a subject for literary material. My book was now displayed in New York bookshops of the Soviet persuasion whose directors saw in Hearst's quarrel with me matters of significance and had ordered several thousand copies. The sales were accompanied by passionate harangues delivered by unshaven men who spoke for hours on what had been my fate after having prostituted myself for a system which was engulfing me with J. P. Morgan and John D. Rockefeller.

CHAPTER II

WASHINGTON had become a beehive of "dictators." In every Government office I visited in the course of my work, Senators and Congressmen, hands clutched behind their backs, paced the floor talking incessantly, their faces frozen into the grimace which the effort to think usually results in when politicians concentrate. This was the time of dictation, and orations resounded through the halls of the House Office Building and raced through the fingers of stenographers into notebooks. Nearly all speeches consisted of demands for money. Lawmakers were agreed that this was the only way to end the depression—and, maybe, prevent revolution.

There were a few veterans of the Congress, however, who were not convinced that spending would effect a cure. Privately, John Nance Garner, the Vice-President, could not discuss the subject without resorting to talented swearing. When the final rap of his gavel stopped the flow of millions for the day, he retired to his suite with a group of followers, prepared himself a Bourbon highball, downed the first draught of it and shook his white head.

"Why," he stormed, "I got a man I started in the banking business down in Texas, Bruce Holsomback, who runs the Zavala County Bank, who knows better than this. You can't keep taking it all out without putting it back."

Speaker Joseph W. Byrns of Tennessee, who toiled in the powerhouse of the New Deal's financial Niagara until he was weary and bent, and eventually died under the burden, struggled through the early years of the Recovery Administration in apprehension of the outcome.

"This is the people's money," he told me, "but they're not getting any fun out of spending it. You can have a hell of a good time blowing in your own money if the supply seems inexhaustible. We found that out under Hoover. We thought we were all getting rich and didn't give a damn. I'll

stick to our program till the cows come home, but it isn't
the lark that it was before we went to hell in a handbasket in
1929. We can't spend forever."

Sirovich was dictating when I saw him again. Over
the bowed head of a secretary, he was refurbishing a speech
to appear in a pamphlet to be mailed to his thousands of
constituents.

". . . So long as the profit motive is the animating and
fundamental concept of capitalistic rugged individualism, so
long will the few, at the expense of the many, control the wealth
of our nation, and unemployment must always prevail. (Applause) Despite the sunshine which floods the road of the high-
way of life, the path of human progress is lined with rocks,
thorns and thistles. . . ."

He put the speech aside reluctantly to discuss my affairs.
The hearings on the Department of Art were taking up so
much of his time that he had decided to let me go ahead to
prepare for the investigation of the aircraft industry. This
was a monumental task, as he trusted no one else with the
subpoenas, which had to be obtained from the Speaker of the
House, whose signature made them powerful documents. I
was to serve them personally on the heads of vast corporations.
But here the chore only began. The subpoenas entitled me to
demand stacks of papers, books and records which I was to
study and condense into reports to be used for purposes of
questioning the witnesses when these harassed gentlemen took
time out from $150,000 a year jobs to snarl their answers back
from the stand.

Sirovich's art scheme, however, dominated his thoughts.
War being horrifying to him, airplanes represented in his mind
a symbol of death and destruction.

"Do you know," he said, "that if Hitler had received any
encouragement when he was a starving artist in Vienna, he
might have been satisfied to spend his life painting mediocre
pictures? Just imagine what that would have averted for
mankind! The same thing can happen here. This department
of arts will pacify the restless imagination of the artistic and
a lot of other dangerous creatures. It may prevent all sorts
of terrible happenings."

Sirovich was typical of the law-makers I had to deal with—
hard working, honest, but without humor. The Congressman

accepted as excellent publicity a long satirical article in the *Herald Tribune* which carried the headline:

Sirovich To Put
Cultural Dream
Up to Roosevelt

Later, the *New Yorker,* in the same acid vein, presented the Doctor to its readers in a seven-page description in its department of "Profiles." He had copies of the article mailed to his East Side supporters as a tribute accorded to a man of prominence. Printed satire had become praise in politics. Most of the Congressmen I knew were deeply grateful for such stories and used them to advantage at election time. Sirovich occasionally found me convulsed over speeches in the *Congressional Record* which he perused solemnly, and then informed me there was nothing funny in them because the word "laughter" in parenthesis had not been printed between any of the sentences.

Presumably he had discussed his art project in a general way at the White House as it seemed to be in line with the ideals of the more abundant life. Now he was anxious to sound out, through someone other than himself, how the President felt disposed about it and he suggested that I see Roosevelt about this matter and other committee affairs that were simmering. I had seen him two or three times during campaign celebrations after my luncheon with him at Albany and I had received one or two cheerful notes from him. I readily agreed to avail myself of the opportunity of seeing him again.

Before my appointment at the White House I dropped in on Charles Michelson, Director of Publicity of the Democratic National Committee, whose quiet ability had an untold influence in the President's effectiveness in striking a common ground with the public. Michelson sat hunched over his desk, his lined face peering into an entirely predictable future. Although twelve months were to go by before the next campaign, he already was planning for four more years of the New Deal.

"People vote to throw a man out," he said. "They seldom vote to put a new man in. The nation will never request Franklin Roosevelt to leave the White House."

His face shrouded with alarm at the possibility that overwork might in time force the President to give up his duties. He was convinced no one in the country had the capacity to carry on the vast program of changing the country to conform to what he called an indescribable evolution molding a Democracy to be fit to survive.

The same fanatical faith pervaded the White House. Here one caught the resentment of any criticism of New Deal policies. And the editorial tirades were, by now, abusive. In my talk with Stephen Early, a self-contained secretary of fine integrity and grave countenance who handled the press in masterly fashion, I gathered that, at times, some of the newspaper attacks got under the Presidential epidermis.

"The majority of the people are sincere," Early said. "They know the President's purpose and appreciate it. Tell him so when you see him. While shouldering his burden, it helps him."

I chatted outside the President's door with Marvin H. McIntyre, a more jovial secretary who carried his office ballast in lighter fashion and who found occasional time to enjoy Washington's social life. Members of the cabinet entered the private portal in twos or threes, some emerging with smiles, a wave of the hand, others walking out in silence. James A. Farley, the Postmaster General, bounced out and greeted me in a laughing mood. A second term for the President furnished no problem for him.

One man waited until the President was alone. This was Harry L. Hopkins, then Works Progress Administrator, the country's biggest "employer," with 3,500,000 persons on his payroll. At the White House I was introduced to Hopkins who quizzed me about some impossible item in Winchell's column, for which a kind Providence had made me no longer responsible. From slippery ground the Broadway gossiper was beginning to make weird prophecies about Washington officials. This was read by the Capital's credulous, who loved to be deceived and were seldom disappointed.

Hopkins was an interesting man. The underdog has always had a fascination for me, and the Works Progress genius might have been so described. He was undergoing a terrible lambasting, and not only from the press. Democratic veterans, still in a quandary about the new shape the mold of the nation was to assume in the President's hands, resented the Hopkins type. From the howls I heard at the parties of some of the leaders, the resentment had grown into an abiding hatred of this social worker in politics. New Deal coteries spent hours at night making his ears burn and wondering where Roosevelt had dug him up. I soon discovered that the idealistic way-farers who were to guide us to a better existence had not aban-doned the passions of human nature when they packed up for Washington.

To study the career of Hopkins was to know more inti-mately the head of the nation. Hopkins, a harness-maker's son, had devoted years of his life helping the poor as a relief worker. Running into him in the White House, without know-ing him, one might have left with the impression that he was some useful person who had come up from downstairs where he was fixing something in the cellar. His carelessness in dress was part of him. But when he talked to you, the strange power of his intent eyes and his strong, square cut chin left something in the memory about the man.

Roosevelt had met Hopkins before the days of the Gover-norship, when the social worker was going through his most formative period in his contact with helpless humanity. They had become close friends and worked together to help the underprivileged. Here, perhaps, began the ten-billion dollar dream to make provisions for social conditions which ought not to exist. Both men sought to redistribute the goods of life without the overthrow of society. Hopkins believed passion-ately, every word of the philosophy which Roosevelt had ex-plained to Emil Ludwig and which had appeared in his book, *Roosevelt: A Study in Fortune and Power*:

"It doubly becomes the duty of those born rich to try to do that. [To seek to redistribute the goods of life.] Wasn't I able to study, travel, take care of my sickness? The man who doesn't have to worry about his daily bread is securer and freer. The man who comes up from underneath carries into his later life bitter memories of his youth, and so he has less love for me. The man born poor retains resentments. I can't have any. That is the personal motive in me."

Somehow, in Hopkins' devotion to his chief I discerned traits that reminded me of Louis McHenry Howe who had con-ceived the idea of making Roosevelt President. I had talked to Howe during the campaign of 1932 and I saw him for the last time during a celebration in honor of the President-elect who was watching a jubilant crowd dancing. Howe, a little gnome-like figure, looked fondly at the victorious candidate.

"Carlyle is the only man who could have explained him," he said. "Reporters who want to know their next President might save themselves a lot of time by reading *On Heroes, Hero-Worship, and the Heroic in History.*"

I do not know whether Hopkins sought an explanation of Roosevelt in the writings of the great thinker of the nineteenth century, but as an adviser to the President the gaunt relief worker grew closer to him than any man in the Administration. The White House became his home as it had been Howe's up to the time of his death.

I was to attend a conference of Washington correspondents in the President's office and remain with him after they had retired. Sixty or more men crowded about his desk. Older reporters seemed to form the first rank, mostly grizzled veterans, tolerantly cynical, who represented the papers which were certain that the New Deal was ruining the country. Behind them were men much younger and eager-eyed who saw in Roosevelt a daring leader. They worked for that part of the press which felt fairly certain the nation would survive if the New Dealer did not stay too long in office.

Behind an expansive desk sat a large, graying, tanned man in a white suit, attentive and cheerfully smiling. There was no doubt in his mind about the direction the country had taken. He had set the course. While pencils flew he lashed out at Wall Street and talked of an emancipation proclamation for stock-holders who would have a chance to live instead of being sent to the death house of poverty by having the profits of their investments absorbed by holding companies. He answered a reporter in the rear, calling him by his first name at the sound of his voice. Right and left he turned, with a ready word. He knew down to the smallest detail the answers to the questions fired at him in this self-imposed third degree. Check dams built by the Civilian Conservation Corps? He knew the number of dams, the number of men enrolled, how much money was sent home by CCC enrollees to dependents. He described the material with which New Deal roads were being built. He snapped his answers after the fashion of a star in a spellin'-bee. He puffed at a long cigarette holder at a cocky angle.

The men filed out and the President asked me to sit down, recalling our long luncheon talk at Albany.

My impressions of Franklin Roosevelt, as I saw him in the White House may be of more than ordinary interest because of the psychological stimulation and of the implications my few encounters with him left in my mind. As a man he had overcome the same affliction which had cut me down as a boy. Years after my Fourth of July accident, when I could afford to do so, I had consulted specialists who informed me that the explosion was coincidental with an attack of infantile paralysis. My own struggle had taught me something about that merciless enemy which sought totally to disable without necessarily killing. When finally the victim fought it off, Nature stood aside, watching to see how much he could do with the power it had grudgingly left him. The courage required to lick that enemy explained the unconquerable mind of the man who was to guide the nation during the gravest period in world history.

CHAPTER III

THE President lit a cigarette for me from one of the many gadgets that lay before him. The thermometer outside was registering in the upper nineties and the circular office in which we sat reflected the temperature, unprotected by cooling devices, which he abominated. He blotted the perspiration from his face with a white silk handkerchief. The small working space on his desk was encroached upon by a growing jungle of gimcracks and trinkets, all manner of things presented to him as tokens by admirers. He disliked to cast aside the little gifts, which reminded him of the thoughtfulness of the givers, and the accumulation had spread into a humorous collection.

I recalled that President Hoover had wanted his desk clean, as the Standard Oil executive in Brisbane's story, with nothing in front of him but a virgin pad on which Hoover drew wandering designs as visitors talked. He then expressed an opinion and the interview was over. H. G. Wells, who wanted to chat with Hoover, found he had to be led to him by Sir Ronald Lindsay, the British Ambassador, who sat close to Wells, "during the encounter, rather like a gentleman who takes a strange dog out to a tea party, and is not quite sure how it will behave." President Coolidge had observed almost the same principle, but on his immaculate desk added one or two newspapers folded in such a way as to prevent those who saw him from surmising what articles he was reading.

Roosevelt sat smiling, and unperturbed, enjoying a "breathing spell" during a task that never ended, that he could never really catch up with, that he had to pursue within four walls to the limit of his endurance. But to him, it would never be the "hair shirt" that Hoover had described it to be, nor Harding's "prison sentence that you couldn't forget even in a hot game of poker."

"You never got to Warm Springs," said the President, recalling the invitation he had extended to me at Albany, to induce me to take more exercise. I explained the purpose of my visit, a few of the things that had happened to me since last I

saw him, and Sirovich's anxiety about the art project. The
President listened attentively. Of the art project he said: "All
these things will come in time. If they are for the public good
there is no harm in trying to accomplish them. People ask me
why I am trying to do so much all at once. There is hardly
enough time to do all the things I have set out to do. And yet,"
he added with a laugh, "I don't think the people are going to
send me back to Hyde Park, delightful as that place is, before I
finish most of this job, do you?"

I agreed with his conclusions, which were also those of
Jim Farley who had assured New Deal leaders that the second
term was "in the bag."

"And so you're through with Hearst," said the President.
"You look better than you did the last time I saw you. It re-
minds me of what happened to my old friend Jimmy Montague
who covered Albany politics for the Hearst papers while I was
up there. I liked Jimmy, who was a little fellow not much
bigger than a pint of cider. He was sincere and conscientious
and we used to have fine chats. Suddenly the Hearst papers
decided to attack me and Jimmy had to write the stories. He
explained to me that it was part of his job and he had to do it.
He began to droop, and after some time went around pale and
haggard. Later Jimmy was announced to me. He seemed
like a new person. His face had filled out and he greeted me
with a joviality that he had completely lost the last time he had
called on me.

" 'Why, Jimmy,' I said, 'what's happened to you? Have
you been down to the Fountain of Youth?'

"And Jimmy said: 'No, but I've gone through an experience which is the next best thing to it. I'm through with
Hearst!'

"And I said, 'Jimmy, now you're your own master!' "

Our talk reverted again to the art project. It was all part
of a pattern, he said. It fitted in with a system of changes to
come, quietly working in the human mentality because events
conspired to bring such changes about. He struck at those
whose faith still clung to economic anarchism, to an endless
succession of trade cycles, for better or worse. All this led to
inevitable reconstruction for a new Democracy. It was the task
before all rational people. He brought in a dramatic symbol of
the millionaire hoarder to illustrate a point.

"Years ago," he said, "long before I ever thought of being Governor of New York State, I began the pursuit of a hobby still fascinating to me—the collecting of old naval prints. I allowed myself about $500 a year for that purpose. I was walking down Lexington Avenue in New York, one day, when I saw in the window of an art shop three old prints which would have added great value to the sequence of my store of pictures. I went in and priced them and bought them but while the clerk was wrapping them up the proprietor ordered them unwrapped because they had been already sold. I was disappointed and I was naturally curious to know who had bought the prints which would leave a permanent hole in my collection. The owner of the shop told me they had been picked up by collectors for William Randolph Hearst.

"Many years went by and one day, while I was Governor of New York, I was informed that Hearst wanted to see me on a matter of great importance to him. An appointment was made and he visited me. He wanted a favor and he was obsequious about it. He was extremely anxious to receive my endorsement, as Governor, of a campaign he was conducting in his New York papers. It was of a humanitarian nature and I saw no objection to it but before I agreed, in his eagerness to obtain my approval, he said:

"'I shall consider this a great personal favor, Governor. Endorse this campaign and I shall do anything you ask me to do for you which is within my power.'

"I thought of the old naval prints which he had bought years ago and which I still longed for. Here was an opportunity to restore the gap in my collection. I told him the story of my disappointment. I pointed out to him that if he wanted to exchange favors I would gladly buy the prints from him, pay him whatever price he had paid for them and the interest on the money from that day to this. That's how badly I wanted them.

"His face fell. He was grieved because, even though it was trivial to him, it was the one request he could not grant. He said he undoubtedly owned the prints but that he had never seen them. Such things were bought for him in all parts of the country and Europe, and put away.

"'Why, do you know,' Hearst said, 'that I have storehouses filled with art objects, paintings, sculpture, prints, tapestries, museum pieces and what not, that must have cost hundreds of thousands of dollars and which I have never seen. These things are all bought for me by collectors and packed away in warehouses. I don't know what I have. It's a great pity because it would be like looking for a needle in a haystack to find your little prints.' "

The President lit another cigarette, leaned back, inhaled and blew out a funnel of smoke through curling lips.

"That," he said, "is the type of static wealth I should like to break up."

The talk led to Hearst's publications and other papers training their armament on the President. Hearst had started a new tirade against Roosevelt's social program. While the Communists claimed the New Deal was bolstering up Capitalism, Hearst shouted angrily that the Administration was destroying it.

"Hearst is making his usual noise," said the President. "A number of others are yelling fairly loudly. I suppose Hearst is already planning deafening broadsides for the next campaign!"

I told him that from what I knew of the political policies of some of the publications we were discussing, Hearst's in particular, I believed that the arguments to come would place emphasis on the money the Administration had spent. It was obvious that the President's opponents would pounce on the promises he had made in 1932 when, in his campaign against Hoover, he said: "Let us have courage to stop borrowing; stop the deficit. It is my pledge that this dangerous kind of financing shall be stopped and that rigid economy shall be enforced by a stern and unremitting Administration policy of living within our income."

The smile which the photographer caught, the complacent and confident voice of the "fireside chat," which confounded his detractors, did not always prevail when in his office Roosevelt studied the mounting criticism poured out by those from whom he had expected sympathetic understanding. The story of his decision to forget a balanced budget, regardless of his campaign promises will never be told until he tells it. He sincerely believed such a step had saved the nation from chaos.

Only three months after he had moved into the White House the *New York Times* had begun to look dubiously upon the temporary recovery and to doubt seriously that the new Administration had brought it about. It was inclined to agree with "the greater number of experienced business men" who believed a distinct turn for the better in the course of industry to have been a normal probability in the late Spring of 1933. Said the *Times* of the New Deal on June 25, 1933: "It undoubtedly contains much that is good, but also some things that are doubtful. So far as they contradict or affront the long experience of mankind, they also will fail."

All this from the *Times* when Roosevelt had hardly had time to get started. And now, after he had stood for sound money, he had swept the country off the gold standard. He had stood for government economy and was piling up the largest gross peacetime deficit in Federal history.

The President exhaled jets of smoke as I outlined some of these points which, as a newspaper man, I believed would be used for editorial targets. It all got down to the purpose for which the hundreds of millions of dollars were being poured out.

Suddenly he brought his large, powerful fist down upon his desk with such force that it made the gadgets jump.

"Don't they know," he asked, "why I had to spend this money? Don't they realize the situation I had to face when I got behind this desk? We had to be headed in a new direction. *Don't they know what would have happened if the money had not been spent?*"

Obviously he held to the thought that the country had survived the shock of a bloodless revolution. He may not have realized it but HE was the revolution. The time has not yet come to measure Roosevelt. Historians will forget about unbalanced budgets when they write about him.

We discussed Brisbane, and Hearst's castles and stored-up art.

"Somehow," said Roosevelt, "I feel Brisbane isn't as bad as the others."

Before I left the President he added:

"Some day it may be that Hearst's palaces at San Simeon will be visited by people as strange museums."

Perhaps he had in mind the great estates then going by the boards. Such thoughts may have inspired his wife to write later for her newspaper column, the following paragraphs on this speculation after visiting on the Hudson the Vanderbilt estate which had been acquired by the Government to be administered by the National Park Service:

"Individuals are not going to live in houses like these in the future, partly because few will have any desire to do so, and partly because our social set-up will be so changed that it will not be possible. Historically, however, it will be interesting to see the various steps through which we have come in our development.

"I wonder if we have really grown to the point where the size of a house in which a person lives will have little interest to his neighbors, but what he contributes in mind and character to the community will bring him respect and admiration? If we have, we are entering an era where the arts, science and cultures of every kind may come into their own."

CHAPTER IV

I BECAME immersed in the investigation of the Aircraft Trust whose ramifications reached back to the shocking Air Service Scandal of 1918. The people had long forgotten that, during our participation in the World War, only 196 airplanes of American manufacture had been delivered to the front in France up to the time of the Armistice. There was a little matter of $1,500,000,000 that had been spent for those 196 machines but that had been forgotten, as well. Assuming that such a situation could have been possible in a totalitarian state, the responsible participants would have been shot.

There was one man in command of the American Army air forces in France during the World War who still remembered what had happened. He had received the 196 airplanes, most of them unfit for use, and he found that they killed more American pilots than did the Germans. He returned to devote his life to the task of convincing the American people that without leadership in an air force as a main arm of defense, this Democracy would not survive. He had become such a vitriolic critic of the Air Service and his superiors that he had been court-martialed for violating the ninety-sixth Article of War. He was convicted, but had avoided a five-year suspension from the Army lists by resigning his post. He was probably the most prophetic judge of the future that this country's soldiery ever produced. Laughed at, reviled, surrounded by enemies, he had pursued his mission doggedly.

This man, who died almost in my arms during our investigation, was General William Mitchell. He had nursed the American Air Service from its infancy, when the Army, being in a quandary as to what to do with the early military planes of the Wright brothers and Glenn H. Curtiss, had flung them at the young air enthusiast, as one might throw a bone to a dog. In France he had shown them what could be done with a plane, even though it was nothing but a crate. He was the first American officer to fly over the battle lines and finally there were not medals enough to distinguish his "repeated acts of extraordinary heroism," as the Government described them.

The investigation of the pooling of patents of the aircraft industry had been inspired by Mitchell as a final effort to make our air force dominate all other problems of national defense. In 1935 he was convinced, by his own investigations in Germany, that Hitler, in less than five years' time would seize Europe by air supremacy. He had revealed in his testimony before the Committee on Patents of the House that Germany and Italy were building subterranean bases for thousands of airplanes, to prevent bombardment, to get out quickly, to protect and to have as "gas tight" as possible, huge fuel deposits for the coming war of the air. The Italians, he had discovered, had an immense underground airplane factory in the Alps. Airplanes could be hauled clear through a mountain, coming in or out on each side. The Germans, he said, had twenty-one of these subterranean airdromes. He pleaded for a study of these plans by the Army. No attention was paid to his testimony. It was called "war-mongering." From his own experience he believed that no future war could be effectively fought by the United States without a department of national defense, headed by a Secretary of Defense in the Cabinet, under whom would operate the Army to defend the land, the Navy to defend the sea and the Air Force to defend the air. He had fought and pleaded for this belief and faith. It had prompted from his lips the gravest charge ever made against the heads of the armed forces of the United States by an American Army officer. "The high command of both the Army and Navy are guilty of incompetency, criminal negligence and almost treasonable administration of the national defense." He had been broken for it, but relentlessly he shouted out his warning.

General Mitchell was convinced that the pooling of patents of the aircraft industry was a menace to national defense because it gave a monopoly complete power to control inventions and to sell engines or implements of war to totalitarian powers which might eventually use these American weapons to attack the Democracies. The purpose of our investigation was to reveal the menaces of the patent pool and pave the way for protective legislation by disclosing any agreements of the combination which might be against the public interest.

To the man on the street who supports out of his own

pocket the arms of defense that safeguard his home, the technicalities of this investigation may have been too boring to absorb. An innocent citizen begins to understand these affairs when bombs rain about him and blast his house to match-sticks while he cowers in an air-shelter with his helpless family.

To familiarize myself with this situation I had studied hundreds of documents and a large part of the testimony of the previous investigations on the subject. I had become convinced that the patent pool of aircraft, as it affected the defense of the country, was a dangerous industrial conception. The individual acquiring ownership of a large number of patents usually has in view one of two objects. Either he seeks to gain control of the industry to which the patents relate and thus eliminate competition, or he intends to suppress such patents as he believes would be detrimental to him in their exploitation. In either case the public suffers, in proportion to the importance of the invention involved, and the true purpose of the patent laws is violated.

Under the aircraft patent-pooling arrangement, not only was the Government forced to buy what the manufacturer offered but factories operated under this system were open, under certain mild restrictions, to the agents of foreign powers. As the Government had no control over the plants, any secrets might easily leak out. As a matter of fact I discovered that *many of them did*!

According to expert testimony the Government could have built aircraft cheaper by fifteen to twenty percent, than the prices it had paid. On large orders these savings would have amounted to vast fortunes. According to General Mitchell a foreign agent could visit any plant manufacturing aircraft in this country and could keep himself informed of all progress. The General's records, in 1936, showed that between seventy and eighty percent of the airplanes made here were sold to foreign countries. Our best airplane engines were being sold to the Japanese. Foreign governments were buying the right to manufacture American airplanes under license and employing our own men to do the work. Hidden in the archives of the Patent Committee is Mitchell's testimony that in 1933 the United States did not have *any pursuit group that could have kept up with the late Marshal Italo Balbo's mass of flying boats* which flew to America from Italy on a pleasant journey. The engines of the Italians had been stepped down to 950-horse-power from 1,500. This was just a friendly visit.

"We are like so many hitch-hikers thumbing a ride on the road to hell," the General said. "I sometimes wonder how this nation has survived the thick-headedness of our Regular Army, and I have served on the General Staff. We are spending more money on our national services than any other country in the world and we are organizing for defeat.

"What we have known as the hostile army in the field will become the false objective in the next war. The real objective will be the vital centers. Armies will be disregarded by air power which will destroy areas where food and supplies are produced. A greatly superior army numerically will be at the mercy of an air force inferior in numbers. In the next war a nation ambitious for universal conquest, and which gets off to a flying start, may be able to control the whole world more easily than a nation has controlled a continent in the past. We will soon discover that the destinies of all people will be controlled through the air. I hope that we never have to find out that it will be too late to organize an air force after war begins. We will wait until the last minute and blow in billions of dollars."

The testimony of ruined inventors who came to Washington to offer their help to break the patent pool did not have a pleasant ring for the hearers who loved to contemplate America as a land of opportunity for the imaginative. Newspapers paid little attention to James V. Martin, owner of the Martin Airplane Works at Garden City on Long Island, whose tragic story filled countless pages of Government records. He was an aircraft pioneer, a pupil of the famous Augustus M. Herring, who had been Professor Langley's chief engineer in 1895. Herring had taught the Wright brothers the use of current surfaces from which are derived the lifting characteristics that enable airplanes to fly. Herring claimed to be the real inventor of the airplane in its essential combinations, but he was a forgotten man.

Martin had conceived seventeen airplane inventions. His type of wing, for instance, was in universal use on practically all classes of heavier-than-air craft. His retractable chassis had been spurned by the aircraft monopoly because it was the idea of an independent inventor. During the World War he had offered his services to the pooling combination but had been informed that his inventions were not wanted. He was asked to build a machine known as the DeHaviland 4, which was later to figure in the billion-dollar Air Service Scandal, and which he had already labeled as the "flaming coffin." Convinced that such a machine was a pilot's death sentence he refused to produce it. The DH-4's were aptly named by Martin. The gasoline tank of the machine was located directly ahead of the pilot's seat. The Germans were soon aware of this and shot incendiary darts between the motor and the pilot. The darts instantly turned the plane into a flaming ball, burning the pilot alive in mid-air. Young aviators fighting to make the world safe for Democracy had more than the Germans to contend with.

A year before Lindbergh had even conceived his flight to Paris, Martin had completed, as an independent manufacturer, an airplane which had all of the characteristics and mileage required for a trans-Atlantic voyage. On the night before it was to be introduced to the public it was destroyed by fire from incendiary darts. Martin accused his competitors in testimony in the Government records. The inventor had exhausted his fortune. His inventions had been appropriated, his reputation torn to shreds. After years of struggling, hoping each investigation would bring redress, he was at the end of his rope.

I found the Government records of aircraft investigations full of such sworn testimony. The progress of flying seemed to be marked by staggering recitals of the incomprehensible hardships and frustrations of its pioneers. It is not a pretty story, this one, about an invention which was to alter the social geography of the earth and brutalize mankind. I met almost at every turn men who had contributed to the development of the airplane and had the proof to show it but had come out of the experience with nothing but poverty and disillusionment.

CHAPTER V

RUMORS were soon afloat in Washington that General Mitchell would be restored to active service and the uneasiness occasioned by these reports in both the aircraft industry and the military services became apparent to me when I set out to gather my witnesses. High executives of the aircraft business produced with reluctance the information I required and charged openly that Mitchell had instigated the investigation to become a czar of aviation. The General smiled grimly when I reported this state of affairs. He told me he had discussed the country's airplane status with the President, even to the point of urging action for a separate department of the air.

One evening in August of 1935, having flown to Washington with a mass of records, I found Mitchell waiting for me at The Mayflower with a man who was deeply interested in our work although he preferred to remain in the background of the inquiry. He was Senator Joseph T. Robinson, Democratic Leader of the Senate and from the course of the conversation during dinner I began to understand Mitchell's plan of campaign. The Senator proposed to use his powerful influence to restore the prerogatives surrendered by the former Brigadier General. Such a move had already been attempted but had been thwarted by George H. Dern, Secretary of War, who had told advisers that any plan to help Mitchell or promote a separate department of air would be put through over his "dead body." Mitchell, recalling the incident, cursed the Secretary roundly. It was the first time I had seen the General in explosive anger. He was a man of medium height with an inquisitive nose, set lips, gimlet eyes and a lined, receding forehead which added a tenacious touch to his face.

The General's ambitions plunged me into an unforgettable experience. One man whose services he was anxious to enlist in his battle to revolutionize air defense was Senator Huey Pierce Long whose political potentialities were not comprehended until his assassination. Mitchell's support came from a quarter which looked upon Long as a barbaric menace but the General saw a vital force in the Louisiana dictator which might be invaluable in accomplishing the air objective. He wanted Long's help but he believed it would not have been desirable to approach him personally about it. After some curious maneuvering I was dispatched, during the first week of September, 1935, to New Orleans to sound out the "Kingfish" who was at that time preparing a book to be entitled *My First Days in the White House*. He was seeking the services of an editor outside of Louisiana to suggest whatever final revisions might be necessary in his manuscript. Working through a friend of Mrs. Hattie Caraway, whose re-election to the Senate had been helped by Long, Mitchell, remaining in the background, succeeded in placing my name before the Louisianan as a newspaper man whose experience might be helpful in a literary enterprise. The General saw no hope to obtain what he wanted if I represented myself as a Congressional investigator. This means, he felt, would have aroused the Senator's suspicions. Long was then at the height of his notoriety and power and his ambitions were far from bewildered. He believed he represented a turbulent confusion of inarticulate masses which, once solidified, would place him in the White House. His dreams were dangerous and had disturbed the Administration to such an extent that the President himself planned to take the stump against him in the Fall.

To visit Long in New Orleans during his last days, one followed a routine which was similar to the arrangements which had to be made to see Al Capone before his sojourn in Alcatraz. I was roughly questioned by three members of a bodyguard the night before my appointment, having been quartered in the same hotel with the "Kingfish."

I was a few minutes ahead of time at Long's suite in the sparkling forenoon and was greeted again by the bodyguard who this time comported themselves as those who have the honor of attending at the doors of great men. One of them forgot his dignity sufficiently to pat my pockets before I was led through a door at the end of a brilliantly lighted corridor.

The Senator was in bed in pink silk pajamas, reading a fistful of manuscript, and reaching out to spear mouthfuls of creamed chipped beef from a smoking silver dish. He greeted me with a raucous shout, remembering a meeting we had had in New York. As I was drawing up a chair, he asked:

"Do you ever have breakfast in bed?"

I replied that it was a luxury with which I was unfortunately unacquainted, a piece of information which seemed to dash his joviality.

"Well, honey-child," he thundered, "you're just underprivileged, and I'm going to make you acquainted with one of the pleasantest experiences in life. Go into that cupboard, take your clothes off and put on a suit of my pajamas and get into this other twin bed and I'll order a Southern breakfast. Then we can talk and you won't feel self-conscious, because I'm not going to get up until this conference is over."

Remembering Mitchell's admonitions to humor the Senator I obeyed instructions and crept between the sheets of a bed which he had jerked alongside of his own. While we ate we reviewed his manuscript.

"This is going to be a great book," he said. "It's all part of a plan. The way to do a thing, these days, is to write a book about it and then proceed to do everything that the book says you're going to do. They're laughing at Hitler but that's exactly what he's doing. We've become so hypocritical in this country that when a man announces he is going to do something we think he's going to do exactly the opposite. Then he puts it over."

He handed to me a handful of pages of *My First Days in the White House*, an early copy of which had already gone to the printer, and shouted with laughter while I read of President Long's Cabinet appointments. Roosevelt was to be Secretary of the Navy, and Hoover, Secretary of Commerce. Senator Borah was to become Secretary of State, and General Smedley D. Butler, Secretary of War. Alfred E. Smith was Director of the Budget, a post elevated to Cabinet rank. This departure, Long said, would eliminate all duplicating Government bureaus. John D. Rockefeller, Jr., was to head Long's Share-the-Wealth Commission, after dividing his Standard Oil millions with the people.

Long hated the figures in his imaginary Cabinet and said so. Through mouthfuls of chipped beef he raged over the ingratitude of those in power.

"Roosevelt knows damned well," he stormed, "that he

wouldn't be President but for what I did at the Convention. I know what he's trying to do. I'm sincere enough to keep it out of my speeches in the Senate, because I want to do it myself. Franklin intends to stay where he is by a scheme of his own to share the wealth. If he puts it over he'll stay there until he dies. I'm more open about it. In my book I write about the New York financiers proposing a Government seizure of wealth while private control and operation of the affected businesses and industries is continued. That's why I name Rockefeller, Winthrop W. Aldrich of the Chase National Bank, and even Andy Mellon to help me out as President to draft a plan for the redistribution of wealth. They're doing that in my book to prevent their heads from being chopped off in a revolution. We're all sitting on a lid that will pop off, but the aristocrats don't know it."

The Senator was interested in my association with Brisbane. He thought at first of appointing him, in his book, as head of the Federal Share-the-Wealth Commission, in place of Rockefeller, but gave up the idea as lacking in tact. The irony of it, he feared, might provoke the editor to strike back.

"I pulled my punches with Brisbane," said Long, "when I answered Hugh Johnson in my radio speech. Brisbane is scared about this share-the-wealth business and it's because of his $260,000 a year. He would be one of the first to have to share his money bags with the poor. In his editorials he lied about my plan. I don't propose to give every person $15,000 for a home and its comforts. My plan proposes a minimum of $5,000 for every family, which would come to less than $125,-000,000,000. That is less than one-third of this nation's wealth in normal times, when it is $400,000,000,000."

Long described Brisbane as an arctic horned owl. Several months before, the Senator had captured the fancy of headline writers by likening Roosevelt to a "scrootch" owl and comparing Hoover with a hoot owl. The chief distinction between the two was that the latter raided a roost with fair warning while the "scrootch" sidled up coyly, won the chicken's confidence with sweet murmurings and then proceeded to devour her. The "Kingfish" regretted that I had not been present when he imitated the cries of these birds of prey for the Washington correspondents and offered to repeat the performance privately from his bed. He tossed his tousled head back, pointed his turned-up nose at the ceiling and uttered three sharp, throaty, blood-chilling screams.

A door burst open and a guard looked in anxiously, his right hand in the side pocket of his coat, surprised, I presumed. that I had not been found slitting my host's throat. "It's all right," Long laughed, "I'm imitating the Hoover bird. The other calls representing the Roosevelt owl may be worse, so don't get excited."

I expressed my appreciation of his performance and made some remark to bring him back to his literary work and restore my peace of mind.

"I must have guards around," he explained. "That one can empty a pistol into a four-inch target at fifty feet. You know," he said, as if he were informing me of a foregone conclusion, "I'm going to be killed. They've tried it with bombs through the mails. A bullet could make me President sooner, if I recovered from it, but," he added, frank alarm spreading over his porcine face, "I don't like the idea of waiting for it."

An attractive blonde secretary, the reigning darling of his stenographic staff, was escorted into the room by two of Long's armed servants and we went over the points of the manuscript about which the Senator had been in doubt. He discussed his literary problems with one arm about the girl, fondling her with a fat hand while she sat on the edge of the bed taking her notes with a cool indifference to his familiarity.

The literary conference had left the Senator in an expansive mood and I was able to introduce the subject of Mitchell and soon found that Long believed the General had been outrageously treated. He blamed the entire trouble on Coolidge, whom he had despised, and as the conversation proceeded I had little difficulty in talking more freely about the General's plan which the Senator recognized as a cause of merit. Revealing myself as Mitchell's friend I was able to secure for him Long's complete support. My mission accomplished I made to leave but the "Kingfish" remained talkative. He dressed leisurely while I got into my clothes. He was to spend the weekend at Baton Rouge and invited me to accompany him so that we might further explore the scope of his book. I declined and I have often wondered what fate would have had in store for me had I joined him.

As he donned his apparel he discussed the psychology he

had developed to intrigue vast masses. He was convinced he was an historic American figure. At that moment hundreds of his agents were working to establish throughout the nation groups of the rabble with the announced intention of making "every man a king."

"All I need," he said, "is one hundred thousand of those societies and I'll run the country. Sometimes I'm almost frightened how easy such things can be done. By God, it makes a man decide to be sincere! Suppose the wrong man swept the people in a false direction. Think that over! I'm going to cut loose from a lot of people who are stealing my stuff. I think there's a menace in what Father Coughlin is doing. I agree with a lot of his points, which he swiped from me, but there's something dangerous in the political outcries of a priest. If religion ever sinks to the level of politics, God help it!"

He talked as if to himself, an amazing creature, not now the "plausible punchinello," which one of his opponents had called him. The child of a poor-farmer family, he was still in effect one of the "untouchables" according to the tradition of the better class in the South. And when it rankled, he was no longer satisfied that he could rule his home State as if it were a personally owned province. If this could be done with one State, it could be done with them all. Yet, he would never be able to distinguish the wrongs of his class from the humiliations he himself had undergone before coming to power.

The illiterates of a nation were ready to follow him anywhere because he knew enough not to use the best English unless he considered it safe. It was a great thing for a leader to understand the effect in his speeches of "ain't," "I seen" and "they was" on the plain people. It was so easy to appear to be of, as well as for them. The poor would be the last to see in such a prophet a betrayer and a perverter of the social forces that were their only hope of survival. Of such are the Dictators of these times.

Long looked at himself in the mirror, adjusting a red and green tie. He flicked a speck of dust from his brown and white sport shoes and buttoned his tan tropical-weight suit so that the coat almost covered his lavender checked shirt. He examined his manicured fingernails, and fitted to his head, at a slightly rakish angle, a straw hat with a gay band. It was fun to be the "Kingfish" and the smartest man in "Loozyana." A lot of people were saying already that he was the smartest man in the United States.

"You sure you don't want to come to Baton Rouge?" he smiled. "I'll show you how a future President of the United States runs his home State."

He walked off jauntily to his slaughter.

CHAPTER VI

HEADLINES were shouting the news that Long had been shot down at Baton Rouge while, on my flight to New York, I had stopped off in Washington to tell Mitchell that the "Kingfish" had agreed to support him. The General crushed his forehead in his hands and for some time remained in deep thought. When he uncovered his face it carried an expression strange as tender, as though to convey a meaning to me without too many words.

"Circumstances have changed my actions," he said, "but not my mind. Nothing matters but the country. When you face death in a crate over the battle lines, that's what you think about—the country. It will not survive without the most powerful air defense in the world. I have fought seventeen years for that cause. I'll give every day I have left to it."

He tapped his heart.

"You know what that means. Generals may die in bed but their battle plans remain. Perhaps a reputation is preserved with more ease in death than during life. That isn't the country's fault."

Now he took no note of time but from its loss. He had a horror of putting anything off even for an hour. A day missed in gathering evidence drove him into a fury followed by periods of exhaustion. During his last struggle he was at the same time wrestling with a libel suit brought by an aircraft corporation which demanded $200,000 damages from him because he had charged in a New York address that the company's materials were becoming quickly known to foreign powers, and that it was not free to make its own decisions.

I was still involved in a number of Sirovich's enterprises. One night in Washington he sent me off to interview an obscure Congressman who for some unexplainable reason had blocked a political maneuvering intended to protect the American Society of Composers, Authors and Publishers which collected vast payments for all broadcasted music and songs written by its membership of 50,000 creative artists. A measure which sought to stop "Tin Pan Alley's" financial operations was to have been referred unanimously by the House to the Committee on Patents, behind whose doors Dr. Sirovich proposed to dispose of the bill's remains. He was convinced that the Representative who had sidetracked the motion by one vote had accepted a bribe from a radio combination. Nathan Burkan, a celebrated New York lawyer who represented the musicians had been left speechless by the development. The complications drew me into an adventure which Sirovich described as a "singular experience."

When I hunted up the offending Congressman at his apartment to ask him to explain his motives I found him engaged in a thunderous brawl with a disheveled woman who was hurling crockery. He opened the door amid the din of shattering furniture while fragments of dishes rained down upon us like shrapnel. Behind me a landlady was howling the respectability of the establishment. The man I sought, who was barefooted and stripped to the waist as a gunner in a sea fight, yanked me in, locked the door and flung a typewriter in the direction of his antagonist who had barricaded herself in a kitchenette. He studied my credentials with a sudden imperturbability. This was my introduction to the Hon. Marion A. Zioncheck, Representative from the State of Washington, described later in headlines as the "Seattle Scourge."

He was lean and above medium height and his face reflected the quick intelligence such as is seen in smart animals. His eyes were strange, burning and dilated and as he circled about they enveloped me and never left my face. They carried an expression more than intoxicated and I became transfixed with the realization that I was locked up with a madman.

He leaped to the top of a sideboard where he squatted like an ape and as I held his stare strange noises in his throat gripped me with a fear such as I had never experienced. In a purring voice he said he had raised his objections in the House to let his colleagues know that he understood the rules. He proposed to object to everything. Appropriations for millions of dollars were being passed and he was given no time to study them. He could no longer sleep. Nobody could count the money that had already been spent. His last remarks were delivered with shouts and screams.

He sprang from the sideboard and forced down my throat a cocktail of his invention—a murderous concoction of rum and honey. His eyes softened as I drained the glass fearfully and he unlocked the door, after searching for the key during an agony of time.

Zioncheck's insanity was soon to smear the front pages. Apparently I had interviewed him when he had taken a turn for the worse. He drove his automobile into a throng of Washington shoppers. In New York, before a crowd of enthusiastic photographers he went wading in the pool at Rockefeller Center. He landed in jail after personally delivering to the White House a cardboard box, addressed to the President and containing two overripe bananas. Finally, he leaped to his death from the high window of a hotel.

*   *   *   *   *

Mitchell, who had hoped that the year 1936 would bring a turning point in his struggle for a unified air defense moved into Doctors' Hospital in New York late in January with no illusions about his fate. He lay in bed when the House Military Affairs Committee killed a bill which would have retired him as a colonel with a Government pittance. His personal estate amounted to $5,765.

He had used up his indomitable energy as a witness when Sirovich finally opened the aircraft hearings. The General's testimony had been sensational but editors slashed the stories of his last warning to the nation and pushed them into obscure columns. Lying on a bed when it was over he had flung newspapers aside with a spirit of mockery that seemed to translate everything of life into emptiness. What he said was no longer news. Bombs were not then falling on Buckingham Palace and London had not yet become a city of human moles. It was monotonous reading before the House of Commons met between air raids and Washington was shouting for 50,000 planes a year.

"I won't live to see it," he said, "but New York will soon be employing engineers to plan bombproof air-raid shelters. We will wake up after London has been bombed to a powder. We will then discover that it takes 30,000 parts to make an air bomber. Our 'brass heads' in Washington don't even know that anti-aircraft gunners can be trained only by actual fighting experience. God help England, when she finds that out. She's in the same fix!"

Shortly before Christmas in 1935, there had occurred an incident that I could only attribute to a baffling coincidence, but which had added to Mitchell's distress. Lindbergh and his family sailed from the United States under the utmost secrecy while Sirovich was making private arrangements to have the aviator subpoenaed to appear in the aviation inquiry. The *Times* announced exclusively that the Lindberghs planned to establish their home in England as a place of refuge where they believed they would find greater regard for law and order than in their own country.

Mitchell had sent me a number of reports which may not now be published as they involve aircraft corporations active in building airplanes to the capacity of their plants in the war-aid program of 1941. He accused some of them of being concerned in what he called a conspiracy to make money at the expense of the nation. His views regarding Lindbergh are explained in a letter which he wrote to me from his home, "Boxwood," at Middleburg, Virginia, and which follows in part:

My dear Gauvreau:
As to Lindbergh, he is a commercial flyer. He was a barnstormer and airmail pilot before his flight to Europe. This flight was well prepared and well executed. Of course there was a certain element of luck in it. His deportment after it and the way everything was handled gave him remarkable prominence in this country and over the world. At first the Air Trust didn't know what to make of it. Some articles appeared attempting to belittle him, notably one by Grover Loening, but it was too good a show to pass unnoticed. Therefore, they decided to use him, and immediately upon his return they made overtures to him for employment. He has been used by them . . . for their ventures . . . Lindbergh's influence has been used by these interests against a united air service. . . .
Had Dwight Morrow lived, Lindbergh's reputation would have been used to assist him in obtaining the nomination for the Presidency. It will be remembered that Dwight Morrow was chairman of the Morrow Board under Coolidge, convened at my suggestion that an impartial board be brought together, but it was stuffed by the profiteers, and their find-

ings resulted in practically our whole aviation development being turned over to the Air Trust, and eliminating not only the pioneers in aviation but the very highly trained government personnel which we had developed during and just after the war. Since the findings of the Morrow Board were put into effect, our aviation has sunk lower and lower. . . .

You must realize that this is also a very clever group and that they have ramifications here, particularly in the Navy. It should not be hard for you to establish how they . . . carried out their various designs.

You will notice that this group all along the line has not attempted to support any definite concrete policy . . . under any and all conditions. The people they have picked up and made much of are what might be termed "stunt artists," such as Amelia Earhart, a commercial flyer, and several others in the public eye. These people, while excellent pilots, particularly Miss Earhart, are very much in the nature of theatrical performers as far as their influence on the development of aircraft is concerned. This includes Lindbergh.

I know that you are making good progress and I hope you will not be carried away too far by side issues before you get at the main proposition.

Yours sincerely,
WILLIAM MITCHELL.

Among the records the General had turned over to me was an exhaustive report prepared by Senator Ernest Lundeen of Minnesota who was one of Mitchell's supporters. The Senator believed navies were outdated. He not only advocated a Department of Air Defense but had presented a bill to create a Government bureau to regulate commercial navigation of the air. Charts indicating years of study of the causes of aeronautical accidents, which he hoped by his plan to reduce to a minimum, were included in his appeal for a unified service. He was killed with twenty other passengers in an airplane crash which, ironically, he had described as a type of accident most easily avoidable.

One of the Senator's disclosures which Mitchell had verified threw an interesting light on the ease with which foreign powers obtained modern American-made weapons even though the State Department stepped in to prevent such transactions. In 1935, attachés of Soviet Russia approached American manufacturers of tanks and bombing planes with an order involving

several millions of dollars.   The American firms were enthusiastic but a few days later became suddenly lukewarm.   Vague
excuses were offered that the Russian credit would have to be
investigated and that American factories were already busy on
such orders, which was not the case.   The Russians offered to
place the business on a cash basis but the manufacturers remained aloof, and for good reason.   The State Department had
stipulated that American tanks and planes could not be sold to
Russia.

Nevertheless, Russia obtained both tanks and planes.   She
bought them in England and Germany and they were identical
with those which were to have been ordered in the United
States.   American manufacturers, seeing valuable contracts
slipping through their fingers, sold their patents to British
Vickers and German Junkers and in return received a ten percent commission on the order.   Russia was satisfied and, incidentally, Germany became acquainted with the detailed plans
of some of our most up-to-date weapons.

During the last few months of his life Mitchell was concerned about the military strategy of tanks to be used in cooperation with airplanes and had received information that a
report submitted by Colonel J. K. Parsons to the War Department, five years before, recommending the organization of six
divisions of 486 tanks each, had been pigeonholed.

"Tanks, like airplanes, are something new," said the General.   "They go together and they'll win the next war, but
destruction will have to reach our doors before we realize their
value.   There is something criminal in voluntary ignorance.
Our Army is still fighting the motorization of their cavalry
divisions.   We can't get 'Squads right!' and 'Squads left' out
of our heads."

In the deadly parallel of experience the General might well
have been compared with General Charles de Gaulle who as a
Colonel in France, while Mitchell's life was ebbing, urged the
mechanization of the French Army and the formation of the
very "Panzer" divisions which were later used by Hitler to
crush the French Republic.   For his pains, de Gaulle, who also
had begged for a vitalizing increase in the air force, was dismissed from the general staff.   He went out, and five years
later, the Germans came in.   When that happened the pigeonholed report of Colonel Parsons was dusted off by our War

Department which found itself with only *one mechanized tank brigade* and was amazed to discover that the devastating "Panzer" divisions of the German Army followed the Parsons plan, even to the last organizational detail. In 1941, while the only Democracy fit to use the name hoped and prayed, those whose prejudices, self-conceit and obstinacy had driven Mitchell into exile sheepishly recovered his prophetic trumpet from the dust and, in confusion, struggled to reorganize an army that had little left but its fighting heritage to meet the tactics, weapons and equipment of modern warfare.

I heard from Mitchell for the last time from his hospital after I had informed him that my part in the air inquiry was done. He expressed anxiety about the records we had accumulated and which we kept in New York. He ordered me to fly with them to Washington and lock them up in the House Office Building. The General was concerned about my own safety. He believed foreign forces were at work to prevent his revelations from reaching the public. I attributed his apprehension to his physical condition.

I flew to the Capital with a sense of relief. I wanted to free my mind from a task which at times had been disheartening. Although I was not disturbed by the General's warning as it applied to myself his words crept back into my consciousness. They had been repeated by him several times during the last intensive weeks of our association. I kept the records in my lap on the plane and shook off forebodings which I attached to the effect upon me of his shaking voice. I sensed no danger. There had been a few unpleasant scenes during the process of obtaining some of the evidence. One, I remembered humorously, involved a group of Japanese purchasing agents who had taken affront at my questions and had hissed like ruffled geese. Russian agents with whom I had dealt, masked their resentment with native complacence. The Nazis, whose artificial politeness and stolen English accents covered always a contempt for our way of life, I distrusted instinctively. The suavest of these were the most dangerous and I had never left their doors in Washington, New York or elsewhere without being maneuvered out of reach by chauffeurs trained in the technique of vanishing from "shadows"—so I believed.

Badge-wearing crowds were milling about The Mayflower in the excitement of a convention of unexplained business enthusiasm when I reached the hotel. All rooms had been taken but the management put my brief cases in a safe and permitted me to spend the night in the Vice-President's suite, which he was not occupying at the time. It was a vast place, richly furnished, silent as a tomb. I notified Sirovich of my new domicile.

I fell asleep with a sense of unbanishable solitariness, an oppression of the spirit even more intense than the feeling of loneliness that, as part of my nature, swept irresistibly over me when I saw nothing ahead to grip my interest. I awoke in the forenoon from a depressing dream of a violent tolling of bells which seemed to be telling of some unexplainable mourning, a strange property of the mind that absorbs into the fancies of the subconscious the sounds of life within earshot of the sleeper and compresses an unendurable eternity into a moment. A telephone of melancholy note had been ringing. It was Sirovich, his voice weak and far-off.

"I've been trying to get you since I reached the office. Hurry over to the House Office Building, for God's sake!"

I pulled some of the window drapes aside to find that a winter rain had turned into an icy drizzle. I ordered newspapers and breakfast, reading and eating simultaneously being one of my unbreakable habits.

I left the food untouched when I saw the headings. Mitchell was dead. Columns of type were freely given to his predictions, his struggle for an adequate air defense, his heroism, his warnings of national peril, his unique assault on the *Frankfort* and the *Ostfriedland* off the Virginia Capes to prove that air bombers could sink warships. It was all fresh news again—now that his heart had broken and he was gone. Tears made my eyes smart while I dressed. I collected my records, swallowed a brandy and drove to the Congressman's office.

Sirovich was slumped at his desk, his cheeks hollow and pale. He was recovering from a paroxysm of the heart, brought on by the discovery that a dollar-a-year assistant in our investigation had written to one of the aircraft corporations under our scrutiny a letter that would have compromised our enterprise had it reached the press. Although, happily, it had been the only occurrence of its kind among our group of patriots, I saw in the episode an example of the foolhardiness of placing temptation before politically-minded schemers whose motives of working for nothing often produced the opportunity they sought for shake-downs and even extortion of jobs from those whom they threatened with Congressional credentials.

Although shocked by the General's death, the Congressman was still dominated by his arts and science project which he hoped to leave as a monument to his career. As it would have required a new post in the Cabinet, he planned to recommend three men from whom he hoped a choice would be made— Arthur Brisbane, Dr. John H. Finley of the *New York Times* and Dr. Robert M. Hutchins, President of the University of Chicago. No one was stunned but Sirovich when the House swept his cultural dream into the dust heap, leaving him mumbling about a civilization that threw aside what was best for it.

He was to be spared the horrible confirmation of Mitchell's predictions when bombs, turning the London subways into catacombs, fell on King and cockney, destroyed the priceless relics of English civilization and turned our Democracy into an arsenal. Sirovich was found dead in his bathtub before the war, in 1939. Eulogies hailed him as a statesman, and among the 25,000 attending his funeral were leaders in politics and public life of the nation.

* * * * *

On the day following Mitchell's death, which had occurred on February 19, 1936, Sirovich wanted me to leave on a private mission to Latin America but I felt the need of a rest and begged to be excused for a week. Newspaper work had hardly been more arduous than my dollar-a-year job. My forwarded mail included a friendly inquiry from a social acquaintance of amiable memory, a charming hostess from whom I had not heard for several months. I wrote a letter inviting the lady to dinner at my New York apartment on Washington's Birthday so that I might have a short time in the Capital to tie up essential odds and ends.

I flew to New York barely in time to keep the appointment. I had made arrangements for the dinner in advance. There had been one or two slight changes in my ménage. White Fang had floated off to some lottery heaven and for a time a German housekeeper attended to my wants when I was in town. My bachelor quarters were attractive enough but I paid little attention to its problems. The housekeeper had left for Germany to be replaced by a negro servant.

The death of Mitchell had affected me deeply. At times I felt my emotions turning back on themselves, not leading anywhere. I wanted to talk about what I had done, to hear something from a pretty woman to make me feel not only a little happy but perhaps inordinately smart.

I straightened pictures on the wall, moved a footstool near the fireplace, feeling the temperature of a bottle of fine vintage in the wine bucket, looking at my watch. I lighted some candles on the table as the doorbell rang.

My guest was a little person, with a slight plumpness without which she might have been less attractive. Her laughing gray eyes and her personality could have been described only as jolly, radiating good moods with a caressing soft-lipped smile found with few women in New York beyond thirty. Aptly, she was called Jolly by close friends, and as I had divined the word which best fitted her I was favored with that informal privilege. She possessed intuitions better and readier than those of most men I knew, and I sensed that she felt something venturesome about this meeting, as indeed it was to be.

Jolly gave a little gasp of delight over the fireplace ready for the match and noticed the footstool where I hoped she would sit to watch the flames. Her eyes understood with a quick, grateful glance. She sat down, her hands folded tightly about her knees in some posture of ecstatic feminine snugness as I ignited a wax taper. I was describing some of my adventures and her shoulders cuddled into a slight shiver. "How exciting!" she said.

I had a log-burning fireplace which I liked to poke when the wind howled down the East River. I was pleased with the meticulously piled wood, the paper beneath, ready to be ignited and the well-chosen back-log. I wondered whose thoughtfulness was responsible for these preparations which I usually handled myself. I could not start the fire properly with Jolly so close on the footstool and I asked her to stand behind me as I crouched with burning taper to touch the blaze into life.

I remember a convulsive flash as though a muted cannon had been let off. It was an explosion that reached savagely into every corner although, singularly, it had a modulated sound, a muffled roar which made the room quiver. I was still on my knees, my right hand thrown instinctively before my face which had become like clay in a hot oven. My eyes were burned slits behind the wide glasses which had saved them, but I could see after the paralyzing ferocity of the flaming liquid volley. A fiery foam had shot out from the fireplace. We were curtained with tiny tongues of blue flame and an acrid, chemical odor hung over us.

My right arm dangled uselessly and smoke exuded from my clothes. I swung around to Jolly when I managed to get to my feet. She was a stiffened figure, overwhelmed with horror, her full lips open, her eyes expanded. Little flames licked at her gown and with the fingers of my left hand I reached for the yoke about her neck and sheared the dress from her body. I was horribly burned and my spark of consciousness became dim. It was my first sensation of slipping off into space. My last recollection was of something which reached into obscurities basic in human nature. Jolly was wearing round, wide, old-fashioned garters full of brilliant colors.

BOOK VI

CUBAN INTERLUDE

CHAPTER I

I was on the sloop *El Destino* heading in from Cayo Largo, southeast of Cuba, completing a task which included a private mission to obtain the consent of the Cuban Government to the sale of land to serve as a colony for thousands of Jewish refugees from Nazi Germany. I had inspected part of the south coast of Cuba without arousing too much Latin American curiosity.

The skipper, a tall man shriveled by the sun and shrunk by salty gales, had turned the tiller over to me at midnight and slid his thin form into the forecastle where his crew were occupied with Bacardi and guitars. But now all were drunk and snoring. There was nothing to take up my mind but a sail, a compass lamp and a Diesel engine.

I felt the tug of the tiller with thankful satisfaction. I could use my right arm again. It had been in bandages for four months after the explosion. Competent investigators were agreed that it had been the result of an attempt, at least, to reduce me to total blindness. The pain at times inclined me to the philosophy that the shortest life was long enough if it led to a better. The cause of the attack might have been attributed to various sources as I had stepped on many people's toes as a newspaper man before I began to investigate foreign influences in the aircraft industry. I had not added the affair to my collection of insoluble mysteries.

Winifred, my former secretary, had helped me during the critical stage of my injuries, and when I left New York to recuperate and to reach some decision about my unpredictable future I did not tell her how much a part she occupied in my thoughts. I had begun to discern the difference between heart-service and the lip-service with which I had been surrounded.

I had undertaken a commission from Sirovich who was organizing a financial syndicate which hoped to establish a home for the persecuted Jews. Also he was seeking first-hand information for a measure involving Roosevelt's "Good Neighbor"

policy in Latin America, which was playing an important part
in the election campaign of 1936 then under way. It had been
interesting work at a languorous pace in a new world of people
whose temperament was emotional rather than practical. It
humored my mood.

The moon spread a floodlight on the floor of the sea. Off
to larboard, tropical trees were bathed in a soft glow. Above
the dull pounding of the engine I heard the cries of animals,
the calls of birds. Stars were paling and disappearing and the
water behind me was phosphorescent, full of greenish, luminous hues. I was trying to form the habit of seeing more than
what I looked at. It is an alarming state to be past feeling. I
had wolfed down experiences until every sense of my being
had been overstrung. The business I had been in for years was
heading me toward a thorough and mature insensibility. Perhaps an explosion is the best remedy for the benumbed who are
buried in the rubbish of the daily scramble.

I must have been dozing for hours when I was jarred to
my senses by a flash of lightning which tore clear to the horizon
and in the illumination revealed a mounting sea. The coast
line was gone, the sky filled with heavy clouds. A sound like
the rumble of an express train crossing a trestle announced a
rising wind which lashed the black water into scudding spray.
Beside me on the seat was a large conch shell which the skipper
had blown earlier in the day to summon the first mate. I did
not blow on the conch shell. The tiller had been turned over
to me and I felt I was in charge. For the first time in my life
I decided to enjoy authority which required physical effort.

The boom swung over my head and with all my strength I
pulled the tiller over and the sail bellied before the wind. I
lashed the tiller and pushed down the speed lever of the engine.
The sloop rose and sank in spasms of wrath under her straining
spar. She was close hauled but the strong wind headed her
into the Caribbean. I was drenched in a deluge of rain and
clawing waves.

The roar and the whistle of the tempest seemed to be an
outer event which was wrestling with my inner conflicts. When
I became fully conscious of the gale it was subsiding and vanished almost as quickly as it had come. Soon the sloop was
leaving behind moving gleams in a broad, luminous track. A
profound peacefulness preceded the dawn which touched off

mountains of empurpled clouds. The sun rose like a gigantic sliced beet out of a blue platter, drenching the sail with hues of blood and spattering the waves. I sat back breathing it in and drinking the savor of the green salt mist. Sunrise on the Caribbean after a storm was a magic of nature that gave a meaning to life—that made one ashamed to be weary of living.

* * * * *

I had broached the subject of a homeland colony for the Jews months ago to Miguel Mariano Gomez when he was heaved about New York as though he had landed in a fireman's blanket during an interminable celebration of his election as President of Cuba. As a member of the city committee which welcomed him I was able, during brief lulls of this bewildering affair, to talk to him and the conversation had been hopeful. He wanted to see me in Havana to express officially his appreciation of the sympathetic publicity I had given him when he was in exile. I had learned long before I read *The Education of Henry Adams* that a friend in power is a friend lost and did not attach too much importance to the promises of winning candidates.

The summer of 1936 was not a fortunate time to seek from the Cuban President any answer to the world's despair. Gomez had his own troubles. He looked at me blankly, a trace of annoyance touching his pale face, when I mentioned the plight of the Jews and what might be done for them in Cuba. Even the mention of the money behind the project did not arouse him from his torpor. A great change had come over the man who three years ago had been ready to invade Havana with Waxey Gordon's machine guns. His campaign talks of sympathy for mankind were forgotten. He had been reduced to the emotions of a guinea pig, squirming in the laboratory of the New Democracy. Before I left him I accepted his invitation to attend a formal dinner at the Presidential Palace.

I was stopping at the old Hotel Inglaterra, which faced the Prado Boulevard, and in Central Park across the street, the Times Square of Havana, a military band was playing *La Dance Espagñola*. The musicians in stiff white uniforms, each man armed with a six-shooter in his belt, played in a standing position. I stood near the piccolo player who aroused in me an

undying interest. He was young and he had mastered a skill-
ful tonguing. He was doing what I had done with equal fa-
cility twenty-seven years ago. I was riveted like a country
yokel and cast my eye from his music rack to his face when I
knew he had to turn a page. He glared at me over his little
stick of an instrument and I retired across the street. I sat in
the Andalusian patio of the hotel listening to the band playing
None But the Lonely Heart, whose sense of loss and despair
mingled with my enjoyment of its lament. I inhaled music as
I had seen practiced addicts breathe in opium. It stimulated
old memories. Sometimes it produced haunting anxieties.
Over my wine swept the disturbing thought that Sirovich
whose premature enthusiasms often betrayed his discretion,
might let it be known in the mysterious channels which reached
the oppressed Jews of Germany that they would be welcome
in Cuba.

I was seized by the same feeling days later when my inter-
views with those who, I had hoped, might be inspired by
humanitarian feelings for the refugees, resulted in nothing
but a total lack of encouragement. The Jews in Cuba, with
whom I had discussed the plan were thrilled with its possibilities and talked about it. Even unofficial word of it might
bring boatloads of exiles, clamoring to land, only to be turned
away to a creeping death. The picture of this calamity in my
mind began to assume spectral proportions and I sent a warning
cable to Sirovich which reflected my increasing anxieties. He
replied that he would come to Cuba himself if I failed to report
progress within a month.

The word had spread, however, through those underground communications which reach the despairing. I remembered my presentiment long after I had returned, sick to death,
from this forlorn mission. Sirovich had followed my trail
with the optimism of the Jew who never gives up, his faith
still undimmed, before the first, unauthorized boatload arrived off Havana on the S. S. *St. Louis*. He wept when, after
twelve days of agonized waiting in the broiling sun, the ghost
ship of hope pulled up anchor for Europe, with its 1,000 exiles
praying for Divine intervention to find them a place of refuge.
The railings and portholes were crowded with faces distorted
into fantastic masks, burning with haunted, staring eyes taking
a last look at a world of narrowing freedom. Their plight

aroused less consideration from the crew than the human decencies accorded to cattle. The news of their hopeless wanderings reached hundreds of distraught Jews who were sailing for Cuba from Constanta, in Rumania, on the Panama Steamship *Rim,* and 150 of them plunged overboard into the Black Sea in a mass suicide. Dispatches said a number had been rescued. Perhaps those who went down in the oily waters were able to reason in their dying moments that drowning was at least an end of their own choosing, though the tropical waters, to die in, might have been closer to liberty.

My arrival in Havana had provoked a little demonstration which stirred my mind, still overcharged with the excesses of my yesterdays. Brushing aside uniformed greeters, a little group had pressed through the formalities, and an aged woman in black embraced me, followed by two younger women who kissed me tearfully, laughing and crying. Behind them was a little man whose bearing implied a degree of daring and physical courage. He had a grim mouth with the eyes of a patient saint. I was puzzled as he gripped my hand.

"My mother and sisters are indebted to you, and so am I," he said, "for saving my life when I was going to be shot in the Revolution when I was Mayor of Batabano. I am Doctor Louis Henriquez."

I stammered an acknowledgment and, as we drove to the Inglaterra with his relatives, I tried to awaken my memory by segregating his name from the insane episodes of my New York existence. It was a few moments before an account of his experience revived my recollections. He was to have been shot at sunrise at Cabañas Fortress but when his cell door was opened early in the morning, he was marched by the wall where men were usually stood for that ceremony, and told to go home. A New York editor had interceded for him through Ambassador Welles.

I recalled the cablegram I had almost forgotten to send to Sumner Welles, a note scribbled on the back of an old envelope which had fluttered as a signal from my pocket while I was fishing for a piece of paper to jot down a telephone number, during a merry wine-drinking dinner.

"You were our only hope," Henriquez said. "I was to be shot but my family knew that my cousin, Carlos, was acquainted with an editor in New York who might intercede with the American Ambassador. It was more than one could expect of a busy man to do for someone he had never seen, so far away. It is another evidence of the humanitarian spirit of the American citizen. But I prayed hard. Maybe that helped."

I told him I believed the prayer had everything to do with it. He suggested that our meeting called for a celebration with his family and appeared stunned when I insisted that I would pay for it. I never explained to him why the check for the party seemed to be the most appropriate bill I had ever settled.

I was not to forget Doctor Henriquez again, nor the underside of the Cuban tapestry he revealed to me. At first I was inclined to attribute his morose reaction to the gayety of Havana to the boredom of a familiarity with its life. I found myself relaxing to the pleasures of this atmosphere with an enjoyment I had seldom felt. I liked to watch the Sunday evening flirtation parade on the Prado. Youths strolled in one direction around the park while dark-eyed girls in their finery walked in the other, exchanging coy glances and sometimes words which led to warmer affections than friendships. I thought I discerned among the young, a happiness, a sense of security such as I had never seen.

The well-to-do lived here with an intensity I had not discovered anywhere, even in Vienna during its pre-Hitler twilight, or gay Warsaw before her officers fled from her rape. Havana flocked to the midget-car races where machines invariably piled up, killing its drivers while the crowd shrugged its shoulders. The ferocity of Jai Alai, the Basque game of handball, aroused mobs into a passion of betting. Society led the pace at the Oriental race track, the night clubs, yacht clubs, country clubs, the cockpits and the gambling casino where one forgot there was such a thing as Luyano, the Beggars' Village, whose inhabitants made merry in their own way at night, in the satisfaction of existing without working.

Doctor Henriquez recommended sea water for my burned arm and while enjoying the remedy I marveled at the exclusive beaches of white sand where the wealthy pampered themselves after nights of excess. Here, under an azure sky, the method of sex attraction seemed to be reversed. The voluptuous maiden, her fingers laced behind her head, lay in little, spent waves of emerald, watching the Cuban male, his hands on his hips, walking with that ease of well-built men who are never embarrassed. Occasionally she beckoned. Madame did not have to drop her shawl.

"This is not Cuba," Doctor Henriquez said, his sad eyes roving in displeasure. "I have got to go back to my troubles. If you want to study conditions you will learn something if you come with me. You will see the knots and tangles under this false embroidery."

The next night, in the Batabano region, we were ministering to the dying in the workers' hovels, hopeless people amid rags and misery, the smell of sickness and damp, of moldiness, of fever which made the air quiver. Typhoid and diphtheria raged through this area. Victims were suffocating, some dying alone, panting, emaciated, their eyes glistening as they tore at their tangled hair. Maddened by suffocation, children buried their heads in the straw bedding, screaming in terror at a touch. The water was contaminated. To drink it was to die. I held instruments, bottles, trimmed wicks in sputtering lamps as I listened to the wheezing breath of dying life. The children were taken with a languor, the women said. Then came pains in the stomach and the final agony.

We went from house to house in streets of anguish; at every door the same faces in the weak lamplight which deepened the shadows of sunken cheeks, the deep hollows in thin, strained necks. The men sat in corners, telling their beads, the little black pellets slipping slowly through gnarled fingers.

On a pallet, a pretty golden-haired child lay gasping and her breath was fiery against my face as I held up her head while Henriquez peered into her throat from which he pulled out a false membrane, a strip of white stuff which he examined under the lamp her mother held. She gulped from my flask of boiled water and cried. On another pallet a boy was convulsively grabbing at rags of potato sacking thrown over him. His sister, a young mother, sat quietly nursing her feverish baby, fitting its eager lips to her breast, her great dark eyes regarding us without curiosity. A swampy chill laden with the choking spume from the cane swept through the open door mingling with the odor of pestilence. Pale rays of light settled on a crucifix on the wall.

"This is Cuba," Henriquez said, as we left after the first night of my explorations. "Heads of these families have to work on the plantations for nine dollars a month. That

amounts to thirty cents a day. You can't buy medicine with
that and have food. Beggars in Luyano can make seventy
cents a day holding out their hands. Here, a man who tries
to live by the dignity of work to raise a family, makes less
than half a beggar's allowance and watches his children die.
These hovels have no outhouses. That is how the water is
contaminated. We are doing what we can but there are not
enough of us. Thank God, we don't expect to be paid."

Day in, day out, the little doctor fought his battle, winning
here, losing there. In other districts I met more of his type,
outnumbered, but dogged, persevering in the services of others.
I would not forget Henriquez. Perhaps a hand, whose mercy
was not of this sphere, held for a moment the fluttering paper
that had jogged my memory to telephone a few words to save
his life.

CHAPTER II

THE formal dinner which Gomez gave at the Presidential Palace impressed me with a pomposity hard to reconcile with my knowledge of the conditions in the interior. Surrounded by intriguers who had taken advantage of his neurotically meek nature, he presided almost with a gesture of bravado; but after the gold goblets had been raised in his honor, the hostilities rushing him to impeachment seemed slight compared to the lush and impregnable gayety of the evening.

Among the señoras, who preened and glanced over their powdered shoulders in the Hall of Mirrors, the gossip of the plotting and bickerings which trailed their host was as succulent as the imported delicacies waiting for them on the glittering table. Here, the challenges and impending duels among the gentlemen at the Capitolio, the bombs that occasionally jarred the touring Daiquiri sippers at the sidewalk cafés were all part of the romance that colored a new administration before it settled down to divide the spoils. The starvation in the cane country never intruded into the wide-eyed small talk of the sugar rich.

Gomez, at the head of the table, beamed at the señoritas, young women quaint in their simple-mindedness, their ready laughter coming from voluptuously full lips, whose piquant charm might have been called lustful in other girls of a profession not wholly ignored in Havana. On their shapely heads were graceful towers of black hair which caught the glint of the chandeliers, and beneath the glistening tresses dark eyes smiled in their depths. I observed it all with a feeling of loathing I could not shake off. The awful scenes through which I had passed had quickened my imagination for the incongruity of this studied luxury. In the finely wrought silver-plate, the gold-plate, the jeweled bowls of fruits and ices of this sumptuous dinner, I saw nothing but the reflections of the deathbed in the hovel. Every luscious course seemed to pass by a grinning Lazarus lying on a dunghill at a rich man's door.

Rouged grand dames ate the choice morsels and drank the rare wines with animal spirits. Under their smeared cheeks was the glossy mother-of-pearl whiteness of skin more familiar behind the latticed windows of Old Spain. Through their laughter they flashed a regularity of teeth that caught the eye with little flashes of diamonds in the fillings. Turmoil never interfered with their resources of elegance. Their arms still tapered, and the use of their jeweled ostrich feathers was a beguiling game older than Cuba itself. Above the quivering fans, ageless black eyes searched the man at the head of the table for a strength of will and the strong passions that women like in the tropics. And the ostrich feathers hid questioning eyebrows.

I strolled about the ornate Palace with Gomez, hoping to find a quiet corner for a chat under some palms. We had been followed by two officers, in glistening white uniforms and gold braid, who walked closely behind us, almost by stealth.

"They are officers of the guard," he explained. "They are sent to the Palace to see that I am protected. They are the men of Colonel Batista and," he added wryly, "they are very thorough."

"Have you had any dealings with Batista?"

"No," the President replied. "He is running the army and he is trying to get used to my methods." He bent over slightly and made the motion of a spirited horse accustoming himself to tight gear. "Batista is fitting himself into the new harness," he said. "He will learn to pull."

I thought I heard a low chuckle behind the palms. We resumed the discussion of my mission for the Jews and made little progress.

"There is an old Cuban saying," the President said, "that we had rather do and not promise, than promise and not do, but," he gave a little start, "you must not take that as meaning anything."

Experience had taught me to make allowances for the sons of accomplished men. But the chasm between General José Miguel Gomez and his son, Miguel Mariano, seemed wider than usual. There were those in Cuba who shook their heads when they remembered the great rebel leader who had defied Spain, thirty years before 1898, by leaving his plow, like Cincinnatus, to lead his countrymen in their first blow for freedom. His heroism in the Spanish-American War was a warm legend. He had reaped the reward of the Presidency of the nation he had helped to create, and had died leaving wealth. But he had started from the plow. His son would not have known the difference between a furrow and a political rut. Rattling in his father's shoes, he was light, skeptical, captivating, and irresolute. I retired to my hotel smothering my usual disappointments when I found such people out.

Early in the morning I was awakened by the manager of the Inglaterra who filled the telephone with excitement. A lieutenant of the army was downstairs with a message, and the manager urged me to abandon formalities and receive him at my bedside. A dapper officer entered with a deference which covered a suavity of command. He presented the compliments of Colonel Fulgencio Batista who expressed a desire to meet me at Military City. The appointment seemed to be governed by the impulse of a man of large affairs, and I jumped out of bed when the officer, drawing his watch, added pointedly that an army car was waiting. I lost no time in dressing, and in a few minutes we were off.

Within a half hour we drove into a lavish suburb not far from the gulf, flickering in the sun. In the colorful foliage tropical birds sang, to be suddenly silenced by shrill trumpets and the roll of drums. A sentry stopped us, then waved us into Military City, a vast arsenal enclosed in barbed-wire fencing, its borders protected by machine-gun and field-artillery emplacements and rifle pits. Sentries with fixed bayonets were posted at regular intervals of the road. Soldiers swarmed about. We entered a building of castle-like design after passing the homes of the officers, palatial quarters of Spanish style with colored tile roofs, cool arches and balconies, high ceilings and grilled gates.

Behind a desk in a mahogany-lined room, an office filled with books and pictures which could have served a New York corporation lawyer, sat a short chunky man of broad features, straight black hair and the high cheekbones of an Indian. Beneath his bronzed skin were traces of the yellowish tinge of the Oriental but in his racial blend, the white Cuban strain predominated. His deep-set black eyes, under thick brows bordering a receding forehead, sparkled with cordiality. This was Colonel Batista.

Our conversation had hardly begun when I discovered that he was acquainted with the details of my mission and all there was to know about the dinner at the Presidential Palace. I expressed mild surprise and his laughter accentuated the curiously Mongolian cast of his features. He spoke briefly in Spanish to an orderly, who snapped at attention, saluted and clattered down a tiled corridor. Two officers appeared, saluted the Colonel, exchanged a few words with him, turned to me and grinned a greeting. They were the white uniformed, gold-braided escorts who had followed me about with Gomez. My impression of the chuckle behind the palms became a certainty. An explanation of their introduction would have been superfluous. The byplay was typical of Batista's naïve but impressive boldness. The Colonel penetrated me with an ironic glance, which might have said: "You have wasted time in finding out who runs Cuba."

Roosevelt had made an important pronouncement with relation to the "Good Neighbor" policy, and I used it as an entering wedge of our discussion. I found that Batista had completely digested it and he gave me cogent reasons for his agreement with its main points. He knew apparently that I had sounded Gomez on the subject.

"Did his views agree with mine?" he asked.

I had to admit that Gomez had not even read the headlines because of the pressure of social responsibilities.

The Colonel gave me a glance full of calculation.

"Right now," he remarked, "that is important reading for a President, don't you think? It was important enough for me to keep my lights on, after my work was done."

"Perhaps that is why—" I hesitated.

"Why, what?" he asked sharply.

"—why you are closer to Cuba than the President."

"If I wanted to," he answered, quickly, "I—but I did not ask you to meet me to discuss Gomez." He moved things about on his desk in the manner of clearing it for a fresher topic.

Although he could sway, with oratorical skill in his native tongue, vast masses of people which stretched from the Palace to the harbor of Malecón, he spoke English slowly, but with a correct choice of words. His eyes glittered with interest when I described some of my conversations with President

Roosevelt, particularly when they referred to the New Deal's social program.

"He is for the people, but not from the poor, because, first, he was a rich man; a rich man who felt sorry for the masses. The people will not let him get away. He must have studied Lincoln."

He talked about the Emancipator, his struggles for self-education, reading in a log cabin by candlelight. The Colonel pointed to his books.

"I have much reading to do," he said. "You know I have not had much time to read. It is never too late. It is a good way to be prepared. You know about me?"

I knew what he meant. He gazed through tall French windows at brilliant blooms sparkling in the sun. Not many years ago he had been chased away from public gardens by soldiers who were later to cheer themselves hoarse when he addressed them as the people's President. Lincoln had a peculiar meaning for him. American Presidents have come from log cabins but the Cuban hovel in which Batista had been born was on a path which led in a different direction from the Presidential Palace. Reared in a shack, a ragged orphan at thirteen, cast adrift with little schooling, to struggle or starve, he worked in cane fields until he dropped in the sun. No type of labor had been too low for his boyhood drudgery, a port worker, a roustabout lugging rails in the jungle, a tailor's assistant, a barber, a mechanic, a carpenter.

He joined the army and after two years as a private he discovered that superior knowledge had its rewards. He went back to civil life, learned stenography and rejoined the army as a court-martial reporter, which gave him the rank of sergeant working at headquarters where orders originated. The "Revolution of the Sergeants," which he led on an island suffering from centuries of misrule, now added an interesting footnote in Latin-American history. He chose the title of Colonel. Other Colonels who had been inclined to look upon his sudden rise in rank as a subject for debate were reposing in a place which made discussions unnecessary. The leap from Colonel to the Presidency was to be less hazardous.

Batista broke through his reverie as though it had been an unfolding narrative.

"I know the people," he said, slowly. "I worked with

them. They are Cuba. They produce for others but get
nothing for themselves. I want to make Democracy a reality
for them, like Roosevelt. But they will not yell 'Viva la
Democracia' if the government permits them to starve. Free
society is a fine thing but one does not spend much time thinking of liberty when his only freedom is to die of want, while
others squander. I do not care what labels my program in-
vites so long as it helps the people. Striving for the poor is
often called Communism. Your President is not unacquainted
with that type of slander. On the other hand if you insist
on discipline to stop strikes against the public good, you are a
dictator. Once we had a strike of the doctors. City and government hospitals, first-aid stations, private hospitals had no
doctors. A sick man could not get his medicine. That will
not happen again."

His gaze no longer had the liquid gentleness which comes
from the Siboney Indians enslaved by the conquistadores. It
was piercing and, behind it, I was to learn, a realistic brain
was in constant operation, feeding a pigeon-hole mind that
turned with lightning rapidity from one problem to another.
He talked as though he belonged to a period of change, sensing
with a native instinct, the coming of a new trend in Democracy,
a new philosophy of social thinking which was to transfigure
the world of ideas with dramatic suddenness. This man was
more than a military chieftain who had leaped from the gutter. The army was the machinery he needed and it would
always be useful. It fitted in with the intuition of his destiny.

Close to the French windows drums rolled, fell into march
time and, beyond the garden, a platoon filed by. The Colonel
watched the men fondly. I thought of Laurence Sterne's observation that the honor of beating a drum was likely to be
its own reward and I explained the sentimental Irishman's reflections. Batista looked at me shrewdly.

"It is what the drum means," he said, "that counts. It becomes important when it is beaten for a reason. All this," he
waved his arm about, indicating the vast armed camp, "is not
just a plan to teach 22,000 men the manual of arms. Maybe
you have been told at the Palace that the National budget for
the armed forces has increased under me in proportion to the
total budget to operate the nation. But the men in the army
are learning that education and discipline will liberate Cuba

from her shackles of ignorance and poverty. Meanwhile, they are eating! It is regeneration through the stomach.

"In Cuba on a smaller scale," he continued, "it is the same problem you find in your own country, people out of work, low prices for the producer who furnishes employment and, on top, wealth which insists on living as it did during the good times and refuses to make sacrifices which it would not even feel."

"Perhaps our new Lincolns will have to be a little more Napoleonic to make the people listen for their own good," I suggested.

"To a certain extent," he replied through grim lips. "But too much of a Napoleon would be the end of Democracy. Finally, these men don't know when to stop until they come to their Waterloos. One does not have to cut a way through life like a cannon ball."

I knew the temptations of his leadership, and his reference to Napoleon interested me. He was dropping little hints that there were times when the cries of dictatorship had to be risked if weak points in the way that Democracy worked were to be strengthened for the good of the whole system.

"A leader generally creates his own Waterloo," he said. "If he heads a Democracy today he can only save himself by realizing that Democracy itself came from revolution and must provide more than liberty if it is to be a government of the people. Conditions may force Democracy, if it is to survive, to become much more revolutionary than the Constitution that gave it birth. You have a saying that 'you can't eat the Constitution.' When the people decide to get something to eat in an unconstitutional manner, because they can't eat otherwise, it is time to look over the Constitution. When the belly cries for food it sounds much louder than the free expression of the individual's intellect which, of course, is guaranteed by Democracy. When the Constitution becomes a diet it no longer interests the hungry man. That is why you will see some changes in ours."

He explained his solution with a native insight. Large estates would have to be prohibited. To insure progressive steps and end hopeless debates, the structure of government would have to be semi-parliamentary. If Cuba was to remain free to conduct its affairs, the acquisition and possession of land by foreign persons would be restricted and State lands distributed to tenant farmers. If the government knew its way ahead it must have Constitutional power in a labor code to give it full control over relations between employer and worker.

"What will commerce and industry say about that?"

A grim smile flashed across Batista's face.

"They will have to look upon discipline as a friend of Democracy," he said. "They will have to understand it as well as the illiterates in the rural districts where one thousand schools are being opened by the Army. The teachers are sergeants and teach in their uniforms. When a soldier reads a lesson and talks sanitation, the people listen. In the obscure regions our first lesson in Democracy is to show the ignorant and half-starved how to use outhouses which we are buying for them. That is Democracy starting from the bottom, and it will eliminate epidemics. That is an elementary lesson in Democratic principles which commerce and industry have been too busy to teach to the rural slaves who produce for them. There is money in Cuba for these renovations and those who have more than enough will pay for it."

His words reflected the bitterness of his early life and his eyes flashed in anger.

"Certain people will find out," he rasped, "that there is something going on in Cuba besides Sans Souci."

I knew the story of Sans Souci, a gathering place in Havana society, devoted to the pleasures of life. One evening, when Batista and his wife had appeared in the charmed circle, the aristocracy had snubbed them by departing in a body. Those who had taken the Colonel there to witness his discomfiture were now in prison and society groveled at his feet. There were others, behind the bars, who had interfered with his program for a disciplined Cuba. Some 4,000 persons, mostly terrorists, were crowded in ancient castle prisons and there had been drumhead courts-martial and firing squads. Perhaps that was to be expected if a philosophy of authority were to be evolved from the chaos precipitated by the breakdown of civil government.

"You have seen enough already," Batista added, "to be convinced that we must first consider the troubles of our own people before we can think of helping the Jews start a colony in Cuba. The world is full of suffering and our four million people have their share."

His eyes narrowed when I asked him if he intended always to wear a uniform. The question was put to his liking and carried an implication with which his Cuban mind could play and produce an answer in the same vein. Since his Revolution he had made and unmade Presidents. That power, it was natural to assume, might find some satisfaction in operating from a more impressive center, around which one expected Democracy to revolve even though in less gaudy attire.

"One must be well prepared here," he replied slowly, "to be able to use authority in civilian clothes when he hangs up his uniform. These are times in Latin America when it is a good thing for a government to parade itself. People prefer to know those who govern them, at least by sight. I am studying the great men who have ruled without uniform. Lincoln is the best example and my uniform will be on for some time before I have read all about him. The people would not have recognized him if he had worn other than plain clothes. To be cheered and followed without gold braid is a tribute one wants to make sure he can keep alive before he lays aside the sword."

It was dinner time at Military City and its soldiers and officers were sitting down to the best that the island could afford. Millions had been spent on the construction of their quarters, on their modern military equipment. Gomez had been notified that his Administration was expected to impose a special tax of nine cents a bag on sugar produced in the island for more money for the Army. During the previous year of 1935, $14,000,000 had been appropriated for the armed forces, about one-third of the national revenue, but those who paid the taxes did not stop to consider that it fed and occupied 22,000 men and put an end to any threat of revolution. It was as good as the WPA. The rich Gomez had let it be known that he would use the demand for these new Army taxes as the occasion for a showdown.

As I left this city of the soldiers, driving by its butcher shops, its schools, clean domiciles with healthy children, and finally its machine-gun parks, masses of artillery, armored cars, units of modern tanks which our own army might have envied; airplanes and anti-aircraft guns, there was no doubt in my mind that Batista would get his nine cents a bag, and later feel as comfortable in mufti in the Presidential Palace as he did among his cannon and salutes.   His warm-hearted cable to me after his election gave some indication that the orphaned roustabout had not forgotten the rail-splitter. Through the roar which greeted his first speech as President four words rang out from Batista repeatedly: "With malice toward none."

BOOK VII

A MADMAN'S MANUSCRIPT

CHAPTER I

I was conscious of a deep change in myself when I returned to New York. Sunsets on wide horizons unpierced by sky-scrapers, birds calling in the morning, had won my mind from the parasitical jealousies of command and the intolerable futility of business. There had been time to read and absorb good things which I enjoyed much as the tasteful move their tongues about a mouthful of choice wine before the swallow. Wordsworth's last words on the boat held me fast: "By all means sometimes be alone . . . dare to look in thy chest, and tumble up and down what thou findest there." Much tumbling had taken place.

Winifred had greeted me at the pier with a handful of flowers. She was not ready to believe I had no intention of resuming executive work. "You'll take a final fling at it," she said. "I should like to walk out with you again when you really quit it." I took her bouquet to my apartment and arranged the gay blossoms myself on the mantelpiece over the scarred fireplace.

I walked by newsstands as impervious to headlines as a cured addict. I was something like a fisherman whose fingers no longer tremble with eagerness when his line vibrates. I was not going to run daily newspapers—perhaps a quiet corner in one of them later, where I could inhale the smell of the shop.

The friends in my trade were too busy for good talks. Most of them were engaged in tempestuous attacks on Roosevelt of whom they spoke with venom. Conversations about the new humanism wound up in curses. Hearst suavely predicted Landon's election, and Alfred E. Smith, at last in agreement with the aging publisher's political hatreds, repudiated the old friend who had taken up his crutches to nominate him in 1928. The *Literary Digest* was running its last poll, to be buried with it. I could not understand how anyone of social maturity of judgment could have doubted the outcome in 1936.

375

The *Saturday Evening Post* featured long articles by Garet
Garrett, later to become its editorial writer in chief. He already had developed a sense of apprehension about the future
of the nation. I visited him at "Bleak House," his Colonial
mansion, at Tuckahoe, N. J., where he sat in his study, late at
night, performing his editorial devotions in the creamy robe
of a Carthusian monk, his sharp, sensitive nose protruding
like a beak from the depressing cowl drawn over his head, a
long-roped girdle looped about his middle. He wrote, against
the inexorable ticking of a grandfather clock, long warning
pieces about the man in the White House, decisive things you
had to read, whether or not they agreed with your digestion.
Concealed in his hood, he had turned his hunched figure from
his work as I came downstairs for cigarettes. I halted on the
landing as I saw him. Like a Savonarola of Righteous Business, about to expose the incompetency of a new Piero de
Medici, he said in a sepulchral voice:

"I have it! He wants to put the Nation in braces!"

I saw La Guardia briefly. Gene Fowler would have described him as busy as a moth in a lighthouse. The Mayor
went about in a car equipped with a collapsible desk, dictaphone and telephone, an office on wheels which reduced Brisbane almost to the horse and buggy age. Phone calls from
the car were handled through the Fire Department's short-
wave radio station and the little executive went to all the good
fires. He ran the largest city in the world with the energy of
a dynamo. He saw in the times something symptomatic of
an impending change, explosive forces at work. He reminded
me of other men whom I had met, who believed destiny had
made them important. Office saturates them with a characteristic of perpetual attention to themselves, but they perform prodigious tasks in these uncertain days.

I had heard La Guardia conduct the band of the Department of Sanitation and I wanted to tell him that, with his usual
impetuosity, he had rushed the musicians at such a pace through
The Stars and Stripes Forever, that the piccolo player was
unable to put in his work. It was enough to make any man
throw his broom down in the gutter and quit. Sousa's masterpiece had been ruined for me. But the Mayor was in the
middle of a headlong holus-bolus and I did not delay him.
He was hurrying down to posterity and I wasn't going any-

where in particular. I knew he would never cook spaghetti for me again, and I left him with a feeling of my small importance in the cosmic scheme.

Kobler still owed me $2,500 of my Hearst bonus check and I hunted him out to collect it. He was doing business in a little office on Madison Avenue near the Ritz whose expensive Japanese Garden he still frequented for lunch. He was in a fever of excitement about a new project and looked upon my arrival as an act of Providence. A melting smile spread over his moon face, which put me on my guard, but I was touched by the signs of strain he had undergone. His light blue eyes had grown dull and faded to a steel-gray color and his inflamed rims looked as though they had shed tears of blood.

He revealed his plans during luncheon. Moses L. Annenberg, multi-millionaire, had bought the *Philadelphia Inquirer* as one might buy a horse in a stable. Kobler was to revolutionize its Sunday edition by adding to it a new magazine section to drive Hearst's *American Weekly* supplement to the wall. Already he had signed up fifteen papers on an ambitious syndicate arrangement. Soon the *Inquirer* magazine would appear all over the land as a Sunday supplement. Its huge circulation would attract quantities of advertising. Money would pour in. I was to be the editor of this new publication. Later there would be greater opportunities. I might become editor of one of the great papers of America, with power, influence and a salary commensurate with the position—if I played my cards correctly.

I was ready for his choleric outburst when I demurred. I told him I would not mind a peaceful cubicle on the paper but I wanted no intensive responsibilities. He seemed shaken, but recovered himself. Apparently he noticed in me something he had never seen before, perhaps a quiet determination to keep out of any struggle for money. I was turning over in my mind a plan which would require a steady, but low income and I agreed to meet the new owner of the *Inquirer* on my own terms. I wanted to leave New York and I embarked with Kobler for the "City of Brotherly Love" to be led into the most hilarious adventure of my newspaper experience.

The *Inquirer* had been convulsed into a bizarre activity by its change of ownership. The oldest families of the city were thunderstruck by the invasion of the new publisher, who, over night, had acquired one of the oldest symbols of Philadelphia's character and conservatism. With millions of dollars from an apparently inexhaustible source of wealth—a monopoly of race-track information and pool-room tips on the running horses—he now dominated one of the great institutions of the American press. I was amazed at the building in which the celebrated newspaper was housed, a massive white structure covering a city block, with a great tower from which innocent chimes rang the quarter hour. At noon from the sky the tune of *Auld Lang Syne* was hesitantly played, and I never determined whether this added touch of musical irony came from Annenberg's Taj Mahal or from a reproachful quarter close by.

Kobler stalked about the edifice swinging his cane as though he were already part owner. We waited in a pretentious office, a room rich in memories of journalistic decisions. The walls were covered with the inherited art of the passing regime: nostalgic gold-framed paintings of mid-Victorian rectitude, smiling people going to church or strolling through the park. Annenberg hurried in, his head extended forward from his shoulders, walking as a man pursuing a purpose always slightly ahead of him. He was eating oranges, and flung the skins over his shoulder as though they were discarded projects whose substance he had devoured. He had a lantern-jawed face whose lines somehow reminded me of the smart horses which had made him a millionaire. But here the resemblance stopped. His features had a mixture of jovial brutality and rapid perception. He was tall, rangy, with the nervousness of a gray wolf and during business hours wore the alpaca coat which drapes the individual behind the counter of a pawnshop.

Kobler presented me in an unctuous introduction, designed to intrigue the millionaire who held me with a cold and fascinating glance. There was a sinister suggestion of strength and rapaciousness in his thin frame. His humid eyes, rather close together, seemed to darken from a grayish color, and mingled cunning and suspicion behind their penetration. He blinked when Kobler laughingly remarked that I had scruples of honesty which at times provoked arguments.

Evidently Kobler had discussed my future status with the publisher. My salary was fixed at a nominal figure, which I accepted as it did not indicate I was to hold a position of full responsibility. I was still determined to find seclusion at reduced pay.

"We already have an editor for the Sunday magazine," Annenberg said in an abrasive voice, "but maybe two would be better, considering the way the thing is going. Muscle in as an associate. If you peel off your coat right now it won't be too soon. We're working fast, as some of the deadwood in this joint will find out."

Kobler gave me a dig in the ribs.

"He's used to running things," he said. "You'll get action."

Annenberg continued to stare at me, his hands in his pockets.

"You ought to know your stuff by this time," he said. "I think you got somethin' on the ball."

Kobler's magazine plan of campaign proposed to outgeneral Morrill Goddard, editor of the *American Weekly,* the master of this type of Sunday concoction, absorb his formula, blend it with ideas of our own, but not to deviate too much from the Hearst technique.

I went immediately to work, to discover that my associate was Moses Koenigsberg. The fates could not have conceived a more ironic whim than to back us into the same harness. I had met him years ago when he was the able head of Hearst's syndicate, King Features. It had been established by Koenigsberg's energy and had been named after him. At the height of his success as a high-salaried Hearst executive he had been awarded the Cross of the Legion of Honor by the French Government and had been forced to resign as a result. Hearst had announced that he would not permit his employees to receive foreign honors. The episode had occurred after Marion Davies, the motion-picture actress, whose career Hearst encouraged, had gratefully accepted the Award of Merit from the French Dramatic Academy, a decoration of crossed palms which is not recorded as having been returned to the nation that a few years later informed the publisher he was an unwelcome visitor.

Koenigsberg returned his insignia to the French as an act of protest of the debt situation. The gesture apparently had not softened Hearst to the point of rehiring him. While I was editor of the *Mirror,* Koenigsberg had visited me for the purpose of obtaining a position but because of Kobler's private instructions I was unable to take him on. It became evident, as soon as I began to work with him, that he had not forgotten our last meeting. He was a large, fat man busily engaged in a glass cage from which he surveyed a line of writers bent over their tasks in separate compartments. Down his damp forehead fell a Napoleonic lock, which he twisted about with a nervous forefinger. After the manner of Kobler, he was addicted to telephonic hysteria, answering two calls at one time, necessitating desperate pantomime with the help of underlings waving papers and signaling. I did not dislike Koenigsberg, but apparently he had conceived the idea that I had moved in to supplant him. My jousts with him on this strange field of journalism can never be anything but a haunting memory.

While I was trying to acclimatize myself to an atmosphere which was loaded with enough calamity to fell an ox, Kobler distressed me with the announcement that he intended to place me in full charge as the editor of the magazine under his direction. This plan he hoped to accomplish by picking a deliberate quarrel with Koenigsberg and forcing him out. He expected my full cooperation to bring about the explosion. Although I refused to have anything to do with the scheme, the battle soon took place, the glass partitions shaking under the roar of the cannonading. I was called into a frightful wrangle while Kobler was accusing my associate of trying to "carry water in both pockets" and sending his staff out on a "wild gooseberry chase." Both men were livid with rage amid bellows of volcanic wrath.

"Look at this headline!" Kobler screamed while he pointed with his cane at one of Koenigsberg's page proofs. "How can I syndicate this? 'The story of one woman and her fight for happiness!' What woman? We want to sell personalities and what do we get? Chambermaids! Sawdust apples we give the readers! They'll only bite once."

I had more important reasons than my respect for Koenigsberg's years of experience to keep out of the brawl. I was making every effort to avoid full executive responsibility and long hours which would have made impossible the settlement of my personal affairs. A tender thought had penetrated through the crust of my dulled understanding to convince me that my former secretary and I had a common purpose which seemed to have welded us into one will. Winifred and I were alike in our pleasures and sorrows. Her marriage had been no happier than mine.

My decision to make her my wife was devoid of the delirium which turns the brain and finally spoils enjoyment. I admired the venturesome courage of a woman ready to share my undertakings while I settled down, almost defiantly, into as much peace and happiness as my questing spirit could ever hope to find. I had finally been able to cut through the complications of a double divorce with the usual amount of money which seems to be required under these circumstances to bring about the desired results. I was glad to surrender anything for contentment. All I wanted was a quiet nook on a newspaper where I could collect a modest income and go home as a normal human being when my stint was done.

Kobler, who was unaware of all this, dragged me to his suite at the Warwick Hotel after his row, for a final conference to win me over to his strategy. He ordered an enormous luncheon which he could not touch because his rage was still in him. As he talked I knew his plot would tie me hand and foot in detail and confine me to days and nights of toil in a grip for supremacy with Hearst in the Sunday field. He spoke of the money to be made, the success and the glory, which left me cold. He sat in a reverie of past victories and ideas which floated through his mind without reflection. He had taken the *American Weekly* with 2,000,000 circulation and had increased it to 25,000,000. Its revenue had jumped from $35,000 a year to $16,000 a page. It had been a fight, but victories that are easy are cheap. He had amassed a fortune and lost it. He would start over again. Annenberg had the organization and the millions and knew circulation inside out. If he loaded the dealers with a new supplement they would sell 'em and call for more! Moe would see to that! What a satisfaction it would be to turn about and beat Hearst at his own game! We would all be rich.

As I looked at this unbowed Jew I knew it was the contest that delighted him, not the victory. It was the contest that he talked about as he drew on his last reserve of energy. It was his life, and his heart was full of it, but mine groaned for him, because somehow, before it was too late I had learned what happened when his type of victory was pursued too far.

"And another thing," he said, his hand trembling on my knee, "Goddard won't live much longer and Brisbane may drop off any time. Nobody can follow these men up. I was one of them. I know what it takes. We'll break through, I tell you. We'll dominate!"

His predictions of the deaths to come soon were to be confirmed with tragic accuracy but in foreseeing the end of two of the greatest trio the Lord of San Simeon ever had, his best salesman failed to include himself. One never does.

I listened to his dreams of future triumphs with a patient indifference which he perceived with growing uneasiness. Why was I not enthusiastic? All the cards were stacked in my favor. Then I told him.

He rose in a passion and drained the dregs of his fervor to change my mind. He opposed my plans to remarry. This was a time for deadly strategy which required hours away from home. This project was not to be interfered with by my personal affairs. Big enterprises came first, women second. He noticed the anger burning in my face and his expression changed into the smile of a Medicean Cardinal, as much compassionate as disdainful. Where was my ambition? Was I such a fool as to scorn money?

It was a sales talk against my happiness, a threat to my hope of finding out how it felt to be master of my own life, and I fought him down. There were bitter words, a parting shot of recriminations, which I was to remember with regret. I left him fuming behind his table of silver covers, dishes of untouched food and coffee pots. As I shut the door I thought his eyes were moist, for, in his heart, and he had one, he knew I was right.

CHAPTER II

ALTHOUGH it was not known at the office that Kobler and I had had a violent disagreement my former association with him added to my discomfort. Koenigsberg, apparently clinging to the conviction that I was engaged in a cabal to seize the magazine department, became openly hostile. A managing editor who offers to reduce himself to the ranks is looked upon with open suspicion around a press. Nobody would have accepted the story that I wanted to marry my secretary, live simply on a Pennsylvania farm and enjoy the luxury of peace that comes from a minor job. Every move I made to efface myself from any position of command added to Koenigsberg's disbelief of my motives.

Perhaps I should not have endured the agony for seven months but for a friendship which I made with a staff member who was the only man I ever met with a complete sense of fun in a newspaper office. Had I been his editor years ago I might have fired him as a disturber of morale. Now his philosophy was my daily tonic. He was a daddy-long-legs sort of person known in every news shop worth its salt as Hugh Fullerton. No task in the game had been beyond him and a touch more of pompousness might have carried him further but he had laughed himself out of city rooms for forty years because of his unsuppressed passion to dethrone dignity. He resembled an old-time Shakespearean actor, with a long, sad face in constant conflict with a pair of sharp eyes full of impish raillery. He was suspicious of any subject which would not bear the poke of a jest.

It was Fullerton who had been assigned by Brisbane to reform the business of picking winners at race tracks by having the heart of each horse X-rayed before the start, to show through the wonders of science that stamina was bound to win. Frightened by the machine which Fullerton hauled in a black wagon near the stables of the Derby entries, the attendants called the police and had him chased off. Realizing the impossibility of his project, but not at his wit's end, Fullerton produced for the editor an exhaustive portfolio of X-ray pictures which he had taken of the heart of a broken-down horse which was ending its days drawing a garbage wagon. Brisbane picked a photograph from the batch which Fullerton carefully identified under a magnifying glass as that of the heart of a Derby favorite. The editor printed the picture in large dimensions and devoted a column explaining his new method of scientific prediction of horse-race winners. He boldly announced that nothing could stop the animal from winning. The wonder was, that the horse picked by Brisbane won the race, which convinced the editor that science could explain anything. It also astounded the gambling fraternity.

"And it cost me ten per cent of my salary for six months afterward," Fullerton drawled, "to keep the dawggone driver of that garbage wagon quiet."

Koenigsberg believed in the conference method of editorial progress, and each morning called the staff into his ample cage to suggest future stories for our supplement. He leaned over his desk, facing us, cold and tense, taking up all matters with an oppressive seriousness. We sat in front of him in a straight line, like the surviving members of Lew Dockstader's Minstrels, Fullerton and I holding down seats at each end, much like the grinning end-men of that bygone musical attraction. It inspired the humorist to address me as "Mr. Bones," a practice which ruffled the editor's dignity and was not too subtle to draw a laugh from the Philadelphia writers. Each man would outline a magazine story to be developed from a clipping. If approved by the conclave I inaugurated the research and gave the article its first impulse into type.

Fullerton, who had suggested that we appear each morning in blackface, occasionally upset the ritual by calling for an old-fashioned roundelay to be sung by the entire company. He drove the conference into hysterics by challenging Koenigsberg's debatable pronunciation of *fin de siècle,* an expression still in favor with a surprising number of Philadelphia readers.

Finally, I detected the reason for Fullerton's forenoon buoyancy. On the eighth floor of the building he had discovered a seductive bar, used for club purposes, an oasis reached by the simple means of sliding into an elevator, five yards from his cubicle. It was a luxury Annenberg had probably been unaware of when he had gobbled up the whole establishment and was frequented by philosophical editors resigned to Philadelphia. It was there that Fullerton expounded the philosophy of a rugged school which believed that Scotch before breakfast was the best drink of the day.

Annenberg, meanwhile, had thrown the building into the high-voltage excitement one experiences at Churchill Downs on the eve of the Kentucky Derby. The place was seething with rumors of his circulation schemes to dominate the reading public. He hurried through the establishment with a loping stride, always restless, with perpetual nervous movements. Occasionally he patted me on the back. "Keep your eye on the ball!" he would shout. "Keep your eye on the ball!"

He hurried in one morning to recommend that a writer be sent to New York to obtain an exclusive interview from the survivor of an operation on Siamese twins, who had been cut apart from his dead brother and who seemed to be recovering as by a miracle. He managed to live for a short time. It was a case unparalleled in medical annals, involving the celebrated theatrical performers Simplicio and Lucio Godino, natives of the Philippines. I turned myself into a reporter and landed the story with an enthusiasm which I had not felt since I had covered Polish wedding murders in New Haven for twelve dollars a week. It was the sort of piece that would have made Morrill Goddard's mouth water as editor of the *American Weekly,* and Annenberg was aware of it.

Back in Philadelphia, I got into the meat of the yarn with the zest of a newspaper man who knows he owns the shop because he has the hot feature of the day in his pocket. My notes were on the margin of encouraging letters from Winifred, on the back of laundry bills and brokers' slips recording losses I had been forced to take to settle my private affairs, but nothing mattered but the story that danced into the typewriter. The words sang out, 8,000 of them, my fingers snapping the keys, my hat on the back of my head, my shirt open at the throat, a cigarette dangling from my lips. The movies do not exaggerate this. Perhaps there are other thrills as profound in business experience, but I don't believe it. Those who have never been through it must try to understand. It would be something like describing colors to a blind man.

Illustrations were being prepared for my double-spread by George Kerr, a noted Hearst veteran who could draw anything from a seraglio in dissipation to Saint Elmo's fire and who was always talking about retiring to invent a patent medicine. I was meeting a deadline. Two and a half standard-size pages had been held open for me and the hands went around the clock. Koenigsberg was pulling the copy out of my machine and reading it. His eyes seemed to glow in his fat face, which had the mark of good fellowship, of illness, of care and wine. He felt this thing, as well as I did, deep down in the bowels where that ruffle of excitement begins before it jumps the pulse when you are slamming out an extra and forget that you are surfeited with sense impressions. We were part of the same breed. I would always have some hidden depths of sublime affection for the most cantankerous of the lot.

My story was done and I gulped black coffee with a dash of cognac which Fullerton had palmed down the elevator from his oasis. Koenigsberg summoned all the minstrels, seated me on the end of the line, read the words of my copy aloud in a tone of lofty disdain, interrupting himself to hack at my sentences as though his blue pencil had become a machete in the hands of a macerating Cuban. I never knew whether this was, on his part, a conception of calculated torture. I had turned out a competent job, but I set my teeth and took it. Anyhow, tomorrow would be my day off. Milton Diamond, my lawyer, had telephoned me that my personal problems had been cleared up. Winifred was to meet me at the train and we would be married in Virginia before noon.

*   *   *   *   *

Brisbane died on Christmas day of that year, which was 1936. He had weighed accurately his importance on the scales of news value. The *Times* announced his passing with a single-column head on the front page but made up for it by continuing the account of his career in inside columns under a five-column banner. The lamentations of the leaders of the nation were carried in a section adjoining. Roosevelt sent a careful message recalling the delight which he had enjoyed in exploring with the great pragmatic millionaire-philosopher, the teachings of history and the philosophy of our civilization. Hearst described his extinct partner as the most powerful factor behind the social and political progress of the country, going through life with kindness and understanding, and deeply sympathetic with the struggles and sorrows of humanity. La Guardia said he had been inspired from boyhood by the journalist's editorials and called his death the nation's loss. The *Herald Tribune* crowned the news with a two-column head which the departed editor might have endorsed as a more competent handling of the calamity, but its long account of his acquisitive idiosyncrasies would have been less pleasing to him, a quaint journalistic custom which prevents the truth or faults of an individual from being discussed until death has taken possession of him. I was interested in the great man's last words, which his son-in-law had caught with bended ear: "Everything is for the best in this best of all possible worlds." Readers examining the economic aspect of the editor's final journey were informed that he had left thirty millions of dollars.

At the office all the talk was of the passing of the Master. Annenberg expressed his opinion at a round table at lunch time in the *Inquirer's* eating hall, where employees milled about in a hubbub for sustenance. This was a tumultuous place, full of the odors of food and the dynamic expectancy of a railroad restaurant. Executives sat at the favored table with the publisher who described this noon experience as "eating with the common people."

"How much did Brisbane leave?" Annenberg shouted through the clatter, "thirty million or so?" He went on to explain that he had read the editor's column to his children for years and obtained comfort out of it for himself. Brisbane had introduced him to Spinoza down in Florida and he dipped into the works of the savant when he had a chance.

"He's got something on the ball," he observed, referring to the earlier philosopher, "but he spends too much time watching the bases instead of throwing to home plate."

He was in an expansive mood, banging the table as he talked of the melancholy prospect in store for his competitor, little Dave Stern, who conducted the *Record* across the street. Money would dominate, as usual, and he, Moe Annenberg, had more of it than all of them put together in the Philadelphia newspaper business. He was about to offer $50,000 for the most appropriate name for his new Sunday supplement. There would be all sorts of prize contests. Had he not been the one to start the circulation rackets by giving away silver spoons as souvenirs, thirty years ago? He laughed over the outlook of the battle he intended to wage around the country against his brother, Max Annenberg, who was circulation director of the New York *Daily News*. He was not on speaking terms with his brother and referred jokingly to Max, who was struggling along on the modest salary of $150,000 a year, as one of the Annenbergs who had not made good. The new owner's boastfulness was at times indescribable, his personal anecdotes too robust for polite repetition. Wythe Williams, a gentleman of no raw sensitivity, a foreign correspondent of note, had been induced to come from New York to be interviewed as a prospective editor, and after a puzzling session around these uproarious boards left for his train with the remark: "I'm afraid this journalism is a little too primitive for my school of thought."

Back in New York, leaders in finance, industry, politics and journalism, and in that order, filled the exclusive Park Avenue church where Brisbane reposed in mortuary magnificence under a blanket of violets and lilies of the valley, whose grandeur failed to dull the simple cheerfulness of the Christmas decorations the house of prayer still displayed. Those privileged to attend as honorary pallbearers observed with decorum the notable tradition which governs wealth's last tribute to a fallen captain of the rich, and of necessity were all millionaires whose top hats were dusted off for first-class funerals only. They were kindly disposed gentlemen, some approaching the Bible's score of longevity, possibly more than casually interested in the preview of a ceremony in which, one by one, they would sooner or later play the major role. Girdled by a crowd which represented ten billions of dollars, the impressed rector's streamlined invocations for Divine intercession melted into the strains of *Parsifal*. As the coffin was moved out, the organist played *Hark, Hark My Soul*. A police motorcycle escort led the cortege through the Holland Tunnel with all reverent speed and the great editor was locked up in a steel vault, on his 3,000-acre New Jersey estate, on a little knoll from which you can see the ocean which roars at night, sending out lashing waves that strike the beach, recede to come back again, and make little pebbles disappear.

Brisbane was already making considerable progress toward oblivion when Kobler died six days later, on the eve of the new year. Defying illness to accomplish his syndicate purposes he had literally worked himself into his grave. He had wagered Annenberg a sizeable sum that a score of newspapers would be signed up to carry our supplement as part of their Sunday editions by January 1, 1937, and with his last breath had won the bet. The *Times* closed the last chapter of his life with an obituary reviewing his accomplishments as a super-salesman. Those who knew him well could not have escaped the touch of irony which hovered over his funeral. Standing among the sincere at the bier of this tireless slave of business, who had surmounted the brutal prejudices his race always has had to face, were those who had kicked him when he was down and contributed to his financial ruin. I went back to Samuel Butler for a perfect description of these mourners: "They buried their faces in their handkerchiefs to hide their lack of emotion."

Kobler's death was a body blow to the syndication of our supplement and nipped his work in full flower. The man who had put millions of dollars in Hearst's pocket left an estate of less than $5,000, and his art objects were sold for a song.

CHAPTER III

DURING the winter Winifred and I were looking for a Pennsylvania farmhouse. We had created a mental picture of a home nestling in a valley, near a rippling stream; no lordly hall, but a place surrounded by trees with rest of heart. We found this right spot of earth forty miles from Philadelphia while we were driving along a road skirting an old canal which seemed to be resting from a long voyage at the foot of a range of hills. We crossed the canal over a small rustic bridge, landing on a plateau overlooking the Delaware River which danced into rapids around a wooded island. The private road from the bridge led to a rugged Dutch Colonial stone house smiling under its eyebrows of icicles. Here the only sound came from the mirth of the romping, prankish waters.

It was for sale, one hundred acres, including the sheltering hill and the sprawling island forking the river. We picked our way down to the water and stood looking at the island. In three months the hills would be green, giving off a warm half-light at sunset. Now twigs shook off their clots of snow as broken cake frosting, snatched by hungry gusts of wind hurrying by, but soon robins would sing, red-breasted in the sun, standing on the bridge railing, cocking their heads.

The agent of the property was a calm, portly gentleman with the cacophonous name of J. Cooper Pidcock, that rare type of honest man in business who freely enumerates the faults of what he means to sell. I bought the place in three minutes although he preferred to cook the deal over a slow fire. The papers were signed in a sleepy town with a name of peculiar meaning to me. It was called New Hope. Quite unconsciously I had become a property owner in Bucks County, occasionally described in the *Times* as the "genius belt," the landing place of a writers' migration which, it is said, has unnerved many of the old Pennsylvania settlers.

Now nothing seemed to matter but our plans to move to the farm in the Spring and restore the old house which had been

390

built during the Revolution. It was a saving anchor. In the ruling camp of the office Kobler's passing had created the impression that I had lost my chief ally and my woes increased like Job's. As months of petty needling dragged by I waited for the climax which I knew would send me on my way. The imps of the perverse had provided all of the ludicrous elements conceivable for my exit.

One sparkling May morning during a gathering of our minstrel board, Fullerton submitted a clipping which, according to his analysis, contained all of the desirable requirements for quiet Sunday reading. A bridegroom had driven his frantic bride to the divorce courts during the honeymoon by reading at her bedside every night a story which was described in the newspaper as *A Madman's Tale* by Charles Dickens. As the complete account of the Dickens fantasy had to be obtained to develop a magazine feature and give our inventive artist an opportunity for his handsprings, a debate arose to determine the name of the book in which it had appeared. The arguments convinced me that Dickens had almost been forgotten in our little hermitage and I groaned at the end of the line.

Koenigsberg, who was tired and querulous during the conference turned on me sharply, having noticed my expression, which may have been one of malicious skepticism upon his announcement that he read *A Tale of Two Cities* once a year.

"I suppose you think *you* know what book it appeared in," he said; "but a man who has spent years poisoning the imagination of the young by running tabloids should not be expected to be familiar with the immortal Dickens."

The enduring traits of human temper being what they are, I answered him in similar vein. I told him it was not a separate short story, as he had suggested it might have been, but could be found under the title of *A Madman's Manuscript* in *The Posthumous Papers of the Pickwick Club*. Somehow, I had not forgotten Dickens, never dreaming that he would escort me from the most miserable job I ever had.

Two stalwarts were rushed out to find copies of *Pickwick Papers* and the staff settled down to watch the outcome of this duel of the intellects. Three dog-eared tomes were passed around, one of which was flung on my desk without a table of contents. I sat back in my chair to endure with one of my favorite authors the brief time which remained to me as

Koenigsberg's associate. We were now working in adjoining cages separated by a door and an immense glass partition such as may be found in an aquarium to keep back the curious who study strange forms of life. Fullerton, who felt responsible for the upheaval, came in to console me, as I appeared to be submerged in *Pickwick Papers* for the rest of the day.

I did not find *A Madman's Manuscript* immediately. I was surprised by the size of the book which was almost 1,000 pages long. The delightful illustrations by the lamented Seymour delayed my investigation and revived recollections of my early struggles as an embryo cartoonist. I riffled through four or five hundred pages, suddenly finding myself in court attending the memorable trial of Bardell against Pickwick. Samuel Weller had just stepped briskly into the witness box.

Koenigsberg, who, through the partition, had seen me break into the first laugh I had had in months, opened the door to catch me red-handed reading Dickens for enjoyment in the face of the time clock. He stood there looking at me with an expression of deadly calm, his cheeks slightly trembling, his hand on the knob. I told him the madman was still at large.

The race to find the hidden tale had turned the staff into literary detectives whose solution of the mystery, they hoped, would brighten their future prospects. Twice again Koenigsberg yanked open my door and glared, his lips curling in silent accusation. I looked up almost without seeing him. I was immersed in the fate of Pickwick held in the clutches of the Bardell woman. The jury had come back. Mr. Pickwick put on his spectacles and gazed at the foreman with a beating heart to hear the outrageous verdict which millions had denounced from the time it had been described by the master's pen.

I fell into a silent soliloquy about the deeply human experiences which were missed because Dickens was no longer read. He was frowned upon as much when people had time to read as he was during working hours. And yet how much altered the outlook of the world would be if he were still the favorite author. Thousands had waited in America for boats to arrive from England, to find out from installments what had happened to Little Nell. I fondled the old book in my hands and blew the dust from its withered binding.

But Mr. Pickwick was not finished with his adventures at

the trial. He had carefully wiped his spectacles, put them in his pocket and had drawn on his gloves, staring at the foreman. How many times had I not seen this myself in court when injustice held down the scales! Mr. Pickwick mechanically stepped into a side room where the court fees were paid and where he was joined by his friends after the verdict.

> *Here too, he encountered Messrs. Dodson and Fogg, rubbing their hands with every token of outward satisfaction.*
> *"You imagine you'll get your costs, don't you, gentlemen?" said Mr. Pickwick.*
> *Fogg said they thought it rather probable. Dodson smiled, and said they'd try.*
> *"You may try, and try, and try again, Messrs. Dodson and Fogg," said Mr. Pickwick vehemently, "but not one farthing of costs or damages do you ever get from me, if I spend the rest of my existence in debtor's prison."*

My face must have reflected the admiration I had for Mr. Pickwick as the door of my partition burst open, this time almost taken off its hinges. Koenigsberg stood framed in it, shaking with fury. During the next few moments many things happened. A mysterious note had been slipped on my desk which said:

"Look on page 190, then let's drink a toast to Martin Chuzzlewit."

I rippled the pages back and, sure enough, there was *A Madman's Manuscript*. I had reached the line, "Hurrah for the madhouse! Oh, it's a rare place!" when the storm broke. Koenigsberg had decided to make a final issue of the situation and I stood as a man under a tree in a tempest waiting for the lightning. When his explosion had subsided I closed up *Pickwick Papers*, gave him the book and told him what he could do with it, which was to read it slowly to assuage his soul. I picked up my hat and quit the place.

Fullerton, who had missed nothing of the scene, having experienced these sudden departures a hundred times, stood before his cubicle, after the manner of a *fin de siècle* tragedian, his right hand over his heart.

"What ho!" he sounded off sonorously, " 'One woe doth tread upon another's heel, so fast they follow.' "

That night Winifred and I fled to the farmhouse and dropped to sleep to the undertone of the rapids babbling their little secrets. We cooked breakfast in an old fireplace over blazing maple chunks. The faint sting of wood smoke was sweet to the nostrils on the light breeze of a new day. The sun was coming over the river. Winifred sat on the hearth, crossed-legged, watching me, a faint smudge on her little nose. She wore a pair of slacks and one of my shirts and looked like a mischievous gamin. But suddenly she sighed and her face softened with a smile of languishing tenderness and peace. The glowing maple chunks burst into new life and the smoke curled lazily up the chimney. Morning had come.

And so the summer went. Soon workmen were rejuvenating the old house. It had been known since 1783 as "Tinicum Pines" and now it would never have to worry again for fear that its old name might be changed to "Doneroving." I could hear the hammering, the scraping and the sawing from an inlet where I learned to swim. I remembered that H. G. Wells had not achieved that accomplishment until he was in his forties and I could appreciate his delayed struggles. Training my muscles to this new response was something I should have done defiantly as a boy, when I was told to give up all thought of sports. I had never learned to play and, therefore, never really understood the desire of others for free movement and organized games.

The discovery that I could swim led to a strange experience with a book which I had been trying to read for many years. It was W. Somerset Maugham's *Of Human Bondage*. I had started it five times but I could never get beyond the fifty-eighth page which described the lamed Philip praying in a nightgown in an icy room with the feeling that his prayers were more pleasing to God when he said them under conditions of discomfort. Once I managed to get to the next page which told of the boy's hopes after his prayers, his heart leaping as he saw himself going in for school races like everyone else. Now I read the book with intense enjoyment, at times with a peculiar satisfaction, recognizing its savage flash of life as a superb work of art, perhaps because it described my own experience better than I could ever tell it.

I wanted to write but, under the most agreeable conditions imaginable, the words would not come. The sharp taunts of a swaggering cock-pheasant failed to bring them out. I stalked across the field to hear more plainly the liquid notes of a crimson cardinal. I discovered there was quiet music in the slightest breeze that rumpled the apple blossoms. Lying in the grass I saw an "angle shot" that no camera shutter would ever catch—a daisy leaning upon her stem while a lazy bee swung above it, window-shopping and undecided. I fell asleep dreaming about these important trivialities of life.

A mile from "Tinicum Pines" there is a curve in the long winding road, and to the right you thread it to Doylestown, or continue to the left along the canal and follow it beyond New Hope to a Dukedom where restored farm houses are reported to have gold doorknobs and artificial moonlight. This region is bounded by box-office royalties and golden rains of checks from motion-picture moguls and the publishing houses of best sellers which water the good earth and buck the encroachments of those less inspired who live in reduced, artistic circumstances. The inhabitants of this domain seldom escape public notice when they get back to the soil from New York.

There are hardier folk, such as George S. Kaufman and Moss Hart who stay even beyond the time when the wind scuffs the yellow leaves that cling to their transplanted maples. They are held there by the annual necessity, as the *Times* has expressed it, of writing a Broadway smash. They can take a house guest like Alexander Woollcott, cut him apart, and turn him into a play crammed so full of interesting criminal libel that you have to order your tickets ahead for months to be able to see it. They recoil from any plots of social significance and make money so fast they can hardly count it, possibly because many people prefer to let others worry about the social significance cluttering up the world.

Dorothy Parker came to visit "Tinicum Pines." My wife had conceived a perverted idea of her talents from the notations of the gossip columnists and may have expected to hear masterpieces of unstudied profanity from the literary wit. But the author talked to our Bedlington Terriers, no fools, from whom she withheld the slightest trace of her brittle cynicism. She wore a folk costume of the Slovaks and her black hair in a razor-sharp bang. She might have been "Judith, and Jael, and Madame de Staël." Each time I met her studying gaze I groped for something penetrating to say and I quailed. Some of the biting lines of her books had interpreted with an undying acid the era I had survived, while I rushed through the years writing headlines about it. Giving the title of *The Little Foxes* to Lillian Hellman's thunderous stage hit was as easy for Dorothy Parker as it was for most of us in the "genius belt" to toss off a dry Martini. Now she was among the commuters to Hollywood, doing with her husband, Alan Campbell, some of the better pieces for the films.

We went to their farm to visit "Hortey" Campbell, Alan's mother. The writers, at the time, were 3,000 miles away preparing something for the screen. I am a rummager of books, a nuisance about the shelves of those who have written things that I like. Here I found some of the old friends I had in my house, outside of the little red *Elsie* books. Dickens took up his required space with all the other solid folk who serve you a good meal of meat and potatoes. There was not a wisecracker among them.

One book was upside down. It was the story of Flaubert and *Madame Bovary*. I took it down to right it, so that it wouldn't have to stand on its head, and it opened up and a pressed four-leaf clover dropped out. I felt as if I had broken a cloisonné vase. I picked up the clover and put it back tenderly where it had been between two pages which described the flaming moment of the love Flaubert experienced before he wrote one of the greatest novels of all time.

Across from the fireplace in the cheerful room was a large frame on which a Smyrna rug was trying to emerge into life. Some of the exuberant flowers which had managed to bloom followed a design that danced with the colors of a peaceful Spring. A strand of brilliant wool hung from a long needle that might have been a final dart flung into a target.

The lady working on the rug was no longer the same person who had written:

> *"Three be the things I shall never attain*
> *Envy, content, and sufficient champagne."*

The rugmaker was the author of *Big Blonde*, the Dorothy Parker who, while recovering from a serious illness, had

climbed up on a piano to address a crowd in an appeal for
Loyalist Spain. "The humorist," she said, "has never been
happy anyhow. Today he's whistling past worse graveyards
to worse tunes. If you had seen what I saw in Spain, you'd
be serious too."

I looked back as we left the rambling stone house which
reminded me of an old woman, weary of her crying over a
great story she had to tell while the finest writer in Bucks
County was too far away from her unfinished Smyrna rug to
hear it.

It was a dark year for book writing when I saw Dorothy
Parker again. The world seemed morally paralyzed and overwhelmed, but the writer who had seen it all pour out of Spain
was working tirelessly for a cause in which no one may con-
fess he is beaten until death rattles his wind-pipe. "We
haven't lost character," she said. "There's a lot of it lying
around. Wait and see! There could be no better time to live
in. I'm glad I'm in it; aren't you?"

*   *   *   *   *

Fall was coming, but at night the air still rang with the
orchestral underbreath and twitching woodnotes of the little
creatures that drone sound into stillness. My ears were pitched
to it by now as I sat at my typewriter, puffing a pipe near the
fireplace, but my thoughts produced nothing. I was still waiting for a deadline. Finances had to be considered. The
settlements with which I had had to agree before I could
marry and quit my high-salaried treadmill made it necessary
for me to earn at least a modest income. If I intended to
barricade myself on the farm for the winter until the words
came I would have to throw away my remaining securities at a
beggar's auction.

One night something happened that forced me to reach
a decision. I received a crisp wire from Annenberg. He
wanted me to transform the rotogravure of the *Inquirer* into
a tabloid picture-magazine of national scope on his color
presses and drive his Sunday edition up to a million circulation. I could "write my own ticket."

Winifred eyed me curiously as I walked about with the
telegram in my hand. Perhaps it offered the solution of my

immediate problem. Stocks might climb a few rungs while I functioned in an editorial post and then maybe I could sell my holdings and get some of my money back.

"This is the final fling I've been expecting," Winifred said. "Perhaps you need it. I'll go back with you and be your secretary while you get your last million readers—but we will live on the farm. It will be a lark!"

The man who marries his secretary should not assume that he has found out the sum of all that makes up the woman who worked shoulder to shoulder with him for years breathing life into his orders. Perhaps it is the other way around. She has had more time to study him. I did not have to be told that it required more than a summer on a farm to forget the fiddle-string tension between the news flash and the roar of the extra or the pungent odor of the acid that bites its magic into the copper under the blue lights of the photo-engraving shop.

BOOK VIII

EENIE MEANIE MONEY MOE

CHAPTER I

Moe Annenberg received me in his office of Victorian art. This repining gallery had become the *Inquirer's* chief sanctum where the publisher sat behind a rambling desk of the nineties, studying the editions of his local contemporaries which he called the "opposition." He was spoiling for a circulation brawl. Beside him stood his son Walter, tall, dark, of sombre countenance, in his early thirties. He had a nervous manner and occasionally brushed back his oiled, black hair and plunged his hands into the pockets of his smartly tailored clothes. He spoke with an impediment of speech which occasionally made his phrases hesitant. He looked at me dourly and began to argue the point of my sudden resignation during the affair of the *Pickwick Papers,* but his father shut him off with an arrogant sweep of the hand.

"The hell with *Pickwick Papers,*" said the gray publisher. He wanted to know where I had been. He listened attentively to my enthusiastic description of "Tinicum Pines" and its island, but suddenly he interrupted me with a raised palm.

"I need you here on an important proposition," he said. "I'll show you what a sport I am, by taking the farm off your hands. I'll give you $5,000 more than you paid for it."

Selling my country home was unthinkable. My wife and I were happily settled there and I greeted Annenberg's overture with laughter. His shrewd eyes blinked when I rejected what he undoubtedly looked upon as a quick profit in a real estate deal. I told him the farm would continue to be my home and I intended to drive there every evening when my work was done. He accepted my terms but with some uneasiness. "Tinicum Pines" had won its first skirmish with a millionaire.

Moe's invitation to me to "write my own ticket," I discovered, was a bit vague, not to take place at once. This, he said, would come when I had established his new magazine and increased his Sunday circulation to a million copies. I had faith in pictorial journalism, and furthermore, Moe now controlled some of the finest color-rotogravure presses in the world. I took him at his word and accepted the new editorship at a modest salary. He told me I would have a free hand, that everything would be serene. To my regret Fullerton had disappeared. Koenigsberg also was gone. Mr. Pickwick apparently had cleared the scene.

Six months on the farm had renewed my energy and my wife and I plunged into our work with the enthusiasm of pioneers in a constructive adventure. But we returned to the farm every evening to inhale the smoky fragrance of the maple chunks which chuckled in the fireplaces.

Moe had definite ideas about the physiognomy of his new tabloid Sunday pictorial. He believed all rotogravures were in a rut and that its editors were hypnotized weekly by photographs of kittens lapping milk out of saucers. He proposed to change all this and blast his way into a new field, clearing a path to the inarticulates of the primitive and the abysmal, which is the only way publishers of his type can bag a million readers quickly. His son who relished the prospect of his first Sunday million, was timorous, almost fearful, when Moe unfolded his plan. Walter was concerned about the effect it would have on the old readers of the *Inquirer* but his father silenced him. "We're not going to do anything raw," he said, "and we can tone it down when we get the million." It sounded like the old formula.

I found myself in the middle of a cross-fire of arguments about pictorial policy between the swashbuckling father and his soft-pedaling son. Walter, as vice-president of the corporation, was acquiring some social prestige in the community. He was paying taxes in Philadelphia on a million dollars' worth of personal property. He lived the life of a gentleman bachelor, inclined to be influenced by the intelligentsia, and in New York was pointed out in café society. He was far removed from the Chicago junk shop over which the immigrant Annenberg family, including Moe, lived in 1885, a domicile whose photograph was to be printed later in *Collier's* to illustrate a frank interview of Moe's early struggles. Walter, after a day's work, retired in the Rittenhouse Plaza to an apartment described by its decorator, the noted Terrence Robsjohn-Gibbings as "Sans Époque." Those who could afford such luxuries believed these ultramodern abodes to be sounding the doom of period houses and other traditions. In Walter's vast living room, any books to be seen were beyond reach near the ceiling and bound in colored linen to harmonize with walls of beige. Draperies and fabrics on the furniture were native-spun in shades of beige and tanagra pink. The library walls were of bleached teakwood, the carpet of chrysoprase green. Above it all a gigantic, ancient Hindu-Chinese figure dominated the abode. Some said the bathroom had been turned into a Capri Villa with tub and washbasins of marble and bronze and all faucets with the heads of griffins, but I could not verify this from the photographs which Walter asked me to reproduce of his resting place in our new rotogravure supplement.

Meanwhile, Moe lived near his office in a place more familiar with the comforts of life than with rebellions against periods, past or present. Whatever social status he may have possessed in Philadelphia he threw over his shoulder by rounding up a dozen attractive red-headed and blonde stenographers in his counting room and taking them all for a harmless but rattling good time in an uproarious rendezvous known as "Benny the Bum's" where he gave the orchestra leader ten-dollar bills to play *I'm Only a Bird in a Gilded Cage*. In the midst of the merrymaking, while he listened to the old song, tears would come to his eyes, but he shook them off with a laugh.

At times the heir apparent had his way about the pictures we selected but more often his father roared his disapproval of any conservative ideas for the early numbers. As the magazine was to be a part of the Sunday *Inquirer* I watched developments with considerable trepidation. From past experience I knew that if something went wrong all the blame would be flung into my face. Some weeks before the deadline, Walter called for a pictorial series on the world's great waterfalls, a picture in color of the Taj Mahal and a spread on the birds of America by John J. Audubon. He wanted two pages of color photography of the glazed fruits in silver bowls and other delicacies of bright hues served to the gourmet at the Warwick Hotel. Moe punctuated his son's desires with a scornful snort. "Audubon!" he shouted. "What the hell did he ever do for circulation? And pictures of food, with millions starving! Do you want to start a revolution?"

He countered with an idea which left us both gasping. I was ordered to take actual photographs of the butchering of a bullock by a Rabbi and use two pages to cover every phase of the sacrificial ceremony. Moe said he had been trying to do this for years and now would have his way. He knew every point of the kosher ritual, from the testing of the spotless blade, which is called the cholof, to the two deft slashes of the knife across the jugular vein, the first stroke traditionally forward, away from the Rabbi, the second backward, which completes the slaughter. He illustrated all this with vivid motions, making me note it all down. I assigned a photographer with a strong stomach who took twenty pictures of the time-honored rite and returned spattered with blood. This presentation was scheduled for the first issue in a brown tone, Moe reluctantly abandoning his original plan of printing it in full color which, he agreed, might spoil the Sunday breakfasts of several hundred thousand Philadelphians who like to eat their scrapple undisturbed.

The balance of the initial number was made up largely of the publisher's ideas of what the public wanted. All contemporary happenings were ignored, as though we were living in a world with the medieval flavor of rapine and bloodshed. We carried a page of pictures of a Zulu wedding in which the happy warrior stands his bride against a tree and marries her by ceremoniously knocking out her teeth with his fist, to show her how much he loves her. This strictly was an inspiration from Moe himself. He gave me the particulars from his mysterious store of information and scrutinized the photographs with satisfaction before they were sent to the rotogravure plant, allowing me no time to verify this strange marriage custom. The buxom Negro lass, whom we had hired to pose for it, visited me after the magazine appeared, complaining of her jaw, which she rubbed tenderly, and asking me what I proposed to do about it. Another page revealed the festival ceremonies of cremation, as they are celebrated in Bali and India. Two pages were given over to the bloody duels of German students. Still another showed an unconcerned gentleman in a state of hypnosis, his cheeks being pierced by long hatpins, pushed through by a cooperating friend. Ten photographs explained the "Psychology of the Peeping Tom." A lady was exhibited while enduring the tortures of a beauty treatment under a mask of hot lead, guaranteed to remove wrinkles. Those interested in the mysteries of nature had, all to themselves, a page entitled "Murderers in the Animal World," starting off with the photograph of a horned viper devouring a rat. Others, inclined toward art and sociology, could ponder over "A Day in the Life of an Advertising Model" including her morning shower, or pictures illustrating bad honeymoon manners and "how they can wreck your marriage at the threshold of happiness." A page in color showed Alice Faye mooning in lingerie and the "center-spread" gave, in brilliant hues, full play to the antics of George M. Cohan, then appearing in *I'd Rather Be Right* and making fun of Roosevelt. This piece of enterprise was described as a "slashing political satire." From the cover of this concoction the ventriloquist dummy, "Charlie McCarthy," peered out in top hat and monocle.

Moe liked this mélange to such an extent that, at the last minute, he ordered me to add eight more pages of the same formula to this incredible mixture, a process which threw the rotogravure shop into a panic. When the presses began to roar he sent the first copy to Captain Patterson of the *Daily News,* with a laconic note telling him of the great revolution which had come over rotogravure. In this indirect manner Moe presumably wanted to inform his brother, Max, that a national circulation brawl was on. I went home tired after this accouchement, but ringing in my ears were the publisher's words:

"There's not a monotonous page in the whole damn book. The hell with monotony! If we don't go over a million with this I'll kiss my brother Max in Macy's window!"

On occasions, during this publishing upheaval, Moe permitted his son to intrude his oar although Walter's ideas took milder form and drew lofty but yet tolerant sneers from the patriarch. Among the works of art which stood out in the memories of Walter's boyhood was the colorful painting of "Custer's Last Stand" which the brewer Adolphus Busch had presented to the Seventh Cavalry Regiment in 1890 in a burst of benevolent patriotism. It swept me back thirty years when my father brought home a large reproduction of it on a calendar from his favorite saloon and hung it in the kitchen where it remained long after its monthly record had been ripped away. Walter wanted to reproduce it across two pages of the rotogravure in full color and I had almost given up hope of finding it when I discovered a copy of the venerable lithograph hanging behind Mike Welsh's old sawdust bar in Lambertville, across the Delaware from New Hope, where a nip of Bass' ale was always procurable. I explained my problem to Mike who took down the huge affair in its frame, and as a man highly honored he permitted me to take it to Philadelphia after I had promised my life as a forfeit for its safe return. Mike ordered many extra copies of the paper in advance although he had been looking at the picture for twenty-five years.

Perhaps for the last time in American journalism this masterpiece was reproduced in full color although I abandoned any thought of trying to explain to the reader the reason why it had been exhumed. Moe saw no point to it, but I pacified him by adding a full-page picture of the vivid Indian massacre of a family of stalwart American settlers in the Wyoming Valley in 1778. This led to more promptings on the same subject and I managed to unearth an old print of the last fight of the Pequots, a terrific harquebusade which took place in Connecticut in 1637 when the Pilgrims killed 800 of the tribe, watching them perish in the flames of their Indian village and losing but two of their own men. The effect of this sanguinary encounter on the reader was softened by Pocahontas in the act of saving Captain John Smith, about to be brained by the warriors of her merciless father, Powhatan. In my grapple with the redskins I thought it fitting to devote the cover of this historical number to Sitting Bull, whose grim countenance appeared against a flaming-red background brandishing all his feathers, with two bluebirds perched on his head. Philadelphia palefaces greeted by this challenging gospel of forgotten hate and strife on their quiet Sunday morning may have concluded that Moe, unpredictable in a circulation rampage, suddenly had declared war on the Indians.

Although Walter grinned his pleasure over this bloody history, Moe told me privately to forget about the Indians thereafter. We received a large number of letters of approbation from readers who urged us to continue our researches of the warpath, but our trail led elsewhere.

The Thanksgiving issue was to put our modern photographic equipment to an unusual test. Moe implored me to shun any photographs of motherly creatures peering at turkeys roasting in the ovens or jovial people sitting around a table in happy expectation. This he called "monotonous tradition." As 1937 was one of the years under Roosevelt when the date of Thanksgiving had not yet become debatable, we were able to plan ahead. A farmer agreed to chase a turkey for us, running after it over a wooded acre with an ax in his hand before our "magic-eye" camera which could catch the fastest movement of this early American ritual, including the bird's head flying off in its blood from the chopping block. The publisher liked the pictures but declined to pay for the gobbler.

Moe recognized all holidays in our rotogravure magazine, believing such traditions should be recalled to the minds of the American people but garnished with a few well-peppered side dishes. Our Thanksgiving issue carried, among other things, two pages of pictures on the "Run-in-the-Stocking Bugaboo, and How to Prevent It." This opened the doors for all sorts of photographic possibilities. It attracted wide interest among women readers, and presumably did not escape the notice of the men. I discovered in this research that the run in the stocking is responsible for the yearly sale of 35,000,000 dozens of silk hose, costing an average of seventy cents a pair, a most important item in the working girl's apparel budget. Moe told me that he believed the manufacturers made stockings in such a way as to cause runs, which increased the sales.

We exposed the wildly-spreading evil of the marihuana plant, "as a timely warning to American youth" with the cooperation of the narcotic squads of the United States Government. Old readers of the *Inquirer* howled to high heaven when this smoking menace was depicted. A Philadelphia Main Line debutante of complete respectability, although she was out for a lark, and smoked a less harmful form of cigarette, posed for the pictures, and when her father, a wealthy industrialist, saw them in our Sunday paper his daughter's career as a model came to an abrupt end.

Walter's ideas dominated the color section of the Christmas number and we devoted two pages to the Adoration of the Magi. Moe, however, insisted that some of his own ideas be included, although they clashed a bit with the significance of the season. I appeased him with a department called "Cannibalism Among the Reptiles" and fourteen pictures under the heading, "Fifty-one Feet of Film for Hollywood's Longest Kiss." He went home happy when I produced two pages on "The Mad Klondike Rush of 1898," bringing back to life the whole fatal scramble over the Yukon Pass. He was always interested in stories of privations leading to fortune and often regaled me with anecdotes of his early days as a saloon roustabout. "But," he wound up, "before I got through with that job, I turned that bar into a profit."

Moe spent much of his time in my corner, looking over masses of pictures. He had a highly developed sense of the incongruous and the futile gyrations of the "upper crust," as he called it. His eyes glittered over photographs of expensive human-like funerals for dogs and cats, some of these ceremonies in animal cemeteries costing up to $500. Motion-picture stars were among the best clients of these rites. He burst into profanity over the ritual as he studied pictures of pets interred in mausoleums.

"One hundred dollars," he shouted, "to bury a canary! Put that in the paper! When I think of what I had to go through to move out of that place over the junk shop this barbarism makes my stomach turn. That's what breeds Communism!"

He smothered his rage with a new inspiration. He wanted two pages drawn to illustrate a story he had heard years ago when he was building up circulation for Hearst, tooth and claw. John L. Sullivan, the Boston Strong Boy, while in a drunken condition, had jostled a young woman escorted by her sweetheart on her way home to her aged mother on a snowy night. The captions for this art were prepared under Moe's explicit directions and took me back to Frank Merriwell.

"You clumsy oaf!" snaps the stripling. "Doubtless you learned your manners in the bar from which you were just thrown! Apologize at once, sir!" The world's champion blinks in amazement. Is this a dream? "D'ye know who I am?" growls the voice that makes men's hearts turn sick with fear!

"Zounds! I don't care who you are!" cries the youth in ringing tones. "A man who fails to respect womanhood is no man at all!" And planting his heels on the icy pavement, he

brings up a smashing uppercut flush on the point of Sullivan's granite jaw. The champ's feet slide—he's down! He's out!

Moe's headline for this inspiring legend, based on his own philosophy of life, was: "The Bigger They Come the Harder They Fall." Three years later it was to have a strangely prophetic ring for him.

CHAPTER II

ALTHOUGH the circulation of Moe's Sunday paper jumped spectacularly from something under 700,000 to a mark clear over a million, at one time 300,000 above it, Philadelphia's "best people" were determined to oppose the boisterous pictorial supplement whose clamor disturbed their Sabbath mornings. The increase in sales had grown to such an extent that the Sunday *Inquirer* in its weekly field could boast of the largest number of readers of any standard-size paper in America. It sold 200,000 copies in Canada. In the city of Toronto it sold 30,000 copies, and the Toronto *Star,* to meet the competition, turned its rotogravure into a tabloid magazine, sending an editor to Philadelphia to absorb our technique. All over the country sales were booming and Moe was jubilant and defiant when he read the letters of complaint which poured in from the Main Line, the blue-stocking segment of his adopted community.

Analyzing the new supplement, which was called "Picture Parade," I saw nothing in it to justify the wrath of the bailiwick. By no stretch of the imagination could it have been classified as offensive. It may have been excitable but it was recognized as an important medium by advertisers and finally led the field in advertising lineage among rotogravures. Those who said there was neither wit nor method in its harmless turbulence were ignorant of the millions who buy Sunday papers mainly for the colored comics or picture entertainment. Perhaps Moe had "something on the ball" when he said, "the hell with monotony." The magazine reflected his mind and his knowledge of the average man on the street. The millionaire who had progressed from the junk shop displayed his wares as he liked them, and more than a million people agreed with him.

The "rags to riches" publisher knew that old Philadelphia would never accept him, nor his harlequinades, but would read his paper if it knocked the Democrats occasionally and refrained from exuberance. The old families of power and money, whose cupboard skeletons were safely removed from the candid camera, had nothing to be proud of about the state of affairs in the city which had become the nation's scandal. Their political ineptitude could never be overestimated. But they wanted no outsider to disturb them, and their resentment of Moe was mostly concerned with his antimacassar audacities which stirred the backwaters of the frisky nineties, when life was piquant in the burlesque shows and beer gardens. Moe produced a costly blue and silver brochure about himself, in which he attempted to explain his character and purpose. In it he described Philadelphia as "deep-rooted in a curious admixture of quiet reserve and studious skepticism which it inherited from its Quaker founders." This expressed his ideas of the region he had invaded somewhat charitably, and had been written by a highly paid advertising copywriter who evidently knew what he was doing.

Nothing was done by the influential and wrinkled conservatives on the *Inquirer* to check the rising tide of hostile criticism of Moe's Sunday baby. They encouraged the outcry although they enjoyed the additional revenue from the million circulation. Some of them had been on the paper for forty years, through its lights and shadows, never aware that there might be new tastes and moods in the world. Moe called me into his art gallery during the agitation. He had a new picture inspiration and his eyes were alive with the devil in him. He outlined to me the history and the evolution of the dread "Micky Finn" and what had befallen the celebrities who had partaken of it from the time of Diamond Jim Brady, who appeared to be its first prominent victim, in Moe's recollections. To the innocent reader, a "Finn" is a doch-an-dorrach which is served slyly to a customer after its purity has been deplorably contaminated. Its effect makes seasickness seem like the pleasant reaction from a pheasant and wine dinner.

We reserved four rotogravure pages for this scientific subject. I revived the heroic Lillian Russell who, according to Moe, had saved Brady hours of agony by detecting several "Finns" that were handed to him by certain jealous cutthroats of the nineties. In my research I came across Carrie Nation and discovered that she endorsed the "Micky Finn" for all drinkers. I brought her respectfully out of the past with her hatchet and Bible.

Moe reveled in this historical adventure, examining old photographs of Jack's Café on Sixth Avenue, near Forty-third Street in New York, at the turn of the century, and Steve Brodie's famous Bowery saloon at the time he laid claim to jumping off the Brooklyn Bridge. Many a deadly "Finn" was passed over Brodie's bar and my explorations drew a flood of reminiscences from the millionaire. He remembered Jack's particularly, before Prohibition had fallen upon it with its blight. I recalled a description of Jack himself, from long ago, by Carl Van Vechten who, in a piece for H. L. Mencken, had described the proprietor as gray-haired and gray-mustached, immaculate in evening clothes, a carnation in his buttonhole, wandering about like the host of a yachting party, while the Irish waiters exchanged pleasantries with the customers. All this had to go with the passage of time.

"Gone," said Moe, sad-eyed, his long face in his hands, as though his experience had convinced him that nothing worth while in life remained stable. "They were all regular people, doing great things, and rubbing elbows. No snobbery. But they're gone. A big change has come."

His Sunday bill of fare of a mourned era might have been accepted by Philadelphia's dyspeptic readers if Moe had been satisfied solely with its historical significance. But he added a dramatized embellishment which required additional posed photographs showing what happens when a respectable, married man, attending a convention, unsuspectingly meets his downfall at the hands of a fair charmer who pours the evil powder of the "Finn" into his drink to stupify him, then takes him to her rooms where an angry intruder appears, posing as her husband. There, the sickened victim, by means of blackmail, is stripped of his money and prestige. I had reported this sad story years ago for the public prints, but Moe said the moral would never die. With characteristic thoroughness he made me pry from a reluctant bartender, the secret of the malevolent mixture, as it is used down to this day, a powder of ipecac blended with magnesia and saturated with croton oil. We printed the formula.

"It's the same dope," said Moe. "It never changed. It's handed down from one generation to another."

This pictorial project drove our department into new bursts of activity. Our photographer made the mistake of taking a picture of a near-by bar over which a church deacon was enjoying a quiet whisky sour. The deacon ran into our marble halls and set up a fearful clamor after the bartender had informed him proudly that the photograph was to appear in the Sunday *Inquirer*. We destroyed the plates, which were to be used as background, and saved the deacon's reputation. We published the ramifications of the "Micky Finn" as the main feature of our rotogravure which carried other sparks from Moe's mind: a department exposing the old "shell game"; another depicting the fantastic funeral of the King of Borneo, a gentleman whose illness had escaped my notice, and a page entitled "Wearing a Dead Friend's Clothes and Dancing at his Funeral." The issue, incidentally, contained the largest volume of advertising we had yet received. Moe was so impressed with the pictures of the model who posed as the siren of the poisonous potion that he asked me to obtain her telephone number, so that he might show her his Victorian paintings, but I was never able to bring about this social contact.

The storm that followed the pictorial history of the "Micky Finn" raged as much among the creaking gentlemen dusting themselves off on the *Inquirer's* shelf as it did along the Main Line. Old timers on the paper served upon Moe a mandate of moderation, predicting all sorts of disasters if the rotogravure continued to shun the cat and the saucer and the meetings of the Daughters of the American Revolution. Letters of protest were mailed in, full of vindictive hostility from Philadelphia groups, a number of them, I learned later, having been inspired by notable fixtures on the paper. Meanwhile the circulation continued to increase.

Moe read the letters contemptuously. One of them, written by an officer of the corporation, put the blame on me for the upheaval and the publisher cast it in my direction with a sardonic grin.

"What this town needs," he meditated, "is a couple of dozen first-class funerals. I bought this paper before I had seen the building. I thought I could do something with it. I was looking over the balance sheets on a boat. The proposition looked good if some ginger could be put into it. And so I walked into a $15,000,000 deal without knowing anybody in the damned town. I think I know what people want and nobody's going to stop me."

He was working himself into a state of agitation, but soon had a grip on his rising anger; but his eyes were cold and his lips might have been the ruled line of a red pencil.

"I know how to compromise when it's the best thing to do temporarily. We can tone the magazine up a couple of notches and still hang on to the million, but don't make it dull." He sighed resignedly. "Give 'em their God-damned Taj Mahal!"

While renewing my acquaintance with Audubon, the birds of America and India, the land of mystery and enchantment, I received a surprising telephone call. It was from Miss Frances E. Barnes Linton, Executive Secretary and Treasurer of the Women's Christian Temperance Union of Philadelphia, and long an admirer of Carrie Nation. Miss Linton wanted to buy several thousand copies of the paper containing the history of the "Micky Finn" and requested permission to reproduce the pictures of this object lesson on huge posters to be exhibited at lectures on temperance around the country. She complimented me on our crusade and said we had struck a great blow at the forces of evil. When Moe heard of this new turn of affairs, he bellowed: "You couldn't want any better people than those on our side."

Walter's ideas now prevailed in the color section. Many things of a narcissistic streak were selected. His pictures of the gastronomic feats at the Warwick soon appeared in blazing hues, covering two pages and surrounding the face of the late, lamented food authority, George Lamaze. All captions describing the culinary creations were printed in French, from the menu of the famous hotel, exactly as they were read through the lorgnettes of the Philadelphia illuminati. A large photograph of the *pièce de résistance* was called "Caneton de Long Island à la Sauce Bigarade garnie de paniers d'orange et fonds d'artichauts Clamart avec cylindres de pommes douces."

Moe studied the picture of this masterpiece for some time and grunted in disgust over the caption.

"Hell," he said, "that's just plain damn Long Island ducklin' with peas and sweet potatoes. They charge more for it in French!"

Our rotogravure covers were chosen from colored films

made from the Dufay and Kodachrome process from which
all colors of the spectrum may be reproduced. These films
specialized in the pictures of motion-picture stars, in every
conceivable pose, from Dorothy Lamour in her sarong to
Shirley Temple painting Easter eggs. They were mailed to
us by the hundreds from Hollywood and cost us nothing.
Walter selected them after long ponderings, scrutinizing the
beauties of the screen over a glass-topped table under which
a strong light could be turned on. He picked them through
a secret formula of his own, about which he never informed
me. I was to discover later that it was largely influenced
by the varying degrees of business friendliness which existed
between the motion-picture houses owned by the Annenbergs
in the Middle West and the reigning dukes of the screen companies. I imagine the fluctuations of motion-picture advertising also had something to do with it. My recommendations for
covers were useless, although I clung to my own movie
favorites. Joan Crawford, for instance, might be in our
good graces, suddenly to be banished to some mysterious
purgatory. We used so many pictures of Dorothy Lamour
that I recoiled from movie theaters whenever she was billed.
I saw so much of Hedy Lamarr, Olivia de Havilland, Anita
Louise and Norma Shearer, fully clothed or ready with set
smiles for their swimming pools, that these pleasing creatures
had no more appeal for me than aged crones.

The subterranean picture warfare came to the surface in
realistic fashion when Walter ordered me to turn over an entire page to the feet of Greta Garbo and the hands of Leopold
Stokowski, two artists who had given me joyful moments
and who, according to the public prints, were seeing much of
one another. I went through hundreds of pictures of Garbo,
hunting for the largest photograph that could be found of her
feet. This quest disturbed me. I felt it was holding up to
ridicule the most talented actress in cinematic art. Once,
Greta had been one of my suppressed desires. I finally found
a print of her feet in stout shoes with straps and buckles.
Walter enlarged it to a half page in size which gave Garbo's
extremities a gigantic appearance. Beneath them he printed a
picture of the hands of Stokowski in similar dimensions. He
chuckled over the headline he prepared for this combination:
"The Romance of the Year as Seen in a Photographic Close-

up." It was printed in more than 1,000,000 copies of the paper.

"That'll bring somebody around," Walter added, mysteriously.

This fighting in the dark with Garbo, who had no chance to defend herself by implanting an effective kick in somebody's pants, threw me into such a state of distress one evening, when I was examining the offending supplement at Mike Welsh's bar, that I decided to resign my position. Upon thinking it over when I got home I concluded to compromise with life. There was something more absurd even about throwing up my job over the size of Garbo's feet than there had been when I walked out over Mr. Pickwick. Such gallantry rarely was appreciated in this materialistic world. Garbo would never hear of my sacrifice. I went back to work the next morning.

The picture of Garbo's brogans produced decisive results. From out of the West came a man of high talent for diplomacy, who introduced himself to me as Barrett C. Kiesling, representing Metro-Goldwyn-Mayer. He was an official "troubleshooter" who spent much time pouring oil on the agitated waters which divided Screenland from the publishing world. For two days he whipped the well-stocked streams of Moe's estate in the Pocono Mountains and when he returned I was informed that Garbo's feet were to be respected.

In my office, Kiesling demonstrated what a Movie Metternich could do as an executive in action. He tore off his coat and paced about in long strides. What did I want in pictures? Leg art? Sex in a nice way? In a few moments Western Union messengers were rushing out with long telegrams on these subjects, my wife taking down the dictation, her shoulders bowed as though under a storm. Some of my assistants crowded the doorway, to see how Hollywood attained results. How about pictures of historical association, or Frankenstein monsters jumping into boiling lava? More telegrams, more messenger boys pushed out, bug-eyed, to the elevators. The film statesman then bowed low, looked at his watch, and leaped for the door to catch a plane.

Ambassador Kiesling's visit brought to an end an extensive research we were making into the high salaries drawn by the chief executives of Metro-Goldwyn-Mayer, whose pictures were to be printed over the figures of their staggering incomes.

All this was dropped like a hot poker. Walter asked me, instead, to prepare three pages on the triumphs of Darryl Zanuck and the miracles he performed on the two-hundred-acre "lot" of 20th Century-Fox. In this history, Walter ordered a large picture of Joseph M. Schenck, who was described as the financial genius of the enterprise "who tore up a $5,000 a week contract to rise to fame." A photograph of the trusting face of the president, Sidney R. Kent, was reduced to the circumference of a dime, not much larger than Brisbane's diminishing NRA duck. President Kent appeared to be a hard-working man, but I never inquired into the laws governing these violent pictorial contrasts. He was in the "dog house," Walter said.

Moe's son was interested in elaborate conceptions illustrating wealth. He liked pictures of millionaires who spent $30,000 a year to fly to work in Wall Street in $60,000 planes operated by $100 a week pilots. Our supplement showed a number of these weary commuters landing at the Downtown Skyport in the East River, in New York. It cost them a dollar a minute to reach their offices. A reporter told me that what they had to say about Roosevelt was unprintable.

My researches, under Walter's directions, launched me into the fantastic fortunes of the Rajahs of India who live in splendor beyond imagination. Moe's son was familiar with the annual incomes of most of them, rattling off the figures at his fingers' ends, like a table of multiplication. We printed the pictures of all these princes of enchantment who were still alive, beginning with the Nizam of Hyderabad, who had an annual income of $33,823,097.

"Jesus!" Walter commented, while he studied a photograph of the turbaned gentleman. "Have you figured up what that amounts to by the day? That's what I call money!"

Moe, meanwhile took a fling at the pictorial helm to see that we did not veer completely off his course. I could always please him with illustrations of "The Night Stranglers of Paris" or under-sea photographs of a death battle between an octopus and a shark. He liked particularly a picture serial which ran from week to week entitled "Midnight Money," a potboiler which I had hoped to sell to the motion pictures. It had to do with the vicissitudes of an influential racketeer who controlled night clubs, but whose heart was bursting for understanding. In disguise he distributed some of his questionable wealth to the poor. I gave him the name of "Big Frenchy Quintus." Into his life I maneuvered an innocent girl from a small town and saw to it that he never brought a blush to her cheeks. She reformed him and married him and he turned his talents to more legitimate enterprises.

Moe studied many proofs of these pictorial chapters, which I prepared at my farmhouse at night. I received no extra pay for the additional effort, and Walter informed me that I could reserve the motion-picture rights. His father, however, was visibly impressed by "Big Frenchy" and my understanding of "hard guys with a human streak." It might have been the story of Moe himself, although I managed to keep my tough hero out of prison. It seemed to bring me closer to Moe, who told me a number of stories of the grim battles he had survived. He liked stories of action and read himself to sleep at night with the advanced proofs of his own lurid detective magazines, often unable to curb his curiosity until the coming serial installments had been published. When he had devoured all of the horrors he could find in his own publications he went to sleep with Spinoza.

At times Moe's mind turned to matters historical. We fought the Battle of Gettysburg in pictures, from Pickett's last charge down to the Brady photograph of the amputation of a soldier's leg without anesthetics. We invaded Valley Forge to photograph its famous relics. Said Moe: "Show the people all the things Washington used, like everybody else, his razor, his plate, knife and fork. I understand his pants are hanging up out there. Take a picture of those."

Being familiar with the professional callousness of staff photographers, I supervised this delicate assignment personally although the custodians of the museum, timid little ladies, shivered as we removed Washington's breeches from the wall in a forbidding glass case.

My camera man, somehow, reminded me of Izzy Kaplan, the *Mirror's* unabashed shutter hound who had photographed Queen Marie of Rumania when she arrived in New York. Izzy would have parted with a limb rather than turn in an ordinary print. Finding the royal visitor in the proper light on deck he had shouted:

"Hey, Queenie, sit on the rail, cross your legs and smile!"
There was every indication from his photograph that the Queen had complied.

The modern press methods of prying brought about a renewed public interest in the priceless collection at Valley Forge. Our million circulation drew an army of visitors for months to the museum, and I received a tender note of thanks from the relieved custodians.

Beneath a cushion of colored comics, features of murder and the high jinks of bachelor millionaires on their Florida yachts, a vast number of readers had found the pictures of the relics, had been touched, and had driven for miles to see them for the first time. Moe, who had accumulated the greatest individual cash income in the country, promptly forgot the illustrations he had conceived and which, as a result of his whim, had reached a Democratic people hungry for great examples.

CHAPTER III

MOE now developed the imperial hunger which was to hasten his downfall. He was rolling in unlimited profits from a world which was not recognized by polite society. His activities as the czar of racing information were never discussed in the *Inquirer* building, but, quietly, by telephone and conferences outside of his office, he ruled a monopoly which served the needs of thousands of law-breaking gambling joints and clients beset by gang warfare.

He had been a member of the inner council of the Napoleonic Hearst, and at the entrance of his sanctum he hung a framed letter from Brisbane which included among other paragraphs of high tribute, the following:

"You remember that when I persuaded you to come to New York and presented you to Mr. Hearst, I told him I was doing him a much greater favor than if I had given him one million dollars in cash."

To such people, little in life was of value unless it could be compared with a million dollars. Moe felt a certain exultant pleasure when he pointed to the framed letter which was attached to a photograph of himself, standing with Brisbane in front of some exclusive portal at Miami Beach—two millionaires close together, planted solidly on their feet on a piece of real estate worth $1,000 an inch. But Moe was no longer satisfied with this recognition from the predatory philosopher. The junk shop prodigy's ultimate standards of success had been pushed far beyond his baronial nod, without which no bookie joint in America could open its doors. In his mind had grown the conviction that what other publishers had done in the way of placing their own candidates in office, he could do, and with more power for himself.

He spent many hours in his office, ignoring his magnificent estates at Kings Point, Long Island; Pike County, Pennsylvania; Sand Creek Canyon, Wyoming, and Miami Beach. In New York he lived at the Waldorf-Astoria, and in Philadelphia he maintained exclusive apartments at the Warwick

Hotel. He was responsible for a flow of income which has been estimated as high as $6,000,000 a year. Someone at this time asked Moe if he were worth $40,000,000. He laughed but did not deny it.

His exclusive wires ran into twenty-nine race tracks, then to thousands of bookie joints in 223 cities in thirty-nine states. He was the fifth largest customer of the American Telephone and Telegraph Company. He paid half a million dollars a year in wire tolls. He published between twenty or thirty racing papers distributed in large cities, led by *Racing Form,* including a volume called *Systeology* which announced that "the horse player is sure to find that corner around which prosperity lurks if he has the intestinal fortitude to stick to his selected system and play it through to the bitter end." But, as Brisbane had once written, Moe never bet on the horses. He sold the "dope" to the gamblers of the nation.

Walter told me at this time that the Annenbergs gathered their money from forty sources of income and that he was thankful he had studied a business course. A reporter during an interview had once asked him: "To what do you attribute your success?" Walter had replied that the main reason was that he had been fortunate enough to have been born the son of Moses L. Annenberg. He was feeling his way about the labyrinthine corridors of his father's enterprises, and there were enough of them to occupy his mind apart from the colored pictures he selected for the rotogravure.

Aside from his race-track information monopoly, Moe owned a paper in Massillon, Ohio; the hundred-year old *Morning Telegraph* in New York, the only daily newspaper that sold for twenty-five cents a copy; the hundred-year-old Philadelphia *Inquirer;* hotels, office buildings, garages, motion-picture theaters and an insurance company. He was a large shareholder in banking institutions. At one time he owned a brokerage firm, wholesale and retail liquor stores, a laundry and bowling alleys. In the field of quick-selling literature he produced such newsstand adornment as *Click, Actual Detective Stories, Official Detective Stories, Radio Guide, Screen Guide* —and what not.

After I had established the new rotogravure Moe came into my office with a newspaper man whom he had been trying to place in a suitable spot on the paper. The publisher had received no encouragement about him from other department heads who looked with suspicion upon any journalist with wider experience than Philadelphia afforded. The newcomer was John J. Fitzpatrick, a competent editor of New England training, who had found himself without a berth when Moe, who had hired him to be the managing editor of the Miami *Tribune*, one of the millionaire's trinkets, had disposed of it suddenly like a bag of unground feed in a mill chute.

I took Fitzpatrick on as my assistant. He was a man of middle age, well informed, with a bubbling Irish humor which was to be completely knocked out of him. Among the notable writers he had trained as reporters was Kenneth Roberts, author of *Northwest Passage* and *Oliver Wiswell*.

My collaboration with Fitzpatrick pleased Moe and he visited us frequently with a pocketful of ideas. He had asked me to criticize the daily *Inquirer* and I wrote an analysis of it which might have been described as "brutally constructive." Fitzpatrick, after reading it, commented dryly, "He will either appoint you as managing editor or throw you out the window."

But Moe was not offended. He thanked me for "exposing a cancer," as he called it, and appointed Fitzpatrick to the post, a selection which received my warm approval. I was no longer interested in putting morning papers to bed and waving to the milkmen on my way home.

"Fitz" soon had the "daily" humming, drawing upon his New England newspaper experience, which is among the best. His responsibilities were heavy and he had taken the position at a benevolently meek salary with the promise of more money soon. When the increase arrived he imparted the news to me over the luncheon table.

"Moe is a tough man about pay," he said, ruefully. "He's going to put my name on the editorial page and give me twenty-five dollars more a week."

I saw the shrewdness behind Moe's decision to print the Irish name of Fitzpatrick on the masthead. The publisher wanted to please the Catholics of his city under all circumstances, and there were, in Philadelphia, many thousands of them, whose Archbishop, Denis Cardinal Dougherty, stood for no publishing nonsense. Any article or picture spreads prepared for the *Inquirer*, referring to Catholics, were taken to his office for inspection or approval, either from his Emi-

nence (to whom Moe referred respectfully as "his Immense")
or subordinate prelates. This precaution was due to a still
remembered contretemps which had happened on the Philadelphia *Public Ledger* years ago when something in print
of a nature offensive to the Catholics had slipped by and the
paper had lost a large number of readers before it could make
amends.

Fitzpatrick's increase of twenty-five dollars a week was
another matter, however, which made me wonder what might
happen when I took Moe at his word and "wrote my own
ticket." I found out, soon enough. The new rotogravure
was well stabilized, recognized nationally as a success and had
developed into a lucrative publication. Our formula, which
now included matters of significance as well as entertainment,
was widely copied.

Walter finally stammered out the reward for my efforts,
which was fifteen dollars more a week. By this time my
securities had righted themselves. I liked the work I was
doing, which enabled me to come home to my farm every
night and I accepted the donation, which the publisher's son
referred to impressively as "almost a thousand dollars more
a year!" To show that his heart was in the right place he
bought me a five-dollar sport shirt and gave me two tickets to
hear the Philadelphia Symphony Orchestra. The convenience
of the forgetfulness of the rich was by no means a new experience for me. When I told the story to "Fitz" over a glass
of ale, he covered his face with his hands, peered at me through
his fingers and lapsed into the cold, dawn silence of an Irish
wake.

I became impressed one morning with the fact that Moe's
viewpoint was definitely headed in a political direction when
he stormed in with a suggestion that evidently had alarmed
Walter, who ran into my office on his father's heels, arguing
with him to change his mind. The publisher wanted two pages
of photographs of the notorious political bosses of the country
with a sardonic history of their background.

"It will look like a rogues' gallery," Moe shouted. "Put
them all in, from 'Bathhouse John' Coughlin to Jimmy Hines
under the headline: 'Take a Look at Who Runs the Nation.'
Let's show the country who these bruisers are who get out
the votes and elect Mayors, Governors and Presidents!"

Walter listened in speechless nervousness. Later he ordered me to put the whole matter aside. "It's dynamite," he
said. "For God's sake, forget it. I'll get my father to
change his mind."

But Moe had another idea which he may have regretted.
We printed the least flattering photographs we could find of
eleven of President Roosevelt's chief advisers to whom we
referred as "Coach Roosevelt's All-American," under the
headline: "The New Deal Hand-Picked Eleven That Dishes it
Out but Never Takes It." One of these officials was Robert H.
Jackson, then Solicitor General. Later, as Attorney General,
he was to listen to frantic pleas to keep Moe out of prison.

Moe directed vindictive political engagements on several
fronts against the Democrats. His Washington bureau poured
in a barrage of shrapnel which was unloaded on the New Deal
under crackling headlines. From the State Capitol at Harrisburg special correspondents of the newspaper let loose a
steady fire on Governor Earle's Administration. Moe began
to accumulate powerful enemies. In Republican camps it
was open gossip that he would select the next Governor of
Pennsylvania. From my reserved seat in the rotogravure
department I watched the performance with the interest of a
spectator who holds a good ticket at a three-ringed circus.
I did not anticipate that this warfare was to plunge me into
more broiling activities. Working with Moe could not be
described as monotonous.

The publisher had moved the entire staff of his string of
magazines to Philadelphia from Chicago, where in Plymouth
Court, known to race-track experts as Annenberg Alley,
Moe's countless publishing enterprises about the horses were
spread about. For days the *Inquirer* building was in a hulla-
baloo while invading editors rushed in looking for working
space and rushed out again to move their families and sign
leases for apartments. Moe then discovered that the Pennsylvania taxes to be imposed on this caravan of endeavors were
higher than he had expected them to be. Overnight he
ordered distracted editors, assistants and artists back to
Chicago.

Among Annenberg's national magazines affected by the
upheaval was the pictorial monthly known as *Click*. Moe had
gone to Chicago early in 1938 to launch it personally, and

had added so much hot spice to it that in two issues, its circulation had reached 1,600,000 copies. It carried no advertising but already was producing a surprising profit. It expressed the publisher's explosive character and crudities, and the sensual mob had been quick to extend its paws for it at the same time paying out its hundreds of thousands of dimes. It was never seen on the beige coverings of Walter's furniture at "Sans Époque."

The first editor of *Click* was Curtis Mitchell, an alert gentleman well known in the pulp-magazine field, who possessed the suavity of a junior Grover Whalen. I never blamed Mitchell for the plight in which *Click* found itself after four issues under his editorship. He had given Moe what was demanded. Such circulation triumphs could be accomplished every day if there were no laws to curb them. Walter had hoped that his Indian pictures would appear in the first number but Moe flung Custer and Sitting Bull into the wastebasket with Pocahontas. The magazine's *raison d'être* may be explained by its three pages of pictures showing what a woman should do when in danger of being raped. I still remember the admonition Mitchell added to the illustrations of this problem: "Keep calm, don't run—but scream whenever you can."

Moe returned from Chicago elated over his latest success. He wanted to drive *Click* to a circulation of 2,000,000 by methods even more sensational and announced in its pages an offer of $50,000 in cash prizes for picture ideas. He desired a series of consecutive photographs showing a Caesarean operation and asked me to produce the pictures from a local hospital. Illustrations of the birth of a child had never been printed outside of the pages of a medical journal, and photographs of delivery by section of the abdominal walls and the womb of the mother were even more unthinkable in newsstand literature. For a time I thought Moe was off balance, and to convince him of his proposed folly I secured a motion picture of the operation, projecting it on a screen in my office. Among those who attended my clinic was Walter who emerged with a greenish pallor. Moe then abandoned the idea. "I guess the public wouldn't stand for it," he said.

Click's pictorial policies aroused a storm of angry protests in all parts of the United States. The Canadian Government banned the magazine immediately. It became a violation with

a prison penalty to send it through the mails. The Catholic
Church blacklisted it nationally. Campaigns were begun by
leagues of decency to exterminate it. The Annenbergs became thoroughly alarmed. The magazine now was being
printed on the *Inquirer* rotogravure presses and at any moment copies of it might be flashed at Democratic campaign
meetings, arouse Philadelphia Catholics and destroy the political prestige Moe was trying to build up.

I was sent for by the Annenbergs during this crisis. Moe
explained the painful problem with crisp sentences. Walter,
pacing the floor, was frankly frightened and wanted to knock
the magazine in the head. His father, however, thought it
might be rescued by some process of repatriation and the glint
of greed was in his eyes when he said to me:

"Take it under your wing and clean it up. It still has
1,500,000 readers."

As this was a good-sized job in itself, aside from my
rotogravure editorship, which I was to continue, I asked him
what the additional remuneration would be. He seemed surprised.

"My word is good," he replied in exasperation. "Put this
thing on its feet and you'll be handsomely rewarded."

I added dryly that I was glad he hadn't offered to let me
write my own ticket again, and he caught the point with a
wince.

"There's a lot of vicious talk about my thrift but it's just
malicious slander."

In the process of protecting Moe's political reputation by
establishing *Click* on a legal foundation, I lost 600,000 readers.
I was given a free hand, perhaps because I was accomplishing
the desired results without a penny of additional compensation.
I have found in my working experience that a happy independence in toil may be reached if your fabulously rich employer feels that you are doing much more work than you are
being paid for.

I soon had an issue prepared which was acceptable to the
mails without incurring the risk of arrest of all those responsible for its publication. I was able to satisfy the Canadian
Censor, the Honorable J. S. Roe, Examiner of Publications,
who had banned *Click* from the Dominion. After a long
diplomatic correspondence, Mr. Roe accepted my word that

future issues would comply with common decency. I had to send my chief pictorial assistant, John Miller, to Ottawa, who informed me that Moe's promises were received with open skepticism. The magazine was passed into Canada, however, and Miller and I were held personally responsible by the Canadian Government with regard to subsequent numbers. At the time two other flaming creations from Moe's literary stables were on the Canadian banned list. Mr. Roe inspected our proofs every month, before our press output was released. He was a gentleman of cultural background whose tastes inclined toward the *Manchester Guardian* and the *Times* of London. The veteran censor examined every page of our periodical and frequently turned it upside down to scrutinize the pictures over again before he gave it his final approval.

The Annenbergs produced an impressive brochure of my career, illustrated with my picture by James Montgomery Flagg. It announced my new editorship to thousands of people of importance in the world of the Church and in the marts of advertising to whom it was explained that *Click* would be conducted on a constructive policy. Moe saw me during these increasing labors, expressing his satisfaction, but avoiding any remark that might open the subject of added pay. In the account of my experience he had noticed that I once held the title of checker champion of the Town of Hamden in Connecticut, when I was a boy. He offered me $100 to teach him the fine points of the game on his estate in the Pocono Mountains. But my job of editing, simultaneously, a weekly and a monthly pictorial gave me no time to make him acquainted with the advanced science of this pious pastime, which, later, might have helped his social contacts with fellow inmates in prison where his only hobby, that of making money, was beyond his reach, and mocked him.

Weeks of delicate negotiations were to pass before the Catholic Church was to agree to remove *Click* from the proscribed list of indecent literature which was affecting its circulation seriously, as well as that of other publications throughout the country. National campaigns had been launched against newsstand trash of a corrupting nature by religious groups of all denominations. Indecent literature in the United States had been the subject of a conference between the Pope and the American Cardinals who had recently returned from

Rome. Vigilance committees were organized and dealers who handled offensive reading matter were denounced from the pulpit. The crusade affected magazine publishers, high and low. *Life,* for instance, which was doing a superb pictorial job was condemned in high Catholic circles because it had printed a series of pictures of the celebration of a solemn high mass at St. Patrick's Cathedral in New York, and followed these photographs in the same issue with a feature on birth control.

I carried on an extensive correspondence about Annenberg's situation with numerous prelates. The Most Reverend John Francis Noll, Bishop of the Diocese of Fort Wayne, Indiana, was extremely helpful, and by conforming with his recommendations *Click* cleared the hurdles. All that the Church required was a show of the proper spirit. High Catholic dignitaries believed that sixty-four percent of the people of America had no religious beliefs and saw no reason why the remaining thirty-six percent should permit themselves to be dominated by the perverted tastes of the majority.

Click now made its own way unmolested as a popular pictorial, avoiding the shoals of criticism and satisfying a mass readership of 850,000 to 900,000 monthly buyers. Although advertising came in slowly, the magazine was enjoying a sizeable profit from its circulation. I had given the publication a sense of direction, keeping in mind that such periodicals must provide entertainment but I added an editorial page with a serious note, and whose policy was stoutly American. In pictures we exposed vigorously the Nazi Bund Camps, the underground Communist movement and the Fifth Column brigades, already evident many months before the European War of 1939. These features took hold and we received a heavy mail of approval.

Rescuing *Click* from the mire had required a year of grinding work and I decided it was time to ask for the reward which had been promised to me. Apparently the Annenbergs had an impression that I did not depend on my salary for a living and took full advantage of that assumption. Walter offered to add thirty-five dollars a week to my rotogravure pay, ignoring the time I had spent to save his magazine from ruin. He was completely surprised when I flung the enterprise in his face.

CHAPTER IV

Moe's interest in his monthly pictorial had been dampened by the campaigns of the decency leagues which had prevented him from driving his magazine's circulation to 2,000,000. He grew cold overnight to projects that engrossed him but which, for some sudden turn of affairs, ceased to have panoramic possibilities. He enjoyed the revenue which *Click* continued to produce in spite of its weathercock swing toward respectability but it lacked the gambler's thrill. Nevertheless, he did not want me to abandon it, and he ordered Walter to make a more equitable adjustment of my salary. The year of work I had devoted to this additional duty went unremunerated. These dealings appealed to Moe as "smart money," many of which were to be described later by John T. Flynn in his articles about Annenberg in *Collier's*.

I doubt that those involved in the unctuous negotiations which delivered the *Inquirer* to Moe for $9,000,000 in cash and the balance of $6,000,000 on the installment plan were aware that this fortune was part of an accumulation protected by feats of shyster legerdemain in Chicago which had defrauded the Government of the largest individual tax in American history. As a newspaper man, reasonably familiar with the Midas rackets of the country, all I knew about Moe was that he owned a racing-news service and published race-track publications. I had rubbed elbows with reputable people at the great tracks, including Governors and Senators and I saw nothing wrong in the thrill of a well-run horse race.

Others on the paper may have felt about the owner's business ramifications as I did, including John T. Custis, the editor in chief, a man of editorial integrity who had served the *Inquirer* for forty years, and Charles A. Tyler, president and general manager, pillar of the community, who had worried his way to the top of his profession and after the sale of the paper drew a salary which was reported to approach $65,000 a year. Tyler, a smallish man with a round, shrewd face and the figure of a Toby jug, functioned on strict business principles in a financial sanctum also decorated with mid-Victorian art. He saw to it that expenses were kept down, an honorable practice of all great journals. Moe admired his general manager's two-fisted watchfulness though it interfered at times with some of the publisher's circulation gambles. "Charley is all right," Moe said, while we were discussing a copy of the rotogravure choked to such a point with advertising that it had forced out a number of pictures. "With one eye closed he can spot a penny rolling in the wrong direction faster than any man I ever saw. That's good business policy."

We were to forget expenses for a time, however, when Moe plunged us all into a volcanic ferment to destroy the New Deal Administration in Pennsylvania and elect a more or less obscure judge as governor of the state. The Honorable Arthur H. James, whom the *Inquirer* decided to support as the Republican candidate for the Governorship in 1938, grasped Moe's political alpenstock with alacrity and made ready for the climb. He was honestly ambitious and he accepted his wealthy sponsor's background as ruggedly American and industrially legitimate. All he saw was what appeared on the surface. He was a little man with shrewd eyes and a red, wrinkled face and his days as a breaker boy in the mines impressed the publisher who still posed as a disciple of the early struggle.

As the campaign grew in excitement the Judge was soon hurrying in and out of Moe's office. I shook hands with the candidate on occasions which I probably remember better than he does. A man running for office will shake hands with you every time he meets you, if it were a dozen times a day, having so much on his mind that he may believe he is adding a different voter each time to his cause.

Moe asked me to prepare a three-page spread of pictures on the life of James for the rotogravure. In the Judge's rise from obscurity, the publisher said he saw a curious and significant parallel to the story of Abraham Lincoln. I took this problem home with me and decided, at all events, to leave Lincoln's kindly face out of it. Moe, however, wanted the Lincoln parallel in the captions. I could find no illustrations of the Judge as a rail splitter. We exhumed his rusty mining lamp and printed an old photograph of a group of boys, with their backs to the camera, picking coal in long chutes. One of the boys, the Judge's publicity manager said, was little Arthur at the age of twelve. The Judge once sang with the Shawnee Warblers and we found a picture of that vocal body. James had been lieutenant governor of his state. He was also the first president of a Kiwanis Club. There were other homespun activities recorded in an album. We pointed out that, like Lincoln, he understood the common people. Moe was disappointed, but I could do no more. Lincolns are not uncovered by millionaires.

The publisher was confident of victory and discussed with gusto the political horizon which lay before us. He believed the country was headed for a Republican landslide in 1940 and that as the Governor of Pennsylvania, a strategic state in a national election, James, who preached budgets and who was beginning to talk more and more like Coolidge, every day, would have an excellent chance of going to the White House. What Moe would be in those great days to come was beyond prediction. Perhaps he might begin by accepting an appointment as Ambassador to the Court of St. James's. I suggested this to "Fitz" during the battle, but he was too busy to laugh.

And Moe's ambitions were no laughing matter to the political opposition. He was probably the most important single factor to place James in the governor's chair, but his fight was not to be easily won. In an open contest he was completely vulnerable and Custis was hard put to it to answer, with lofty editorials, the denunciations of his old newspaper and its rambunctious owner. I marveled at some of the thrusts of the aging editor, backed to the wall, giving blow for blow on the old sheet which had recorded more than 100 years of American history. He wore a tired, sad expression. For years his integrity had counted in journalism and his comments had been reprinted all over the land. The *Inquirer* had been part of a great voice. But now, Custis, a man of sensitive refinement, a disciple of Dana and Godkin, had to defend the baron of the bookies.

The President's attention was drawn to the *Inquirer's* assaults on the New Deal, and he sent a letter to a friend in Philadelphia denouncing Moe and treating him with contempt. The communication received nation-wide circulation. Harold Ickes, Secretary of the Interior, went to Philadelphia at the height of the campaign and revealed Moe's past history in Chi-

cago. From every direction enemies of wide influence descended on the publisher. The attack by the President seemed
to inflate Moe's ego who assumed the attitude of a man suddenly transformed into a figure of national stature. At the
round table of his cafeteria he was combative and boastful, and
a number of us heard him say:

"Roosevelt figures the people are going to lose their form
of government anyhow, and so he thinks he might as well stay
in as long as possible. He doesn't want his organization destroyed, because he wants to run again in 1940. He'll never
get out until he's pushed out!"

Among those in Philadelphia who looked upon Moe as a
national menace was a wealthy, civic-minded gentleman named
Albert M. Greenfield. He was financially interested in the
affairs of the *Record*, which led the defense of the New Deal
in Pennsylvania and he had been attacked personally by the
Inquirer. In an address, broadcast by two radio stations, he
branded Moe as a panderer to gamblers from whom he had
gathered millions of dollars to buy the *Inquirer* to cloak himself
with respectability. He accused the publisher of having used
the fist and the blackjack to build up circulation for Hearst.
He charged that Moe was not satisfied with the clean competition the *Record* offered him but that he was out to destroy its
publisher, David Stern and all opposition. Greenfield had a
rugged, Biblical command of English and described Annenberg
as "a dog who had returned to its vomit." He completed his
lecture by warning the people that Moe had prepared a five-
year plan to take over the nation by buying political power in
pivotal states and establishing himself as an American Hitler.
Publisher Stern saw to it that the illuminating address, which
filled about three columns of type, appeared in the *Record* without any typographical errors.

The diatribe drove Moe into a fury and he called down upon
Greenfield all forms of malediction. I was not among those
who considered the broadcaster's prediction as completely fantastic. I had been required to approach, already, two or three
high officials in outside states, to flatter them with their life
stories in pictures in the rotogravure. In this way Moe might
open the door to some form of understanding to extend his
race-track wires where they were prohibited. One of those to
whom I had been asked to offer this form of publicity, which

guaranteed more than 1,000,000 readers, was Attorney General David T. Wilentz, of New Jersey, an honest and competent public servant. He politely rejected Annenberg's philanthropical proposal.

I remembered the methods which had turned the country over to the Harding gang, and the stories of their operations which had filled the press with scandal. The late Boss Roraback of Connecticut, who had played his part in returning the nation to "normalcy" had spent painful moments trying to explain to me when I was managing editor of the *Hartford Courant*, that there was no idealism in the ballot battles to gain political control of the nation. He had a realistic definition of it which, I discovered later in my experience, came closer to the facts. On set dates, prescribed on the calendars of our Democracy, an organization of men got together in an effort to seize the offices of government, not by some principle, necessarily, but by laying out the cash on the line. If you won, it would come back to you ten-fold, when you got into power. It was a great game! Annenberg was beginning to understand the first moves on its time-honored checkerboard.

But Moe was plagued by the facts of his dubious business background. The *Record* printed accounts of the investigation of a Legislative Commission at Harrisburg which disclosed that the publisher was the directing head of a nation-wide race-wire network that had competed with the notorious Waxey Gordon and once used the services of Scarface Al Capone. I saw Judge James, our gubernatorial candidate, the day after these revelations, as he hurried out of the publisher's office. His red face was a bit pale and he appeared to be staggered with surprise.

Moe wrapped himself in a smug cocoon of martyrdom. He became the main target of the campaign. His paper fought back with poisonous broadsides and the courtesies of libel suits were exchanged between mud-spattered contenders. Among politicians there was much gossip about the money he was pouring out of his inexhaustible coffers. He was sitting in a stiff poker game, but he had the chips. Occasionally he referred to the attacks aimed at him as "blows below the belt." He sat on the rim of his copy desk, reading headlines before they were sent to the composing room, often adding some of his own paprika to them. I passed by him one night in the city room as I was going home. He was scanning an edition of the *Record* which was boiling him in oil. "It's the penalty of leadership," he said resignedly.

The *Inquirer's* Taj Mahal had never before experienced the pandemonium that made its walls tremble on the night Judge James was elected. The sanctum of Victorian art resounded to the popping of champagne corks. Moe, flushed with victory, the floor of his office covered with bulletins of the returns, sat behind his desk, as if on a throne, in the middle of a cheering mob. With a roaring laugh, he shook his fist at Stern's paper across the street. Goblets of the sparkling juice that goes well with triumph were passed around to the politicians, the nattily-dressed, oily-haired promoters, the race-track enthusiasts, who slapped him on the back, urging him to greater heights. Moe proclaimed his impregnability by shouts of defiance. His huge white building was bathed in a blood-red waterfall of flares and, on the roof, cannon were shot off, their detonation reverberating up and down the squares of Broad Street, and making the *Record's* windows rattle. The king-maker was ready for the royal toboggan.

CHAPTER V

THE comet that was Moe flashed briefly in the political firmament. In the summer of 1939 he was indicted by a Chicago Federal Grand Jury in what was described as the largest income-tax fraud in the history of the nation. His son, Walter, was indicted with him. Moe's local contemporaries spread the tidings with the maximum of information and the minimum of comment, their headlines adding a revealing quality to the genius and morals of their new fellow townsman. Readers of the *Inquirer* were not kept in ignorance of the developments. Moe had to admit that the news was selling papers and printed it on his front page with the announcement that he "welcomed a court trial." A long statement said his bookkeeping system had not kept pace with the growth of his business. He told cronies that it was "the usual headache suffered by a leader in vast enterprises."

Matters reached a more realistic point when the publisher was fingerprinted after additional indictments charged him and a group of his colleagues with collaborating in a gigantic race-betting lottery, conspiracy to bribe a government witness and numerous other sins of omission and commission involving his projects. Father and son and their racing business associates surrendered to the United States Marshal in Chicago, pleaded not guilty, posted bonds totaling $175,000 and were released to await trial.

Moe assumed the attitude of a persecuted patriot and discussed his case freely, comparing himself with an innocent bystander harassed by scalawags jealous of his pursuit of happiness. When the final indictments fell on his head he was asked for a statement with regard to his feelings, to be used on the press wires. Looking the reporter in the eye, he said: "Like Nathan Hale, my only regret is that I have but one life to give for my country." This expression of unselfish sentiment was printed all over the nation.

Nathan Hale's patriotic sacrifice had slipped Moe's mind,

435

however, when he dictated to L. Stanley Kahn, one of his
numerous sons-in-law, a self-revealing letter, produced before
the Grand Jury which had branded the Annenberg race-infor-
mation service as an illegal monopoly and recommended that it
be killed by legislation in the states where it operated. Kahn
had apparently urged his father-in-law to widen his operations
in the racing scratch-sheet territory. To those unfamiliar with
the exhilarating literature of the scratch-sheet and the run-
down sheet, it may be explained that it is the latest information
furnished about the tracks to the bookie joints and the poolrooms, and provides the betting parlors with final developments
considered indispensable by gamblers before the races are run.
Internal Revenue agents were informed that this branch of
Moe's business alone had a gross return of $2,000,000 a year
and its profits were at least half of that sum. The publisher
was evidently satisfied with the *status quo* of this particular
realm when, sitting in the center of his web of activities, he
replied to his son-in-law:

"We simply cannot have everything, and like Mussolini
when he started out to grab Ethiopia, he had to carefully consider what he might be plunging into; but Mussolini had nothing to risk because Italy was on the bum and those who might
have opposed his ambitions had, by far and away, much more
to risk than Mussolini.

"Our position is similar to that of the English nation. We
in the racing field own three-quarters of the globe and manage
the balance. In other words, the few little nations that are
left have to pay us tribute to continue. Now, why isn't that
the most beautiful and most satisfactory position to be in which
ought to satisfy even me?

"Have you ever stopped to figure our earnings and how
they might be upset by a little mistake? For example, we have
a number of enemies with unusual ability that are eager for a
chance to get even with us and upset the monopoly, who would
be willing to work for almost nothing just for revenge, and
who would contribute their talent more enthusiastically than
our own people just for a chance to upset our applecart."

One fact soon emerged on the *Inquirer* and all that followed turned upon it. It became clear that Moe would not
weather the storm. He had established an unfortunate prece-
dent in a legal wrangle with one of his racing-business partners

who had sued him for an accounting of the profits. Moe's staggering answer, which presumably left the judge petrified, was presented as follows:

"It appears on the face of the complaint that the subject matter of the lawsuit is a division of profits made by supplying operators with certain essentials in the conduct of said gambling or handbook business. Equity will not take jurisdiction of an accounting between participants in *AN ILLEGAL BUSINESS*."

A collaborator of Moe's in the litigation, put the matter even more bluntly:

"From the facts alleged, it appears that the subject matter of the suit is the *DIVISION OF LOOT*, alleged to have been procured by supplying the instrumentalities indispensable to the operation of poolrooms and handbooks. A court of equity will not entertain an application for accounting between alleged coadventurers in an alleged *CRIMINAL ENTERPRISE*, nor aid the participant therein to recover his alleged *SHARE OF THE LOOT*."

Moe's smart practices had returned to haunt him. Still he talked of facing trial, but he exploded into sudden rages, blaming his troubles on Greenfield who, he said, had induced his competitor, Stern, of the *Record,* to see the President and start the avalanche.

"I wrecked the New Deal in Pennsylvania to show the people how to get back to sound, business principles of government and I'm going to be crucified for it. That's the kind of country we're living in!"

He had forgotten the news printed on the front page of his own paper which disclosed that the indictments climaxed two years of investigation by Internal Revenue agents and nine weeks of Grand Jury hearings. Fifty auditors had been employed to break down the complicated and surreptitious bookkeeping of the many dubious companies he had spawned. He was like a man who had set out to round up a swarm of bees and who was blindly fighting off the raging inmates which the hive of his past let loose upon him.

Moe, now an example of humility and submission, went to Washington with his son and a brigade of lawyers to see Attorney General Frank Murphy in an effort to effect a settlement and keep out of prison. Belated but properly planted donations to religious charities evoked dignified gestures of clerical magnanimity from high church dignitaries who joined with powerful politicians in an appeal to men in power to permit the publisher to pay the Government the millions of which he had defrauded it, and go free. But the grim, bushy-browed Murphy told the press that nothing could soften the fervor of his prosecution. Moe could not understand why a man whose brains produced an income larger in one day than the yearly salary of a Cabinet officer should have to endure the indignities of a trial. Murphy, on the other hand, wondered how Moe, who owed the Government an income tax of $313,000 in 1932 had got around the matter by paying only $308. He was charged with owing income taxes of $1,692,000 in 1936 and paying only $475,000. Altogether the Government claimed he owed $5,548,000 in income taxes and penalties from 1932 to 1936.

Respected Jews in high places in the nation, many of them leaders in their professions became deeply concerned over the relentless warfare going on between Stern and Annenberg, two Jewish publishers of important newspapers. Efforts to settle the feud, or at least to soften its overtones to pianissimo, were useless. Moe insisted upon a last-ditch fight. He had become sharp of tongue in his desperation, and he injured himself even further among the religious of his community by insulting in his own office a rabbi of national reputation who had visited the publisher with the hope of obtaining a contribution for a synagogue. I have it on the authority of a man of unimpeachable character who was present at the conference that Moe turned upon the learned preacher and said:

"You'll get no money from me. Religion is a racket! It's the greatest racket in the world. I know all about it because I have read every book on the subject!"

Walter, who had told friends after the election victory that his father's considerations included a path to the White House for the *Inquirer's* "mining Lincoln," became a saddened figure. The millions that would have to be paid to the Government was a subject whose contemplation was even more painful to him than it was to Moe. The latter, who thoroughly enjoyed trampling upon the bowels of his foes, was less downcast than his son before the final blow fell. To be sure, he exploded into a torrent of talented profanity in his Victorian gallery when, his troubles apparently having been rocked into a delicate sleep in the press, alert reporters of Frank Knox's *Chicago Daily News*, nudged the Attorney General about the progress of the case. This enterprise spread the story all over again on the front pages of the nation. Knox, one-time general manager for Hearst, was familiar with Moe's trails, and the powerful Chicago paper illuminated long accounts of the scandal with photographs of the bookie-baron's estates and Roman swimming pools.

These developments naturally had an influence on the *Inquirer's* operations. Its city editor, one Elias Z. Dimitman, suddenly was promoted over Fitzpatrick's head to the post of executive editor and soon was the oracle of our shifting policies. He had attracted Moe's attention by accepting responsibility for the bootlegged publication of an important State Supreme Court decision before it was officially handed down. The incident made Pennsylvania newspaper men gasp. The news had been siphoned in some mysterious manner and Moe denied all knowledge of it when he was hauled to the witness stand in an investigation of the affair, and which he privately considered a smart piece of strategy. Dimitman was a tall, gangling man with a trim, sandy mustache. His devotion to Moe seemed to have taken on the form of physical imitation and he stalked about, head thrust out, his hands deep into his hip pockets while he peered through large eyeglasses with a knowing look.

During this excitement I had been left pretty much to myself as the head of Annenberg's two pictorials, and they became a laboratory for my experiments in satisfying mass readership. The monthly served as an outlet for my penchant toward editorial crusades. The response from vast groups grasping their messages through the eye, from a series of photographs telling a story, was immediate. It accounted for the fact that millions of people attended the movies every day, and listened to the radio, an enjoyment requiring less mental effort than reading. The weekly rotogravure and *Click* were studied by 5,000,-000 people each month and I was having an interesting time conducting experiments up and down the backbone of the nation.

My only hope of holding *Click's* circulation and attracting advertising above the grade of Lydia Pinkham's compound,

reducing tablets and hair dyes lay in pictorial crusades of national interest. In this respect I took advantage of my loathing for the Nazis. When Lindbergh accepted a decoration
from the Hitler regime I reviewed his career in pictures and
roundly denounced him. Instead of ruining the magazine, as
the circulation director had predicted, the condemnation of
the flyer created such a newsstand demand that the pictorial's
entire issue of 900,000 copies was sold out.

Some of my crusading enterprises took queerly ironic turns.
I was anxious to place a photographer on a large gambling
ship, anchored under the name of the *Rex*, three miles from
the coast of Southern California. The idea I had in mind was
to expose the entire enterprise in a series of pictures showing
clamoring patrons playing roulette wheels. I believed the assignment would encounter serious difficulties. When the chief
agent of the ship, a seasoned gambler known as Tony Cornero
Stralla, heard that our cameraman was on Moe's payroll, the
photographs became immediately available and our photographer received the consideration of an honored guest. Among
the conveniences on the ship, which had a daily attendance of
2,500 persons of irresponsible wealth who were transported
from land in swift, sea-going launches, was Moe's racing-news
service which was received by radio telephone. We printed
four pages showing the gambling operations in detail. Stralla
looked upon the feature as advertising of incredible value and
ordered several thousand copies of the magazine. The publicity, however, caused an unexpected stir and Government
authorities put the gambling ship out of action in a bloodless
engagement.

I had time occasionally to ponder over the achievements of
some of my friends who were trying to enjoy the rewards of
concentration and perseverance. Joseph Connolly, with whom
I had begun my newspaper career in New Haven, had become
general manager of Hearst Consolidated Publications, at a
salary of $65,000 a year. As *Time Magazine* described it in
its scalpel style, he was striving to put Hearst's empire in
order "before the old man died." During Joe's widespread
activities he found himself in a burning airplane, prayed for his
life and landed safely. His prayers appeared in various publications. *Time* referred to the episode as a modern miracle.
It was the only case ever recorded of a Hearst executive hav-

ing received an answer to such a supplication, and I became interested in the phenomenon. My prayers had never been heard, apparently, when I was a Hearst editor, and some of them were of a rather high order. Furthermore, it was the first official revelation that one of Hearst's "little Turks" actually had prayed.

I wrote a piece about the matter for *Click* and printed Joe's picture, handling the details with the preciseness which might have been used by Ernest Renan, whose explanations of miracles are still first-rate reading. I was pained to learn that Joe interpreted my comments as a fling of Voltarian cynicism. Joe's health soon cracked under the pressure of his job and for weeks his recovery seemed hopeless. This time there were many, including myself, who prayed for him and when he was able to get out of bed he retired to a less strenuous post at the age of forty-four, presumably with more leisure to reflect upon the thing called success.

Stanley Walker, once my fellow inmate, had come to Philadelphia to edit the *Evening Public Ledger* under an impressive fanfare. After his hideous experience on Hearst's *American* he had led a gallant sortie as editor of *The New York Woman* before repairing behind the portcullis of the *Herald Tribune*, where he belonged. To the shame of those who pried him loose again, he embarked this time on an undertaking which was to make his explorations on the *Mirror* seem like editing the old *Youth's Companion*.

With a blunt naïveté Walker proceeded to make a newspaper out of the *Ledger* and had soon given it a sense of alertness which shook off its years of pithlessness. It sparkled at times with his satire and mordant wit. However, the saying that no thoroughly occupied man was ever yet very miserable does not necessarily apply to Philadelphia newspaper work. After being made use of in good earnest, to the limit of his endurance and capacity, Walker was informed that expenses had to be cut to the bone. He found himself much in the situation of a native of India during the monsoon period. The management imported a budget balancer who, for years, had been going about the country pulling papers out of the red and editors out by the roots. With exemplary gratitude, publishers paid him well for his results, dictated by the methodical calculation of profit and loss, but which invariably left a trail of anguished journalists who suffered from the delusion that they were indispensable. I had always managed to be one job ahead of this pursuing economist.

Stanley, finding himself surrounded, fought bravely to save his staff, with the tenacity of Gordon of Khartum holding off the tribes of the Mahdi. But the strategy of the counting room always wins such battles. The disgusted Texan, who had been named by *Time* as "the most famed city editor in the land," left in a manner which the *Ledger* (had it not ignored the episode in its columns) would have described as "posthaste," and flung himself into the club car of a fast train for New York. Joining him in the flight was his columnist, Joel Sayre, who, on the wing, interviewed his erstwhile chief about Philadelphia. Both agreed that it was full of the remains of our past civilization and Sayre's article was given full space in the *Record* which, apparently, had reached the same conclusion.

I turned my attention to the Nazis for the last time before I was to be shorn of my powers as a crusader under the banner of Annenberg. The German American Volksbund was sowing its poisonous seed on camp sites in seventy counties throughout the country and the most sinister of these outposts, where Fritz Kuhn, the "American Fuehrer" held forth, was twelve miles away from my farm. I had been visited by irate neighbors who wanted to put the Nazi nest to the torch. As an investigator accredited to a Congressional Committee I decided to make an inspection of the local Bund.

The Nazis had acquired 130 acres of Bucks County property, two miles from the town of Sellersville, and met undisturbed in a club known as "Deutschhorst" (The Eagle's Nest), a venerable stone building used as a mill by Pennsylvania patriots during the Revolution. It was as snug as a fort. Close by was a shooting range where storm troopers indulged in target practice with high-powered rifles.

I got into the place by means which need not be revealed here as they may be useful again. Publicity was the only thing really feared by the tribal rats occupying these staked-off claims on the soil of freedom, but American journalism was not yet much excited about such portents of worse things to come.

The brown-shirted Bund lieutenant, whose suspicions I dispelled at the door of "Deutschhorst," said to me: "The passvoit is Chawge Vashingdon." As I walked by his raised arm

held in the gesture of a salute now familiar to a crushed continent, he barked: "Heil Hitler!" The cry was taken up by the
target shooters and the air echoed with it, twenty-five miles
from Independence Hall which shelters the Liberty Bell that
rang out the news of the Declaration.

Inside the stone building a drinking crowd was celebrating
the rape of Czecho-Slovakia, bellowing the *Horst Wessel Song*
and banging beer mugs. The walls were bare but for an enlarged, framed photograph of Hitler, draped with swastika
banners. When Fritz Kuhn was arrested later near the Pennsylvania border during his last flight before his imprisonment,
he was attempting to reach this hide-away. "Deutschhorst"
was the camp where Kuhn had referred to Roosevelt sneeringly
as "President Rosenfeld" and had made a ringing speech in
which he said that "Hitler would lick the world." Kuhn had
participated with Hitler in the Munich *Putsch* of 1923, and I
reproduced from a German magazine a photograph of the
"American Fuehrer" being greeted by the Dictator.

I was informed that in certain Bund meetings the American
flag was used as a carpet covered with cuspidors. Photographs
of these orgies were being taken and sent to Berlin where they
were printed in publications directed by Joseph Goebbels to
show the brazen contempt displayed for Democracy by the
Nazis in America. I produced a full-page illustration of this
desecration in *Click* and the anger that it aroused in many quarters brought about a number of results, not the least of which
was the closing down of the Bund camp near my farm, amid
scenes of old-fashioned American wrath. Newspapers copied
the picture and I was told by Federal agents that its influence
in wiping out other foul nests of the Bund was considerable.
As my name appeared on the magazine which I had used as a
medium to give its readers a glimpse of the "wave of the future" the personal threats I received were to be expected. In
New York, the office of *Click* was menaced to such a point by
inhabitants of the Yorkville district, which was, and is, infested
by Nazis, that it was forced to call for police protection.

These campaigns were considered beyond my jurisdiction
as a circulation builder and the excitement they caused had a
direct effect on my pictorial activities on *Click*. I received a
memorandum from an important figure in Moe's magazine organization requesting me to stop my attacks on Hitlerism. I

put the little, yellow order away among my curiosities of Americana. I learned that a number of Philadelphia politicians opposing the New Deal believed my crusades were offending the so-called German vote which, in Pennsylvania, as elsewhere, was ready to swing to anyone opposing Roosevelt in the approaching Presidential election. The Republican candidate, a fine patriot, has long since repudiated the thickly accented cries of "Ve Vant Villkie," occasionally noticeable during the Convention of 1940 in the "Cradle of Liberty," where the "passvoit of Chawge Vashingdon" once had an American ring.

CHAPTER VI

As months went by it became evident that Moe, out on bail, was maintaining an attitude of defiance with visible effort. He appeared occasionally at the head table of his cafeteria where he sat like an inscrutable Caligula who had bestowed the priesthood upon his horse Incitatus and challenged the world to criticize him. His millions of dollars had become useless to him. He could not undo what had been wrongly done.

His mind turned to circulation schemes, vast projects to make his paper dominate over great areas. He became contemptuous of expense with proposals that made his advisers shudder. He plunged about the building, his head extended as though under a yoke with which he had dragged his army of relatives for whom he had amply provided, his many corporations and the whole load that had brought him his fortune.

He remembered a memorandum I had sent him about a prophecy made by the far-seeing Kent Cooper, general manager of the Associated Press who said that the increasing importance of pictures in newspapers eventually would reach a point when photographs would occupy half the space of the dailies. The prediction had given Moe a stupendous idea for an experiment on a wide scale but his executives were too alarmed about his future to encourage him. He came to my office to discuss it. He wanted to launch the first daily rotogravure magazine in America. It would have contained photographs in color and the latest pictures of the world's news, printed as rapidly as the intricate process would permit, with advanced production. I told him his great presses made the project possible. The color pictorial would have been, to my knowledge, the first of its kind in the history of world printing and in all probability it could have given his daily the largest circulation of any standard-size newspaper in the country.

"They think I'm crazy," Moe said, pathetically. "They're not 'yessing' me now; everybody says 'no,' and I know why. They think I'm going to jail!"

445

And it was true. The timorous people around him already imagined that he was behind the bars. They would not have understood that he was not entirely to blame for what he was. He had desired to compensate himself for his early poverty and by hard work, imagination, and then by cunning, had accumulated a fortune which was worse than the privation that had created his lust for gain.

Moe began to break. At times he couldn't shake off the conviction that he was going to prison and would spurt out the thought during conferences, where his associates hung their heads. "I'm going to jail!" he moaned. "I'm going to jail!" Old men on his paper, fixed like lichens to the stones of the building, could not understand the convulsions that were going on.

I attended the last conference in which Moe took part with his chief executives before he got into prison garb. Suave gentlemen from the poll-distilling laboratories of Dr. George Gallup were telling us why people read the *Inquirer*—and why some did not. The publisher listened tolerantly to the lecturers while they turned over pages of huge circulation charts. His careworn face broke into a twisted smile when one of the Gallup gospel-guides propounded the theory that photographs of trim-figured Hollywood stars in one piece bathing suits drew more women subscribers than men. This reversed a number of conclusions on the subject and pulled Moe out of his lethargy. He wanted an explanation. The chalk-talker explained, according to his research, that women who worried about their proportions indulged in the pastime of mentally transplanting their own heads on the pictured forms they envied, and thereby absorbed much satisfaction. The findings, coming from a Gallup apostle, received grave consideration although they were opposed to years of Moe's calculations about the value of sex appeal in pictorial art.

"Well, by God, that's something new, anyhow," he commented; "but I'll stick to the old theory."

Slowly the charts were unfolded before us while the Gallup examiners, in bland voices, droned the reports of the populace. The interpreters stood in front of the exhibit like tutors who recognize originality and love to encourage it. They described newspaper work as "traffic in readership." The proceedings seemed to irritate Moe, restless in his chair. He knew circulation in the raw. Finally he swung with a bewildered expression from the gigantic guide books.

"Traffic in readership—hell!" he grunted. "This business is getting to be too damned scientific!"

The remarks he usually made about his troubles were not long delayed. The European War had already begun and when the charts reached the news of horse racing the Gallupers informed us that readers of track information were increasing by larger degrees than those interested in the outcome of the battles.

"See that!" Moe exclaimed. "People want to know all about the race track and I'm going to be put in jail for it!"

The publisher became more indulgent toward his fellow human beings. When Premier Edouard Daladier had ordered labor uprisings in France to be put down by armed force, Moe told Fitzpatrick to "give that guy 'Della-dear' a good play." He believed the French statesman's defiance of the organized workers was setting a good example for American employers. But now, Moe said it was unfortunate that the underprivileged of California had lost their "ham and eggs" campaign.

"The country will have to do something about the down-and-outers. There's getting to be too many of them. That's how all the troubles began in history. You got to feed those people."

These views, however, were not reflected in the *Inquirer's* editorial pages.

The haggard millionaire wandered into my office to discuss the frustration of his daily rotogravure project. He had seldom been balked, and talked as though he had received advance information of the annihilation of the universe. I believe that he had already made up his mind to plead guilty to the charges against him and he carried himself with the appearance of a man who was slowly being crushed. The conversation led to topics we rarely discussed—my farm and the offer he had made three years ago, to buy it. He was curious about the fact that I could drop office matters every night and go home. He was familiar with the intensive life I had led in New York.

"I know now why you wouldn't sell the farm. I suppose you live in a little cottage where it's quiet, away from everything."

He looked at me curiously with a long sigh of defeat and resignation.

"You get home there, every night, and nobody bothers you and you can forget everything—no worries—and you can sleep. And when you wake up, the sun shines. Jesus!"

He rose in utter weariness from his chair and walked with dragging steps to the door where he turned around slowly.

"You know," he said, "you're not such a God-damned fool, after all! What is money, for Christ's sake?"

A newspaper of high momentum invariably functions from a central spark and when Moe's light grew dim the *Inquirer* proved that old printing theory. Whatever might have been his faults, Moe had never been accused of being super-sensitive and he had given his paper a punch which now was going out of it. His indifference to departmental problems became more pronounced day by day. While I continued to conduct his monthly pictorial and weekly rotogravure he gave no attention to what I was doing but for an episode in which I unwittingly offended him. I had projected a feature on national defense to appear in *Click* with the reproduction of a painting of Roosevelt in color on its cover. The management threw the President's picture into the wastebasket and I received word that Moe said:

"I don't want that guy on any cover of my publications. I'm not going to give people the impression that I'm trying to get a favor out of him."

In its original conception *Click* had included a section of risqué cartoons in color, an idea Moe had appropriated and enlarged upon from the magazine *Esquire*. For the early issues he had personally selected from this form of art a number of drawings which conformed with his goatish humor and they had been largely responsible for the boycott by the Catholic Church. My assistant, Miller, had made the interesting discovery that the daring drawings in *Esquire* were passed by the censors, including those in Canada, because the colorful fifty-cent publication carried an imposing list of authors whose prominence acted as a soporific upon criticism which might be aroused by pictures which, at times, were unusually gay. Another theory upon which the censors operated was that little boys whose purity had to be protected could not afford a half dollar to scrutinize a magazine showing ladies in deshabille.

The drawings were undoubtedly printed with the high purpose of attracting subscribers to the works of writers of intellectual quality. Whatever may have been the case, *Esquire* circulation was not retarded by the boudoir scenes which appeared "to the reader's intense delight and disapproval," as Mark Twain once remarked about the novels of Elinor Glyn.

Click could not consort with prominent authors and had to pick its humor gingerly, a task which Moe's son supervised because he thought he knew how far one could go along those lines. Walter would select a drawing and with mirthless laughter, dictate a caption for it which invariably pitched me into abysmal gloom. Indictments had been exploding like bombshells over our marble shelter one afternoon when I entered his office with a batch of humor to submit to him for his approval. He examined the drawings apparently without seeing them, his mind distracted by the impending calamity that was to send his father to prison and deduct millions of dollars from the family fortune. Suddenly, he thrust the cartoons at me.

"Take them away," he said. "How the hell can I laugh?"

Moe, who stood at the door of his sanctum, across the anteroom from Walter's office, stopped me to look at the pictures under my arm. He peered dejectedly at them, discarding many, but, unexpectedly, he pounced on one that gripped his interest and, to see it in a better light, he took it near a window where he emitted strange sardonic howls.

"Here," he said. "Print this one. It's funny and, by God, it's the truth!"

The drawing in his hand reflected the bitterness and cynicism in his face. Perhaps it recalled early struggles for existence. The picture represented two gaunt charwomen, on their knees, looking up from washpails at a group of haughty females in gorgeous array, glittering with jewels, and escorted through a mopped lobby from a soiree by leering gentlemen in evening dress. One scrubwoman was saying to the other:

"What did virtue ever get us?"

I continued my work with an odd dispassionateness. My last crusade in the monthly took the form of an attack on the hypocritical pact between Stalin and Hitler. Dimitman informed me that the management wanted all editorial comments thrown out of the magazine. *Click*, which reached a large

audience became spiritually homeless and among the advertising agencies remained in the situation of a fallen woman
who deeply regretted her past and was trying to be helpful at
a church supper.

The war immediately added to my complications on the
rotogravure.   Travel-bureau executives complained that the
advertising of the French Line and the Italian Line was being
jeopardized by pictures of fortifications, armies on the march.
Advertisements appealing to American tourists to "come to
sunny Italy to relax amid an Old-World culture" were twisted
into ghastly irony by the photographs of destruction which surrounded them.   Walter was fearful of the possibility that the
Sunday *Inquirer's* large output in Canada would be barred by
the censors because of pictures which showed nothing but
Allied reverses.   The blitzkrieg had not yet struck France and
huge spreads were produced of the "impregnable Maginot
Line" to comfort panic-stricken business men whose foreign
commerce had fallen under Hitler's shadow.   War hid in our
photographic darkrooms, so hideous had it become to print.

I turned from the murder of mankind to photographs in
color of paintings by famous old masters and here I received
my worst setback.   I wanted to reproduce a series of pictures
of the priceless art collection of Joseph E. Widener, noted
Philadelphia capitalist.   He owned an awesome gallery which
included Rembrandts, Titians, Raphaels, Gainsboroughs, Van
Dycks, Holbeins, Millets and countless others.   But Widener
was also interested in racing, being the principal owner of the
Hialeah Track in Miami and had refused to permit Annenberg
to enter it with his wires and staff, so that Moe had to float a
balloon over the racecourse and absorb his news from the air
through binoculars. Moe never forgot this inconvenience. For
this reason I was prevented from using our great color presses
to show a million people some of the finest paintings the world
had produced.

Moe reduced his organization to a state of hypnotic gloom
in the Spring of 1940 when he pleaded guilty to his tax fraud.
He announced the decision after pacing the floor of a Chicago
hotel suite for an entire night.   "It's the best gamble," he said.
"I'll take the rap!"   His legal staff told the press that he hoped
to soften whatever blow might fall upon his son, who had
pleaded not guilty.

It was "the best gamble." The publisher was sixty-three years old and had been indicted seven times and billed for $5,548,384 in unpaid income taxes, penalties, and interest which brought his personal liability for his crime to more than $9,000,000. He was liable, upon conviction on all charges, to 100 years in prison. As one of his convicted colleagues remarked on his way to jail: "Nathan Hale should live that long!"

Moe returned from Chicago thinner and grayer, to await final disposition of the case which was to be made by Judge James H. Wilkerson of the Federal District Court, who had sent Al Capone to Alcatraz. The publisher described the judge as "a tough baby." Sentencing was delayed to permit Annenberg's busy lawyers to confer with Government authorities in an attempt to reach an agreement on the exact amount and manner of payment of the millions of dollars Uncle Sam demanded.

The *Inquirer's* Taj Mahal became a temple of voiceless woe. Executive editor Dimitman issued a memorandum warning everyone on the paper to refrain from discussing Moe's dolors. One paragraph of the gag rule carried a peculiar implication regarding the integrity of the Government's investigators:

"Efforts may be made to entrap employees of this newspaper into statements or actions which, however innocent or well meaning, COULD BE TWISTED BY GOVERNMENT AGENTS to charges that attempts were being made by employees of the *Inquirer* to interfere with the case."

The Annenberg fraud was treated by the public prints as a national scandal. *Time Magazine*, in its quaintly readable fashion, reviewed the matter under the subdivision of "Crime" and reprinted a cartoon by Daniel Fitzpatrick in the *St. Louis Post-Dispatch* showing a pigmy Annenberg fleeing a gigantic Uncle Sam. The caption, which made old *Inquirer* executives squirm, was "Anybody Making Book on This Race?" Moe had become "picture material" and found newspaper photographers merciless. *Life* reproduced his photograph in a "candid," full-length shot as the camera had caught him pacing in agitation the corridors of the court. It became part of my task to weed out from the country's outpourings of the picture services, scores of photographs, for which Moe had to pay, and which illustrated the latest phases of his plight. These were not printed in the *Inquirer*, but were taken down in baskets to our department of archives, whose bewildered librarian never knew whether his job would be safe if, faithful to his duty, he should file them, either under "Annenberg" or under "Crime," for the guidance of future journalistic historians. Moe had personally crashed into the only kind of news that really interested him, because it had the quickest circulation turnover—and that was crime news.

"Even Winchell is jumping on me," he said, referring to the following item in the gossiper's syndicated column in the *Ledger*:

"Overheard in 46th Street where the bookmakers were groaning about the new ban on wager-making via phone: 'It's gettin' tougher and tougher to make a crooked dollar!' "

Moe preferred to avoid any retaliations about this comment and warned me in a memorandum to disregard the tattler's shots. I recalled that Kobler had turned over to me, during our *Mirror* regime a warm letter of protest from Walter Annenberg who asked protection for his relatives from the snooping columnist's innuendos.

Meditating upon Winchell, while my wife and I were riding with Moe in his limousine, he said:

"He's got something on the ball and he knows too many things about too many people. Hearst will not get rid of him in a hurry."

It was the final discussion I was to have on the paper about Winchell whose voice I heard for the last time on the radio, which Winifred accidentally tuned in one evening. The peeper was offering $100,000 in cash to anybody who could prove that his real name is Lipshetz. He was then acquainting his audience with the Bill of Rights, whose privileges he had almost exhausted years before he had perceived their existence. But what was in a name, now that he had uncovered the benefits of a freedom which made the Americanism of Lipshetz as precious as that of Honeysuckle Lapides?

CHAPTER VII

I now became part of the magnetic vortex of Moe's rotating litigation which seemed to whirl us all about, faster and faster, like little planets and satellites. The publisher's capable lawyer, Weymouth Kirkland, and his platoon of sweating pleaders had reached a settlement with the Government, cutting down the sum to be paid to $8,000,000. The agreement had to be signed by Annenberg and Henry Morgenthau, Jr., Secretary of the Treasury, which may or may not have flattered Moe when he affixed his name as the joint signature of a document with a Cabinet member. Frank Murphy, now far above the problems of Moe's financial vivisection was occupied with less sordid reflections in the robes of a justice of the United States Supreme Court and had been succeeded as Attorney General by Solicitor General Jackson, whom the *Inquirer* had lampooned in its New Deal pictures. Moe, who had pleaded guilty to one count of his income tax fraud, found himself in the role of a self-confessed criminal and was told to return to Chicago to be sentenced. Jackson ordered a number of the charges dismissed and one of the defendants released from future claims was Walter who was saved from further embarrassment.

Sudden changes in policy were invoked on the *Inquirer* to create a halo over the publisher's character and moral purpose when he appeared in court again with the hope of escaping prison. Editorial attacks on the New Deal were pigeonholed. My tabloid rotogravure section was changed over night to what is sometimes described as "respectable size" and a full page in color was devoted to a photograph of Cardinal Dougherty, Archbishop of Philadelphia, in his robes of office. Moe had founded an award for police heroism, and Philadelphia's "finest" circulated petitions asking clemency for him. His pictorial vaudeville was banished from my Sunday offering which almost immediately fell back upon the cat and saucer art he had abhorred. Gone were his "Micky Finns," horned vipers and the "Stranglers of Paris." Remaining on my hands were the photographs of the Berber beauties of North Africa, smiling innocently and bared to the waist, and which Moe once said we could print because the *"National Geographic* got away with it."

The *Inquirer* announced itself, according to the legend at the top of its front page as "An Independent Newspaper for All the People," New Dealers included. Above its editorials appeared a platform which was closer to the Ten Commandments than anything I had ever seen under a masthead:

> To print the news accurately and fearlessly, but never to be content with merely printing the news : to strive always to uphold the principles of our American Democracy, to war relentlessly against alien "isms," to fight intolerance, to be the friend and defender of those who are persecuted and oppressed; to demand equal justice for employer and employed . . . to expose political hypocrisy and corruption; to be just, to be fair and above all to be unswervingly independent; to fight and never to cease fighting to maintain the sanctity of personal liberty and the inviolability of human rights.

Moe's adversities caused all sorts of complications in his editorial department. The daily carried the syndicated outpourings of the largest assemblage of columnists that ever capered about a press. Among the better known of these Indian drum-beaters who kept the faithful informed were Dorothy Thompson, Mark Sullivan, General Hugh S. Johnson, Raymond Clapper, Westbrook Pegler, Paul Mallon, H. I. Phillips, Emily Post, and a menagerie of war experts. As Annenberg's affairs had become the talk of the nation, some of these soothsayers felt inclined at times to interpolate Moe's woes for the vast public which believes that a department that does not agree with the paper that prints it must be telling the truth. *Inquirer* editors struggling with this material yelped in agony when some of the syndicated fulminations, for which Moe had to pay under signed contracts, began to hint he was the worst bandit at large since Jesse James. On these occasions the offending columns were removed from the paper without any explanation of their disappearance, readers being left to assume that the analysts had temporarily fallen into some cosmic hole. My old friend Harry Phillips' pillar was pitched out permanently over some piece of humor which Moe said was "too spontaneous."

Westbrook Pegler, whose indignation is proverbial and often justified, wrote a sermon about the income-tax scandal that has yet to be equaled as invective against a newspaper publisher. He said Annenberg's character was low, cunning and criminal; and charged that his racing-news monopoly was in league with the underworld; and that he had been willing to corrupt the form of government which had given him his chance to become a rich man. This matter appeared in many parts of the country but was deposited in the wastebasket by Moe's editor who handled it after the manner of grappling for a hot potato with a pair of tongs. While Westbrook vanished from his usual corner during this episode our delivery trucks were rushing about Philadelphia with huge red signs which announced:

READ PEGLER!
EXCLUSIVELY IN THE INQUIRER
HE DOESN'T PULL HIS PUNCHES!

General Johnson adopted a more philosophical attitude regarding the upheaval, being inclined to sympathize with anybody in a fatal struggle with the New Deal and produced an article which Moe apparently interpreted as some vague mitigation of his conduct. It appeared under a three-column heading in large type.

Soon the entire establishment was floundering in an eruption of cost cutting that might have made Stanley Walker's monsoon seem like a playful breeze. Money had to be saved. The American Telephone and Telegraph Company had withdrawn its wires from the Annenberg racing-news service, and Moe's great bonanza was dead. In the ensuing uproar I had to abandon *Click* which flung itself on the altar of sex to hold a circulation which no longer had to be hindered by Moe's political reputation. The extra salary I had been receiving to direct its operations had not been too small to escape the attention of General Manager Tyler who sliced it off. I saw him for the last time in a conference about extra labors for which I had not been paid and which he described as problems beyond his jurisdiction. He was carrying out the faithful duty of embalming every dollar that could be rescued, his task of trimming here, cutting and squeezing there, being reflected in his strained face.

Moe became responsible for a number of queer things before he was sentenced, and I attributed them to some final spark of defiance when the incumbrances of his troubles narrowed his sphere of activity and forced him to truckle to conservative tastes. While the *Inquirer* was cast into a mold almost angelic to serve as a silent character witness for him in court he filled the street-floor windows of his building with the most remarkable assortment of murderous weapons I had ever seen. Each carried on a label a description of the crime in which it had played its part: the blood-stained saw with which a mother had hacked her baby to death; the revolver taken from Al Capone when he was arrested in Philadelphia; the machine gun used by "Slick Willy Sutton" in the holdup of the Corn Exchange Bank. The police which had furnished the exhibit controlled the mobs of morons and riffraff of the town drawn as though by a magnet to view the gruesome collection. For days, strange, pushing creatures plastered their noses against the glass. A smaller window adjoining, hardly noticed, displayed bulletins describing the fall of nations.

Unmindful of his paper, which held rigidly to the path of virtue, Moe launched a ghastly affair which he called *Intimate Detective* whose covers in color featured pictures of undressed females in the throes of a horrible death, invariably choked by a clutching hand. One issue, which I was looking over at home as something unique, gave my wife a nightmare. Its main display was occupied by a mystery entitled: "Trailing the Hooded Rapist of Los Angeles." A photograph of full-page size showed a nude model standing in a bathtub in an attitude of petrified horror while a frightful figure in a black cowl climbed through her window, his fingers reaching out. Annenberg's *Wholesaler's Guide* reproduced this bone-chilling conception with commercial candor under the announcement: "This Ad Makes for Sales in Los Angeles."

Moe finally appeared before Judge Wilkerson to hear his fate pronounced. The publisher's lawyers, an array of brains gathered from Chicago, New York, Washington and St. Louis, fought with exemplary courage to keep him out of the penitentiary, but their ringing defense assumed the quality of a diminishing echo when the Government, in unhoneyed words, presented its evidence. The facts filled many columns of the press and historians of these legal radiations could only point out it was fortunate for Moe that he never had any social aspirations.

Painful to me was the revelation that the wedding of Moe's daughter, Harriet Annenberg Ames, an event which I had been instructed by Kobler, when I was editor of the *Mirror* to recognize as a matter of the utmost social importance, was entered in the books of Moe's chief track publication as the expenses of a racing convention. It had been held at the Hotel Pierre in New York and celebrated by a series of dinners and entertainments for hundreds of guests, with special Pullman cars chartered at Chicago to transport crowds of them. Society news has always been my worst disillusionment.

Other disconcerting matters made themselves known while the judge rocked patiently back and forth behind the bench, occasionally asking questions to satisfy himself that the intent to defraud had been plain. In the ramifications appeared the name of a woman who received from Moe a handsome weekly check which any of his editors would have envied. The money was charged to *Racing Form*, for which the Government said she had never performed any services. The money, amounting to several thousand dollars in one year, appeared on the publication's books as expenses for "track hustling." According to Government evidence large sums used to pay the family household expenses of the publisher, were charged to *Racing Form* also as the salaries of "track hustlers." At any moment I felt I might be described as having hustled in a similar manner as editor of *Click*, a disclosure that would have been less surprising to me than to the stern bishops with whom I had engaged in a long correspondence in Moe's behalf.

A more fantastic picture of brutally selfish wealth could hardly have been painted by the Government prosecutor who described Moe as a money-obsessed man whose desire to evade his taxes was equally as keen as his zeal to expand his fortune. His famous Wyoming "ranch," whose expenditures involved an unreported income of $109,000 used for swimming pools, riding stables, guest cabins, electrical cooking equipment, sheep liver for trout feed, riding clothes and other assorted luxuries drew a final outburst of wrath from the District Attorney, an irate Westerner, who shouted:

MY LAST MILLION READERS

"Not one dime was even spent for a cow on this stake of the lone ranger!"

Eventually the judge stopped rocking. He had heard enough and he sentenced Moe to three years in Federal prison. The publisher received time to adjust his affairs and he returned from Chicago to ponder over the fact that he still had to pay $8,000,000 to the Government in seven years from the day he entered the penitentiary. When his presence had not been required in court during the arguments he attended the Republican Presidential Convention then being held in Philadelphia. He posed for cameramen with some of the delegates, many of whom believed that he was a walking example of business persecution at the hands of a dictatorship. One or two of these photographs got to the judge while he was being told that the publisher was a broken old man, bewildered by financial details and practically bedridden. The New Deal, whose Pennsylvania Governor, Annenberg had supplanted, now seized among the convicted man's possessions as security for the $8,000,000 payment, his majority stock in the "independent newspaper for all the people." The *Inquirer* promptly turned its guns on Roosevelt, praying for a Republican victory which, it was hoped, might bring about a Federal pardon for the publisher as a political martyr. Moe, however, never again mentioned Nathan Hale.

Before he left to give himself up the publisher called many relatives to a banquet and sat at the head of the table. As a fictional character he might have been described as an incarnation of a splendid iniquity, looking down grimly upon the feast which was no scene of rejoicing. Those who wept into their wine over his humiliation were sharply reprimanded by him. This was not an occasion for tears, he said. It was a time to show an insensibility to all human vicissitudes. To the last he believed he was persecuted because he had had the courage to break certain rules which he thought were observed only by the timid who never got anywhere. That his type was doomed never entered his mind. The significance and the challenge of a new era, which had come to save Democracy from the bestial degradation of the money-mad, would always be beyond his comprehension. He may hold the distinction of being the last multi-millionaire to be sent to prison by a people so awakened that it will have no more of his kind. He may find the new

America difficult to recognize without blinking when he gets out.

When the clock was ticking off the time to go, Moe sat behind the big desk of his Victorian sanctum, staring at the paintings which surrounded him. He had never used a moment to study those nostalgic depictions of sturdy folk going to church, of an old Philadelphia that had embraced those precious hours of our short span whose real meaning lies in the simple, honest things of life. He remained staring curiously at the gallery recording an age that was gone, a fresh, optimistic America that had given him his start. About his mouth lay a bitter, ironic smile—a smile of scorn for those who would never have brains enough to make a million dollars. He got up from his chair, lifted his head high and his chin became firm and protruding.

At the door he found himself facing one of his capable editors, an old Hearst grenadier, Guy Norton, whose nickname, "Stud," implied that he had obtained it in some informal baptism during a poker session of a bygone time. "Stud" could make the Sunday *Inquirer* appear in San Francisco two days before the Sabbath on which the same issue was read in Philadelphia. But "Stud" had not come in to discuss this feat of publishing magic. With tears rolling down his face he wanted to know if something could be done to enable him to serve the time for his convicted boss. Moe's eyes were rarely moist, but now he had to control his emotion. He put his arm around the shoulders of his "old mustache," and pinched his ear, after the manner of Napoleon saying good-by before Elba.

"Brace up, 'Stud.' I'll serve my own rap," he said hoarsely. "But don't forget the Sunday's got to hold that million. I'll have more time now to think up some ideas."

Before he left, he corrected the proof of a unique farewell announcement which was to appear the next day on the front page of the *Inquirer* which he would read in his cell. If he meant what he said there may be hope for him and for those of his ilk who are finding out that occasional human kindness is of no avail when combined with brutality and double-dealing.

"With so many serious problems now facing our nation I should have been glad to be in a position to be helpful, as I have sought to be in the past. I should have liked to remain personally active on the firing line, fighting for the things I believe to be right and in the best interests of my country."

Moe was locked up in the Government penitentiary at Lewisburg in the state over which his "mining Lincoln" presided. The multi-millionaire became known as No. 10197. He draped his long, thin form with the drab garb which his changed situation required and had his $250 tailored suit wrapped up and addressed to himself at the *Inquirer* building. His secretary opened the package in his son's office and burst into tears, but Walter set his lips and got down to his task with the inherited stamina which had lifted his father from the junk shop—for Moe had faith in himself, but faith is a two-way force and somewhere along the road he had misdirected it.

The name of Moses L. Annenberg remained on the masthead of the *Inquirer* as "chairman and publisher" while he conducted his paper's policies from his cell, writing out his orders painfully in longhand, no trim secretaries being around to take his dictation.   He set his circulation department on edge by a blistering letter when he discovered that *The New York Times* was being delivered at the prison, three hours ahead of his own newspaper, an unforgivable state of affairs, as he pointed out, because it took less time to travel from Philadelphia to Lewisburg than it did from New York.   This condition was promptly remedied.   He had the history of his accomplishments removed from *Who's Who in America*, a tactful decision which made unnecessary any embarrassing references to his new address. The only editorial comment that pleased him about the interruption of his activities was written by William Randolph Hearst who now authored his own column in a style which never quite succeeded in duplicating Brisbane's.   Hearst described his former circulation captain as the victim of vindictive New Deal persecution.

Moe now met a number of interesting gentlemen upon whom had been bestowed the recognition of *Who's Who*, and who were paying their debt to society, as it used to be quaintly phrased about people of less importance.   The millionaire occasionally rubbed elbows at lunch time with the Honorable Martin T. Manton, former senior judge of the United States Circuit Court of Appeals who was "doing a rap" for selling justice.   Both compared notes on their philosophy of life, about which, presumably, they found themselves in agreement.

After a time Moe was appointed assistant to the librarian of the prison and was brought closer to Spinoza. Now he could rest a little longer in the dining hall where a twenty-piece orchestra composed of the inmates played Beethoven and Bach. Whether he was ever tempted to ask for a rendition of *I'm Only a Bird in a Gilded Cage* becomes a matter for private speculation.

CHAPTER VIII

It might be anticlimactic to attempt to explain at this stage of my narrative why the presses are made to roll faster by "Terry and the Pirates" and "Orphan Annie" than by the news that the swastika is flying over the Acropolis. Little editors, whirling on microcosms of the whole turbulent racket for readership seldom have time to reflect upon the sociological aspects of their hurried contributions to a million readers. The responsibility for this development of the law of supply and demand may be shared, presumably, by a segment of our society whose seat of thought impels it to tune in the orchestral style of boogie-woogie rather than the tidings of world engulfment. Publishers interested in satisfying such a market are not greatly concerned about the significant if not admirable effect of sensational journalism on American life.

Even Moe, who now had more time to be subjective, found that he could increase his vast circulation from his prison merely by ordering one new comic page in color piled upon another until his *Inquirer* advertised the printing triumph that it had "more comics than any other newspaper on earth." They mummified his Sunday issue, forming a tattooed wrapper for the whole concoction on whose cover the number 100 appeared three inches high in yellow on a red background, the figures dwarfing the name of the century-old paper, itself. The number, however, was not used to celebrate 100 years of American journalism. It indicated the total of comics for sale, and newsdealers no longer asked: "Do you want the *Inquirer*?" Instead they responded to the call: "Gimme the 'Old Hundred'!"

And circulation grew from a ripened formula which has seldom disappointed those who can afford to use it. Through it one may make enough money to fill warehouses for years with fabulously-priced works of art and relics of armor finally to be offered at bargain prices in a department store where the masses, whose pennies helped to make the collection possible, may discern in the examples of genius something greater than what they see in their funny papers. They may even appreciate the incomparable irony of the sale for they are far from the slap-happy Hooligans they used to be. A loyal follower of "Popeye," now privileged to tell a clerk to wrap up a sixteenth-century battle helmet, marked down to $29.49, and once worn by a Duke, is getting back to certain American fundamentals. And the way things are going, the headgear may prove to be of practical use.

One could not have found in Moe's "Old Hundred" any indication that such trends gave the publisher pause for reflection. His Sunday publication became stuffed with everything from a two-dollar novel on the ramifications of love, to departments which told you how to utilize a whole ham, or what to do to keep a dancing husband home when the babies begin to arrive. The paper tipped the scales at two and a quarter pounds, was two inches thick and fell on Philadelphia doorsteps with the cold thud of a side of beef. My rotogravure effort and the news of a crashing world were entombed under "Toots and Casper," "Superman," "Flash Gordon" (who rescued a semi-nude beauty every Sunday), "The Lone Ranger," "Buck Rogers" and even those unlayable ghosts, "The Captain and the Kids." Readers still interested in the fate of mankind after buying this deposit had to peel it like leaves from artichokes before they could keep abreast of the terrifying progress of a mechanized Attila.

I made what effort I could to inform the world pictorially of what was going on. My contacts with London illustrated publications, the finest of their type, were cut off. Dimitman suggested, with a certain eagerness, that I might make more satisfactory arrangements by flying to Europe, a journey which my wife opposed. But there were problems of a closer nature with which I was soon to contend.

The entire staff of the *Inquirer* had joined the Newspaper Guild, becoming an active part of the Philadelphia-Camden unit, probably the best-directed group for the protection of its workers in American journaʼism. I was not a member of it, having been excluded as an executive, but I had not forgotten the orders I had received in years gone by, to slash my working force because a millionaire was buying castles in Spain. The Guild movement was the swing of the pendulum from such whims. Now it was no longer considered a good baronial joke in a newspaper office to fire a man on Christmas Eve.

Back in New England I would have been intolerant of unionism in the city room, although I believed that organization was the only hope of the man who worked with his hands. But collective bargaining, in those days was not even contemplated as a remote national privilege, let alone the legal right that it was to become. My father used to talk about it quietly at home, to avoid being called an anarchist at the factory.

Journalism, I thought, was a different matter. The opportunities it offered for success, in which free individualism counted more than anything else, made it unnecessary, I felt, for the chosen souls of the press to band together. When I became a managing editor well under thirty I discovered there was a price to pay for such advancement, on some papers, at least. To keep things going one cut salaries, reduced budgets, and grinned agreeably when the man who ruled the counting room flung into the street old printers who insisted upon carrying union cards.

I had changed my views about organization in the city room long before Heywood Broun began to point out that the newspaper man deserved a better break, but by that time I was in the executive group, labeled as the type that hires and fires. I talked these things over with Broun before he died. He had sought many answers but eventually could find only one, which was in the strength of union with something greater than himself.

A situation had arisen in my office which brought these matters home to me again. Winifred, perhaps intuitively, had resigned as my secretary to supervise the development of our farm where we began to grow much of our food and produce our own eggs from a self-supporting flock of New Hampshire Reds. Milk from Nubian goats was also a part of our little industry. I had to find a new secretary and I promoted a hard-working young woman whom I had hired as a receptionist. Her name was Edna Berger, an attractive brunette with deep, limpid, black eyes, in which, perhaps, some future boss might notice little candles that burned in them, and tell her about his discovery.

Edna was a member of the Guild, and after she had worked several months in my office the *Inquirer* management was informed by her local unit that she was entitled to the scale of wages specified by a contract between the organized group and the newspaper. I no longer had the power to regulate her salary. She had become more than a secretary, really, and was carrying on a number of editorial duties, including her old job. In the Guild contract, a salary of thirty dollars a week was specified for a secretary. Edna was receiving five dollars less than that amount. Moe's $15,000,000 corporation decided to fight the case to the last ditch, apparently having forgotten our editorial platform which, every day, demanded "justice for the employed."

The struggle over the five dollars reached such a stage of bitter argument that it developed into arbitration hearings presided over by Dean Herbert F. Goodrich of the Law School of the University of Pennsylvania. During this climax I was subpoenaed by the Guild and before I testified I was informed by the management that it would claim Edna was a receptionist only. I felt I would have perverted the facts had I not supported the Guild's contention and from the witness seat I crowned Edna with her full title, which proved to be my last official act as an *Inquirer* executive. No one tagged with the label of a boss was supposed to translate "justice for the employed," as our masthead called it, into such literal meaning as to fight for a girl entitled to more than twenty-five dollars a week. Blows began to rain down on my head from every plank in our platform.

I remember Executive Editor Dimitman's knowing look as he watched, with his hands in his back pockets, two well-paid lawyers of the management's legal staff who had unleashed upon me a venomous argument, drawn up with detailed acrimony and delivered with vindictive relish. I was trying to concentrate on the immediate engagement although my mind was filled with the news of another conflict of more decisive nature raging at the moment, and which was sweeping an irresistible horde on to Paris to raise the swastika above the Eiffel tower. Perhaps the patient Dean, who had been scanning headlines with his face in his hands, hardly heard the red-faced men who were bellowing with impotent fury about him. When they had retired he readjusted Edna's battered, but nevertheless secretarial tiara, and awarded her the five-dollar increase.

I abandoned the witness chair, somewhat like Mr. Pickwick, carefully wiping my spectacles, and left the hearing room to encounter for the last time Moe's "Dodson and Fogg," who had not yet heard they had lost the case and were "rubbing their hands with every token of outward satisfaction." They deserved whatever fee they charged their imprisoned client. Nobody could have fought harder to keep a five-dollar bill in the cash box of a $15,000,000 corporation.

On my way to the office, reflecting upon the action Mr. Pickwick might have taken under the circumstances, I reached the only conclusion appropriate to his memory. It had to come and it might as well have come as it did. I said good-by to Edna, whose experience with changing bosses had begun early in life. She wept a little when I dictated my resignation. They always do.

Outside I stood looking at the great color presses which one could see from the street, through the front windows of the paper. The machinery was pouring out the million comic sheets, operated by highly privileged characters in overalls who knew two weeks in advance of the public all that was happening to the mythical people that sprang from the drawing boards to hold a large part of the population in suspense. Pressmen casually looked at the sections, examining the registration of color combinations and then, with nonchalance, cast the papers to the floor while the presses thundered with new momentum. These activities always have had a fatal fascination for me and almost immediately I forgot I was no longer a part of them.

The boss of the press was studying, with more than professional interest, the front page of the supplement on which I recognized the familiar grin of my old friend, "Joe Palooka," whose prosperity had never removed "ain't," "I seen" and "they was" from his speech. The foreman, evidently a "Palooka" fan, scrutinized intently every panel of "Joe's" latest history and with a grimy smile put the section in his pocket. "Palooka" had done well since I had given him his first job in New York. It had not taken him long to learn that he was the counterpart of untold thousands of living "Palookas" who now knew as much about him as they did about "Skeezix." But, yet, if they were all as honest and as courageous as "Joe," the country could not be so badly off. He possessed gratitude and had never rested until he had put his proud father, "Ham" Fisher, in *Who's Who in America* where the President of the United States exceeded him in space by hardly more than an inch.

"Palooka" now took up more room in the funny papers than "Mickey Mouse." But I had faith in "Mickey Mouse." He always seemed to be closer to things that were going on, and, I had no doubt, led his followers through tunnels of comics to the buried pages inside, which soon were to carry such words as "blood, tears, toil and sweat" and the brave reassurance of a sad King, who had to pick his phrases slowly, but who told the world from his bombed palace that there would always be an England. "Mickey" knew that was so. While British soil broke into yawning wounds he was cheering people up in London. The President would never have to call him a "Copperhead."

Through the din of the presses which tumbled "Mickey" about in a cascade of color I was sure I could hear his tinkling laughter. Everything would come out right in the end if a shaken mankind could only muster half of his confidence and dominating spirit. The laughter grew closer and I turned to find my wife tugging at my sleeve. She had been shopping and we were to drive home.

"You're out early," she said. "Are you finished for the day?"

Her warm, gleeful voice rang clear above the steady roar of the machines when I shouted to her the news of what had happened.

"We can talk right through it, now! We can hear each other."

And suddenly the intensity of the sound enveloping us became like the cold moan of a blizzard in the dark. I had never heard it that way before when I had said good-by to it. Winifred pulled me to the car.

"I'm so glad," she said. "It means we can get back to the farm in time."

"What's the excitement about? I don't have to hurry."

"You'll have to, for this occasion," she laughed, stepping on the gas. "Something important is happening. Our Nubian goat is going to kid."

FINIS

INDEX

A

Coughlin, "Bathhouse John", 423
Coughlin, Rev. Charles E., 165, 339
County Cork (Ireland), 219
Cox, James M., 75, 171
Cranmer, Thomas, Archbishop of
Canterbury, 289
Crater, Justice Joseph Force, 145,
155
Crawford, Joan, 415
Crompton, William, 176
Cuba, 181, 195-196, 355, 357-362, 364,
365-371
Cuff, Sergeant, 53
Cunliffe, John William, 93
Curtis, Cyrus Hermann K., 309
Curtiss, Glenn H., 329
Custer, General George Armstrong,
405, 425
Custer's Last Shot, 38
Custis, John Trevor, 429, 431
Czecho-Slovakia, 189, 443

D

Daily Mirror (New York), 108-109,
125, 137, 139-149, 152, 154-156,
158, 160-162, 164-165, 168, 172-
174, 176-178, 182-183, 191, 195-
204, 210-214, 219, 221-223, 225,
228, 230, 236, 239, 243-244, 249,
251, 259, 261-272, 274-276, 278,
280-281, 287-295, 297, 309-310,
314, 379, 418, 441, 452, 457
Daily News (Moscow), 189
Daily News (New York), 86, 109,
123, 138, 193, 221, 236, 237, 243,
256, 272, 275-276, 310, 388, 405
Daily Worker, the, 174, 292, 314
Daladier, Edouard, 447
Dana, Charles A., 55, 68, 86, 431
Dance Española, La, 357
Daniels, Alfred, 155-156
Dante Alighieri, 45
Darrow, Clarence S., 126
Daumier, Honoré, 46, 250
Davenport, Homer, 46
Davies, Marion (Douras), 112, 160,
379
Davis, Forrest, 183

Davis, Richard Harding, 61-62, 227,
299
Debs, Eugene Victor, 58
Debussy, Claude Achille, 11, 13, 64
Declaration of Independence, 443
Delaware River, 390, 406
Della Robia, Giovanni, 137
Democracy, 188-189, 191, 319, 324,
329, 333, 349, 368-371, 433, 443,
458
Democratic National Committee,
318
Democratic Party, 72, 88, 93, 170,
411
Dempsey, Jack, 85, 238-239, 246, 259
Denlinger, Sutherland, 118
Depew, Chauncey M., 43
Dern, George H., 334
Detroit (Michigan), 239
"Deutschhorst", 442-443
Dewey, Dist. Att. Thomas E., 155,
167, 281, 284-286
Diamond Dick, 39
Diamond, Milton, 166, 386
"Diamond Queen, The," 65-66
Dickens, Charles, 74, 391-392, 396,
465-466
"Dime Novel," 38, 130
Dimitman, Elias Z., 261, 439, 449,
451, 463, 465
Dinty Moore's Restaurant, 226
Dockstader, Lew, 384
Doctors' Hospital (New York City),
343
Dodd, William Edward, 182
"Dodson and Fogg, Messrs.," 393,
465-466
Doherty, Edward, 168
Dollfuss, Engelbert, 189-190, 196
"Dooley, Mr.," 309
Dougherty, Denis J., Cardinal, 422,
453
Downtown Skyport (New York
City), 417
Doyle, Ray, 163, 251
Doylestown (Pennsylvania), 395
Dreams of the Rarebit Fiend, 208
Dufay Film, 415
Dunne, Finley Peter, 159, 309
Durante, Jimmy, 224
Dusenbury, G. W., 148